Portugal and Africa, 1815–1910

A publication of the
FOOD RESEARCH INSTITUTE
Stanford University

One of a group of
STUDIES IN TROPICAL DEVELOPMENT

Portugal and Africa
1815-1910

A Study in Uneconomic Imperialism

R. J. Hammond

1966
Stanford University Press
Stanford, California

Stanford University Press
Stanford, California
© 1966 by the Board of Trustees of the
Leland Stanford Junior University
Printed in the United States of America
L.C. 66-17561

Contents

Illustrations and Maps

Preface

This book, as the "and" in its title should suggest, does not profess to be a history of Portuguese Africa between the dates mentioned. It is at once something more and something less: a study of Portuguese policies and attitudes concerning Africa, as affected by events in both Africa and Portugal and by the policies and attitudes of other powers, especially Portugal's long-standing ally, Great Britain. Its subject is the scramble for Africa, viewed from a Portuguese standpoint; its aim, to evoke the political and economic atmosphere of the time and to set out the way in which a seemingly doomed dominion was enabled to survive and even to consolidate itself. Such a purpose does not require the historian, in the words of R. G. Collingwood, to work "against the grain of his own mind" and study subjects merely because "they are 'in the period' which his own misguided conscience fancies he ought to treat in all its aspects." If he should do so, Collingwood adds, he will produce not history, but dry bones.

Together with Karl Popper's advice to historians, that they study only subjects in which they are interested, this seems a sufficient answer to any who might complain of my omissions. I would add, however, that in the case of Portuguese Africa the existence of Professor Duffy's pioneer work provides additional justification. My debt to him is, in fact, considerably greater than my direct references to his work would indicate. Not merely did his bibliography guide me to sources of which I might otherwise have remained unaware, but the appearance of his book, at a time when I had already resolved on writing this study, has affected its form. I have presumed that my readers will be acquainted with his *Portuguese Africa*; and I have, where covering the same ground, deliberately done so on a much larger, or much smaller, scale. I should also like to say that no one who has not encountered the exceptional difficulties of working on any subject connected with Portugal is likely to realize what a tour de force Professor Duffy's work represents.

My purpose, however, is diametrically opposed to what I imagine his to be, namely, a didactic and moralizing one. He seeks to appraise Portuguese performance in Africa by reference to what it has done for the African; he weighs it in the balance and finds it wanting. Though many will be found to differ with me, I do not think that this is the historian's job. I am not raising the standard "Back to Ranke," or saying that the historian should confine himself to narration and explanation; only that his comments on the wisdom, expediency, or morality of a course of action should be related to its historical context, not to some arbitrary external standard, however meritorious. Equally misconceived, in my view, is the demand that historians dealing with African subjects should avoid the sin of "Eurocentrism," and for the same reason: it seeks to impose on them a historically irrelevant criterion derived from a possibly transient political situation. The sole test to be applied to a historian's approach is one of intelligibility—whether his narrative makes sense from the point of view he takes. Looked at from a Portuguese point of view, the subject of this book makes sense; looked at from, say, a British point of view, it makes some sense; looked at from an African point of view, sympathize however much one may with the toad beneath the harrow, it would make no sense whatever. That is the historian's loss: for instance, one would very much like to know from Gungunhana's side what his policy toward the white man was, instead of having to infer it from the white man's records. But the hiatus is not to be filled by using what Sir Alan Herbert once called "witch-words"—words like *exploitation, colonialism,* and *racialist,* which have no precise historical connotation and explain nothing.

Of course, when I say that I adopt a Portuguese standpoint, I must qualify that statement by adding "so far as it is possible for one who is English by birth, citizenship, and training, and working in an American university." I should like to think that I have steered a successful middle course between the nationalist apologetics that characterize much, though not all, Portuguese writing on these topics and the unseemly tone of patronage that has afflicted so many of my fellow countrymen, past and present, when writing of things Portuguese. In this respect, even historians of the caliber of the late Sir Charles Webster have reflected all too faithfully an attitude of mind which has become traditional, and which, together with the resentment it has understandably provoked, goes far to explain the want of warmth in the traditional alliance between Great Britain and Portugal. The feelings that are still aroused in educated Portuguese by the British ultimatum of 1890—an event that not one Englishman in ten thousand has even heard of—are something that the historian has to reckon with in more ways than one, for documents relating to it are still, as Warhurst discovered a few years ago, withheld from him in Lisbon. Indeed, none of the archives of the Ministry of Foreign Affairs there after 1850 have been thrown open to inspection.

The writing of recent Portuguese history can hardly be said to have reached the stage at which the absence of this material would be a major handicap, for the mass of contemporary evidence that exists in print has yet to be thoroughly worked over. One of the reasons for the shape this book has taken is that I could find no modern work of scholarship that set out the political history of nineteenth-century Portugal in sufficient detail to make it intelligible to non-Portuguese readers. Contemporary Portuguese writings, as one might expect from a society in which no politically conscious member was really a stranger to any other, present an opaque structure of personal and institutional allusion that is hard to penetrate. The brilliant and pointed cartoons of Raphael Bordallo Pinheiro, four of which are reproduced in this volume, are all but indispensable to an understanding of the period, but many of them now require minute research to interpret. Side by side with this allusiveness goes an absence of organized factual information such as is to be found in contemporary British Blue Books. It is not so much that facts are lacking, but that they are liable to turn up in the context of political polemic, or for isolated years in which government reports happened to come out; one comes across them in the course of reading, not by systematic research through works of reference.

In the study of nineteenth-century Portugal there are few bibliographical aids and no shortcuts. The best way into the labyrinth is shown by foreign observers, whether they be descriptive writers like the Frenchmen Vogel, Marvaud, and Poinsard, or British diplomatic and consular officers. It is not so much the degree of detachment they display as the ignorance they perforce presume in their readers that makes these observers so useful to the historian. In particular, the British consuls serving in Portuguese Africa, being charged with the extra-consular tasks of helping to suppress the slave trade and keeping additional watch on the Transvaal Boers, were men of far higher caliber than the routine requirements of the service would have justified. Their reports may well have kept the British government better informed about conditions in the territories than was the government in Lisbon. Even were it not necessary to study the British attitude to Portugal in the interests of making Portuguese history intelligible, the Foreign Office records would still constitute a first-class source for the history of Portugal in Africa. What they cannot convey, however, is the flavor of that history. The great historian Oliveira Martins once described Portugal as a nation of Sancho Panzas, the embodiment of Cervantes' kingdom of Barataria. To the outsider, certainly, Portugal's persistent belief in herself as an imperial power appears inveterately quixotic; that, no doubt, helps to explain why her empire was tolerated by the others. It was the achievement of men like António Ennes and Mousinho de Albuquerque to convert quixotry into an effective imperialist force, to confound the prophets of doom, and to make nonsense of the Hobson-Lenin theory of economic imperialism before that theory could even be propounded.

The story of this achievement is worth telling for its own sake and because it may help to explain why Portugal is still an imperial power in Africa when others more apparently potent have crumbled. But its interest by no means stops there. Events in British imperial history, such as the foundation of Rhodesia, the Boer War, and the formation of the Union of South Africa, all take on a significantly different aspect when viewed from the Portuguese angle. The self-satisfaction characteristic of Lord Milner's "kindergarten," expressed in the famous Selborne Memorandum of 1907, is made to look rather foolish by the comments of Freire de Andrade, the governor-general of Moçambique at the time; while the writings of Ennes, of Mousinho, and of Ayres D'Ornellas make those of Lugard seem somehow unsophisticated. The superiority of British empire builders over those of

Portugal lay in their greater national wealth and better routine organization, rather than in individual talent. Indeed, one might regard the modern Portuguese dominion in Africa as essentially the creation of a few determined individuals in the face of a public opinion that could only be aroused from apathy by a crisis like that of 1890; and one might go on, perhaps, to ask whether this was not largely true of the other imperial powers as well.

The plan of the book will, I hope, be largely self-explanatory, though I should perhaps indicate that the first two chapters are intended to be introductory, so that the main story begins after 1875. The terminal date was chosen partly on practical grounds, partly because it marks the fall of the monarchy, an event which seemed, at least at the time, to be a turning point in Portuguese history. I hope I may have the opportunity at some later date to carry the narrative well into the twentieth century.

The translations from Portuguese books into English are my own, and I have striven hard to preserve some of the flavor of the originals. The spelling of Portuguese proper names presented a problem, inasmuch as it was impossible to avoid some inconsistency between the old spelling as represented by the titles of books published before the spelling reform of 1911, the new spelling after that date, and whatever spelling was adopted in the text. As most of the books I have cited were published before the spelling reform, this inconsistency has been minimized by spelling proper names as they were spelled by contemporaries. The differences are, in any case, not such as to confuse the reader. In abbreviating Portuguese personal names and in indexing them, I have tried to follow Portuguese practice, which appears to vary with the individual. For instance, Ernesto Rodolpho Hintze Ribeiro is referred to shortly (and indexed) as "Hintze." On the other hand, in printing the titles of Portuguese books I have used English rules of capitalization, as being more convenient. The arrangement whereby substantive notes are printed at the foot of the page and source citations are relegated to the back of the book was urged upon me by my publishers.

Grateful thanks are due to the Ford Foundation for the grant to the Food Research Institute that alone made possible the research on which this book is based and its publication. Thanks are due also to the Controller of H.M. Stationery Office, London, for permission to quote Crown Copyright material held in the Public Record Office; to Comandante Ernesto de Vilhena, of Lisbon, for permission to use, in translation, extensive quotations from his writings; to Companhia Nacional Editora, of Lisbon, for permission to reproduce four cartoons by Raphael Bordallo Pinheiro; and to Dr. José de Almada, of Lisbon, for helpful advice and the gift of valuable source material.

To these acknowledgments I would like to add a note of my indebtedness to my old friends Sir Henry King, K.B.E., who first introduced me to Portugal, and Luiz Marques, who carried on the process of educating the foreigner. Without the active interest of Merrill K. Bennett, former Director of the Food Research Institute, the book could never have been written. Mary Leder's knowledge of Portugal and of the Portuguese language was of much assistance to me in the earlier stages of research. Mildred Wretts-Smith found answers in the Public Record Office to a number of queries, as well as helping me keep abreast of the "fifty-year rule." Peter Duignan, Lewis Gann, and William O. Jones read and commented on the manuscript. Last, but not least, the pertinacious editorial staff of Stanford University Press taught me more than I thought I needed to know about polishing a book to a fine sheen, and about the innumerable small differences of usage that separate American and British English. The result will, I hope, be equally intelligible on either side of the Atlantic.

RICHARD J. HAMMOND

STANFORD, CALIFORNIA
APRIL 8, 1966

Note on Documentary Sources

The most important manuscript sources for this work are the records of the British Foreign and Colonial Offices preserved in the Public Record Office in London. The original dispatches and minutes are bound up in a number of separate series, which overlap to some considerable extent. The series designated F.O.63(Portugal), F.O.84 (Portugal–Slave Trade), and F.O.2(Africa) contain the incoming dispatches, the minutes thereon, if any, and the outgoing draft dispatches. That designated F.O.179 contains the corresponding material from the Lisbon legation; very occasionally, a document will be found therein that is missing from the Foreign Office series, but the all-important minutes are, of course, lacking. (Warhurst, in his useful study *Anglo-Portuguese Relations in South Central Africa,* used this legation series to the exclusion of F.O.2 and F.O.84, thereby missing some points.)

One cannot always be sure that all the relevant documents are included in the "Portuguese" series (for example, many of those leading up to the Anglo-German treaties of 1898 are found in F.O.64, or the "Prussian" volumes). It is generally preferable to work from the Confidential Prints, the form in which correspondence was circulated for the information of interested persons within the British government. Each Print or series of Prints deals with some general topic and corresponds to the published Blue Books of which the Prints constitute the unexpurgated originals. Documents are arranged in chronological order of receipt at the Foreign Office, and a Table of Contents is prefixed. Comparison with the original bound volumes—which were, of course, made up after the Confidential Prints—shows only minor omissions, mostly minutes. These are more than compensated for by the inclusion of documents whose existence might have gone unsuspected, such as the letter to Herbert Bismarck of December 1888 and the Anderson memorandum of 1890. Moreover, since more than one set of Confidential Prints is extant, I have preferred whenever possible to cite them, even when I have had access to the original documents. In such citations I have used the Foreign Office serial numbers rather than those given by the Public Record Office, on the mistaken assumption that the series was complete, to the copies in its possession. Some of the original numbers were duplicated with an added asterisk, and other Prints appear not to have been numbered at all, so it is doubtful whether an assuredly complete set could ever be assembled.

The relevant Colonial Office records are similarly bound up in two series: one General (C.O.417) and the other "Supplementary," i.e., Secret (C.O.537). It appears that at one time the Colonial Office followed the practice (surely contrary to the Public Records Acts) of destroying documents once they were in Confidential Print, and therefore a great many of the files consist of minute sheets alone. (Unlike the Foreign Office, the Colonial Office did not put minutes directly upon incoming documents, and in consequence its minutes are generally fuller and more informative.) The Confidential Prints (which were printed on the Foreign Office press) frequently duplicate material on the Foreign Office Prints, and I have cited them only rarely. They never contain minutes.

For the sake of convenience, I have occasionally cited the published Blue Books, but I have not attempted any general reconciliation of their contents with those of the Confidential Prints. Much confidential material was included in *British Documents on the Origin of the War*.

The Portuguese government published its diplomatic correspondence in a series of White Books (*Livros Brancos*) corresponding in form to the British Blue Books, and I have used as many of these as I was able to obtain. They are at least as informative as the Blue Books, but perhaps their most useful feature is their reproduction of foreign press comment on matters concerning Portugal, particularly some that appeared at the time of the 1890 ultimatum. (There are also Portuguese Green Books and Yellow Books.) Contemporary Portuguese memoirs and apologia sometimes reproduce official correspondence verbatim in great detail; the works of Ennes, Mousinho de Albuquerque, and the compilation put together by Trindade Coelho under the title *Dezoito Annos in Africa* are especially noteworthy in this respect. Many of the writings, official and unofficial, of the nineteenth-century empire builders have been reprinted, mostly under Portuguese government auspices; the editing, however, has been more often than not perfunctory, and the choice of materials seems to have been dictated by political rather than scholarly criteria. Almeida Ribeiro's memorandum of 1913, the reports of Freire de Andrade, and the classic work of Andrade Corvo would seem to have greater claims for reprinting than some of the minor writings of men whose views commend themselves more to the present administration. Nevertheless, these reprints are something to be grateful for.

Some of the Portuguese official reports and memoranda cited herein bear the imprint of a private publisher. On the other hand, some apparently personal writings have been published by the government printing office. Since it is often difficult to determine whether a Portuguese publication is government authorized or inspired, it has been thought best to designate doubtful cases by a dagger (†).

The following abbreviations are used throughout:

B.D.	British Documents on the Origins of the First World War (eds., G. P. Gooch and H. W. V. Temperley)
B.P.P.	British Parliamentary Papers
C.O.	Colonial Office (Great Britain)
C.P.	Foreign Office Confidential Print (Great Britain)
D.D.F.	Documents Diplomatiques Françaises
F.O.	Foreign Office (Great Britain)

Chapter one

The Sick Man of Western Europe

"An economist or statistician, looking at the diminutive resources of
the mother country in men and goods, compared with the vastness of
the dependent territories and the tenacity with which we maintain,
control, and develop them, would sum up his survey with a single
word: 'absurd.' A mystic or a simpleton, too ignorant of history to
know what we did in the name of faith, but aware of what we
achieved through faith, would certainly declare: 'a miracle.' "[1] Thus,
in 1924, wrote Vicente Ferreira, sometime High Commissioner for
Angola and for forty-odd years a prominent figure in Portuguese colonial affairs. When he died, in 1953, with the fantastic postwar
growth of Angola and Mozambique not yet touched by balance-of-
payments difficulties nor threatened by the forces of African nation-
alism, the miraculous element might almost have seemed to have
eclipsed the absurdity. Gilberto Freyre, writing in 1952, could recount
his experiences as a traveler through the Portuguese dominions in a
sociological eulogy of the "luso-tropical world"—something unique
in its kind that Portugal, alone among the imperial nations, had
known how to create. Ferreira, to be sure, would not have approved of
miscegenation—which for Freyre was not so much an anachronism,
forced on earlier generations of colonists by physical conditions they
had not learned to overcome, as a desideratum—but he would have
shared the Brazilian's sanguine views on the prospects of greater Portugal. That such views—which contrast sharply with the brave but un-
convincing apologetics of most earlier Portuguese writers on the colonies—could seem at least plausible in the 1950's was in itself a mark

of achievement. As the British traveler Patrick Balfour put it in the late thirties, "The Portuguese colonies are no longer altogether a joke."[2]

I

Portugal's tropical African empire, like those of the other European powers, is a creation of the last hundred years, an outcome of the "scramble for Africa"; it differs in that it rests on, and is inconceivable without, territorial claims of long standing. Though it cannot be called a survival, it is certainly built on one. It exists by reason of the past forbearance of others, whether European or African, but not by that alone; the will to survive, if not to prosper, has been every whit as important. This quality of tenacity, seldom absent from Portuguese political leadership even at its most inept, is what has so far falsified prophecies of doom for her African colonies.

It would certainly have been a miracle if Portugal had been able, over the past century, to build up an African empire from scratch, for her economic condition a hundred years ago was backward indeed, and might be termed colonial rather than metropolitan. Appearances on small-scale maps notwithstanding, Portugal is isolated geographically from most of Spain, and a fortiori from the rest of Europe; much of her frontier consists either of natural obstacles or barren *meseta*.[3] Neither the Douro nor the Tagus is navigable into Spain, and the splendid harbor of Lisbon has but a limited hinterland.[4] Even today, when relations between the Spanish and Portuguese governments are as friendly as they have ever been, trade between the two countries is almost insignificant. In earlier times, the Portuguese valued their isolation as an assurance of political independence; the "Babylonish captivity" from 1580 to 1640, when what had started out as a dynastic union of independent kingdoms finished as an attempt to absorb Portugal into Spain, is still looked back on with aversion. There is even a Portuguese *terra irridenta*, the small town of Olivença seized by Spain in 1801 and retained ever since in defiance of an award at the Congress of Vienna in 1814.[5]

A century ago, land communications within Portugal were little better than they were with the outside world. As a Portuguese writer declared in 1866: "The absence of roads was formerly part of the strategic and defensive system of the country. This assertion can be verified by anyone who traveled in Portugal before 1850. The routes between the larger cities were nothing more than beaten and stony tracks, traversed painfully by two-wheeled chariots or litters. In 1849 there were but forty-two kilometers of made road, with sixteen under construction."[6]

Except for a very few stretches of recent construction, including the road from Lisbon to Oporto, there was nothing that could be called a carriage road. The Frenchman Charles Vogel wrote in 1860: "The older highways...traced as though by chance, are roads only in name, and the traveler finds his way as best he can with the help of the *arrieiros,* or muleteers."* From the map it might seem that the rivers might make up for the absence of roads, but this was not so; their navigation was, without exception, impeded partially or wholly by the "prodigious accumulation of sand" that had been allowed to build up, obstructing riverbeds and producing all but impassable bars at the mouths. Coastwise shipping was impeded in this way almost as much as traffic over the land frontiers. As for railroads, none had been built by 1850. Vogel attributed this state of affairs to neglect rather than policy. It was, he thought, the greatest single obstacle to the development of the country's natural resources, and the one most in need of remedy; for although the country was mountainous, the terrain was not unfavorable to road construction and the materials were readily available. As late as 1924 Aquilino Ribeiro, writing in the *Guia de Portugal,* remarked on the insufficiency of roads and railroads and the survival of that "truly archaeological" type of transport, the *carro rural* with wooden wheels and creaking axle, drawn by yoked oxen.

Isolated not only from Spain but from one another, the Portuguese provinces displayed a marked individuality that persists into the present. There may be an element of literary fancy in the distinctions that Portuguese writers draw between the character of their inhabitants—"where the *transmontano* kills a man, the *minhoto* breaks a plate"—but the differences in social atmosphere are still palpable.[7] The depressing, though penetrating, picture of contemporary Portugal drawn in a recent English book, Frank Huggett's *South of Lisbon,* is almost implicit in its title.[8] In the southern provinces of Alentejo and Algarve

---

* Charles Vogel, *Le Portugal et ses Colonies: Tableau politique et commercial de la Monarchie portugaise dans son Etat actuel* (Paris, 1860), pp. 281–82. Vogel's penetrating and detailed study is still helpful in understanding the Portuguese scene.

people take their pleasures sadly: the taciturn Alentejano, says Aquilino Ribeiro, "does not sing when he walks by himself," and the Algarvian *vigilias* lack the noisy gaiety of the *festas* in Minho or Beira—"they are sullen affairs and one does not dance."[9]

These regional differences go far back into history; they have been plausibly attributed in part to the influence of the Saracens, whose dominion, short-lived north of the Douro, endured in the Algarve for more than five hundred years, from the eighth to the mid-thirteenth century. (Coimbra had been recovered by the Christians in 1064, Lisbon in 1147.) But they also reflect wide differences in climate, topography, and the distribution of landed property—differences one might not expect to find within a country measuring 35,000 square miles, the size of the state of Indiana. The extremes are represented by the moist, fertile, northwesterly, coast province of the Minho, with its dense rural population of peasant proprietors, and the semi-arid steppes of the Alentejo, where the farms are huge and the rural population sparse. At the turn of the present century the density of population in the northern districts of Porto and Braga, excluding the urban areas, was 156 and 112 per square kilometer; in the southern districts of Evora, Beja, and Portalegre it was under 10 per square kilometer. Half a century earlier, the relative figures appear to have been much the same, and they have not substantially changed since.[10] The absolute figures have more than doubled since 1860, indicating that the land problem underlying them has steadily become more acute.

II

The Alentejo has always borne the appearance of a no-man's-land between the more densely peopled provinces to the north and south. For much of the twelfth and thirteenth centuries it was a battleground between Christian and Saracen, and thereafter was held as a kind of bulwark against the Castilians to the east. Massive grants of land—not always to native-born nobility—were made by the Portuguese kings to ensure their continued suzerainty over the territory. To attempt its colonization would have been irrational, and was anyway impossible, at a time when the lands to the north of the Tagus were not fully exploited. Hence the picture, well drawn by Ezequiel de Campos, of medieval Alentejo and the neighboring province of Beira Baixa:

A minimum of people sheltered within the walls or dominated by the shadow of castle keeps, rare and tiny hamlets in the open country, solitary farmsteads (*montes*) atop gentle hills; villages and towns barely perceptible on the low table-lands, where the continental climate set fire to the wilderness that the raids and incursions of Christian and Moor alike had created out of once-green fields and olive groves, systematically devastated. . . .[11]

The system of latifundia has persisted there ever since,

as if another Moorish invasion were feared and it were dangerous to multiply villages on the Alentejo plain; and the regime is maintained precisely because our laws favor the dominant cereal monoculture. Levies of seasonal laborers from Beira . . . replace the slaves of a few generations back at plowing and harvest times. . . .

No one comes nowadays from the Minho, the banks of the Douro, or from Trás-os-Montes to the Alentejo; people from thence do not know what it is like . . . or many even that it exists. The *minhoto* or the *transmontano* would not tolerate the semi-nomadic existence, separate from his family, of the *caramelo,* the *algarvio,* or the *ratinho.**

To maintain this system was to follow the line of least resistance, given the existing property rights and the natural conditions of southern Portugal. A land reform that broke up the great estates would not of itself open the way to an intensive agriculture based on peasant proprietorship, such as prevails in the north. It would also be necessary to introduce large-scale irrigation schemes and provide settlers with capital. Until recently such measures of economic development would have been beyond any Portuguese government; as for a massive land reform, it was not indeed inconceivable—they have often been proposed in the past—but politically improbable. Nevertheless one can imagine circumstances in which the pressure of population might, over centuries, have tended to nibble away at the great estates—the more so since their owners were largely absentees—or in which the central government might have promoted some measure of land reapportionment.

Indeed, the distribution of population between north and south may well have been more unequal in the nineteenth century than it was in the fifteenth. In 1422 the population of the Alentejo is said to have

---

* Ezequiel de Campos, *A Conservação da Riqueza Nacional* (Oporto, 1913), pp. 126-27. *Caramelo* and *ratinho* are slang epithets for itinerant workers.

been upward of 300,000, out of a total of one million; in 1535 it was about the same, although the total population had gone up to nearly one million and a half. Population in towns had fallen; Beja, for instance, supposedly had 17,000 inhabitants in 1422, and 7,000 in 1535, compared with under 8,500 in 1878.[12] It is difficult to know how much credence to put in these estimates; the totals are almost certainly too high, being based on multiplying the number of households by five. J. C. Russell has given good reasons, in the case of medieval England, for preferring a multiplier of 3.5 to this purely conventional figure; the mean ratio of households to population in twentieth-century Portugal is roughly 1 to 4.[13] In the towns the ratio is somewhat higher, and this may have been true in earlier periods; but one probably ought to deduct one-fifth from the provincial and national totals.

A relative diminution in the population of the Alentejo, and of its towns after 1422, is consistent with two other known facts: the expulsion of the Jews and Moors, all of them townspeople, in 1497, and more important, the beginning of Portugal's eastern adventure with the arrival of Vasco da Gama in Calicut in the following year. The drain of able-bodied men to the Indies has been put at over eight thousand annually, of whom no more than one in ten returned, so great were the hazards of the voyage. This figure may be an exaggeration: Manuel Severim de Faria, writing in 1655 *Of Remedies for the Lack of People,* put the yearly exodus at no more than two thousand, though by that time the Portuguese dominion in the East was in decay. To some small extent the loss was made up by the import of slaves from Africa and the Orient; but, declared Severim de Faria, "the first cause of the want of people from which this kingdom suffers is our conquests."[14] The second was unemployment; the third, the shortage of land for the common people to cultivate, since the north was overpopulated and the Alentejo composed of large holdings which "are neither peopled nor cultivated." His complaint was to be echoed by reformers more than two centuries later. As António Sérgio put it, in introducing Severim to the twentieth-century reader:

The clear-thinking and observant men who lived in Portugal in the olden days complained of the *same* evils of which we complain today: so that we may say, in rebuttal of those who follow the fashion, that *the great mistake of the Portuguese was not that they broke with tradition, but the very contrary, that they broke with tradition only in its superficial aspects....* In other words, the weaknesses of [19th-century] liberalism, (like those of absolutism) were not the cause, but the consequence of the basic [political] vices from which the motherland sickens....[15]

The result of the Discoveries was thus a decrease in the total population of the kingdom, possibly by as much as half a million during the half-century preceding the union with Spain in 1580. Whereas King João I had easily been able to muster 20,000 men for the capture of Ceuta in 1415, and Afonso V some 30,000 for the expedition to Tangier in 1471, Sebastião had the greatest difficulty in raising a force of 11,000 for the disastrous enterprise of 1578 that ended with the battle of Alcácer-Quibír. At that time the population of Portugal may have fallen to little more than a million, if indeed that estimate is not too high. But the fall had been mainly in the south; the common people of the Minho stayed at home and cared little for a life of vagabondage in the Indies. As Ezequiel de Campos, in literal contradiction of Oliveira Martins, declared: "A mere thirty-seven years from the discovery of India was long enough [for the country] to fall into the utmost degradation, and for the successors of Pedro Alvares Cabral to change completely; but the whole of Portugal did *not* embark for the rape of the Orient in Cabral's fleet." The embodiment of the traditional Portuguese virtues, says de Campos, remained in the north; it was a cosmopolitan, rootless riffraff—"Genoese, Lombards, Aragonese, Mallorcans, Milanese, Corsicans, Biscayans"—and a floating population of uncertain racial origins from the south that departed in search of treasure.

From then on the national madness, what with the freebooting in Asia and Africa and the gold of Brazil, totally upset any policy of settlement. South of the Tagus, the exodus for adventure aggravated the bad conditions for settlement that were beginning to be marked in the period of Roman decline—conditions that the medieval wars and land grants rendered acute and left to weigh endlessly upon a people of mixed blood who were barbarized, without a great tradition in the advantageous use of rainwater, and without any economic policy on the part of government.[16]

One may perhaps question the racial prejudice that underlay de Campos' analysis of the national malaise, past and present, but his main point seems well taken. The Discoveries, with all their grandeurs and miseries—miseries that the dominant group in modern Portugal prefers not to talk about—were in no sense a national enterprise.* They were the work of a minority, and it was a minority that they benefited. The Portuguese peasant did not share in the profits of his king's pepper monopoly, for these profits were neither distributed nor plowed back; they were merely expended in extravagances, temporal and spiritual. "Lisbon," says Oliveira Martins, "presented the double aspect of an orgy of merchants and a congregation of penitent fakirs." By 1568 there was actually a shortage of gold and silver coin and an excess of copper, so that the value of the latter was reduced by decree to a third of its former worth. "The treasure from India had passed through Portugal like wheat through a sieve; the grain went abroad, and only the tares and the dirt of the threshing floor remained."[17] The great plague of 1569, which killed forty thousand persons in Lisbon, or more than a third of the population, was said to be divine retribution for the robbery of the devaluation. It was an all but bankrupt monarchy that embarked upon the crazy and disastrous expedition of Alcácer-Quibír.

III

Move on two hundred years, and the picture is the same. The vanished riches of the Indies were replaced after about 1700 by the gold, silver, and diamonds of Brazil. King João V (1706–50) enjoyed an income of fabulous proportions, but his kingdom had endured half a century of wars of succession, and was (to quote Oliveira Martins again) "depopulated and uncultivated, its villages wretched and naked, without wealth or employment."

The gold of Brazil merely passed through Portugal and cast anchor in England, to pay for the flour and textiles with which [England] fed and clothed us. Our industry consisted of operas and devotions. The Portuguese was fit only to be a shopkeeper; foreign trade was in the hands of English (mainly) and Italians.

Nor did the gold of Brazil suffice; the national debt grew, and if Lisbon wanted to stop dying of thirst, she had to pay for the construction of her aqueduct through a special tax. The Brazilian funds had another, a better destiny.[18]

This destiny can be broadly described as religious ostentation, or holy riches. Symbolic of it is the gigantic palace-and-convent of Mafra,

---

* Compare the account of João Ameal, *Historia de Portugal* (Lisbon, 1942), with that of Oliveira Martins, written in the eighties and dedicated to the memory of Alexandre Herculano (*Historia de Portugal,* 7th ed., Lisbon, 1908, Books IV and V *passim*). It is hard to think of a more unsuitable award of a prize in memory of Herculano than that to Ameal, the inveterate opponent of everything the great liberal historian and publicist stood for.

some twenty miles north of Lisbon, which "devoured in money and men more than Portugal was worth." Built in fulfillment of a vow when the hitherto childless queen of João V gave birth, Mafra took eighteen years to build (1717–35) and cost more than 48 million cruzados.* As many as 50,000 workers were employed on the convent in the peak year of 1729, and 1,338 workers died during its construction. Much of the material and many, if not most, of the craftsmen employed were foreign; the architect was a German.[19] Students of economic development are accustomed nowadays to speak of "enclaves" of modern production within an otherwise primitive economy; but Mafra was an enclave of conspicuous consumption. Even less productive, in mundane terms, than the millions spent on Mafra were the two hundred million cruzados that went to the See of Rome—by way of gift, purchase of concession (such as the elevation of the Cardinalate of Lisbon to a Patriarchate), or the promotion of a favorite dogma—and the unnumbered amounts given to the Church in Portugal and abroad. The king sought to be "the chief almoner of Catholicism." As a contemporary lamented, "Monkery swallows us up, monkery sucks all things dry, monkery is ruining us!"[20]

The great Lisbon earthquake of 1755 was the first of a series of misfortunes under which the ancien régime in Portugal—tough though it proved—was eventually to perish. The dictatorship of Pombal, which followed the earthquake, was an attempt to introduce eighteenth-century rationalism—symbolized by the rectangular layout of the new Baixa, or lower city, that arose on the ruins of old Lisbon—into a society where superstition was the one thing common to rich and poor alike. "What can one expect of a people," Lord Tyrawley, the English ambassador to the court of João V, remarked, "half of whom await the coming of Messiah, and the other half that of King Sebastian?"[21] The phenomenon of *sebastianismo*—the belief among the common people of Portugal that the king, the last of his line, who perished at Alcácer-Quibír, would one day return and bring back the golden age —was to persist into the nineteenth and twentieth centuries.** It was matched by, and in Oliveira Martins' view accounted for, the peo-

---

* At the time of the building of Mafra, the cruzado was worth approximately one-twelfth of a pound sterling.
** The late General Delgado pointed to Dr. Salazar as its latest manifestation. Humberto Delgado, *The Memoirs of General Delgado* (London, 1964), p. 59.

ple's steady indifference to their actual rulers, whether these were the kings of Spain, the Braganças, Pombal, or even the invading French. In this view, the positive Pombaline reforms were bound to be even more rootless than the system they superseded.

In a negative sense, however, Pombal accomplished much. He broke the power of the nobility and so opened the way to a benevolent royal despotism (had there been anyone capable of exercising it); he expelled the Jesuits, who had controlled Portuguese higher education for two centuries; he abolished slavery (within Portugal itself) and the Inquisition; he stopped the flow of private and public wealth into the hands of the clergy; he made all Portuguese subjects, whatever their racial and religious beliefs or antecedents, equal before the law. However, the materials for an enlightened nation, in the eighteenth-century sense, did not exist in Portugal, and Pombal was therefore constrained to import them from abroad in the shape of foreign savants, military commanders, businessmen, industrialists, and craftsmen. Many of his enterprises were thus as exotic, in their way, as Mafra, and less enduring. But, as his admirers and critics are agreed, he opened the way for revolutionary ideas: he showed "the blessed and besotted Portuguese that there was something more in the world than nuns and quince jelly, poetasters' contests and street fights, pious luxury and confused visions."[22]

After the downfall of Pombal in 1777 a sentimental reaction—for which his tyrannous methods were in part responsible—set in under the pious Queen Maria I. There could, however, be no return to the spacious days of King João "the Magnanimous"—to the days of "Portuguese splendor," as a modern writer, without a hint of irony, can describe them.[23] An attempt was made to continue the work of modernization and development by such undertakings as the Naval Academy and the Academy of Sciences. The latter body planned to produce a massive dictionary of the Portuguese tongue; but as Charles Vogel wrote in 1860, the work stopped in 1793 "at its first volume, which does not even reach the end of the letter A.... Thanks to an unlucky if pleasurable chance, it stops at the word *asno* [donkey]."[24] As Oliveira Martins sardonically noted:

Highways were also planned, and the first concern was to set up in Lisbon stone columns marking the leagues. Each milestone had a sundial; but because, on occasion, a league would end in shadow, the question arose which was preferable: to allow the measure to err, or the sundial to do without light. Because no decision could be reached, the roads were not built. In compensation, nine million cruzados were spent in constructing the "New Convent."[25]

The New Convent was the convent and basilica of the Estrêla in Lisbon, built after the style of Mafra and like it the fulfillment of an oath conditional on the birth of a royal child.*

Not all the public expenditures of the reign fell into the category of "pious luxury"; nevertheless, Oliveira Martins' observation carries conviction as a revelation of the state of mind of Portugal's rulers at that time, Pombal alone excepted. For them, the perpetuation of the dynasty was manifestly more important than the economic progress of the kingdom and might more properly have money spent on it. The practical expression of such sentiments is commonly limited, at any rate in the long run, by the realization that the prosperity of a country and the income of its rulers are apt to be interdependent. But it was the peculiar fortune of Portugal that from the sixteenth to the nineteenth centuries no such relationship was apparent. Exotic sources of wealth permitted conspicuous consumption on a scale wholly out of line with what the kingdom's own revenues would have allowed. The ruinous expedition of 1578 would have been impossible without the riches of the Indies; the anachronistic expenditures of the eighteenth century would have been impossible without the treasure of Brazil.

It was wholly consistent with this attitude that when Napoleon Bonaparte's new European order, in the person of Marshal Junot, evinced signs of extending itself to Portugal in 1807, the royal family should have retired to Brazil, along with a retinue of 15,000 courtiers and others. Not even a token resistance was offered to the French invaders, yet the route they took, on Napoleon's explicit orders, along the Tagus valley, was difficult beyond belief to those ignorant of the country: "a series of rocky defiles through an almost unpeopled wilderness," which had to be traversed in pouring rain. With resolute leadership, a few thousand Portuguese could have delayed Junot for months or the very least have forced the French to mount a major campaign. The advance guard that took possession of Lisbon on the morrow of the royal flight was a mere 1,500 men in rags, "their cartridges so soaked that they could not have fired a shot had they been

* According to the authoritative *Guia de Portugal* (Lisbon, Biblioteca Nacional, 1928), Vol. I, p. 336, the cost of this edifice was not nine but sixteen million cruzados; evidently prices had risen over half a century, for the Estrêla, though impressive, is insignificant in size compared with Mafra.

attacked. If the mob of Lisbon had fallen on them with sticks and stones, the starving invaders must have been driven out of the city." Sir Charles Oman, the historian of the Peninsular War, whose judgment this is, comments: "There is certainly no example in history of a kingdom conquered in so few days and with such small trouble as was Portugal in 1807."[26]

In effect, the House of Bragança had abdicated, along with the greater part of the governing class. With their arrival in Rio de Janeiro in 1808 Brazil virtually ceased to be a colony of Portugal and became an independent kingdom. The Portuguese monopoly of Brazilian trade was abolished and replaced by a tariff preference favoring the British as the protecting power. King João VI, when he succeeded the long-mad Maria I in 1816, styled himself "King of Portugal, Brazil, and the Algarves."* But the Brazilians proved less tolerant of the "cloud of locusts," the *mandarinato,* than the long-suffering Portuguese people had been.[27] When João VI returned to Portugal in 1821—reluctantly, for he faced revolution and feared regicide—he left behind a growing separatist movement. Only the attempt of the Portuguese Côrtes to reestablish Brazil's colonial status by the abolition of the central government in Rio was needed to provoke a declaration of independence. With the recognition of the Brazilian Empire in 1825 the ancien régime in Portugal was doomed. "Once again the passing-bell tolled for Portugal, and for a second time the question arose whether or not the country, reduced to the resources existing within her own borders, had the means to subsist as an independent state."[28] It is a question that is still asked when the prospective loss of the African territories is considered. But—*pace* Oliveira Martins—it does not seem to have been uppermost in men's minds in Portugal at that time, and the ancien régime, personified by Queen Carlota Joaquina and her younger son Miguel, was in no mood to go down without fighting.

French control of Portugal had not lasted through 1808. A British expeditionary force landed in support of the Portuguese insurgents and forced Junot and his Spanish allies to withdraw under the terms of the so-called Convention of Cintra. For the rest of the Peninsular War and for five years thereafter, Portugal was virtually a British pro-

---

* "Algarves" in the plural, on account of the long-standing claim of Portugal to the other Algarve—that is, Al-Gharb in Morocco. It is a solecism so to describe the southernmost province.

tectorate under the rule of Wellington's subordinate, Beresford, who reorganized the Portuguese army to fight Napoleon, and "made soldiers of all who were not monks, officeholders, canons and precentors, or eunuchs."[29] The campaigns on the soil of Portugal, particularly the one during which the country was stripped of supplies in the face of Masséna's advance to the lines of Torres Vedras, imposed great hardships on the common people, as did depredations and atrocities by both invading and defending troops. But the lasting destruction brought about by the war has sometimes been exaggerated: Oliveira Martins' claim, for instance, that the population fell by a quarter, or half a million, between 1807 and 1814 seems wrong on more than one count. An informed contemporary estimate put the population in 1807 at 3.2 million and the net war losses at a quarter of a million: these losses, it was said, had been made good by 1822 or 1823.[30] The most populous province of Portugal, the Minho, suffered French occupation only in part and for only a matter of months.

The majority of the Portuguese people, living by subsistence farming, were as much beyond comparatively distant and short-run economic influences as they were beyond external help in case of crop failure. It seems likely that the major economic effect of the Peninsular War was the destruction of roads and bridges, for the gloomy picture of communications painted by mid-nineteenth-century writers like Vogel goes far beyond what one might infer from the military histories about their state half a century earlier. Consistent with this view is the increased dependence of Portugal on imported wheat after 1815, noted by Oliveira Martins; the need can only have been in or near Lisbon and other seaports, for inland there was neither the means of distribution nor the wherewithal to pay for grain from abroad.[31] As late as 1860 it was said that transport costs over the few score miles separating Lisbon from the Alentejo increased the price of homegrown wheat in the capital by one-fourth.[32] The loss of trade with Brazil, considerable even before complete separation, became catastrophic; the total foreign trade of Portugal, both import and export, valued at 50 million milréis in 1796, and 67 million milréis in 1807, was down to 18 million milréis in 1842, and was still under 36 million in 1855.*

---

* Charles Vogel, *Le Portugal*, pp. 341–42. These figures, though official, are given here with due reserve, and probably should not be taken as more than orders of magnitude. (During these years, 4.5 milréis was approximately equivalent to 1 pound sterling.)

IV

Recovery from the Peninsular War might have been more rapid had it not been followed by three decades and more of civil disorders—disorders which began by embodying a genuine clash of principle between the old legitimacy and the new constitutionalism, but degenerated into little more than a bad habit, and were ended only by a combination of foreign intervention and national exhaustion. They had begun in 1820 when, in the absence of the viceroy, Beresford, in Brazil, a revolt against absolutism and British domination broke out (it started in Oporto, always a focus of liberal opinions). A constituent assembly was set up, which drafted a constitution on the lines of the abortive Spanish Constitution of 1812. This would have made Portugal into a crowned republic with a single-chamber legislature and destroyed the privileges of the nobles and the Church. King João VI, on British advice, returned to Portugal from Brazil and was constrained to accept a constitution that would have reduced him to a cipher. His estranged wife, the formidable virago Carlota Joaquina, and her favorite and younger son, Miguel, had different views; and Miguel rapidly became a hero in the eyes of the populace, who cared nothing for liberalism and freemasonry. An English observer, perhaps in jest, remarked of Portugal at that time: "Little or nothing is to be expected of any attempt to introduce civilization among the Turks." For Oliveira Martins, the likeness was just:

The training of three centuries had made the Portuguese into a people fanatical, violent, apathetic, given to intrigue, vile, and weak—just like the peoples of the Orient. . . . To a primitive, visionary, demagogic Catholicism resembling the religious manias of the East; to a ruling class made up of worthless adventurers and bigoted and stupid parasites; to a bourgeoisie of no account, a senile aristocracy, a clergy became a landholding caste, and a populace wretched, cretinized, fanatical, and mendicant: to all these add the endemic violence and the senseless fury of the Portuguese temperament—so like that of the Turk—and one must recognize that the comparison is illuminating.[33]

The constitution came into force toward the end of 1822, and within three months the first of a series of military insurrections broke out against it. For his part in the third of these (April 1824) Miguel was banished from the realm. The king's party now sought a middle course between the Jacobinism of the 1822 constitution, which was declared of no effect, and the absolutism represented by the queen. But King João died suddenly in March 1826, and with the last king of the House of Bragança died any hope of avoiding violent conflict, for the succession of the heir apparent, who held liberal opinions, was ruled out by the fact of his being already Emperor of Brazil.* (The constituent assembly's liberal views had not taken it to the point of granting autonomy to the colonies—hence the complete breach.)

Though Pedro IV was proclaimed king, it was assumed that he would immediately abdicate; but he conceived the notion of first granting his Portuguese people a constitutional charter. This, though more moderate than the constitution of 1822, was anathema to traditionalists, and so Pedro's further design, that his infant daughter Maria da Gloria should become queen and in due course marry her uncle Miguel, who would meanwhile act as regent, failed in its unifying intention. True, Miguel swore fealty both to his niece and to the charter (twice); but the mental reservations underlying these oaths became apparent within a few weeks of his return from exile in February 1828. His adherents greeted him as king from the beginning, and when he was so proclaimed on June 30, 1828, it was amid general acclamation. Only from Oporto had there been any organized opposition, and this rapidly disintegrated; a score of distinguished liberal exiles who had landed there on June 26 made haste to reembark for England; 2500 of their sympathizers reached a British refuge, after first retreating overland into Galicia. Only the tiny garrison of Angra, on the Açorean island of Terceira, held out amid a Miguelist population for Queen Maria and the charter.

With common prudence, the Miguelists might have established their rule permanently; but prudence was a virtue not granted to them. The British would have afforded them recognition—and a loan —on condition of a political amnesty; filled with an idolatrous frenzy, they would not hear of it. An accident in which Miguel's carriage was overturned and his leg broken was blamed not only on the mules, which were put to death, but on the liberals; bands of bravos roamed

---

* It was generally believed, though there was and is no proof, that João was poisoned. Pedro IV should properly be excluded from the list of Portuguese kings, since as Emperor of Brazil he was debarred from the succession; Miguel, no matter what people like Ameal may say, was patently a usurper. The later kings were predominantly German by blood, like so many other crowned heads in nineteenth-century Europe.

the streets of Lisbon, beating with bludgeons anyone suspect of being a liberal or a Freemason. Pamphleteers and preachers lauded the bludgeon (*o cacête*) as a sovereign remedy for these vices. Some indeed went further. A friar, preaching in the presence of Miguel himself, counseled him as follows: "Sire! in the name of God here present, in the name of religion, I ask your majesty to put an end to that vile liberal *canaille,* for they are unbelievers and Freemasons. Your majesty knows that there are three ways of ending them: to hang them, to let them starve to death in prison, and to give them poison—poison, Sire!"*

The government acted as if it relished this advice. Special tribunals were set up to seek out and punish political offenders. In Oporto alone more than eight thousand cases were tried between 1828 and 1832. Comparatively few prisoners were executed, but well over a thousand were transported to the African colonies, and during 1831 the number of those in prison was put at more than 25,000. Conditions in the prisons were unspeakable. The Terror, official and unofficial, did not confine itself to Portuguese citizens. Members of the wealthy British colonies in Lisbon and Oporto suffered arrest and molestation; the Tory government in London turned a blind eye to these offenses, but the Whig government that succeeded it in 1830 did not, and the Miguelists were obliged to pay compensation to those offended, and to dismiss the offenders. The new French government of Louis Philippe went further. In reprisal for the arrest, trial, and sentence of transportation passed on two French residents of Lisbon (one of whom was also flogged through the streets), a French fleet blockaded the Tagus in July 1831, demanding release and indemnification of the prisoners and dismissal of the judges. When this was refused, the fleet entered the river and threatened to bombard Lisbon; the Portuguese fleet, though standing to arms, was hemmed in between the enemy and the waterfront, so that an engagement was out of the question. Without a shot being fired, the French were able to exact, in addition to their original demands, an indemnity of 800,000 francs and the surrender of the fleet as lawful prize of battle.

This humiliation was more than an isolated incident; it was a sign that Great Britain and France were no longer willing to stay neutral

---

* Quoted in *Portugal Contemporaneo,* Vol. I, p. 131. Oliveira Martins' account of the Miguelist terror, pp. 132–56, is almost unbearably vivid.

in the struggle for the Portuguese throne. It was a far cry now from the time in January 1829 when a British warship had prevented an expedition of political exiles from landing in the Azores. In August 1829 a Miguelist attack on Terceira was beaten off, and in the following two years the liberals succeeded in establishing themselves in the whole archipelago. In April 1831 Pedro, the Emperor of Brazil, was forced to abdicate in favor of his son, and left for Europe to fight for his daughter's rights. He spent the winter of 1831–32 raising money and mercenaries, mainly in England, where the government turned a blind eye to infractions of the Foreign Enlistment Act. In February 1832 Pedro's expedition left its base in Brittany and sailed to the Açores; in June it was ready to start for the mainland. The "foreign invasion," as Oliveira Martins, with some justice, calls it, landed unopposed on the coast north of Oporto on July 8, 1832.[34]

The bizarre war of succession that followed was marked by a singular want of military competence on either side. Not a soul rose in support of Maria II and the charter, and the liberals shortly found themselves besieged, though never closely invested, in Oporto, along with an unenthusiastic populace. The siege lasted for a year, and the winter of 1832–33 was one of great privation, but the Miguelist generals failed in attempts to take the city by storm, and Pedro's own determination never wavered. At length the liberals decided on a diversion, in the form of a small expedition to the Algarve, led by the Duke of Terceira and their new naval commander, the English Charles Napier. On learning that the liberal force had landed, the remnant of the Miguelist fleet put to sea, but was utterly defeated by Napier off Cape St. Vincent on July 5, 1833. Thereupon Terceira led his small force boldly across the Alentejo toward Lisbon, ignoring a much larger Miguelist army on his flank, and drove the advance guard of the Lisbon garrison south of the Tagus into the river; the Miguelist army immediately withdrew from the capital and the liberals occupied it without firing another shot. Thenceforth the Miguelists were thrown on the defensive: the British, French, and Spanish governments formed a quadruple alliance with the government of Maria II, and although desultory fighting continued throughout the winter, Miguel was eventually constrained to sign an honorable capitulation at Evora-Monte and to go into exile.* It was a remarkable reversal of

* Not the same place as Evora, *pace* the Encyclopaedia Britannica (11th and subsequent editions, entry "Evora").

fortune for one who six years earlier had been welcomed by the populace as the new Messiah.

v

The victory of the liberals was due in part to the errors of the opposition, in part to the tenacity of Pedro and his leading supporters, in part to foreign help, and in part to the discovery by Napier and Terceira that fortune favors the bold. Its permanent importance, and in some degree its very success, was due to a remarkable man in Pedro's entourage, the constitutional reformer Mousinho da Silveira (1780–1849).* Mousinho, who had begun his career as a magistrate in his native province of the Alentejo, had come to Lisbon as a result of the revolution of 1820 as Director of Customs, a post he resumed in 1823 after a period as Minister of Finance. When the Miguelists took over in 1828, Mousinho sought leave of absence and withdrew to Paris. Neither courtier nor politician, he was regarded by most of his fellow exiles as eccentric, even mad (it is said that he taught them political economy, from the work of McCulloch); and he remained resolutely aloof from the various political factions into which they were divided. For Mousinho, constitutional forms were unimportant; what mattered was the social and economic structure that lay behind them. A convinced individualist and utilitarian, he held that the ancien régime in Portugal, with its congeries of special privileges for the church and the nobility, its mass of obstructions to the free use of economic resources, needed to be completely destroyed if the country were to flourish; and he was prepared, single-handed, to draft the necessary measures. Further, he saw that the time to do this was before the consummation of the liberal victory; that if fundamental reforms were not nailed to the masthead, they would never be imposed on opponents who had already submitted.

It happened that Mousinho was one of the few among the exiles with any experience of government; eccentric as well as deaf he might be, but his political qualifications were indispensable to Pedro,

---

* There is an excellent life by Possidonio M. Laranjo Coelho (*Mousinho da Silveira,* Lisbon, 1918) which supplements classic contemporary accounts by Herculano and Garrett cited here.

Ameal's dismissal of Mousinho in a phrase—"idealista kantiano" (*Historia de Portugal,* p. 649)—is indicative of the extent to which political partisanship can go in Salazar's Portugal.

and in the government on Terceira he became both Minister of Finance and Minister of Justice. There, and in Oporto during the siege, he busied himself in drafting and publishing laws of the most sweeping character. These were dictatorial, in the sense that no one seems to have been consulted on their terms, but their administration was not intended to be arbitary. "Under the usurpation," he wrote, "there are forced taxation, prisons, fetters, tribunals, and gallows; all things are arbitrary, no man is master of his own. Under the legitimate rule, there are no excise duties, no duties on exports, no taxes on fish, no monopolies of wine and brandy, no tithes, no feudal rents, no fourths, no sixths, no eighths." The abolition of tithes, he asserted, would double the value of landed property. The preamble to one of his decrees, dated August 13, 1832, referred to

the sorry picture presented by a hardworking citizen who, after the exertions of an entire year, sees his harvest being taken away by a thousand agents of the greed of the clergy and the overlords (*donatários*) and is left with a miserable residue . . . in order that there may be, at every cloister gate and coachhouse, a flow of alms with which to nourish the city beggars, the sons of the very workers who but for rents and tithes would be hardworking and respectable citizens.[35]

This language was not without its effect on the opposition, even though the liberals at that time controlled no more of the country than the streets of Oporto. The decrees

were circulated and expounded; and the soldiers of absolutism, who were Portuguese farmers, began to see how well it would suit them to be defeated—so that they would no longer see every year the agents of the *comendador* or the prelate, the chapter or the parson, the overlord or the castellan, one exacting a tenth, another a quarter, another an eighth of the gross yield of each crop. . . .*

Nonetheless, the influence of the decrees fell far short of the liberals' expectations, for the war still had to be fought, with political weapons as well as military. Mousinho refused on principle to countenance the seizure of Miguelists' property, or of the stocks of port wine in Vila Nova de Gaia, to raise money to pay the mercenaries. In January 1833 he was dismissed by Pedro from his ministerial posts. He

* António Sérgio, "Introdução Histórica," in *Guia de Portugal* (Lisbon, Biblioteca Nacional, 1924), Vol. I, pp. 59-60. The whole essay, comprising pages 31-62, is a brilliant summary of the history of Portugal from its origins to the early twentieth century.

never again held high political office, and his program was left incomplete for a generation and more.

"Only madmen," wrote Oliveira Martins of Mousinho, "have accomplished truly great things on this earth."[36] The single-handed destruction of the ancien régime in Portugal, rotten though that order was, betokens a singleness of purpose that is terrifying. Mousinho's achievement in the one year 1832 has rightly been compared with that of the French States-General in 1789.[37] Tithes and feudal dues were swept away. A beginning was made with the abolition of entailed, inalienable property (*morgados* and *capellas*), those holdings having an annual revenue of less than two hundred milréis being done away with. Excise duties were abolished or reduced because they interfered with trade, even as morgados interfered with the property market. Monopolies, such as those in soap-making and the export of port wine, disappeared. The jury system and equality before the law were established; judicial and administrative functions were no longer vested in the same persons, and public offices ceased to be hereditary; a new administrative system based on the French model was decreed;* the army was stripped of its second- and third-line nonprofessional elements, the *milícia* and *ordenança*; restrictions on education were removed. Moreover, Mousinho looked forward to the complete abolition of monastic institutions having the right of mortmain, on grounds not religious but economic: after the loss of Brazil, he declared, the nation could not maintain so great a number of persons living directly or indirectly on the labor of others. Unlike other reforms he forecast, this one was promptly effected after his fall: the confiscated monastic lands formed much of the "feast" (*regabofe*) served up to liberal supporters after the Miguelist surrender at Evora-Monte.[38]

Though negative and incomplete, the work of Mousinho da Silveira was decisive and final. As Herculano says, once the stones of the absolutist edifice were reduced to powder and scattered to the winds, its rebuilding became impossible—as it had not been after the revolutionary period of 1820–23 or the "chartist" period of 1826–28.[39] But though the necessary conditions for the emergence of Portugal into the nineteenth-century liberal world were thus fulfilled, the sufficient condi-

* Mistakenly, in the opinion of Alexandre Herculano. See "Mousinho da Silveira, ou La Révolution Portugaise" (in French, 1859), reprinted in *Opusculos, Tomo II: Questões Publicas* (Lisbon, 1904), pp. 175–225. The opinion cited is on pp. 219–21.

tions were not. The victors of 1834 failed to build a new Portugal on the ruins of the old, or even to provide a sufficiency of law and order under which the Benthamite millennium foreseen by Mousinho might have opportunity to work itself out. As his friend Almeida Garrett declared in a memorial essay:

We are placed between a past irretrievably buried under the [new] laws and a future tremendous because obscure, unknowable, and in no way prepared for—in a present so absurd, so disjointed, so incongruous, so chimerical, so ridiculous that if the prospect before us were not such a vale of tears, the way in which we live, in which we tax ourselves, in which we are administered, in which we exist as a people, a nation, a kingdom, would be a matter for uproarious merriment.[40]

Herculano in 1856 put it more bitterly:

Before and after the events of 1831–34, the history of liberalism in Portugal is but a comedy in bad taste, rising, or falling perhaps ... to the level of melodrama.... In our Shakespearian drama there are but two great and noble figures: Mousinho and the son of João VI [Pedro]. The rest are beneath notice: financiers, barons, viscounts, counts, marquesses of new and old creation, commanders, the beribboned, counselors ... gnawing a meager prey called the budget, or crying "Stop, thief!" when they cannot get a share.[41]

VI

What had given the liberal revolution coherence and force vanished with the dropping of its philosopher and the death of its tyrant. Pedro was only thirty-six when he died; his daughter was not yet sixteen when she was proclaimed of age to reign in September 1834. Married, widowed, and remarried (to Prince Ferdinand of Saxe-Coburg) within the next eighteen months, Maria II was to die in 1853 at the age of thirty-four, giving birth to her eleventh child. Neither she nor her consort was a nonentity, but they were inexperienced. Moreover, they were foreign, and so was their entourage—the royal tutor and the royal physician were Germans, the wet nurses and the coachman English, the milliner French, and only the chaplain Portuguese—so ran the compaint of a resurgent Miguelism in 1846.[42] Feeling against foreigners ran high in Portugal at this time. Successive Belgian envoys, sent by Ferdinand's uncle, Leopold I, attempted the role that was played by Baron Stockmar at the court of Leopold's other niece.* The

---

* That is, Queen Victoria. Ferdinand himself seems to have been a more attractive, because less priggish, version of his cousin, Victoria's Prince Consort.

Belgians were suspected of wanting a reward for their assistance and advice in the form of a Portuguese African possession. Furthermore, the British ambassador, Lord Howard de Walden, frequently backed by the Royal Navy, played a part that to many Portuguese leaders seemed equivocal, for all that it stopped short of overt intervention in the country's domestic affairs—or perhaps for that very reason. For an idealist like Herculano, the politics of Maria II's reign appeared to be no more than

a series of squabbles, dishonesties, ineptitudes, and incoherencies linked by a single underlying motive—the enrichment of the party chiefs. Ideas are not to be found, bar those that men of that stamp lap up in the most vulgar and banal French books. Today they are counted progressives, tomorrow reactionaries; today conservatives, tomorrow reformers; but look at them closely, and they will be found forever null.[43]

Of the ruck of politicians, this judgment was doubtless true, though exception ought to be made for two at least—the upright Sá da Bandeira, and the popular hero Passos Manuel, whose defiance of the queen in the name of the constitution of 1822 to which she had signified her assent was the occasion for one of Oliveira Martins' finest set pieces.[44] The queen's assent had been given under duress, following a successful coup d'état in September 1836 by those for whom Pedro's charter, with its hereditary upper house and indirectly elected lower house, was insufficiently radical. The principal political aim of the court thereafter was to find tools with which to overthrow the *Septembrists*. The attempt in November to dismiss them from office failed for want of armed force to support it; indeed, the queen's advisers caused British bluejackets to be landed to protect her person—a panic move which underlined and increased her unpopularity. But the Septembrists appeared unable to put their victory to any constructive purpose, and the queen, for her part, now resorted to revolutionary means in order to get rid of them. A first coup by Marshals Terceira and Saldanha in July 1837 was abortive; in April 1838 the queen was compelled to endorse another constitution, one somewhat more moderate than that of 1822. About that time, however, she at last found her strong man in Costa Cabral, a onetime radical turned moderate, who as *administrador* of Lisbon had put down populist riots with a firm hand. In November 1839 the last of the Septembrist cabinets was dismissed and replaced by one made up of Chartists, including Costa Cabral as Minister of Justice. In January 1842, while still holding that post, Cabral engineered a coup by the garrison of Oporto—of all places—in favor of a restored charter. Various changes of ministry followed, from which Cabral emerged some weeks later as Minister of Home Affairs and the dominant figure of the realm.

The regime of Costa Cabral "was not, nor did it seek to be, a dictatorship, but was merely a way of instituting a form de jure that would serve as cover for an absolutism de facto."[45] These words of Oliveira Martins have a strangely up-to-date ring. For such covert manipulation the restored charter, with its indirect elections, was preeminently suited. The new liberalism of Cabral was to rest, not on the sovereignty of the people, but on the power of money. His new administrative code subordinated elected local councils in parish, borough, and district to officials nominated by the minister. Moreover, public officials might be members of parliament. A formidable engine of patronage and power was thus created, which for a time seemed to sweep all before it. In 1845 the parvenu minister became Count of Tomar and entertained his sovereign at the castle there that had once belonged to the Knights Templar. His pretensions were derided and the malicious accused him and the queen of being lovers. Nevertheless, by a combination of chicanery and brute force he succeeded in winning the elections of that year, though not, of course, in silencing his critics in the House of Peers.

Above all, Cabral had failed to reckon with the common people. In April 1846 an uprising broke out in the rural Minho, the precise origin and leadership of which is a mystery. Its eponymous heroine, one Maria da Fonte, may or may not have existed in fact, but certainly the country women took a prominent part in it. This peasant revolt had nothing in common with the endemic military coups, nor had it any clear political orientation. It was primarily a protest against Cabral, against his tax gatherers sent out from Lisbon, and against a new law that decreed, in the name of hygiene, that the dead be buried in cemeteries instead of within the parish churches. Moreover, it had undertones of Miguelism and clericalism. But as it spread beyond the Minho it took on an urban and slightly Septembrist flavor, though still without a program other than the removal of Cabral and his brother the Minister of Justice. The brothers bowed before the storm, resigned, and fled to Spain. A new ministry was appointed—one containing a Septembrist element—and began the work of national pacification.

In October 1846, however, the queen abruptly dismissed this new ministry and appointed as Prime Minister the old marshal Saldanha, once a radical but now under the influence of Cabral. This was a declaration of war on her political opponents, and it was taken as such; within days the country was at arms on one side or another, with Oporto, as ever, the radical stronghold. The confused and indecisive civil war that followed was mainly remarkable for the ruthless behavior of the government's generals whenever they won an engagement and for the emergence of a sizeable Miguelist element which dominated the Minho for some little time and made common cause with the revolutionary junta in Oporto. This unforeseen development was decisive in ending the war, for it enabled Maria to invoke the Quadruple Alliance of 1834, by which Britain, France, and Spain were bound to defend her regime against Miguelist attack. Britain, in the person of Lord Palmerston, had supported the queen a decade earlier against the Septembrists, who were regarded as radical and, moreover, pro-French.* But her conduct in 1846–47 seemed worthy of Miguel himself. "It would be impossible," Prime Minister Russell told the Cabinet, "to support such atrocities by British arms without bringing disgrace on the British name." "If Portugal is to be governed despotically and by sword and bayonet," Palmerston told the British ambassador in Lisbon, "a man is as good as a woman for such purpose, and it matters little whether the despot is called by one Christian name or another. Pray make this very civilly to be understood by the King and Queen."[46] The British at length succeeded in securing a general amnesty as the price of their intervention. It was then the revolutionary junta in Oporto that had to be coerced by an Anglo-Spanish combined operation. Most of the Septembrist leaders, fearful of the Miguelist specter they had conjured up, seem to have been willing to meet the forces of coercion halfway. The Convention of Gramido, which brought hostilities to an end, was imposed on adversaries who had become too war-weary even to negotiate peace without an outside mediator.

Before long it became evident that the opposing factions in Portu-

---

* C. K. Webster, *The Foreign Policy of Palmerston, 1830–41* (London, 1951), especially pp. 370–85, 479–94. At the risk of being accused of pedantry, one must remark that Sir Charles Webster not only misspells names such as Sá da Bandeira, Vieira de Castro, and Mendizabal, the backer of D. Pedro, but bestows an uncovenanted final "e" on the British Marshal Beresford.

gal had destroyed each other as political forces, and that the apparent victory of Cabralism was hollow. Tomar himself, who while still in exile had become Ambassador at Madrid and so helped to engineer the allied intervention, returned to parliament in 1848; the next year he displaced Saldanha as Prime Minister. Revolutionary opposition to him there was none; but his opponents in parliament and press pursued him relentlessly. Having quarreled with his ally Saldanha, Tomar had him dismissed in 1850 from his honorific offices at court —an error of judgment, for the marshal, though unstable and without principle as a politician, had many friends and admirers. Searching for personal revenge, Saldanha found allies in a group of younger men on the outskirts of politics, among whom Alexandre Herculano was outstanding. Secretly they worked out a political program: direct elections, the abolition of the hereditary peerage and of entailed property. In April 1851 Saldanha, after an initial disappointment, staged a coup among the Oporto garrison and marched toward Lisbon. Tomar's colleagues, and even the king and queen, for whom he had done so much, would not risk civil war on his behalf; once again he resigned and fled abroad, and on May 15 Saldanha entered Lisbon in triumph. His was the revolution to end revolutions; an area of political appeasement, of *regeneração,* had set in.

VII

It was high time, for the treasury was empty and the national debt had soared—in 1848 it was already five times what it had been fifteen years earlier—and the yield from the taxes had not increased. The value of Portuguese foreign trade, thanks to the wars and the loss of Brazil, was less than half what it had been at the turn of the century. Only the population continued to grow: by 1850 it was over three and a half million. For the country's woes the *regeneradores* had a new, or at any rate a different, remedy: not democracy but economic development. Costa Cabral had indeed made a start in that direction but had achieved little; now economic growth was to become not merely an expedient but an article of faith. In the words of the poet Guerra Junqueiro, the regeneradores "sought to irrigate the country with sterling so that a new Portugal might arise, the peer of other European countries and as progressive as they."[47]

The apostle of the new evangel was Fontes Pereira de Mello, a comparative newcomer to politics and an army engineer by training, who became Minister of Finance in August 1851 and retained that post for nearly five years. He once described himself in a parliamentary speech as a "fanatic for means of communication.... If it were possible to pass a law that the whole Portuguese nation should go traveling for three months, it would be our salvation." "This would be ridiculous were it not sincere," is Oliveira Martins' comment.* A few years earlier, Almeida Garrett had derided the whole notion of economic progress:

Go plant potatoes, O generation of steamboats and earthenware; macadamize highways, build railroads, construct the great birds of Icarus.... Go, breadwinner, go; reduce all to figures, every question on this earth to equations of material advantage; buy, sell, play the stock market. At the end of all this, what has it profited the human species? That there are a few dozen more rich men. I ask the political economists and the moralists if they have calculated the number of souls who must be condemned to misery, overwork, demoralization, infamy, crapulous ignorance, invincible misfortune, and absolute penury in order to produce one man of wealth?[48]

This kind of language, both for and against progress, was not confined to Portugal. Its English analogues are to be found in the verses of Tennyson on the occasion of the Great Exhibition of 1851, in the anger of Ruskin against railroads in the Lake District, and in the gibes of Peacock against the Steam Intellect Society. In England, however, as in the Western world generally, the objectors to economic change were a minority; in Portugal, though *fontismo* prevailed at the time, it has become common form to regard it as misguided, even vicious.

The indictment of Fontes' policies may be summarized under two heads. First, in the words of António Sérgio, that Fontes "confined himself to developing the *circulation* of wealth when what was really necessary was to reform the structure of the *productive* organism." Second, that by reliance on foreign capital to build what would nowadays be called the economic infrastructure, he was perpetuating the bad economic habits of centuries: there was no real difference between Mafra and the new ports and railroads. "Utilitarianism was substituted for pomp and religiosity, but the end result ... was the same:

* From a speech given on April 2, 1856, and quoted in Oliveira Martins, *Portugal Contemporaneo*, Vol. II, p. 361.

a society living on foreign or abnormal resources and not on the fruits of its own labor and savings."[49]

Fontismo thus produced—it was argued—a bogus economic euphoria that hid from the nation the facts of life: an underemployment of resources, an overstaffed bureaucracy, a persistent and increasingly adverse balance of trade, and an equally persistent budgetary deficit. The Portuguese house of cards was held up only by the "export of human cattle"—emigrants, mainly to Brazil, whose remittances served to maintain a precarious equilibrium in the balance of payments; in 1890, as its most eloquent critic had foreseen, a crisis in Brazil brought it tumbling down.[50] In the eyes of his detractors, it would have been better for Portugal if Fontes had not been able to accomplish the financial miracles by which he made his name: the consolidation of the national debt and the reopening of the London and Paris money markets to Portuguese flotations. The former feat, accomplished by a decree of December 1852, was essentially a bankruptcy to end bankruptcies: it made an end of the fiction whereby successive loans were termed amortizable and the main purpose of each was to repay its predecessor. The reopening of the money markets was achieved by a variety of concessions to foreign capitalists, which Fontes' opponents thought too generous: this largely accounted for the fall of the regenerador ministry in June 1856. Fontismo, however, was to persist for a generation and more, whatever government might be in office.

Unless Portugal were to remain at the stage of economic backwardness she was in in 1850, there was really no alternative to the liberal policy of encouraging investment from abroad and lowering tariffs on imported raw materials. Economically speaking, the ancient kingdom was a small South American republic that happened to be attached to Europe. As Herculano put it, "In civilization we are two rungs below Turkey and about the same distance above the Hottentots."[51]

The liberals, like some modern writers on economic development, appear naïve in thinking that freedom of trade and the import of capital would of themselves in short order transform the social and economic structure of the country. The same naïveté, of course, was displayed by critics who found national salvation in balanced budgets and protective tariffs. Mousinho da Silveira had known better, though he evidently underrated the ability of a long-established social framework to survive even fundamental legal changes. A recent observer has noted, for instance, the almost impassable class barriers that exist today in the south of Portugal after more than a century of equality before the law.[52] The constant references by Portuguese writers to "the common people" (*o povo*) as a kind of separate social entity bear witness to a state of mind that consciously or unconsciously regards privilege as a natural and inevitable social phenomenon.

The most obvious mark of this extralegal privilege is literacy. In 1864, the earliest year for which figures are available, the proportion of illiterates in Portugal was put at 88 per cent of the population. In 1900, it was 78 per cent.[53] Even if children below the age of seven are excluded, two out of three Portuguese were illiterate as late as 1911, and in 1950, the figure was 40 per cent. Tsarist Russia alone among European nations had comparable rates. The majority of the population, in fact if not in law, were second-class citizens, excluded from effective participation in politics, and acting as a massive brake on any but the simplest types of technical change. At the same time, the education of the privileged minority was predominantly nontechnical: out of 998 students at the ancient University of Coimbra in 1854, 465 were in law, 94 in theology, and 62 in medicine.[54] Not merely was there a conspicuous absence of people qualified to act as industrial managers or foremen—it would have been surprising, in view of the lack of opportunities, if there had not been—but there was no reservoir of literate nonspecialists on which to draw, no potential source of skilled labor outside the traditional handicrafts. In short, the state of Portugal in the second half of the nineteenth century was comparable to that of many "underdeveloped" countries in the second half of the twentieth. The requisite—though not necessarily the sufficient—conditions for development lay not merely in the comparatively easy provision of capital and technical knowledge from without, but in the arduous accomplishment of drastic changes in the social and educational structures: changes that could not come from the people themselves.

If the infrastructure erected by fontismo might better be described as an incongruous and exotic superstructure atop an imperfectly renovated ancient building, the fault lay with circumstances rather than with policy. Railroads, ports, telegraphs, gasworks, and streetcars do not cease to be public utilities because they are owned and managed by foreigners. Much of the criticism leveled at the liberals at the time and afterward seems to have been more or less disguised xenophobia, which virtually amounted to an assertion that rather than take one's economics from the British and one's politics from the French, it were better to have none at all. Resentment against the British especially was so powerful as to deprive many politically conscious Portuguese of the ability to judge their ally's actions and proposals on their merits. Indeed, for all that the first Anglo-Portuguese treaty dates back to 1373, it would be difficult to produce any evidence of genuine amity between the two countries, at any rate in the nineteenth century. The monstrous disparity in wealth and power between them was all too apt to be reflected in a contemptuous patronage on the part of the one, matched by a futile petulance on that of the other. Even a man like Oswald Crawfurd, who was British consul in Oporto for many years and who wrote with sympathy, charm, and penetration about Portuguese manners and customs, could evince an insufferable degree of national arrogance. When, as a result of Salisbury's ultimatum to Portugal in January 1890, there were anti-British riots in Oporto, Crawfurd wrote to a member of the British community there:

I think a good deal depends on us English holding together ... showing a bold front, and at the same time remaining cool and courteous in our dealings with the natives. Above everything, we must not bend the back to them. We are here by virtue of our prestige as Englishmen. ... Let us not imitate the Lisbonian English, who in truth are of another caste ... and have always stood towards the natives in a more subservient attitude than we condescend to use in Oporto. We have held our own way here all these long generations by never bowing down before the Portuguese. For Heaven's sake, don't let us begin now.[55]

The ascendancy and aloofness of the British in Oporto was a matter for particular resentment because of its close association with the famous Methuen Treaty of 1703, which provided for a preferential duty on port wine in England in return for a lifting of the prohibition on English textiles entering Portugal. It became an article of faith with many Portuguese that this was a leonine arrangement by which their textile industry (a recent artificial creation) was sacrificed for no comparable advantage—the presumptive advantage to the Portuguese consumer of textiles being left out of account. Oddly enough, Adam Smith, who singled out the Methuen Treaty for discussion in *The Wealth of Nations,* did not deal with this aspect of it; he held that the treaty was clearly advantageous to Portugal and disadvantageous to Great Britain, in that no preferential treatment commensurate with that afforded to Portuguese wines was secured for the British over other imported textiles.[56] Formally this was true, although it may have been implicit in the treaty that existing prohibitions would be maintained except in the British case. Adam Smith's chief concern, however, was to rebut the mercantilist claim that the treaty was a master stroke because the balance of trade it established [between England and Portugal] was such as to secure the British a constant supply of bullion from Brazil.*

Whatever the precise merits of the Methuen Treaty, there is no need to invoke an element of specific duress in order to explain the dominant position of the British in Portugal in the early nineteenth century. Geography, power politics, sea transport and sea power, along with superior economic development and governmental competence, combined to make it almost a foregone conclusion. That the Anglo-Portuguese partnership was unequal does not mean that it was not advantageous to both sides. But it was hard for the Portuguese to see the advantage when it was embodied in such forms as the viceroyalty of Beresford or the right of British subjects to be tried by a judge of their own nationality. Moreover, though the Portuguese ruling class contained, and still contains, numerous Anglophiles by conviction and preference, the preponderant foreign intellectual and cultural influence in Portugal has long been French—which has often in the past meant that it has been ipso facto anti-British. French writers, for instance, have been foremost in criticizing the Methuen Treaty.[57] In the eyes of the Portuguese intelligentsia, the British, particularly those actually resident in Portugal, have tended to seem not only aloof, but commercial and philistine; it caused offense that residents of long standing should make no effort to master the Portuguese language. One could readily multiply examples of this incompatibility, but it will suffice to say that the greatest magnanimity and tact were required, particularly on the part of the stronger partner, to keep the alliance running smoothly. Marvaud and others erred gravely in dis-

---

* Like a true Scot, Smith evidently preferred claret to port, for he remarks elsewhere that the "celebrated treaty with Portugal" caused Britain to bring in a worse commodity from a country farther off. See *Wealth of Nations,* ed. Cannan (London, 1904), pp. 159–60.

missing Portugal as a "client state."* The lives of the British diplomatists accredited to Lisbon would have been easier, if also duller, had the Portuguese been as subservient as that term would imply.

By the same token, the foreign capital that flowed into Portugal for public works under Fontes and his successors was by no means exclusively British. Belgium, Spain, and France in particular made substantial contributions. Portuguese government bonds, which, in the beginning, were held mainly in Britain, were largely disposed of to European buyers in course of time, so that when the crash came in 1890–92 the bondholders principally affected were in France and Germany. The bonds had always been patently speculative, a fact reflected in the issue price, which was usually fifty per cent or less of the par value, giving a real yield on "3 per cents" of more than 6 per cent, and in one case more than 10 per cent. Hence the remark by one Portuguese writer, after the partial repudiation of the foreign debt, that the foreign lenders had only received their deserts![58] It was scarcely to be wondered at that a government that had not balanced its budget in half a century or more should be reckoned a poor credit risk. What affords matter for reflection on the international capital market in the second half of the nineteenth century is that the rake's progress should have gone on so long, and that the rate of interest was not forced up so high as to be altogether prohibitive.**

VIII

The constitutional changes forming Saldanha's program in 1851 were only carried out in part. The Additional Act of 1852 substituted direct for indirect elections, but retained the existing annual property qualifications of 100 milréis for an elector and 400 milréis for a member of the lower house. The hereditary peerage, and entails, were untouched. The number of registered electors in 1851 was 36,400, or

---

* Angel Marvaud, *Le Portugal et ses Colonies* (Paris, 1912), pp. 54–73 *passim,* adopts this line completely. Morier, writing to Salisbury in September 1879, referred, it is true, to "the docility the Portuguese have always shown to our handling"; but this was neither good history nor did it prove a good forecast of Morier's and subsequent envoys' experience. (Quotation in Roger Anstey, *Britain and the Congo in the Nineteenth Century,* Oxford, 1962, p. 84.)

** In the sixteenth century, the king of Portugal had had to pay around 18 per cent for loans on the Antwerp Bourse. See Richard Ehrenburg, tr. H. M. Lucas, *Capital and Finance in the Age of the Renaissance* (London, 1928), p. 268.

about 7 per cent of the population; those listed as eligible for election numbered 4,509. It is hardly surprising that persons holding office under the crown were not excluded, as in Great Britain, from membership in the legislature, for this would have reduced the numbers eligible still further. The retention of the hereditary element does not mean that the aristocrats of the ancien régime had contrived to retain political power. On the contrary, the great majority of peers were of recent creation, most of the old aristocracy having died or fallen into obscurity. Mid-nineteenth century Portugal was essentially a plutocracy, enriched by the spoil of the monastic houses and possessing that passion for titles and honors that marks a certain type of nouveau riche.[59] Moreover, it was a plutocracy divorced from the land; its members might indeed own large estates, but they rarely lived on them or undertook their management. There was nothing in Portugal to correspond to the British "landed interest," with all that that term implies in the way of benevolent rural despotism, nor was there any cult of country life. As Oswald Crawfurd wrote in 1879:

The Portuguese never play at country life as our people are fond of doing: that is, they do not betake themselves to the country and lead a continuous existence there without having real duties and interests in the land. I think they are in the right, and that to be secluded in a dull country neighborhood ... is the surest of all methods of dulling the social faculties and of slipping back in the race towards culture and the higher education.

He added: "The Portuguese as a rule care not a straw for culture and the higher education, but they hate seclusion of this kind."[60]

A governing class of absentees could hardly be expected to have an enlightened interest in agriculture, or to legislate in a farsighted manner about it. When at length the legislative structure of the liberal state was completed by the Civil Code of 1866—entails having been abolished three years earlier—the possible economic consequences of the new law of inheritance, which formed part of the code, seem to have escaped the degree of notice that was their due. In fact, the parliamentary debates on the code were centered on its provision for civil marriage. In lieu of the previous more or less rigid insistence on primogeniture, the new law of inheritance prescribed that estates should be divided equally among heirs—save that a maximum of one-third might be willed to a single recipient. Some later writers hold that this law has been a potent factor in the excessive subdivision of peasant property that has taken place during the past hundred years. Yet there has not—thanks to the nature of the terrain—been a substantial break-up of the great estates of the Alentejo.[61] Basílio Telles, who wrote with great authority on the land question, denied that the law was responsible for the undue fragmentation of property, which he held not proven; he pointed to purchase, and marriage of heiresses, as factors working in the opposite direction.[62] Later work suggests that a distinction needs to be made between a fragmentation of the land itself and a multiplication of holders. Fragmentation, by the nineteen-thirties, had reached a point where the average parcel in continental Portugal was but four-fifths of a hectare—about half what it had been in the 1860's—and parcels ranged from twenty hectares in the district of Setubal to just over a quarter of a hectare in the district of Viana do Castelo. The average number of parcels held by those liable to land-tax in 1931–32—about 20 per cent of the population—was 8.6; in the district of Bragança it was 16, and in that of Setubal, 1.6; and many peasant proprietors also leased supplementary parcels. Reformers often proposed that steps be taken to restrict further fragmentation, and a decree was issued by Dr. Salazar's government in 1929 under which division of any parcel of less than one hectare, or division in such a way as to produce new parcels of less than one-half hectare, was prohibited. In 1936, however, an authoritative commentator remarked that the decree, though promising, was not being rigorously complied with.[63]

It might seem at first sight that a shortage of land, that was already the occasion for vigorous complaint three centuries ago, when the population affected was perhaps one half what it was a century ago, and a fifth of what it is today, must long since have become so intolerable as to provoke remedy; the more so because, in the words of Oswald Crawfurd, "Farming in Portugal is ... at a standstill, and it has moved very little in some fourteen hundred years. ... The ploughs differ very little from the old Roman type. ..." Crawfurd, who himself farmed in the Minho, and whose account of farming practices there can still be read with pleasure and profit, explained the comparative prosperity of the peasantry in terms of four main factors: a plenitude of water, the intensive use of farmyard litter as manure, the unearned increment arising from a secular decline in the value of the peasant's fixed copyhold rent (*fôro*), and, above all, the introduction of maize soon after the discovery of Brazil. This crop doubled at a stroke the yield of grain from a given piece of land. The same parcel, he noted, was cropped with maize continuously, year in, year out: "Nothing so astonished me, when I first saw a luxuriant Portuguese maize field, as to be told that it had produced such a crop summer after summer for a century, and would continue to do so for as long again."[64]

In Crawfurd's time, moreover, there remained even in the Minho considerable reserves of land not under cultivation. Although some of these *baldios* were already being broken up in the 1860's, perhaps earlier, the process does not appear to have been complete until well into the twentieth century. Elsewhere, the amount of uncultivated land must have been much greater. Authoritative estimates indicate that in 1874 the total land area of continental Portugal (i.e. excluding the Atlantic islands) might be divided as follows: uncultivable, 3.8 per cent; cultivable but not under cultivation, 44.3 per cent; uncultivated but productive (heath, rough pasture, etc.), 23.4 per cent; forest, 7.2 per cent; crops and fallow, 21.3 per cent. In 1902 the respective percentages were 3.8, 17.3, 21.7, 22.1, and 35.1; in 1934, 3.8, 14.9, 15, 28.4, and 37.9. Without entering minutely into the meaning of these figures, or putting excessive faith in them, one may infer, first, that the most spectacular advance during the last quarter of the nineteenth century must have been in afforestation; and second, that by the beginning of the twentieth century the possibilities of bringing more land under crops were at length—given existing techniques—nearing exhaustion.[65]

It may well be more than a coincidence that emigration, mainly from the northern provinces, reached a level during the decade immediately before the outbreak of World War I that was around twice what had previously been considered normal. In the year 1912 emigration may even have exceeded the natural increase for continental Portugal as a whole: "For each child that is born in the district of Bragança," wrote the economist Bento Carqueja in 1916, "an adult escapes to Brazil." To contemporaries the picture looked black from either aspect, whether one were to lament the demographic loss or to speculate on what would happen if Brazil were to close its doors to unskilled and illiterate elements. Two-thirds of those emigrating in 1912 were classed as illiterate; from the district of Bragança, over nine-tenths were so classed. About two-fifths of the emigrants were agricultural workers.[66] In the last years of the monarchy and the first of the republic, the enduring ability of the common man of Portugal, *O Zé Povinho,* to scrape through somehow amid the worst circumstances, whether of misgovernment or natural misfortune, might well have seemed to have reached its limits, and the secular prophecies of national doom to be at long last coming to fulfillment.

Half a century earlier it had at least seemed possible to take a more sanguine view of the prospect facing "the sick man of Western Europe."[67] With civil strife at last ended and foreign capital flowing in, it would have been remarkable if Portugal had not shared in the general mid-Victorian optimism typified by the Great Exhibition of 1851. It was a sardonic pessimism, partly engendered by hindsight, that allowed Oliveira Martins to write, thirty years later:

Precedent ... still governs us. ... Its liberalism derives from calculated passivity: *solvitur ambulando* is its watchword. People think that England is bound to look after us; but what [will happen] when there are no more Africas with which to pay her? Meanwhile, the minhoto goes, the *brasileiro* comes, and the loans are taken up; meanwhile roads are built and landowners grow rich. ... More and more this little Turkey of the Occident, with Lisbon another Constantinople ... loses the organic character of a nation. ... Our farmers and tradesmen are become landlords or lawyers; our proletarians, artisans and bookkeepers for foreign industrialists.

He added, "Truly our situation is that of the Turk."[68]

Chapter two

A Pre-Imperialist Empire

The transformation of metropolitan Portugal into a nineteenth-century liberal monarchy was not without consequence for the overseas possessions which formed, by constitutional edict, an integral part of the kingdom. Both at home and in the *províncias ultramarinas* the habits of the past proved to be stubbornly entrenched.* The frustrations that beset Mousinho da Silveira and his disciple Herculano were indeed almost minor compared with those facing ministers like Sá da Bandeira and Andrade Corvo, who sought to modernize the colonies. For it was overseas that the weakness of Portuguese administration, even in routine tasks, was at its most marked, and the gap between paper legislation and effective execution of laws most evident. Yet the very existence of this gap was something that all but the most upright and candid of the nation's political leaders found it impossible to admit—understandably, lest the admission undermine Portugal's claim to continued sovereignty overseas. The effect of this reluctance, however, was to generate a chronic state of exasperation among their critics, particularly their ally Britain. When what seemed, even to unprejudiced observers, irrefutable evidence of maladministration was met by the citation of impeccable regulations and the flat denial that any blemish existed, the only result was that the Portuguese government failed to gain credit even for good intentions.** That it may at times be politic, if no more, openly to admit imperfection and error,

* *Províncias ultramarinas* is the traditional description of the overseas colonies, revived by Dr. Salazar after World War II.
** See the case of the *serviçaes* on São Tomé, below, pp 312-24.

even to foreigners, is something that few Portuguese leaders have been willing to concede. This deficiency of imagination, this inability to put oneself in the place of an adversary or even an ally is, to be sure, not confined to Portugal. But its prevalence there has had especially unfortunate consequences for a country whose military weakness drives it to depend on diplomacy almost for its very existence.*

I

The Constitutional Charter of 1826 was at pains to specify the extent of the Portuguese dominions in Africa, as elsewhere. Article 2, paragraph 2, lists them as follows: "In West Africa, Bissau and Cacheu; on the coast of Mina, the fort of Ajudá; Angola, Benguela, and their dependencies Cabinda and Molembo; the Cape Verde Islands and the islands of S. Thomé and Principe, and their dependencies. In East Africa, Moçambique, the Rivers of Sena, Sofala, Inhambane, Quilimane, and the island of Cape Delgado."

The charter goes on to say, in Article 7, that all those born in Portugal or its dominions are Portuguese citizens; and in Article 145 it states their rights, including equality before the law. "It is positive," wrote Sá da Bandeira in 1873, "that the Portuguese inhabitants of the provinces of Africa, of Asia, and of Oceania, without distinction of race, color, or religion, have rights equal to those enjoyed by the Portuguese of Europe"—an important assertion of principle, though a cynic might regard it as nothing more for the majority of Portuguese everywhere.[1] Nor, if one takes it to refer only to those persons directly under Portuguese rule at the time it was enunciated, does it appear so absurd as later anti-liberal critics maintained. The Portuguese dominions on the African mainland were quite limited in extent so far as direct sovereignty was concerned, whatever their claims might have been under the vaguer headings of suzerainty or sphere of influence.** Given their military and administrative resources, this state of affairs was inevitable.

The relics of empire that were left to Portugal by this time (apart

---

* The episode of the British "ultimatum" is an outstanding instance (see below, pp. 127ff).

** A nineteenth-century member of the British Foreign Office once remarked that spheres of influence were invented in order to give rights without duties. Sir Villiers Lister, undated minute (c. April 1891) in F.O. 84/2164 (Foreign Office Records, Slave Trade Series). Note: for the meaning of designations such as "F.O.," see Note on Documentary Sources, p. xiii, and list of abbreviations, p. xv.

from the South Atlantic islands) were, for the most part, fortified trading posts dependent on sea or river communication. Their original purpose had been to serve as ports of call on the trade route from the Indies and as naval bases, and their sites were chosen without regard to their suitability for settlement by Europeans. As Vicente Ferreira has said:

What today appear to us as commonplaces of climatology and hygiene were entirely unknown to the navigators and adventurers of the fifteenth and sixteenth centuries, as well as to the statesmen and religious leaders. A confused notion prevailed that the man endowed with sufficient courage and moral strength to wield the sword, wrestle with wave and tempest, and unmask the mysteries of unknown seas could, *a fortiori,* overcome hostile climates by dint of his own willpower.

He goes on:

To choose sheltered harbors, with abundant water and ease of landing, in which to anchor ships, and natural strong-points on which to raise fortresses, was the principal, perhaps the only, preoccupation. . . . This preoccupation had two consequences, at first sight inexplicable, which even today may be observed in the Portuguese African settlements: the one is that the best natural harbors were occupied . . . ; the other is that the most ancient cities are usually to be found on low-lying, almost always swampy sites, but dominated by the citadel and the cemetery—both of them situated on hills or promontories with open views and sea breezes.

It was not that the intention to settle had been lacking: on the contrary, the whole system of land grants (*donatárias*) to the gentlemen-adventurers presupposed that they would take a retinue with them. When Paulo Dias de Novais founded Luanda in 1575, he was charged, as captain and governor of Angola, with the settlement, within a period of six years, of one hundred colonists with their wives and families: some were to be farmers, and were to bring with them "all the seeds and plants that can be taken from this realm and from the Isle of S. Tomé." It does not appear, says Ferreira, that the grantee succeeded in fulfilling this condition, or that he took white women in his fleet, or had them brought from Portugal, during the fourteen years of his governorship. The first white women known to have landed in Luanda, twelve in number, arrived in 1595; all married, but none left descendants. The first governor of Angola to bring his wife with him was the fifty-fifth, in 1772. As late as 1902 there were only just over one hundred white women living in Luanda, of whom all but eight were *degredadas* (wives of criminals deported to Angola). In 1938 it was still Ferreira's considered opinion that the city, though as safe as modern public health measures could make it, with a mortality rate among whites of less than twelve per thousand, was even so not suitable for prolonged residence by Europeans.[2]

The same imperfect awareness, in Lisbon, of the difference between the physical environment of tropical Africa and that of Portugal (or Portuguese India, or even Brazil) appears in the *prazo* system established on the lower Zambezi (the so-called Rivers of Sena) in the seventeenth century. The grant of a prazo by the Portuguese Crown was a formality by which the de facto acquisition of land by adventurers from the mother country was recognized. Many such men had contrived to amass fortunes by trade, licit or illicit, in the *sertão* (backlands); by dint of gifts or services to local chiefs, especially in tribal wars, they had become possessed of large estates and numerous retainers. It was natural that they should seek to regularize their positions vis-à-vis the king as overlord (and his viceroy in Goa, of which Moçambique was till 1753 a dependency); natural, too, that these authorities should seek to adapt land grants in Zambézia to existing practice. The result was a kind of hybrid, stemming partly from the standard donatária which prescribed agrarian settlement, and partly from the practice that had grown up in Portuguese India whereby men who married the widows or orphaned daughters of Crown servants received, by way of dowry, leases of land for three lives. The prazo was to be granted to a female of European descent married to a European settler; both she and her husband were to live on the land and see that it was cultivated. The right of inheritance would descend to her daughter and granddaughter (or failing these, to male heirs or assigns) on the same conditions, after which the land would revert to the Crown; the grant, however, might be renewed for further terms.

The institution thus brought into legal existence was to be a thorn in the side of the Portuguese administration until well into the twentieth century. It has occasioned much misunderstanding, most notably on the part of an investigatory commission set up in November 1888, whose relator was a person of no less distinction than the historian and polymath Oliveira Martins, and whose errors were faithfully copied by later writers on the subject. The policies recommended by this commission, and the extent to which they were influenced by misapprehension of the very nature of the prazo, will be considered in a later chapter. Only recently, in the work of Alexandre Lobato, has a convincing account of the institution appeared. He shows that the prazo derived neither from some existing form of feudalism nor from the landholdings of the coast Arabs; the holder received tribute and services from its native inhabitants, mainly in the form of "the agreeable recreation of war," but enjoyed no judicial authority over them. The *colonos* (as these natives were called) were not in a state of servitude, though the prazo holders both kept slaves as part of their households and acquired them for export. The petty chiefs (*fumos* or *encosses*) retained their authority, though individuals might be displaced. For the rest, justice was reserved to the royal officers of the government, at Sena. In course of time, certain powerful prazo holders succeeded in achieving quasi-political authority. They formed a kind of close corporation, linked by ties of blood and interest, which in effect superseded any independent provincial administration. But this was usurpation and was no part of the original intention.

How many couples were found to comply, even at the outset, with the conditions required for the grant of a prazo appears to be uncertain. There can scarcely have been many, for quite apart from climatic obstacles to the settlement of white women in Zambézia, a substantial influx of Portuguese-born immigrants was ruled out for economic reasons. As Lobato says:

The former concept of settlement (*povoamento*) was not ours. In those days, the present-day settlement by those of small means was impossible; the only colonist who could survive and prosper was he who had money or resources to found a lordly domain, with footmen, governesses, and slaves. Great financial strength was indispensable. The foundation of all social life was trade, sustained by the armed force drawn from the Kaffir population of the prazo. These forces could only be put into operation with money or credit, for the initial investment was heavy.[3]

Inasmuch as virtually all trade was with the Orient, it was natural that many aspirants to the lordship of prazos should be Goans, whether they came to Moçambique in the first instance as traders or as functionaries, and natural too that they should be accepted as husbands for the nominal holders, for want of European Portuguese. "For a long time the Rivers of Sena were a little Indian colony," says Lobato.

Economics likewise dictated that the prazo holder should not engage in agriculture, for except in the immediate environs of the port of Quilimane, there would have been no market for the produce.[4] So too, the large amounts of manpower that were required, whether for warlike operations or for trading or mining enterprises in the interior, meant that a viable prazo had to be large; and indeed at the outset no maximum size was laid down. The decree of April 1760, which sought to limit the area of prazos was "doomed to be completely ineffective, in that it ignored the economic and social realities of Zambézia."[5] By that time the Portuguese dominion on the Zambezi was already in decline and the prazos, which had been the instrument of its original advance, were now contributory to its forced retreat. Much of their original raison d'être had vanished when the Portuguese were driven out of the gold- and silver-mining regions of the interior, on the riches of which the luxurious life of the seventeenth-century *prazeros* had been based. The slave trade was apparently a comparatively unprofitable substitute: Teixeira Botelho estimates the average annual export of slaves from Moçambique in the early years of the nineteenth century at between two and three thousand, and there can hardly have been big money in operations on that scale.[6] At any rate, the characteristic prazero, if he were not an Indian or a half-caste, was by this time likely to be an absentee, rules and regulations notwithstanding. The complaints of extortion, of flights of native inhabitants from the prazos, and of political anarchy and economic stagnation, that characterize official reports of the time are exactly what one would expect of an economy that had lost the great wealth it once enjoyed. "It is a sorry sight," wrote the governor of the District of Quilimane, about 1830, "to see the towns of Sena and Tete all but deserted, with only half a dozen Portuguese ... and the houses that had once belonged to great and even noble families occupied by a handful of despicable Canarins [Goanese Christians] and some natives, who by no means can instill respect for the Portuguese." The same report declared that the people of the Rivers of Sena had suffered a mortal blow in 1807 when "the ambitious and imprudent" Governor Truão made war on the Monomatapa: "The greater part of the residents, their bodies of slaves, and all the companies of regular troops and the militia, were forced to accompany him; and virtually all, to the most wretched disgrace of the Portuguese name, were left dead on the battlefield."[7]

This may be an exaggerated account of a setback by which Tete was cut off from the settlement of Zumbo higher up the Zambesi, but it points up the military weakness of the Portuguese in the whole river basin and the danger of taking desperate measures to relieve it.

The remedies proposed for this state of affairs (strict enforcement of the prazo laws, and the settlement of "poor Portuguese" on the land) were impracticable in any case: the Portugal of the second quarter of the nineteenth century was in no position even to attempt them. The condition of Moçambique had to get worse before it could get better.

II

Zambézia, like the new inland *presídios* in Angola, thus constituted no exception to the general rule that the whole Portuguese dominion in Africa, from Bissau and Cacheu in Senegambia (now Portuguese Guinea, or Guiné) all the way to Cape Delgado, rested on trade: the principal export, of course, being slaves, once the precious metals had been cut off or had given out. The obloquy that attaches to the slave trade has hindered investigation of its economic function and, perhaps, caused its scope to be exaggerated.[8] Today, one cannot assert with early-nineteenth-century confidence that it led to overall depopulation of the African continent, or that it was a source of enormous profit to the Europeans who engaged in it, or that it was infallibly deleterious to the African tribal economies. Slaves were, after all, the most consistently marketable commodity that has ever come out of Africa and hence the most reliable source of the imports desired by the Africans not sold into slavery. Moreover, slaves provided the most ready means of carrying another important export—ivory in the form of elephant tusks—to the coast. The interest of numerous Africans in maintaining the trade was, if anything, even greater than that of the European shippers; and abolition was no light matter unless substitute exports could be found.

Oliveira Martins' views on the slave trade are of interest, for he was a writer of exceptional candor and moral courage. "I do not believe," he wrote in 1890,

that we should worry much about the accusation that we invented the *hateful traffic*. Without the blacks, Brazil would not have come into existence; and without slaves no nation began. In any event...it must be said that we invented nothing. Wherever slaves have existed, they have been [bought and] sold.

Oliveira Martins did not attempt to conceal the horrors of the slave ships, but he did argue that the outlawing of the trade (at British insistence) in the early nineteenth century, while the institution of slavery itself was still legal in Cuba and Brazil, made matters worse. The British had an interest in the abolition of slavery in these territories, sugar from which competed with that from the West Indies, which after 1833* were obliged to rely on free labor. But neither this interest nor that of humanity was served by a measure that merely raised the price of slaves in America and worsened their condition on the way thither. "In former times, one could legislate for and administer a lawful trade. Once the trade became contraband, the shipment of slaves—now that it was done furtively, and the business was a lottery —became repugnant, cruel, and a disgrace to humanity."

Oliveira Martins claimed that the profits of the trade were increased tenfold by its prohibition. The force of his argument is obvious, though one may doubt the ability of pre-nineteenth-century governments, not only in Portugal, to impose humanitarian behavior on slave shippers: these clearly had a greater incentive to keep down losses in transit if the total supply of slaves were ample, than if the losses would merely enhance the price of the delivered article. One may in any case applaud a refusal to fall into the trap that ensnared Lord Acton and so many historians after him: self-indulgent (because merely academic) moral condemnation or approval of actions past and out of reach. However, Oliveira Martins was perhaps unfair in attributing the anti-slavery movement among the British to "a reaction on the part of the temperament of those islanders—a temperament violent, sentimental, and given to excess."[9]

The triumph of the liberal monarchy in 1834 logically carried with it the abolition of slavery overseas, as inconsistent with the Charter of 1826. Likewise, Mousinho da Silveira's decree of August 1832, abolishing various privileged grants of land, had almost casually swept away the Moçambique prazos—on paper. But Mousinho and his disciples had no positive policy for the overseas provinces: preferring that Portugal should henceforth cultivate her own garden in Europe, they were prepared to accept—even to welcome—the fact that the loss of Brazil and the abolition of the slave trade had left the old colonial system in ruins. The logic and unsentimentality of such a view is suffi-

---

* Not 1807, as Oliveira Martins supposed.

cient indication of its lack of political appeal; moreover, the colonial remnants could not just be left to themselves. The one liberal statesman with a positive colonial policy was the Septembrist Sá da Bandeira, "but he framed it in a fashion indiscreetly humanitarian, hoping to construct a Brazil in Africa, with free labor, free competition, and liberal guarantees. In this he showed his *romanticism*. His obsession with colonies was taken for a mania, and that is what it came to be."[10]

This criticism, though in a way not unjust, is tinged with hindsight. Oliveira Martins might well have added that Sá da Bandeira, like his distinguished successors Andrade Corvo and Oliveira Salazar, never visited any of the overseas territories. But if this fact helped to feed the liberals' illusions, the illusions themselves were common to a whole generation of Europeans who believed that the right economic policy would bring about the millennium; and only a lofty idealism could have sustained these men in pursuing it through frustration and disappointment.

Sá da Bandeira, the Portuguese statesman who, more than any other, brought about the abolition of the slave trade and of slavery, was a man of principle; yet it is notorious that British pressure on Portugal for abolition, especially after the advent of Palmerston to the Foreign Office, was unremitting. Palmerston himself publicly accused Portugal of violating earlier promises and encouraging the traffic, and in 1839 the British Parliament actually passed an act authorizing the seizure by the Royal Navy of suspected slave ships flying the Portuguese colors—a flagrant violation of sovereignty which was only withdrawn when Portugal, in July 1842, declared the slave trade to be piracy and accepted a treaty providing for joint enforcement of the law against it.* Anglo-Portuguese mixed commissions were to be es-

---

* H. C. F. Bell, *Palmerston*, Vol. I, p. 234; C. K. Webster, *Foreign Policy of Palmerston*, Vol. I, pp. 490–92. Neither Bell nor Webster attempts to consider that the Portuguese government might have had a case, or that Palmerston's statement of his might not be wholly accurate. Webster's assertion, for instance, that the Portuguese claimed the right to ship slaves between "their Atlantic islands" (unspecified) and Brazil, on the ground that it was "domestic adjustment," is wrong on its face: Brazil had been an independent state since 1825. Again, the "vested interests" in Portugal that were supposedly making money from the slave trade appear to be mythical; at any rate, they had been unable to prevent the issue of the decree of 1836 prohibiting it. A dignified rebuttal of the British case was written at the time by Sá da Bandeira, who by then

tablished in Luanda and Cape Town to act as prize courts (in addition
to the court already in existence in Sierra Leone). Yet to judge by
some Portuguese writers, one might almost suppose that the British
had set out to frustrate idealistic statesmen bent on abolition.[11] The
claim that Portugal had been in the forefront of the anti-slavery movement was quite frequently made in the later nineteenth century, and
evoked a good deal of hilarity in the British Foreign Office.

How could such a claim seem plausible, even to those by whom it
was made? The inveterate Portuguese habit of taking the will for the
deed provides only a partial explanation. The will had been expressed
most recently in a decree issued on December 10, 1836, shortly after the
Septembrist revolution, prohibiting the slave trade everywhere in the
Portuguese dominions; and it appears that Sá da Bandeira was surprised at the extent of the hostile reaction in the African territories and
disappointed that the British would not offer him more assistance in
coping with it. Considering that the slave trade had been a lawful enterprise in the eyes of Church and State for hundreds of years, and that
it was the main source of livelihood for most influential people in the
Portuguese settlements, it was only natural that there should be a
violent outcry when the home government decreed suppression. A
new governor, sent out to Moçambique with explicit instructions to
enforce the decree, found himself unable to do so and had to be content with tripling the tax on each slave exported, to eighteen milréis a
head.[12] The governor of Angola flatly refused to enforce the decree,
and was recalled. His successor strove bravely to do so, even sending
the Luanda judge home to Lisbon to be proceeded against, but was no
more fortunate. As he wrote to Sá da Bandeira in June 1839:

I have done away with the only branch of commerce in which these people were
wont to employ their capital; hence the customhouse was closed, and in consequence there was brought about a deficit in the annual balance of income and
expenditure which may perhaps amount to two-thirds of the latter. The bringer
and executor of such calamities, the reformer of inveterate abuses in which, one
way and another, so many people have a [vested] interest, cannot but be detested.

---

had left office (*O Trafico de escravatura e o Bill de lord Palmerston,* Lisbon, 1840). It
claims, *inter alia,* that the common accusation that Portugal had failed to give the
promised consideration for money received (for example, Bell, p. 234) was baseless:
the consideration had been the abolition of the trade north of the equator, and the
restoration of French Guiana to France.

Such a man, he went on, had better leave Angola in the hope that a successor, free from this odium, might find people more willing to co-operate.* There were no forces available to Lisbon with which to coerce Angola and Moçambique: as events a generation later were to show, the historic right of the government to order its troops overseas had come to be questioned, and anyway the treasury was empty. It is therefore not surprising that at one stage in the negotiations with Britain for a slave trade treaty, Sá da Bandeira should have put forward a clause under which the British would have guaranteed the integrity of all the Portuguese dominions in Africa, and which would have enabled the governors of Angola and Moçambique to call directly for help from the governors of the Cape and of Bombay.[13] This and other attempts to enlarge what in the British view was to be simply a convention with a limited purpose seem to have been regarded in London (and hence by non-Portuguese historians) as no more than devices to gain time or the recognition of territorial claims—a view intelligible but perhaps less than fair.[14] It must have been difficult for anyone not on the spot to realize the extent of Lisbon's impotence overseas. The British reception of Sá da Bandeira's proposals gave color, however, to later Portuguese accusations that the real aim of their ally was to seize the African possessions for herself.

Certainly there can be no doubt that British naval officers charged with repressing the slave trade were frequently high-handed. The proceedings of Lieutenant Kellett, R.N., upon the coast of Senegambia in 1838 and 1839 seem to have been a locus classicus among the Portuguese for actions of this sort, the more so since they brought him into conflict with the famous (and only) colored governor of Guiné, Honório Pereira Barreto.[15] Lieutenant Kellett was accused by the governor of (*inter alia*) kidnapping domestic slaves belonging to a Portuguese major and other residents of the island of Bolama; of seizing a schooner lawfully bound from Bissau to the Cape Verdes Islands with Portuguese residents and their domestic slaves; and, having drunk too much wine he had ordered but not paid for, of insulting the Portu-

---

* The figure of two-thirds was a considerable underestimate of the extent to which the revenue of Angola would have been depleted by abolition of the slave trade. Sá da Bandeira himself quotes sources to show that in the early nineteenth century the export tax on slaves consistently accounted for more than four-fifths of the provincial receipts. See Sá da Bandeira, *O Trabalho Rural Africano e a Administração Colonial* (Lisbon, 1873, Imprensa Nacional), pp. 17–20.

guese flag by tearing it down, spitting on it, and using it to wrap up the bottles. Doubtless the story lost nothing in the telling, but even if not true it is certainly *ben trovato*. Kellett's offense was compounded, in the eyes of the Portuguese, by his assertion that Bolama was a British possession—a claim deriving from an abortive philanthropic attempt at colonization in the year 1792. The following version of this attempt, by Lopes de Lima, whose monumental account (1844) of the Portuguese overseas possessions was commissioned by his government, is revealing:

A private association ... set up an intrusive "factory" on this Island of Bolama, almost within sight of the Portuguese fortress of S. José de Bissau, the Governor of which was so amiable as to agree to it. Not so, however, the natives, primordial lords of the territory. Indignant at the want of ceremony with which those intruders set themselves up in their lands without previous consent, robbing their ancient friends the Portuguese of long-standing occupation, they did not make treaties, because they knew not how to write, but had recourse to arms, because they knew how to fight; nor did they cease from their war of extermination until the last Englishman had been expelled from the territory of Bolama, wherein henceforth the Portuguese continued to cut wood as they had done before, not only without opposition, but even with assistance from [the local chiefs].[16]

A few years later, the territorial claim would have been the only possible justification for Lieutenant Kellett's conduct, for the British government was advised that the destruction of slave barracoons and the carrying away of slaves, undertaken on friendly territory, could be justified neither by international law nor by any treaty provision.[17] The claim was to be a source of friction for another generation; it was at length settled by an arbitration in which President Grant of the United States awarded the island to Portugal. (The award is commemorated by a statue of Grant in the town of Bolama.)

III

The principal threat, however, to the Portuguese position in Senegambia in the second quarter of the nineteenth century came not from the British but from the French. In the eighteenth century Portugal had kept sufficient naval forces in the area to protect its long-established settlements, chief among which were Bissau and Cacheu. The loss of Brazil entailed a withdrawal of ships and crews to form the nucleus of a Brazilian navy, and what vessels remained were occupied in the civil wars or captured by the French in the Lisbon fiasco of

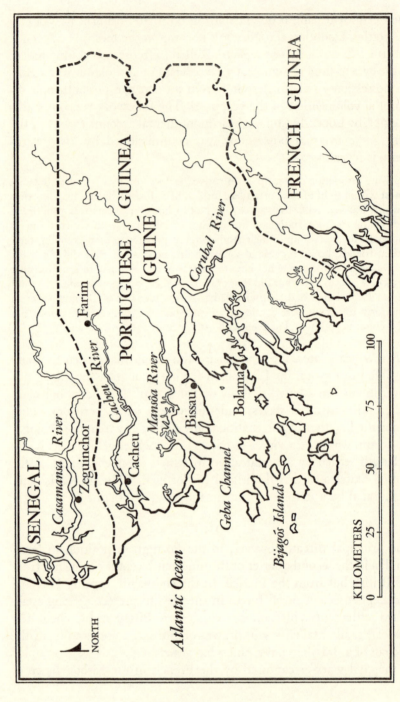

Portuguese Guinea (Guiné) and Surroundings, c. 1850–1900

July 1831. Hence there was not even token opposition to the establishment of French forces on the Casamansa estuary, to the north of
present-day Portuguese Guinea, or at Boké, to the south, and by 1839
the littoral historically claimed by Portugal was reduced by more than
half. That the whole was not lost seems to have been largely due to the
activity of one man, Honório Pereira Barreto (1813–1859).[18] Barreto
a "dark-skinned and obscure African," as he called himself, was a native of Cacheu who had been sent to school in Lisbon. He belonged to
the class known as *brancos da terra* (literally, "whites of the soil"),
descendants of early settlers who in course of time had become almost
completely African by blood, but who took pride in their citizenship
and wished to be regarded as Portuguese. By reason of his descent and
his personal qualities, Barreto came at a very early age to enjoy great
prestige in the Cacheu area, and he was appointed *provedor,* or super-
intendent, of the fortress there at the age of twenty-one. At twenty-
four he was appointed governor of Bissau and Cacheu. Thereafter,
until his untimely death at the age of forty-six, he devoted himself, in
and out of office, to the preservation of Portuguese authority: using
his personal influence with the chiefs, purchasing lands in order to
deed them to the State, and reforming the local administration and
finances. His was frequently an uphill job, not so much on account of
the turbulent tribesmen for whom attacks on the Portuguese fortified
posts were a hobby as because of the frequent indifference of higher
authority in the Cape Verdes and in Lisbon. It was particularly galling
to Barreto that a member of the Côrtes, in July 1840, should declare
that they should not concern themselves with the Casamansa business,
"for that name was barbarous," and that the prime minister, even
when eulogizing Barreto's conduct as governor, should refer to him as
"a colored man."[19] In 1843 Barreto published, in Lisbon, a pamphlet
on "The Present State of Portuguese Senegambia," in which he described the colony as existing "without any security whatsoever ... yet
one reads in Lisbon, in the official gazette, that the Portuguese possessions here are in order and flourishing. ... It can be said that ... there
is a governor and there are commanders, but there is no government."
The officials were military men, who ruled by arbitrary caprice—there
was neither law nor justice. "Contraband is authorized." The fortress
of Bissau, which had never been completed, was mostly in ruins, as
were the lesser stockades of Cacheu, Farim, and Zeguichor. What

trade there was, was entirely in the hands of foreigners. Barreto attributed this state of affairs to misgovernment from a distance:

I am convinced that so long as colonial matters are dealt with by the Ministry of Marine, the possessions will never prosper. . . . It is our misfortune that whatever is proposed in Parliament about the overseas territories gets buried, either in the Commissions or in the Department. It appears that members of parliament are merely representatives of the Kingdom, and not of the nation of which we are a tiny and unfortunate, but integral part.

Barreto proposed the creation in Lisbon of a special Council for Overseas Affairs. Further, he requested the granting of ample powers to the governor of Senegambia, for communications with the Cape Verde Islands were so poor that it was impossible to consult the governor-general there in case of emergency.[20] Each of these recommendations was eventually carried out: the ancient *Conselho Ultramarino* was reestablished in 1851 and lasted until 1868, and in 1879, as a result of military emergency, Guiné was at length separated from the Cape Verdes and given the status of a full province. A contemporary wrote: "We created a new province . . . with two hundred *contos** and an old steamer."[21]

At the time of Barreto's death in April 1859 it looked as if an incident similar to the Kellett affair might blow up into a crisis threatening Portuguese sovereignty. In August 1858 a British gunboat, the *Trident,* commanded by Captain F. A. Close, had landed a force on Bolama Island, declared all the slaves thereon free, and seized the Bissau magistrate and some other inhabitants on the pretext that they were slaving. Early in January 1859 the *Trident* reappeared, with the governor of Sierra Leone aboard, and again behaved in a manner suggesting that the British might be about to seize the island. "If prompt measures are not taken," the governor-general of the Cape Verdes warned Lisbon in May, ". . . Guiné will infallibly be lost. . . . English domination of Bolama will annihilate the trade of Guiné and render our establishments untenable." By dint of repeated representations over nearly a decade, the Portuguese government did at length succeed, after a further incident of the same kind in June 1868, in persuading the British to accept arbitration; thereafter, the little province all but disappeared from history for the rest of the century.[22] The sup-

---

* A *conto* was worth somewhat more than a thousand dollars.

pression of the slave trade caused some economic disturbance, but a substitute export was quickly found in groundnuts, which were being exported from Bissau as early as 1846. The trade might have grown more quickly but for the tax that was levied on exports—a tax that was not levied in the adjacent British or French territories, as the Director of Customs at Bissau pointed out to the Conselho Ultramarino in 1857.[23] In general, there was no disposition among Portuguese public men to do much about Guiné; its climate was notoriously lethal to white men, and not a single Portuguese explorer went there during the whole of the nineteenth century.

From 1842 onward the British Navy was empowered by treaty to search vessels suspected of slave trading, and to bring them before the mixed commissions—a task in which the Portuguese Navy cooperated to the extent of its small resources. The effectiveness of the anti-slave-trade blockade, so far as the parts of Angola and Moçambique under direct Portuguese control were concerned, may be judged from some trade figures quoted by Pinheiro Chagas: whereas in 1825 Angolan imports and exports were valued at 1,088 contos and 830 contos respectively, in 1844 they were valued at 379 contos and 201 contos.[24] Georg Tams, a Hamburg physician who served as ship's doctor on a trading expedition from that city to Angola and the Portuguese islands in the South Atlantic, wrote a detailed account of conditions immediately before the Slave Trade Treaty between Britain and Portugal came into effect. The expedition was led by the Portuguese consul-general in Altona, Ribeiro dos Santos, and consisted of no less than six ships. It was evidently intended for pleasure and instruction as well as profit, for two German scientists, a botanist and etymologist, as well as a six-man band and an expert player of the glass harmonica, were in the party. The flagship's provisions, Tams tells us, were of the best, including pigs, goats, fowls, pigeons, and oysters, and dinner was prepared by an Italian chef. (One of the ships called especially at Lisbon to present Queen Maria II with an enormous iced cake on which was represented the civil war siege of Oporto, "copied with inimitable art and exactitude from engravings by first class artists.")

The party spent five months, from mid-October 1841 to mid-March 1842, in Angolan waters, visiting Luanda, Novo Redondo, Benguela, and Ambriz. Although some of the fine buildings of an earlier century in Luanda were in ruins, it would seem from Tams' account to have been a prosperous place still. The slave trade was still flourishing, though slaves for export were no longer brought into the city in daylight and the activities of the British navy were making the trade hazardous. Persons of a variety of races and antecedents, including criminal deportees from Portugal and former slaves, were engaged in the trade. The social life of the city was equally diverse. Its focus was "a kind of ball" given by the governor every Sunday evening, and attended by a "heterogeneous multitude of blacks, whites, and mulattoes."* Among these Tams noted a woman, richly adorned with gold and jewels, who had come from up-country a few years earlier as a slave, and thanks to her beauty and astuteness had acquired liberty and a fortune; and a man who had been "educated in the Lisbon streets," had been banished from that city as a rogue and vagabond, but had flourished in Luanda and acquired social status. Tams himself was a guest in the house of a Portuguese physician who lived in considerable luxury with numerous household slaves, and whose Spanish wife was notably addicted to using the *palmatória* as a punishment for even minor peccadilloes on their part. This instrument, which was used in Spain and Portugal until recently for punishing schoolchildren, was common throughout Portuguese Africa and was remarked upon by numerous travelers. Made of hardwood, it consists essentially of a disk three inches or so in diameter attached to a handle eighteen inches or more long. The center of the disk has five equidistant perforations, in the form of a cross, such that when the open palm of the hand is struck with sufficient force, the flesh, it is said, enters them. According to some writers this increases the pain of the beatings, though Tams says merely that it diminishes the noise. His particular slave owner was accustomed to order her seamstresses six dozen blows of the palmatória for making a sewing mistake, after which they were ordered back to work immediately. So well disciplined were her slaves that they were highly sought after in the Luanda market. Tams makes it clear, however, that not all slaveowners were as brutal as this one. In his opinion the Europeans were more cruel to their slaves than were the rich native inhabitants of Luanda or Benguela, perhaps because they regarded Negroes not as men but as monkeys, "as they are usually called by the Portuguese."

* Captain Owen, R.N., has left an account of a similar ball at Moçambique in 1825. See C. R. Boxer, *Race Relations in the Portuguese Colonial Empire, 1415–1825* (Oxford, 1963), pp. 126–27.

The main disadvantage for the white man of life in these Angolan coast towns was, of course, the climate. The leader and at least three other members of Tams' expedition succumbed to a variety of fevers within a matter of months. The climate of Benguela was even more unhealthy than that of Luanda, so much so that there were no European women there, and even the half-caste children were commonly sent out of the city to nearby Catumbela to be reared. Tams gives no estimate of the number of European women in Luanda, beyond mentioning ten or a dozen prostitutes from Spain and Portugal. He found Benguela a shabby place: the governor's palace, he says, would have been better suited to house horses or herds of cattle than the representative of a crowned head, and the governor himself had been sent there by way of punishment for some military offense. As in Luanda, the sole form of commerce was the slave trade, upon which the 1836 decree had been without effect. Tams was told that twenty thousand slaves had been exported from Benguela during 1838, and that the trade had not diminished since, though the blockade had diverted it through ports as far away as the newly founded Moçâmedes. As for Novo Redondo, it had only nine or ten European inhabitants, most of them Italians who had been deported to Angola from Portugal twenty years previously. One of these Italians, a Neapolitan named Tabana, virtually monopolized the trade of the place and maintained his own private army, twenty-five strong (the official garrison numbered six). In this district, though not in Luanda and Benguela, it was customary, according to Tams, to employ slaves to buy ivory and slaves in the interior.[25]

Ambriz, the last place on the mainland visited by the expedition, though included in the territories to which the Portuguese Crown laid claim, was at that time an independent African "kingdom," whose ruler expressed great surprise on being told that none of the ships was for slaving: he thought that so great an expedition could not be made to pay merely by a barter trade in merchandise. At Ambriz as elsewhere the trade in ivory, beeswax, and gum was subordinate to that in slaves. Shortly before Tams' arrival, a slave ship had escaped capture by a British cruiser only by deliberately running on the rocks, with the loss of all her human cargo; the ship was the property of a wealthy woman of Luanda, herself a former slave.[26] The incident points up the problem of enforcing anti-slavery measures at that time: even if the will had been present, the jurisdiction was not.

But the Portuguese had an answer to this problem that they thought logical: let them, with British assistance, occupy that part of the African coastline between 5°12′ and 8° south latitude to which they had long laid claim, and which was specified in the Charter of 1826 under the names "Cabinda" and "Molembo." In the view of men like Sá da Bandeira, their right to these territories had been recognized by Great Britain in the Anglo-Portuguese Treaty of 1810 and in subsequent agreements in 1815 and 1817.[27]

Intentionally or not, however, these treaties had been drafted in a way that lent itself to equivocation. To stipulate that Article 10 of the first treaty in no way invalidated the rights of the king of Portugal to Cabinda and Molembo appears almost meaningless, unless a positive act of recognition were intended—the more so since the clause refers to a former French challenge to those rights that the high contracting parties presumably knew had been withdrawn in a treaty of 1786. On the other hand, the Anti-Slave-Trade Treaty of 1815 and its additional convention of 1817 both explicitly distinguish between the actual dominions of the Crown of Portugal and those to which its rights were reserved—that is, Cabinda and Molembo. The relevant clauses clearly stand in lieu of that in the treaty of 1810 (which had been superseded by the treaty of 1815, now that the war against France was concluded), but there is nothing on the face of them to suggest that they constitute an alteration of the former in substance. At any rate, the one interpretation that it would seem impossible to put on any of these clauses is that they constituted nonrecognition of a Portuguese claim to Cabinda and Molembo: yet this was the position unilaterally adopted by Palmerston in the autumn of 1846 and consistently sustained by the British for the next thirty years.[28]

The occasion of Palmerston's declaration was the seizure of a Brazilian slaver by a Portuguese corvette off the coast between 5°12′ and 8° south latitude, and its condemnation by the mixed commission in Luanda on the implied ground that the seizure had taken place in Portuguese territorial waters. In instructing the British minister in Lisbon to make the declaration, the Foreign Office referred to the importance of maintaining unrestricted access to the area in the interests of commerce; and indeed it was true that the Portuguese tariff was high, though British trade with the Congo was as yet by no means large. Palmerston's attitude was, of course, consistent with his earlier rejection of Sá da Bandeira's request for territorial guarantees and his mistrust of Portugal generally: five years later he was to remark that the anti-slavery cause, and British trade, were safer under native chiefs than under Portuguese rule. This view long persisted in the Foreign Office: "It is far better," ran a minute of 1876, "to have to deal with the worst savages than with the best-intentioned Portuguese." Lisbon, however, could hardly be expected to welcome or even to understand a policy that converted an ancient alliance into a form of hostile patronage.[29] As Sá da Bandeira temperately commented years later on Palmerston's action: "It cannot be admitted that one of the contracting parties, of its own accord, without the concurrence of the other, has the right to put in force a new interpretation of treaty stipulations. If so ... [treaties] would become perfectly useless, or would be advantageous only to the stronger of the contracting parties."[30]

Sá da Bandeira surmised that if the governor of Angola had been able to carry out the instructions he had given him in October 1838 to occupy Ambriz, Cabinda, and Molembo, the Portuguese right to do so would not have been challenged; it was the British member of the Luanda Mixed Commission, set up as a result of the Slave Trade Treaty of 1842, who had drawn the point to his government's notice.* The surmise is plausible but academic, since the governor's time was fully taken up with trying to enforce the decree of 1836, but it illustrates a weakness that was to dog the Portuguese in Africa all through the century—their inability to act decisively and in time. They finally did occupy Ambriz, in 1855, when the British were engaged with the Crimean War. Moreover, in rebuttal of British criticism, they introduced a special customs regime there, imposing only a six per cent ad valorem tariff on imports and none on exports. The next year a decree was issued abolishing slavery not only in Ambriz, but also in Cabinda and Molembo; but though the British eventually acquiesced in the seizure of the first, they made it clear that they would tolerate no further advance northward. There the matter was to rest until the late seventies.[31]

IV

In Moçambique, though the slave trade at no time attained the proportions it had in Angola, suppression presented even greater diffi-

---

* The Treaty of 1842 is overlooked altogether by Anstey when he says that the extension of Portuguese authority northward would have prevented British cruisers from hunting slavers in Portuguese waters. See *Britain and the Congo*, p. 40.

culties. A determined governor could, if he would, deal with the objections of those residents within his jurisdiction who were living by the trade; but the jurisdiction itself was, and for another two generations continued to be, pathetically limited in extent. At mid-century it was virtually confined to a handful of widely scattered settlements along the coast and the lower Zambezi: significantly, the seat of government was a fortified offshore island, Moçambique. The more northerly settlement of Ibo was also an island stronghold; the only other places of importance were Inhambane and Quilimane, and the former was constantly beset by the surrounding tribes. The garrisons of such places, composed of black troops with a leavening of degredados from Portugal, were ill-trained, ill-armed, and insubordinate: in August 1850 those of the small presídio at Lourenço Marques mutinied and put the governor in irons, and in December of the same year the help of friendly chiefs had to be called in to repress another mutiny among the degredados there. There had been a similar occurrence at Inhambane a few years before; and in 1849, when the governor there attempted a punitive expedition, his small force was surrounded and he was killed. Elsewhere, Portuguese authority was fitfully exercised: when, in 1861, a considerable expedition was mounted against the sultan at Angoche (a nominal but turbulent vassal), all but a handful of its members consisted of the private army of a prominent prazero of Quilimane. The Zambezi valley between Sena and Tete was dominated for the best part of a century by the Cruz family, of mixed Oriental and African origins, from their stockade at Massangano: not so much rebels as "overmighty subjects" who cherished their Portuguese connection while defying Portuguese authority, they typified the prazo system in its decay. Massangano did not fall to the government forces till 1887; its capture is as much a landmark in the history of Moçambique as that of the Gaza chief in 1896.[32]

Teixeira Botelho quotes a former secretary-general of the province as saying that the slave dealers were everywhere—in the treasury board (*junta da fazenda*), in the town council, in business, in the provincial secretariat—and that each fresh governor had to choose whether he would govern with them or without them. In the latter case he did not last long. In 1839, a separatist plot attributed to the same sinister interests was formed to place an independent Moçambique and Angola under the protection of Brazil. The 1840's seem to have marked the peak of the slave trade between Moçambique and the New World; the abolition of the British import duties in 1846 stimulated the demand for slaves in Cuba and Brazil at a time when their supply from the west coast of Africa was being rendered more difficult. Under the terms of the 1842 treaty with Portugal, and subsequent protocols, British anti-slavery patrols began for the first time to operate in the Moçambique Channel, but their numbers were limited and the vessels employed were seldom, if ever, fast enough for the work. Their captains found ample evidence of open slaving at Quilimane, Ibo, and around Cape Delgado. In the fifties the organized trade with the Americas seems to have declined, though Lyons MacLeod, the first British consul stationed at Moçambique, arrived there in 1857 to learn that no less than seven large slaving vessels had left for Havana recently. In 1861, H.M.S. *Wasp* found that the town of Ibo "swarmed with slaves" (though some of these may have been technically free laborers awaiting shipment to the French islands in the Indian Ocean) and that "every house had a barracoon attached." Two years later the British rear admiral in command on the Moçambique coast stated that four or five large slaving vessels called annually at Ibo; and he estimated the export of slaves at three thousand a year.

With the closing of the main overseas markets—Brazil in 1851, and Cuba in 1866—there was left a residual slave trade which was different in character and more difficult to repress. The transatlantic trade had in a sense been open, though illegal; shipment had been from recognized ports in ships capable of making the Atlantic crossing. What remained—the Arab trade—was more or less contraband; and in contrast to Angola, where the coast was thinly populated, good harbors few and known, and the slaving vessels comparatively large, Moçambique lent itself to contraband of all sorts. The innumerable gulfs and creeks of its lengthy coastline, particularly north of Quilimane, gave ready shelter to the dhows engaged in slave running; the coast population was in league with the slavers; their capture, even when detected, was difficult and hazardous; unlike the Atlantic slavers, they enjoyed the advantage of a short haul to Madagascar, the Comoros Islands, Réunion, and Zanzibar. The process of suppression consisted as much in stopping up these outlets for the trade as in catching the traders en route—and for many years it was a slow one.[33] The chief organized opposition came from the French, whose planters in the

Indian Ocean islands had been accustomed to rely on slave labor from the mainland, and who now strove to circumvent the prohibition by recruiting labor that would be nominally free and on contract for five years. The subterfuge was transparent, for it was not to be supposed that Africans captured in the interior and brought forcibly to the coast would be in a position to enter freely and knowingly into any such contract or to enforce it against an employer. When in 1854 French contractors wished to recruit in this way at Inhambane for Réunion, Lisbon refused them permission; and when, contrary to instructions, the governor-general of Moçambique authorized recruitment, Sá da Bandeira dismissed him. This position was maintained despite representations by the French minister in Lisbon, and the governor of Réunion was warned against allowing ships to come to Moçambique for any such purpose. However, in November 1857 a French barque, the *Charles et Georges,* was captured at anchor in Moçambique waters with 110 so-called free laborers on board, and was subsequently declared lawful prize; the captain was sentenced to fine and imprisonment, the ship escorted to Lisbon. The government of Napoleon III demanded their release, sent warships into the Tagus, and threatened to break off diplomatic relations, refusing arbitration. The British government declined to give more than nominal support to their ally ("You want war, then?" was the reply of Lord Cowley, the ambassador in Paris, to the protests of the Portuguese minister in London) and the Portuguese government was constrained to let vessel and captain go and pay 350,000 francs indemnity. The episode was not calculated to inculcate enthusiasm for enforcement of the law among Portuguese officials, nor to diminish the British reputation for hypocrisy. It is difficult to believe that if Palmerston had still been at the Foreign Office he would not have taken a stronger line, the more so since, according to the private assurances of the French foreign minister to the Portuguese minister in London, the real target was not Portugal, but the British government.*

While repression of the export slave trade slowly proceeded, its

* From the White Book relating to the case of the *Charles et Georges,* published by the Portuguese government in 1858, it appears that Paget, the British chargé d'affaires in Lisbon, had, as late as July 22, 1857, delivered a strongly worded note to the Portuguese government, urging it to stop the export of Negroes to the French Indian Ocean islands. *Documentos Relativos ao Apresamento, Julgamento e Entrega da Barca Fran-*

corollary, the abolition of slavery itself in the overseas territories, was pursued in leisurely fashion: Sá da Bandeira himself notes that sixteen years of effort, from 1842 to 1858, were necessary before the decisive step was taken. The first legislative act in that direction, after sundry efforts had aborted, was a decree of December 1854 which ordered all slaves to be registered, freed those belonging to the government, and instituted the category of *liberto* (freedman)—that is, an ex-slave obliged to work for his former master for a number of years. A little later, the children of female slaves, born after 1856, were put into that category for the first twenty years of their lives. At length, in April 1858, it was decreed that slavery everywhere in the Portuguese dominions should be abolished twenty years thence. Eleven years later, the process was accelerated by abolishing slavery forthwith and fixing the former terminal date, April 29, 1878, as the date at which the obligations of libertos would cease. These moves of the home government, gradual though they might seem, were unwelcome overseas: the president of the general committee (*junta geral*) of Angola declared in May 1865 that abolition would bring upon the province a greater ruin than the invasion of the barbarians brought to Europe, and the vice-president said that slaves preferred dependence to freedom. The Commercial Association of Luanda pointed out that slavery was advantageous to the slaves themselves, inasmuch as if no one bought them they would be put to death by the native chiefs.* However, when abolition was in fact decreed four years later, it passed off in Angola without incident.[34] The reason is perhaps partly to be found in the fact that the internal slave trade was still lawful, for the decree of December 1854, at least as interpreted by some local authorities, merely prescribed that any slave acquired in the interior should be registered

---

ceza Charles et Georges (Lisbon, Imprensa Nacional, 1858), Doc. No. 16A (pp. 24–26). It is difficult not to sympathize with the mingled indignation and contempt with which Lavradio relates the whole episode. Marquês de Lavradio, *Portugal em África depois de 1851* (Lisbon, 1936†), pp. 133–41. (For the meaning of the dagger (†) in the designation of Portuguese documents, see Note on Documentary Sources, p. xiii).

* The acting United States vice-consul in Luanda, a British merchant, had reported to the State Department in May 1876, a few months before the liberation came into effect: "They [the slaves] consider Domestic Slavery no disgrace but rather the contrary, especially when owned by a good master. I have known of instances where, to keep them in order, they have been threatened to be sent to the Government office to be made free —which has had quite the desired effect." Newton–U.S. State Department, May 20, 1876 (N.A.T. 430, Roll 3).

as a liberto when he came within Portuguese jurisdiction. When Dr. Livingstone, in his capacity as consul at Quilimane, reported to the governor in 1862 that one Belchior do Nascimento was recruiting slaves by force, "contrary to the spirit" of the anti-slavery laws, he was told that his interpretation of these was erroneous. The same point was made a year later by the Governor of Tete, Antonio Tavares de Almeida, after Livingstone had taken it upon himself to free some alleged slaves belonging to Portuguese residents: in Almeida's estimation, the residents in question were not liable to prosecution, because they limited themselves to buying slaves "so as to reduce them to the status of libertos." On the other hand, the governor's brother João, who was governor-general of Moçambique (it was he who had seized the *Charles et Georges* a few years earlier) held that such dealings were forbidden to Portuguese subjects and that the law was intended to apply to slaves brought in by outsiders. Neither view was likely to interfere unduly with the supply of captives, taken in tribal wars, for whatever purpose short of formal slavery.

It is easy to denounce the Portuguese for cynicism in such matters, and many have been content to follow Livingstone's example and do so. The flood of moral indignation that was released by the publication of his *Missionary Travels* in 1857 has not completely subsided, even today. Politically it was enormously effective: it influenced Anglo-Portuguese relations for a generation and more, contributing to the failure of the Congo Treaty of 1884 and the ultimatum of 1890. But it did so by darkening counsel and hindering rational discussion. When Livingstone and his followers attacked the Portuguese for slaving, and the Portuguese indignantly denied it, the two sides were clearly not talking about the same thing. The critics were concerned with what seemed to them the economic and social realities of the African scene; those criticized, with its legalities. This situation was to recur in the controversy over the S. Tomé serviçaes; something like it is to be found in the 1962 complaints about contract labor. In each case it was seemingly impossible for one side to see the other's point of view. Livingstone's accusations of bad faith received a tu quoque from José de Lacerda:

The mask is off, and the bold intentions of Dr. Livingstone are apparent even to those who see but little. . . . Betaking himself to Africa under the pretext of spreading God's Word (this being the matter with which he least concerned himself) and of advancing the geographical and natural sciences, he subordinated all his ... efforts to ... fostering elements that, when the opportune moment arrived, would bring about a complete revolution in the present state of affairs, the immediate consequences of which would be a weakening of the moral authority of the Portuguese administration ... and the ultimate results, the loss to Portugal of the lucrative trade with the interior, and thereafter, given favorable opportunity, of the territory itself.*

Evidently, imputation of sinister motives was a game at which two could play; but it contributed nothing to a solution of the problem at issue. The trouble was that slavery and the slave trade were established institutions centuries before they were discovered to be moral evils: "a state of things," as a high Foreign Office official, Villiers Lister, remarked in August 1888 apropos of the Belgian Cardinal Lavigerie's proposed anti-slavery crusade, "founded on religion, custom, profit, and taste, and handed down from time immemorial." Its complete suppression required nothing less than the occupation of the entire African continent willy-nilly by its opponents—something few European politicians were ready to contemplate in 1888, let alone a quarter of a century earlier. As Lord Salisbury pointed out in reply to Lister, "This generation will have done its part if it destroys the *export* slave trade." Kirk, the companion of Livingstone who was afterward consul general at Zanzibar, was equally forthright in private. "I think I shall keep clear of this Crusade," he wrote to the Foreign Office:

There is no use crusading in a country you cannot keep after you have conquered it, and no use driving the slaver out unless you put something better in. The real slavers in Nyasa are the natives themselves, and between them and the coast people there is the closest blood relation. To fight with marauding bands under an Arab is easy, but it is a very different matter when you get the suspicion and ill-will of the people of the country, which is what has happened at Nyasa.[35]

Any Portuguese colonial governor might have said as much, were it not that admission of administrative limitations went against the grain and might be politically damaging. The combination of religious fervor and political irresponsibility represented by the organized missionaries was not one to be taken lightly; even the skeptical Salisbury allowed himself to be influenced by it. Robert Morier might indeed

* The Portuguese side of these controversies with Livingstone was reprinted as annexes to José de Lacerda's monumental *Exame das Viagens do Doutor Livingstone* (Lisbon, 1867, Imprensa Nacional). See especially pp. 481, 485–86, 603–7.

refer in a dispatch to the "foolish chauvinism" of one of their spokesmen, and tell the man himself bluntly that his language toward Portugal was

a gross breach of international comity, and the persons guilty of it are not only wanting in their duty towards their neighbors, but in loyalty to their own Government, whom they place in a most embarrassing position. The British Government . . . has no intention whatsoever of dispossessing the Portuguese of their proprietary rights on the coast of Africa. . . . An insurrection of Negroes supplied with British tracts, British rifles, and British cartridges, and headed by British missionaries, against a nation with whom we are on terms of the most intimate alliance, is not an undertaking that would find much favor with the British Government, and though it might win the applause of Exeter Hall, might not altogether [be] approved by the British public. Whether it would tend to the civilization of the interior of Africa, I leave you to judge.[36]

But such outspokenness was rare: too rare, at any rate, substantially to allay the suspicion of British motives that was endemic in Portugal and that bedeviled relations between the allies for the remainder of the century.

Given the realities of the situation in Portuguese Africa—in which, as Henry O'Neill, the British consul in Moçambique, put it in November 1880, "the Portuguese settlements on the coast rather stand in the position of 'cities of refuge' outside a slaveholding state than as centers of government within a province, where all have been proclaimed free"—it was inevitable that anti-slavery legislation should stand as an earnest of good intentions rather than as an effective instrument of policy.[37] Those whom it was intended to benefit were ex hypothesi unable to invoke it; those who stood to lose were in positions of power and influence, and it was asking a great deal of officials that they should risk odium by uncommon zeal in enforcing the law. The same applies to other paper reforms, such as the decree of 1839 prohibiting the practice, long established in Angola, whereby private bush traders (*pombeiros*) requisitioned native carriers to transport their goods inland from the ports. Such conscripted workers received little or no pay, but the *capitão-mór* or *regente* supplying them exacted a fee from the would-be employer. Frequent attempts had been made in the eighteenth century to stop the practice, on the ground that it led to the depopulation of areas under Portuguese control, but all efforts at suppression were unsuccessful, and the decree of 1839 was no less so— within two years it was virtually withdrawn. In 1856, Sá da Bandeira sponsored a new decree to the same effect, but in 1873 he could still declare: "Even now the abuse has not ceased, although it is practiced under other names. ... For nearly thirty-five years the government has frequently ordained that the right of disposing of their labor freely, which Article 145 of the Constitutional Charter gives to the free Negroes of Angola, as to all Portuguese, shall be respected."

"What has been said on this subject," Sá da Bandeira ruefully comments, "gives an example of the difficulties involved in getting rid of abuses by which many influential people benefit."[38]

v

Pinheiro Chagas wrote of the year 1843: "The colonies, which until then had been a nest of slaves, came to be almost exclusively a nest of degredados," and went on to refer to the "detestable system of populating the African colonies with criminals."[39] The difficulty, of course, was to get others to go there. A trenchant article in the Lisbon *Jornal do Commercio,* written in February 1861, referred to the "race of deluded patriots" who saw in a colony not a source of wealth for the mother country but a monument (*padrão*) "the value of which ought not to be measured by the trivial laws and principles of political economy." Such people "tell us day in, day out that the prosperity of the country must come from the colonies. ... One dreams of our monopolizing the cultivation of cotton. ... Another expects all from the mine of Bembe (Angola). Another puts trust in the rich coalfields of Zambézia. ... All this is but childish illusion."

The article went on to point out that emigrants did not go to the colonies, but peopled Demerara and "swelled the list of deaths" in Brazil:

The reason is obvious. Whoever emigrates is poor, nay, of the poorest. His sole wealth is his labor, his sole capital his personal activity. He needs wages, not virgin soil. He needs an employer, not workers. Whither shall he take his way? To Angola? But what is he to do there? What industries exist there? What activity already established? What accumulated wealth? What cultivated lands? What industry? What trade? Trade—that of the blacks. Industry—none. Shall he go to Moçambique? Worse. ...

The mother country gives land to emigrants. But what purpose does land serve without capital? Few men, given freedom of choice, will resign themselves to be Robinson Crusoe. ...

Does anyone suppose that a man down on his luck (*um desgraçado*) would go to the colony of Pemba [Bay], for instance? He would then be seeking a climate hostile to Europeans, with destitution and misery to boot. For such wretches to die of hunger, the soil of the mother country suffices.

Having asserted that the colonies were useless for Portuguese settlement, the writer went on to declare that the Negroes had gained nothing from three hundred years of Portuguese rule. The handful of whites there had struck no roots in the soil; there was antipathy between them and the blacks, fomented by the errors of the colonial system:

The Negro can have no love for a civilization he knows only through the odious superiority of those who dominate him. The black lives and dies a savage, though within the city; he works like an animal, having surrendered his will, not as one who knowingly exercises his personal freedom. He has no sense of solidarity in a common task.

His condition will not improve if the city grows and riches multiply. For a man to work voluntarily it is necessary that the work appear sanctified by liberty and blessed by religion. But the Negro knows it only as an obligation imposed by force. . . .

After three hundred years Portuguese Africa is virtually as barbarous as it was in the beginning. Indeed, one may well ask whether complete barbarism . . . is not better than this covert barbarism which has all the moral defects of the savage condition covered with the lying varnish of an illusory civilization. One may well ask whether the Negro in his loincloth, ignorant, brutish, without religion and education, is better off in the city carrying loads for his master, or on the plantation working for an alien proprietor, than breathing the free air of his palm trees. . . .

It will be said that we need colonies for our own industrial and agricultural advantage; that we are not, nor do we seek to be, missionaries; that we make use of the Negro as we would of the buffalo, or the dromedary, that we do not intend to civilize him; that we do not seek an Africa civilized for his benefit, but one cultivated by him for our own profit.

Colonial history, unhappily, tells against such desires and intentions. Africa returns nothing to the mother country; on the contrary, the mother country has to bear in part the expenses of its conservation. The colonial budget speaks volumes. . . .

Twenty years later, this disenchanted attitude was shared by other public men than the old colonial hand, António José de Seixas, who judged the article worthy of reprinting.[40] Oliveira Martins wrote in much the same strain in his *O Brasil e as Colonias Portuguesas* (1880) —his skepticism about the *missão civilisadora* being reinforced by his belief in the inherent racial inferiority of the Negro, that "grown-up child."

Are there not ... reasons for supposing that this fact of the limited intellectual capacity of the Negro races, proved in so many and such diverse times and places, has an intimate and constitutional cause? Surely there are, and the documents abound showing us the Negro as a type anthropologically inferior ... between man and the anthropoid [ape]. The studies of prehistoric archaelogy do not authorize the supposition that within a race, i.e., without crosses with alien blood, noticeable progress can be made in cranial anatomy. Are not these proofs sufficient to demonstrate that the civilizing of savages, that vain dream of the Jesuits, was a chimera? If there is no relation between the anatomy of the cranium and intellectual and moral capacity, why should philanthropy stop with the Negro? Why not teach the Gospel to the gorilla or the orangoutang, who do not fail to have ears because they cannot speak, and might understand pretty well as much as the Negro, the metaphysic of the Incarnation of the Word and the dogma of the Trinity?
The idea of educating Negroes is therefore absurd.[41]

At a time when the Portuguese government was hoping, through a treaty with Britain, to make good at long last its claim to the mouth of the Congo, Oliveira Martins declared: "I would not sacrifice a tenth part of a brass farthing (*ceitil*) for the possession of the Zaire." He concluded his survey of the African territories in characteristically gloomy fashion:

To stand on guard—triggerless!—on the walls of a ruinous bastion, alongside a customshouse and a palace where bad and ill-paid officials vegetate, watching with folded arms the trade which foreigners carry on and we cannot; to await every day the raids of the blacks, and to hear every hour the disdain and derision with which all African travelers speak of us—frankly, it is not worth the trouble![42]

After that, it was not very consistent of him, ten years later, to oppose the Anglo-Portuguese Treaty of August 1890, which followed on the ultimatum, in apocalyptic language: "A government that signs such a convention ... presides over a people whose sense of pride and honor has been totally extinguished ... itself the most eloquent symptom that we too are about to be liquidated. *Finis Portugalliae*."[43] The patriot in Oliveira Martins had overcome the critic, the more readily since both agreed in being anti-British. Nor was he alone: one might say that the Portuguese ruling class only began to be consistently imperialist when their title to empire appeared to be threatened.

In the fifties and sixties such threats were peripheral, and interest in Africa—Sá da Bandeira almost alone excepted*—was fitful or absent. The imperialist Pinheiro Chagas later declared that under the regeneradores, preoccupied as they were with economic development at home, the overseas territories "were forgotten."[44] As evidence for this he cited the colonial budget, which appeared as a separate entity for the first time in 1852, with the advent of Fontes Pereira de Mello to the Ministry of Finance. This showed a small but rising deficit overall (e.g., 78 contos in 1852–53, 298 contos in 1863–64) until 1867–68, when the trend was reversed; in 1870–71 there was actually a surplus, which was continued for several years thereafter. Pinheiro Chagas called this "perfectly fantastic . . . a budget of colonies abandoned by the mother country," correctly arguing that they could not be expected to be self-supporting at their existing stage of development. The bare figures as given by him do not lend themselves to analysis, though it is noteworthy that in the sixties the revenue and expenditure of the tiny enclaves making up Portuguese India substantially exceeded those of the whole of Angola, which were in turn nearly twice those of Moçambique. Nevertheless, the trend of both revenue and expenditure was upward, which at least does not suggest a decline in taxable capacity.

Already, by mid-century, one attempt at organized white settlement had been undertaken. In 1840 a small presídio was established at Moçâmedes, on the southern part of the Angola coast, and in 1845 another was set up at Huila, about one hundred miles inland from Moçâmedes on the high, healthy plateau. In 1849–50 a number of Portuguese settlers at Pernambuco in Brazil were removed at their own request to Moçâmedes and given grants of land. Their arrival coincided with a severe drought, making cultivation impossible; they had to eke out a wretched existence on "bad cassava flour and rotten beans"; some moved to Huila, only to suffer such privation that they returned to Moçâmedes. Within a year or so the worst difficulties had been over-

---

* An individual governor-general, like Coelho do Amaral (governor-general of Angola from 1854 to 1860), might essay a more forward policy—as in the occupation of Ambriz —but such men could count on little more than moral support, if that, from the government in Lisbon.

come, and the township has been inhabited continuously ever since. However, the chief sustenance of its inhabitants turned out to be, not agriculture as seems to have been originally intended, but fishing.[45] In the ten years following, a number of fishermen from Algarve found their way to the area, and some established themselves further south at Porto Alexandre (1861) where a presídio had been set up seven years earlier. In 1857 an abortive effort was made to establish a colony of German settlers in the Moçâmedes area, and shortly afterward a company of European soldiers was sent to Huila in a kind of sword-and-plowshare operation, each man being given a dwelling, land, tools, seeds, and pay. However, says Sá da Bandeira, author of the plan, "the colonists were distracted by military operations and the colony dispersed"; and the same thing happened to a similar group sent to Tete, in Moçambique.[46] Successful colonization of the Huila plateau had to wait till the eighties. Yet another attempt at European settlement was made at Pemba Bay in Northern Moçambique (a derogatory reference to which has already been quoted), this time with colonists from the north of Portugal: a mistake, according to Pinheiro Chagas, in that "colonists from Minho habitually go alone, work hard, but always with longing for their native land, and with the ardent desire to return to their families. Colonists from Madeira take their families with them, strike roots in the soil where they establish themselves, and form definite and secure townships."

The group set out in April 1857, but on arrival found that the chosen site for the colony lacked fresh water; another site was found, but it was an hour's journey inland. Libertos from Moçambique Island and Chinese coolies from Macau were recruited to assist, but in vain; the settlement shortly dispersed. In Pinheiro Chagas' view, the failure was due to bad organization, to an ungrateful terrain, and also to the ill-chosen, "detestable" elements making up the settlers. He adds that Sá da Bandeira, for all his devotion to the colonial idea and his efforts to that end, did not execute his plans with the required rigor, dissipated his forces too much, and often attempted to set up "veritable utopias." There was indeed something invincibly utopian about most of the numerous measures proclaimed by successive Ministers of Marine and Colonies during the third quarter of the century. Many of them made sense on paper, whether they concerned an aqueduct for Luanda (to replace the water supply brought by boat from the river Bengo, and allow the installation of sewage disposal), or reforming the prazo system in Moçambique (1854), or attempting to secure by subsidy the running of a regular liner service between Lisbon and Angola. Again, it was a necessary consequence under the constitution of Portugal that, following the introduction of the new Civil Code in 1866, a modified version of the code should be introduced overseas. In 1869 this was duly decreed (by the distinguished writer Rebello da Silva, who was then Minister of Marine), along with a whole series of administrative reforms. However, in default of means to put them into effect they remained a dead letter—"legislative monuments which honor the name of the minister who set them up, which fascinate by the elegance of their preambles and the sound ideas they embody, but which contributed extremely little to the development of the overseas territories."[47]

Given possessions that were so tiny in effective extent, so scattered, and with so small a population that could be counted civilized—less, perhaps much less, than 10,000, at mid-century, for all the Portuguese territories on the mainland of Africa—such waste of effort was inescapable. The disproportion between the pretensions of such centrally enacted legislation and the expense of carrying it out, when compared with its likely effect even if carried out, is all too evident. One might almost say that Portugal was saddled with a dominion that was uneconomic beyond remedy, were it not that the members of her ruling class evinced little desire to change this situation. On the contrary, most of them took the view that what had once been Portuguese should remain Portuguese or, if lost, should wherever possible be recovered, regardless of its economic worth.

VI

The extreme instance of this attitude of mind was the fortified post of S. João Baptista de Ajudá, on the "slave coast" of West Africa at Whydah, in Dahomey. This had been established in 1680 as a dependency of the *capitania* of Bahia (Brazil), in order that an export tax might be levied by the Portuguese Crown on the slaves shipped thence, and to facilitate the purchase of gold and ivory under the Crown monopoly. Its existence in no way implied Portuguese sovereignty outside its walls, and indeed some kind of tribute or quitrent appears to have been paid to the native authorities in respect of it. Throughout the eighteenth century there was a regular garrison there, but as a result of the Napoleonic wars and the separation of Brazil from Portugal, arrangements for its maintenance lapsed. A certain Francisco Felix de Sousa, who had gone from Brazil to Ajudá in the early nineteenth country as a customshouse clerk, within a few years became, thanks to deaths and retirements, virtually "governor, director, treasurer, and all," and, being left to himself, began running the little fort as an independent fief. By 1820 he held the monopoly of the export of slaves from Whydah, and had, moreover, put his own candidate on the throne of Dahomey, being designated in return *xáxá,* or governor, of all the white residents on the Dahomey coast. He seems to have become thoroughly assimilated to the customs of the country, particularly in his marital habits—when he died in 1847 he left 103 recognized children. Though in practice independent of Portugal and Brazil, whose flags he apparently flew indifferently, he seems to have constituted himself the patron and protector of any of their nationals who arrived on his shores.[48] As the slave trade declined, the number of these diminished along with the importance of Whydah, which, having no real harbor, was not well suited to handling non-human cargo. Under the Constitutional Charter of 1826, Ajudá constituted part of the Kingdom of Portugal—having been wrested from Brazil after much argument when the treaty of independence was under discussion —and from time to time it occurred to the authorities in Lisbon and S. Tomé that they ought, perhaps, to do something about it. However (says an account published under official auspices in 1866), if the fort was remembered, it was only so that the government might send there

some Officer, who was thus deported to a place that had been completely abandoned, even though he should go invested with the pompous title of governor. At other times it occurred to someone to get rid of some demoralized black priest, who was named indifferently parish priest or chaplain of the fortress; inasmuch as it was not known whether the chapel there was considered subject to the bishopric of S. Tomé or as a mere chapel to the nonexistent garrison.

The Officers thus castigated with the nomination of governor or commandant went there to suffer hunger and misery, affording shameful evidence of the neglect of our affairs. The xáxá, Sousa, laughed at these commanders of naught, gave them the keys of the fort that they might have a house to live in, and graciously allowed them to eat at his table.... The presence of such officers in Ajudá did us nothing but harm ... for the Negroes could not but lose faith in the greatness of white captains whom they saw penniless, begging from door to door, or shredding tobacco and making it into cigars to earn their bread. (This is historic fact!)[49]

After naming four officers who were forced to live in this way, the 1866 account goes on to quote from the logbook of the fort, in which one of them entered copies of his reports to the Governor of Príncipe, complaining of having to live on the charity of Sousa, without pay or news.

Francisco Felix de Sousa was succeeded in 1849 as xáxá by one of his sons, Izidoro, who was educated in Brazil and England. He appears to have wanted to regularize his position, for he approached the governor of S. Tomé, José Maria Marques. As a result, the governor paid a ten-day visit to Ajudá in 1852, confirmed Izidoro in his post as governor and justice of the peace for the European residents, and provided him with a clerk-notary. Proposals were made for establishing a garrison and a company of militia, but all that resulted was the dispatch to Ajudá of a second lieutenant and a drummer, "to sound the reveille to the crows and the lizards." In 1858 Izidoro died, and no other member of the family took over; the poor clerk, Pinheiro, hung on alone in the bastion, not knowing to whom to report, and faithfully keeping record of all the doings there and of his vain efforts to get messages through to S. Tomé or to Lisbon. As Pinheiro Chagas remarks, he sounds like a character out of a novel.[50] In 1859 a ship was sent from S. Tomé on a visit of inspection which disclosed this state of affairs, but her commander was not empowered to take any action. Not until 1865, by which time Pinheiro had died at his post, was a further ship sent, as a result of rumors reaching S. Tomé that the king of Dahomey had handed over the fort to some French missionaries. The reports proved correct, but the French did not dispute the Portuguese title; a solemn act of repossession was enacted, and the reigning xáxá Francisco Felix de Sousa II (grandson of the original) was appointed lieutenant colonel and governor. Even so, no regular provision appears to have been made for the garrison, comprising a second lieutenant and five soldiers, that was left behind.

Indeed, the whole status of the little place appears to have become matter for doubt. When, toward the end of 1882, the Portuguese set on foot the negotiations that eventually led to the abortive Congo Treaty with Britain, the British Colonial Office, with an eye on French activities along the Slave Coast, suggested that the cession of the fort to the United Kingdom should form part of the quid pro quo for recognition of the Portuguese claim to the coast north of Ambriz. Hertslet, the Foreign Office librarian, thereupon went so far as to question the existence of any Portuguese possessions, properly so-called, on the Slave Coast. He cited an occasion in January 1877 when the commander of H.M.S. *Sirius,* patrolling off Whydah, had prevented a Portuguese gunboat from relieving the garrison, on the ground that there was not a fort but only a trading post there. In March 1877 the British Minister in Lisbon had been reminded that his government did not recognize that a fort existed. The point does not seem to have been pressed at that time, and once the Portuguese showed the least disposition to cede the right to Britain—as they did during the negotiations for the Congo Treaty—it was no longer in the British interest to deny its existence. Though João de Andrade Corvo, the Portuguese Foreign Minister, had referred in conversation with the British Minister (Morier) in November 1878 to "this miserable fort of Whydah," which, since the abolition of the slave trade, had become "a mere source of expense and vexation," he had also indicated the constitutional difficulties in the way of getting rid of it.[51] When it came to the point, moreover, the king of Dahomey might have had something to say about a transfer of the property to the British. Article XIV of the Congo Treaty did in fact give them a right of first refusal in the event of Portugal's giving it up; however, the treaty fell before ever reaching the stage of Portuguese ratification, and so the Côrtes was never confronted with the conflict between its provisions and those of the Charter of 1826.[52]

The story of the Ajudá fort provides something more than a locus classicus for the connoisseur of historical survivals (this particular one was to last well into the second half of the twentieth century) or the collector of strange quirks in political human nature. For it was not a unique instance of the attitude it represented: one might quote, for example, the abortive effort in 1862 to reoccupy Zumbo (the isolated settlement far up the Zambezi abandoned in 1836), when communications downstream between Sena and Tete were still dominated by the Cruz family at Massangano.[53] One might even cite the series of ill-organized punitive expeditions against Massangano itself in 1866, 1867, 1868, and 1869, all four of which ended in fiasco. A fifth, proposed for 1871 and postponed repeatedly, had to be abandoned at the end of 1873, when the forceful governor-general Coelho do Amaral died and the metropolitan troops sent to take part in it flatly refused to march, on the ground that their term of service abroad had expired. Coelho do Amaral himself is said to have been of the opinion that the defeat of the Bonga, lord of Massangano, was called for on grounds of prestige, not because there was a serious interference with the trade route to the Upper Zambezi. What these disasters showed was that a small expedition, such as could be mounted by a local governor (as in 1866), was liable to be ambushed and wiped out, while a larger one, based on the coast and including European or Goanese troops, was beyond the administration's power to organize, supply, and protect against a hostile climate. The expedition of 1868, for instance, which took six months merely to march from Quilimane to Massangano, was demoralized before it ever came face to face with the Bonga's men.[54]

By any rational calculation, the disproportion between the resources (not in themselves large) used in these activities and the tangible benefits they would have secured even if successful should have ruled them out of court from the beginning, even in a much wealthier state than Portugal. They are instances of *uneconomic* imperialism (which, perhaps, taking human history as a whole, is a commoner phenomenon than the economic kind). When Oliveira Martins described Sá da Bandeira's colonial enthusiasm as romantic, he referred to its liberal, optimistic aspect; but he might more fittingly have applied the term to the kind of sentimental, nostalgic behavior of which the poor clerk Pinheiro of Ajudá was the hero-victim. On a small scale, the expeditions against the Bonga are reminiscent of the spirit that led to Alcácer-Quibír;* they represent one more example of the point made by António Sérgio when he argued that the fault of Portuguese liberalism was that it broke insufficiently with the past.

Much petty skirmishing with tribesmen was, of course, unavoidable if the hold of the Portuguese even upon the coast were to be maintained; and it is true that the opportune establishment or reoccupation of some small presídio in, say, the hinterland of Luanda did not call for the same sustained effort and expenditure as measures of public works or economic development. With luck it might even pay for itself out of the taxes on local trade. But such holding operations, in an

---

* Analogous efforts in Angola are described in detail in the recent unpublished Ph.D. dissertation by Douglas L. Wheeler, *The Portuguese in Angola, 1836–1891* (Boston University, 1963). He does not indicate their scale, but it must have been small.

age of *fomento,* seemed inadequate to those influential Portuguese concerned for the overseas territories; and despite disappointments—like the copper mines at Bembe, inland from Ambriz, which proved too expensive to work—a trickle of projects continued to be put forward and even attempted.*

In 1864 the Banco Nacional Ultramarino was floated by a group of Lisbon capitalists, but it was unable to raise its statutory initial capital of 4,000 contos, and had to be authorized to begin operations in September 1865 with a capital of 500 contos. It was given a monopoly of banking and of note issue in the overseas territories (except for banking in Macau) and was exempted from taxation. The maximum interest it might charge was set at 8 per cent for mortgages (*crédito predial*) and 12 per cent for other operations: rates that were regarded by the colonists of the time as a "marvel," considering the shortage of capital and the usurious rates of interest then prevailing. These maxima continued in force until 1900, when they were reduced to 7 per cent and 9 per cent, respectively. The scale of the bank's operations remained small for some considerable time; even twenty years after its foundation, the total value of its notes in circulation in all the territories in which it enjoyed the right of issue was less than 600 contos.[55] But in the seventies British consular reports from Luanda paid tribute to the usefulness of its branch there (managed by a British subject named Tobin), which was steadily increasing its business: cash turnover, for instance, rose from 432 contos in 1865–66 to ten times that amount ten years later. The rate being charged on all loans, including mortgages, was stated to be 9 per cent.[56]

The growth of legitimate trade in the Luanda area from the midsixties onward is also attested by the foundation of a line of steamers, plying from Luanda coastwise to the mouth of the Cuanza and thence up that river some 200 miles to the market center of Dondo. Permission for this enterprise was granted to an American, Augustus Archer da Silva, in 1865, but from the outset of operations in 1867 it appears to have been financed by British capital. Thanks to the steamers, the transit time from Luanda to Dondo was reduced to five days (about a third of what it had been previously), and the amount of produce

* For the Bembe mines, see J. J. Monteiro, *Angola and the River Congo* (London, 1875), especially pp. 189–97.

brought down the river increased sevenfold between 1867 and 1873, the most spectacular increases being in palm oil, palm kernels, coffee, and groundnuts. But the annual total, even at the later date, was less than 9,000 tons. Moreover, the Cuanza was still the effective southern limit of European settlement in the Luanda hinterland. The total exports from Luanda, Benguela, and Moçâmedes, in the early seventies, were officially valued at round about double what they had been in 1825, when they consisted almost exclusively of slaves: exports and imports combined amounted to about one million pounds sterling, a figure considerably more than the estimated trade of the Congo ports not yet in European occupation. These ports north of Ambriz, however, were gaining trade on account of the high import duties charged in Angola on "trade goods" destined for the interior: ivory in particular was being exported through Ambrizette and Kinsembo rather than Luanda. As late as 1882, it was British Consul Cohen's opinion that were it not for the river steamers to Dondo "the trade and commerce of Luanda itself would be nil."[57]

Moçambique was more backward. Until 1853 all foreign trade had been channeled through the one customshouse in the port of Moçambique, but in that year the remaining ports on the coast were declared open to oceangoing ships, and customshouses established. Nevertheless, as late as 1874 the capital accounted for about 70 per cent by value of the total foreign trade, which amounted to rather more than half a million pounds sterling. By far the most important export was ivory, which went mainly to India; its very prevalence would suggest, even if there were no other evidence, that a clandestine slave trade was still going on. The Banco Nacional Ultramarino did not open its first provincial branch at Moçambique until 1877; and even then there was little economic justification for doing so. Not even the beginnings of a plantation agriculture for export existed. The British consul and explorer Frederic Elton, reporting in 1875, declared flatly:

Although the greatest agricultural capabilities exist, no advantage of them has been taken in the past, and the want of protection and security prevents any advantage being taken of them in the present....

Emigration, colonization, capital, and enterprise will continue to draw back from Eastern Africa so long as there is no material guarantee for security. The system of the occupation of fortified settlements at distant points upon the seaboard of a coast, with no jurisdiction over the intervals or over the interior country (except upon the Zambezi) cannot in 1875 be properly termed the effective colonization of the vast and fertile districts known as the Portuguese possessions.

The principal cultivation, Elton noted, was that of the cashew tree, from the nuts of which was distilled liquor for sale to the natives in "small drinking houses usually kept by convicts in the towns of the settlement, with the result that drunken slaves and libertos are constantly to be met with in the streets, whilst broils and theft are matters of daily occurrence...."[58]

Even the modest promise shown by Angola in the seventies seemed absent; Moçambique appeared to be caught up in a vicious circle of poverty and maladministration (or no administration at all). The total provincial revenues were less than sixty thousand pounds a year, and the salaries of many officials, reported Consul O'Neill in 1880, were from one to eight months in arrears—a standing invitation to abuse of office.[59] Clearly, escape from the circle could only be effected through a far-reaching change in economic circumstances; it would not, for instance, have been enough merely to adopt the solution of the disciples of Livingstone and substitute British for Portuguese rule, for the economy of the colony would have been unable to support the extra expense entailed by British administrative standards and requirements. Such a decisive change was the inauguration of the Suez Canal in 1869, which put Moçambique on a direct sea route to Europe for the first time in history, and ended its seclusion in the Indian Ocean trading area. Within a few years, trading houses from Marseilles had established themselves along the coast. In 1879, the Eastern Telegraph Company's submarine cable reached Moçambique Island and Lourenço Marques, en route between London and Cape Town—making it possible for Lisbon to exercise effective and immediate supervision over the provincial authorities. A similar cable reached Luanda in 1886.[60]

Southward, more dramatic developments were taking place: in April 1867 diamonds were discovered in Griqualand, near the Orange River; in December 1867 gold was discovered at Tati in Matabeleland. Attempts by the Boer Republics to annex areas that had become valuable overnight were frustrated by their British suzerain. Griqualand was first declared a crown colony and then annexed to the Cape, at the expense of the Orange Free State; and the attempt by the Transvaal to annex a corridor of land from Tati down the Maputo river to Delagoa Bay, immediately south of Lourenço Marques, was disallowed in November 1868 in view of Great Britain's own claim in the area. Thus began the struggle between the Boers and the British for the control of South Africa, in which the Portuguese were to become inextricably involved; thus began, also, a shift in the balance of economic forces that was to make the all-but-forgotten presídio of Lourenço Marques the commercial and political capital of Moçambique.[61] The rise of Lourenço Marques and the foundation of Beira, farther north, symbolize the function of Moçambique in the heyday of European imperialism: a satellite, though a virtually indispensable satellite, of the more obviously rich, more readily exploitable areas in the high interior of southern Africa. For Portuguese statesmen at the time, however, this rosy, if not altogether dignified, economic prospect before the territory was concealed behind a political threat: that the price of economic development would be the sacrifice of sovereignty. It is a price that few, if any, rulers have willingly paid, and those of Portugal were no exception: the more so because of the prevalent belief among them that the overseas possessions constituted in some way a guarantee of the independence of Portugal itself. The question, for the remainder of the century and indeed for some time thereafter, was whether the sacrifice could be avoided.

Chapter three

The Abortive Treaties, 1878–1885

One would never guess from the majority of Portuguese references to the scramble for Africa that the kingdom ended the nineteenth century with an acknowledged title to a considerably larger area of African territory than it had possessed a quarter of a century earlier, and a great deal more than it could readily digest. On the contrary, the period is commonly represented as one of spoliation in which the British ally took a leading part. One of the salient events in it—the ultimatum of 1890—is supposed to have contributed decisively toward the downfall of the Portuguese monarchy twenty years later, and is a source of resentment to this day. (Nevertheless, it is Royalist writers like Costa Lobo and Vieira de Castro who show little or no anti-British sentiment.) One would likewise have to look hard and long at the Portuguese literature before finding any acknowledgment of the assistance the British gave in consolidating Portuguese hold on the territories before 1914. Perhaps Lord Salisbury had Portugal in mind when, in another context but a day or two before he sent the ultimatum, he remarked that "gratitude is not an international emotion."* The very sending of it might seem to bear out a Foreign Office minute by Villiers Lister nearly four years earlier: "I am afraid we shall never get

---

* The context was a dispatch from the British delegation to the Slave Trade Conference at Brussels suggesting that the right of search be relaxed outside the slave trade zone, in order to secure it inside. Salisbury minuted, "No objection . . . but I would not give it absolutely without an equivalent—gratitude is not an international emotion." (F.O. 84/2101, c. January 9, 1890.)

anything out of the Portuguese by negotiation. They will accept a 'fait accompli' but will never abandon the dogma that Africa belongs to Portugal.''[1] He might have added that they appear to have had no notion of the cumulative exasperation their behavior was building up in the Foreign Office—an exasperation which found release in the crisis of 1890, and which goes a long way to explain why the crisis was so severe.

I

No amount of sympathy with the Portuguese will enable one to regard their foreign policy in the late eighties as other than misguided, for it rested on profound miscalculation of the diplomatic forces at work. Only one of their leaders, João de Andrade Corvo, who was Foreign Minister from 1871 to 1877 and from January 1878 to June 1879, displayed statesmanship in this field; and Corvo ("perhaps more of a philosopher than a man of affairs," as a critic remarked) could not, in the end, carry his countrymen with him over the so-called Lourenço Marques treaty, and was virtually thrown over by his chief, Fontes, and his party.[2] His monumental essay on the overseas provinces, *As Provincias Ultramarinas,* published after he had been forced into political retirement, constitutes a kind of testament: its high-minded liberalism is consistent with his previous acts.[3] In 1870, a few months before becoming Foreign Minister, he had published *Perigos* (Perils), a lengthy political tract inspired by the Franco-Prussian War, in which he warned his countrymen of the implications of Prussian militarism and the absence of political principle that it and the defeated empire of Napoleon III alike represented, and lamented the breakdown of the Concert of Europe.[*] He was shocked by the failure of other countries to stop a war which was "a blot on this century, a peril for the whole of Europe, and a great crime against civilization": even granted that the French had started it, Prussia had no right to deny them an honorable peace or to proceed with a "war of extermination." He attacked the notions of race by which Prussian policy was justified ("The theory of *races,* applied to the formation of Empires in Europe, is a singular fantasy, but an eminently dangerous one"), and went on, not unnaturally, to argue that the maintenance of small states, if they were

---

[*] João de Andrade Corvo, *Perigos* (Lisbon, 1870), pp. 116–58 *passim.* I am indebted to Dr. José de Almada for drawing my attention to this remarkably prescient pamphlet.

viable, was in the interests of Europe as a whole. "The history of the formation of great states in Europe is the history of despotism, war, oppression of peoples by force, and violent attacks on law and social morality."

In these perilous circumstances, Corvo looked for help to the enlightened self-interest of the British, whose influence in Europe and whose overseas possessions would be endangered by the growth of great empires there, and to the United States, whose intervention in favor of immediate peace he hoped for. It was with these two powers, he urged, that Portugal, "which needs good alliances as well as good government, good policy, and good administration," should align herself. He acknowledged that Great Britain's foreign policy had often shown "egoism, ingratitude, inconstancy ... scorn for the weak and complacency toward the strong," and that she had frequently disregarded her ally's legitimate interests. Nevertheless, both tradition and community of interest dictated that the Anglo-Portuguese alliance should not be weakened. A convinced free-trader (among his writings is a primer of political economy),* Corvo looked forward to profound changes in Portugal's commercial and colonial policy that might make her "the first and foremost emporium of commerce between America and Europe."[4]

Magnanimity is a rare and lonely virtue in politics, and in Corvo's case it was also a virtue that had to be its own reward. Even on the plane of expediency it is clear that he was right and the policy he advocated the only practicable one. (Lavradio, who is generally opposed to the British, remarks that they were aware of this and took advantage of it.)[5] But he was surrounded by the small-minded, and was incapable, it seems, of the kind of worldly wisdom that tries to make virtue more palatable by cloaking it as self-interest. Only one man with whom Corvo had to deal—Robert Morier, British Minister in Lisbon from 1876 to 1881—shared his breadth of vision, and Morier also was hampered by indifferent and unimaginative statesmanship on the part of his government. Moreover, it seems that Morier overplayed his hand and injured his partner in the matter of the Lourenço Marques Treaty, even though the ultimate abandonment of the treaty was due as much to a change in British colonial policy—the retrocession of the

---

* João de Andrade Corvo, *Economia Politica para Todos* (Lisbon, 1881).

Transvaal—as to the hostile reception the treaty was given by Portuguese public opinion.

Although Corvo's career ended in disappointment, he was able to do much to promote Portuguese imperial interests, especially during the short periods when he held both the post of Foreign Minister and that of Minister for Marine and Colonies. He and Morier pushed through a treaty providing, inter alia, for the construction of a railway across Portuguese India to the port of Mormugão—a treaty that calls for mention because it was intended to form part of a package deal along with the Lourenço Marques Treaty. He completed the formal abolition of slavery in the overseas territories. He arranged the first subsidized mail steamer service (by the British-owned British India Line) between Lisbon and Moçambique, with connections to Quilimane and Lourenço Marques. He gave official backing to the Lisbon Geographical Society, which was to become a formidable engine of imperialist propaganda. At his instance, a new and liberal tariff, including a transit duty of only 3 per cent, was introduced in Moçambique in 1879. He answered in dignified fashion the accusations of slaving made by Lovett Cameron and others, and he authorized the expeditions subsequently undertaken by Capello and Ivens, and by Serpa Pinto, across central Africa. He arranged for the Eastern Telegraph Company's submarine cable to serve Moçambique (town) and Lourenço Marques. He instituted a series of public works planning missions to the African provinces, and authorized the first loan ever raised for public works there. He established Guiné as a separate province. Not all his projects bore immediate, or indeed any, fruit; yet, with the possible exception of Sá da Bandeira, he did more than any other man of his century toward promoting the establishment of a truly liberal Portuguese colonial dominion.[6]

Corvo's principal diplomatic achievement was the settlement by arbitration of what the British call "the Delagoa Bay question." During the years 1822 to 1825, Captain Owen, R.N., was engaged in making a survey of the East African coast for the British Admiralty; in September 1822 he accepted the cession to King George IV of what he described as the "kingdom of Temby" (Tembe). He did this, he explained, to please the "king," who was aggrieved by some proceedings of the governor of Lourenço Marques, which was and is separated from Tembe by the Rio Espirito Santo, or what British navigators called the "English River." Owen returned in March 1823 and made a similar arrangement with the chief of the neighboring territory of Maputo, after which he notified the Portuguese authorities in Lourenço Marques and Moçambique that he had taken these measures, and added that they enjoyed no jurisdiction beyond the boundaries of the fort of Lourenço Marques. In Owen's absence, however, the two chiefs were prevailed upon to repudiate their concessions, and the British flag was hauled down. The next year (1824), Owen returned and hoisted it again, and the year after he once more asserted sovereignty by forcibly releasing a British ship which the Portuguese were holding for alleged contraband. By this time Portuguese protests at Owen's proceedings were being made in London, with inconclusive results.* Both sides based themselves on the ipsissima verba of the Treaty of 1817, by which the territories possessed by the Portuguese Crown on the east coast of Africa were defined, for the purposes of legitimizing the slave trade south of the equator, as being "comprehended between Cabo Delgado and the Bay of Lourenço Marques." The question was whether this description was inclusive, as the Portuguese claimed, or exclusive—in which case it could only be construed as saying that the settlement of Lourenço Marques, which was unquestionably situated on the bay of that name, was outside the Portuguese dominions. Since the British never claimed that this was so, their whole argument appears even more strained than Palmerston's over the Portuguese claim to Cabinda and Molembo.**

Little more happened until 1860, when Vice Admiral Keppel, in H.M.S. *Brisk*, sailed into Delagoa Bay and formally laid claim to its southern portion. The following year, another British warship hoisted the British flag on two islands in the bay, and the official gazette at Cape Town announced that these islands were annexed to the Crown Colony of Natal. To the fervent protests of the Portuguese Minister in London, the Foreign Secretary (Russell) replied, "in very bad

---

* A detailed account of Owen's expedition and its consequences will be found in M. V. Jackson, *European Powers and South-East Africa*, pp. 108–53, which makes it clear that the British claim was weak and was so regarded by Palmerston. The Portuguese side of the case is given in José d'Arriaga, *A Inglaterra, Portugal e Suas Colonias*, pp. 264–78; Marquês de Lavradio, *Portugal em Africa depois de 1851* (Lisbon, 1936†), pp. 54–62; Mário Simões dos Reis, *Arbitragens de Lourenço Marques* (Lisbon, 1936), pp. 46–51; and, most important, in Visconde de Paiva Manso, *Memória sobre Lourenço Marques (Delagoa Bay)* (Lisbon, 1870, Imprensa Nacional†), pp. 43–47.

** Paiva Manso's argument in *Memória sobre Lourenço Marques*, pp. 51–52, appears conclusive on this point.

French," that this action had been taken by way of suppressing the slave trade: to which the Portuguese Minister retorted that it would be only logical in that case for the British to annex the whole of Portuguese Africa. "I could not restrain myself from saying to Lord Russell, 'Be at any rate frank and say openly: We want the Portuguese colonies and have the necessary force to take them.'" But again no decisive move was taken to resolve the question.

In June 1869, Portugal and the Transvaal Republic signed a comprehensive treaty, which two years later was ratified by the Côrtes. By it, the Transvaal recognized Portugal's claim to the territories in dispute, down to south latitude 26° 30'. The British had already protested against this clause of the treaty; but the administration of Mr. Gladstone was less intransigent in such matters than that of Lords Palmerston and Russell, and it now expressed willingness to accept arbitration, which had been offered by Sá da Bandeira in January 1869. The chosen arbitrator was President Thiers of France; it fell to his successor, Marshal MacMahon, to deliver sentence on July 24, 1875. The verdict went in favor of Portugal: on the evidence as presented it is hard to see how it could have gone otherwise.[8] The tendency in some British newspapers, and even in British official circles, to impugn the fairness of the arbitrator can only be attributed to disappointment following upon wishful thinking. Oddly enough, on more than one later occasion the British press seems to have been under the delusion that the possession of Lourenço Marques itself was at issue.*

II

The importance of the MacMahon award was that it put an end to any hopes, whether on the part of the British or the Transvaal govern-

---

* Simões dos Reis, *Arbitragens de Lourenço Marques,* pp. 51–117, gives a detailed account of the arbitration proceedings, prints the more important documents, and analyzes the findings from the point of view of an advocate rather than a judge; this vitiates, but does not wholly invalidate, what he has to say.

For subsequent misunderstandings of the arbitration issue, see Arriaga, *A Inglaterra, Portugal e Suas Colonias,* p. 291 (quoting *The Morning Post,* May 17, 1880); and (most extraordinary because included in an official British publication) the statement in the so-called Selborne Memorandum of 1907 that "the British and Portuguese Governments both laid claim to Delagoa Bay . . . and in 1875 the debated territory was awarded to Portugal": where it is clear from the context that Delagoa Bay is identified with the port of Lourenço Marques (p. 53 of reprint, ed., Basil Williams). The Selborne Memorandum is discussed below, pp. 327–31.

ment, of establishing a port on Delagoa Bay outside Portuguese jurisdiction. The Portuguese government promptly concluded a revised
treaty with the Transvaal in which specific provision was made for
financing the construction of a railway from Lourenço Marques to
Pretoria. But in 1877, with this treaty awaiting ratification, Great Britain annexed the Transvaal. The action was in no sense motivated by
the MacMahon award, but once consummated it had a natural corollary: an attempt to gain in substance, if not on paper, what had been
denied the British in 1875, and what could at least be represented as a
means of carrying forward the policy of cooperation contained in the
Portuguese treaties with the Transvaal. In August 1878, the Colonial
Office set the ball rolling by suggesting to the Foreign Office that an
understanding with Portugal was desirable about such matters as
transit dues, and that perhaps—as had been provided for in the Portuguese treaty of 1875—the customs revenues at Lourenço Marques
might be used to pay the interest on the capital cost of a railway
thither. This suggestion was transmitted to Morier, with instructions
to sound the Portuguese government; but by the time it reached him,
on October 1, Corvo had independently raised the question of the
railway. By the beginning of December, the two had reached tentative
agreement in principle on four points: Portugal's share in the cost of
the railway; the rates of duty to be charged at Lourenço Marques; the
import facilities to be granted the British there; and the passage of
British troops through the port and railway. On all these questions
Corvo was prepared to be characteristically accommodating.[9]

However, when news of the negotiations reached the Colonial Office in January 1879, the immediate reaction was that Morier had gone
too fast and too far, particularly in the matter of the railway. No funds
existed in the Transvaal for railway construction, and not enough was
known about the prospects of the line to allow the Colonial Secretary
to propose that the British government assist in its building. When
Morier elaborated the general bases agreed on with Corvo into a formal treaty that, inter alia, should bind the contracting parties to build
the railway jointly, the Foreign Secretary told him that he had mis-
understood his instructions: "I certainly never meant to convey to you
any intention on the part of Her Majesty's Government to pay for
the making of a railway, and I cannot find any words that imply it."
Such a commitment, Salisbury went on, would require the prior con-

sent of Parliament. Morier replied, with some force, that without British cooperation in building the railway (which he had never intended should be offered unless it appeared a sound proposal), the Portuguese would be getting nothing equivalent to the concessions being sought: "Public opinion . . . is waking up to the fact that the . . . Treaty is one far more to our advantage than to that of Portugal."[10]

Morier therefore amended his draft treaty so as to provide in the first place for an inquiry into the feasibility of the railway, to be followed by a separate Railway Convention, the terms of which were nevertheless specified in the treaty itself. This met the objections of the Colonial Office; but in the meantime, Sir Bartle Frere, British High Commissioner in Southeast Africa, had involved the British in a war with the Zulus, and the spectacular disaster of Isandhlwana (January 22, 1879), when eight hundred British soldiers were surrounded and massacred, had taken place. The shock it produced was out of all proportion to its military importance: the Colonial Office averred that the British were "engaged in a very serious struggle with a nation of great military capacity . . . . The primary necessity, to [sic] which all other matters must be postponed, is that of bringing this struggle to a completely successful issue, but this work may not improbably be both costly and protracted . . . ."[11]

Hence, it was declared, there could be no more talk of railways for the present: Senhor Corvo would have to wait. "The security of persons and works during construction and after it," Salisbury telegraphed to Morier, "could not be guaranteed, possibly for many years." "I did not," Morier drily observed, "assign the reason given in the telegram for this suspension because I was afraid lest the admission . . . might cause an undesirable panic, and a loss of confidence in the omnipotence of British prestige over black men."[12] Moreover, he argued, the Zulu war made the military provisions of the treaty more, not less, urgent. After Morier had visited London and explained his views in person, he was authorized to resume negotiations, and indeed to sign the treaty, on the understanding that ratification would be postponed until the situation in South Africa was clearer. A week later, on May 30, Morier telegraphed that the treaty had been signed, but that the Fontes government had resigned.[13]

That the treaty was signed before the government fell was due mainly to Corvo himself, and bears witness to the importance he attached to it. By all the rules of the political game, however, in Portugal or anywhere else, a "deathbed" signature smacked of sharp practice, and the numerous opponents of the treaty made the most of it. The struggle by Morier over the next two years to secure ratification, in spite of the weight of Portuguese public opinion, can be read in his numerous, argumentative, and lengthy dispatches to the Foreign Office—few of which received more than formal business replies. In one reader, at least, these dispatches arouse sympathy for Portuguese ministers, writhing under pressure as relentless as the decencies of diplomatic protocol allowed. It was not as though the treaty presented obvious immediate advantage to Portugal. As was admitted in the Foreign Office, it was a treaty *"qui n'engage à rien* on the British side," but that was to secure the United Kingdom "real and substantial advantages." The Portuguese, on the other hand, were to

give up what might prove a great source of revenue, viz., the right to impose a transit duty, which if moderate, would not stifle the export and import trade of the Transvaal through Delagoa Bay. They give up a great deal also in the Zambezi clause (Article III) [which provided for free navigation on that river and its "affluents"]. They get nothing in exchange beyond the hypothetical advantages to be derived from the joint construction of a harbor and railway.[14]

It was this absence of an obvious equivalent for the concessions made by Portugal that was fastened on by the more moderate critics of the treaty there: why, asked one such, had not Corvo taken the opportunity to press for the recognition of the old claim on the west coast? The answer, which may or may not have been known to the critic, is that Morier, who sympathized with that claim, had persuaded Corvo that it should be left in abeyance pending the completion of the rest of their joint program.[15] When Braamcamp, Corvo's successor, broached the question of the Congo behind Morier's back—through D'Antas, the minister in London—Morier advised the new Foreign Secretary, Granville, to agree in principle to talks, but only on condition that the Lourenço Marques Treaty was first ratified. It is hard not to feel that in this (and perhaps throughout) his oft-expressed contempt for the Portuguese caused him to misconceive the position in a way that London had not. Confident of his ability to force the politicians to ratify in the teeth of public opposition, he saw no reason to take steps to disarm that opposition by gestures of conciliation: "The Portuguese," he wrote at one stage of the negotiations, "are not so much men as weak-brained, hysterical women, and when they fancy that they have had the best of it in any transaction or encounter, they become wholly unmanageable." He had written earlier in the same dispatch:

The belief is ingrained in the Portuguese mind that England requires Portugal even more than Portugal requires England: that for the maintenance of our position in the Peninsula and the safety of Gibraltar, the independence, autonomy, and friendship of Portugal are necessary conditions of our policy. Consequently, that whatever their language, and even their acts, we must for our own sake bear with them, and never show anything but the most tender regard for their feelings.[16]

It is a moot point, however, whether Morier was any better than the Portuguese at seeing himself as others saw him. There was something to be said for the critic, already quoted, who regarded the railway clauses of the treaty as being closefisted: he could understand a deal in which the British contributed capital and Portugal the geographical advantages of Lourenço Marques, but not a meticulous apportionment of costs and expenses between the parties that would burden the meager revenues of the colony for "a work of pure English speculation." "This," he went on,

is really to presume too much upon our incapacity to understand or deal with business matters, to seek by sheer audacity to turn the unlikely into reality. The note of avarice that runs, like an operatic *motif,* from beginning to end of the treaty of Lourenço Marques, made it at once antipathetic to our national susceptibilities. The astute English negotiator, by dint of his very ability, ruined his own handiwork, or at the very least rendered it repugnant.[17]

One will, indeed, look in vain in Morier's dispatches for any imaginative appreciation of the affront to Portuguese national sentiment represented by the establishment of what was virtually a British customshouse (for the transit trade) in the port of Lourenço Marques, or by the unprecedented proposal that the treaty should run without limit of time. His treaty was a thoroughly practical job that ignored such imponderables at its peril: for it was not to be expected that, patriotic objections once aroused, the critics would pay scrupulous attention to the precise wording of the text. Moreover, there were no powerful interests in Lisbon itself to organize support for the treaty. The endemic suspicion of British motives had free play in a political atmosphere that favored its exploitation, for the fall of Fontes in 1879

marked the end of an epoch in which the regeneradores had dominated the country by reason of the division of their opponents. The
progressista party, which had been formed but three years earlier by
what was known as the "pacto da Granja," had achieved its first political success. There was to follow the period of *rotativismo,* defined
by Ameal thus: "Regeneradores and progressistas govern turn and
turn about: when things get difficult, the ministry falls. Nothing more
simple—and nothing more automatic."[18]

The automatic element was provided by the control that any government, of whatever complexion, had over the composition of the
Côrtes: rigging in the elections to the Lower House (elections which
always followed, not preceded, a change of administration), and creation of peers in the Upper House. For the latter, the consent of the
sovereign was indeed required, but how much discretion the constitutional kings of Portugal had in such questions is not very clear: King
Luís, whose long reign (1861 to 1889) coincided with the heyday of
fontismo, was not one to offend the politicians by undue insistence on
the prerogative. As a modern disciple of absolutism puts it: "King
Luís ... lets everything pass. And why not? The Charter allows him
to do little more than to watch, undaunted, in the front row, from the
royal box, the circus of vanity and disorder. It allows him, too, in his
spare time, to play the violin or translate Shakespeare."[19]

Nevertheless, Luís was too intelligent to be a complete cipher, and
doubtless knew when to exercise his influence. It was to this influence,
if the accusations of the rising Republican party are to be believed, that
the progressistas owed their advent to office in mid-1879.[20] Part of the
price they paid, it seems, was that they did not enjoy a free hand over
Corvo's treaty—on behalf of which Morier, as well as Corvo, had made
haste to enlist the king's support.[21] Such was the extreme factiousness
of Portuguese politics at this time that the duty of the progressistas
was to attack the treaty, if only because it had been made by their political opponents—and despite the fact that in opposition they had
been enthusiastic proponents of a railway to Lourenço Marques. Their
leader, Braamcamp, a man respected for the constancy of his liberal
opinions (Oliveira Martins dedicated his *Portugal Contemporaneo* to
Braamcamp's memory), but now aging and infirm, was thus in a most
difficult position: he had undertaken to secure ratification for the
treaty, but was unable to control his followers and reluctant to carry

the thing through with regenerador votes. Moreover, the delay in the spring of 1879, plus the stipulation that ratification be delayed, had left time for a formidable agitation to develop, in which the Republicans did not scruple to involve the person of the king.

Whether Braamcamp could have forced ratification through the 1880 session of the Côrtes was a matter of opinion. Morier, of course, held that he could; but Morier (as a Portuguese minister, goaded, once told him) was not a principal, but an agent. At any rate, Braamcamp, in the face of the growing unpopularity of the treaty, dared not (or at least did not) make the vote one of confidence, and early in June the treaty was referred to a committee on technical grounds—that is, decision was postponed till the following session. Significant of the state of public opinion was Morier's plaint in a dispatch of May 20:

By far the worst danger I have to face is the unfortunate coincidence of the ratification ... with the Tercentenary Jubilee of Camoëns, on the subject of which the whole population of Portugal has gone mad. The opponents of the Treaty have artfully used this juxtaposition.

The principal feature of the Camoëns festival is to be an allegorical procession, composed of triumphal cars, representing everything that can be allegorized in heaven and earth, and in the water under the earth. ... The [enclosed] cartoon* suggests that the Colonies shall be represented by a huge beer-barrel containing the Treaties, drawn by Senhor Corvo, in his quality of Maître Corbeau, and on which Her Majesty's Minister, as representative of John Bull, is seated with looks of extreme satisfaction. The car is attended by starving Indians.[22]

Even before the ratification debate opened, the Portuguese government (again behind Morier's back) had sounded London on the possibility of adjourning the matter till next session; and with adjournment accomplished, D'Antas was charged with securing amendments to the treaty that would make it more palatable in Portugal.[23] It became evident that there was some genuine misunderstanding within the Foreign Ministry itself about certain clauses, notably one relating to the passage of British troops over Portuguese territory. But even after Morier had performed prodigies of explanation, one stumbling block remained: the perpetuity of the treaty, which, it was claimed, was without precedent. The British were willing to concede that, in general, the treaty should run for twelve-year periods, at the end of each of which it would be automatically renewed unless denounced;

* This cartoon, by the remarkably gifted Raphael Bordallo Pinheiro, perhaps the most powerful of all Republican propagandists of his day, is reproduced in part facing p. 112.

but they balked at abandoning perpetuity for the provisions that would affect the railway—particularly the one exempting goods in transit over it from dues and charges. Amortization of the cost of construction, it was argued, might take over a century, and ought not to be placed in peril by the possibility that free transit might be abrogated. The question, Morier told Braamcamp in October, was "one not of national susceptibilities and confidence, but of pounds, shillings, and pence"—particularly because the British taxpayers' money might be involved.[24] Eventually D'Antas was instructed to propose that a period of 99 years be set for free transit, and this London agreed to. Unfortunately, Morier's instructions to this effect were delayed in arrival, so that he was left insisting on perpetuity after his principals had abandoned it, and the episode could be represented in Portugal as a triumph for Braamcamp over the British negotiator.[25]

The Additional Article and Protocol were signed on the last day of 1880, just in time for the new session of the Côrtes; but in spite of Braamcamp's guarantee that prompt action would be taken to ratify, inordinate delays occurred. To what extent these were deliberate, given Portuguese methods of conducting any sort of business, is hard to tell; but the progressista ministry was by this time tottering to a fall by reason of the unpopularity of its domestic policy, and hence might well have sought to transfer to its successor the responsibility for ratification. By the time debates had actually begun, near the end of February, an insurrection had been going on in the Transvaal for two months, and the minor but humiliating defeat of Majuba Hill was inflicted by the Boers on the British before the vote came to be taken.[26] Naturally, this suggested that the treaty might be a dead letter even if it were ratified; and though the Lower House, on March 8th, voted 74 to 19 in favor of ratification, it was in the midst of violent public demonstrations in which the consistently hostile Republican element was abetted by others whose motives were purely factious. An excuse for the demonstrations was a routine visit to Lisbon by a squadron of the Royal Navy, which, it was alleged, had come to overawe the government. Feelings were further aroused by tactless reports in the London press that "the treaty ceding Lourenço Marques to Great Britain" had been approved by the Côrtes. Two weeks after the vote Braamcamp resigned, before a vote could be taken in the House of Peers.[27]

As the treaty had originally been made by the regeneradores, who now came into office, it might seem that there was no question of its not passing. But Fontes, their leader, was apparently determined not to incur the odium of voting for it, and hence that it should not come to a vote in the House of Peers, where he would be morally obliged to do so. He therefore declined office himself, leaving a colleague, Rodrigues Sampaio, as the nominal Prime Minister. A story had already been put about to the effect that Corvo had made the original treaty not as a responsible minister, but merely as a plenipotentiary, and that the party was not now bound to support it. In face of this charge, Corvo himself remained silent, and an appeal for written evidence was answered by the claim that none could be found. Eventually the minutes of the Cabinet Council authorizing the signature turned up among Corvo's own papers and were published—too late, however, to prevent Fontes from obtaining his object.[28] D'Antas, the minister in London, was appointed Foreign Minister ad interim in the hope that he might secure Morier's assent to further adjournment—the very monarchy itself being at risk, it was claimed, if the agitation against the treaty were not allowed to die down. Failing in this, he resigned and returned to his London post. There he was more fortunate: the proposal for adjournment commended itself to the Colonial Secretary, for the negotiations with the Transvaal Boers, concluded in the Pretoria Convention of August 1881, were even then in progress. Granville, the Foreign Secretary, who seems to have cared little about the whole question one way or the other, fell in with his colleague's views.[29]

That was the end of the Lourenço Marques Treaty: for the terms by which autonomy was granted to the Transvaal, though they left not merely the supervision, but the conduct, of its foreign relations in the hands of the suzerain, took out of those hands any responsibility for such matters as the construction of railroads. Without the railway and transit clauses which were the core of the treaty, the appendages (such as free navigation on the Zambezi and naval cooperation against the slave trade) which the ingenuity of Morier had contrived to attach to it were left without means of support. But the blistering dispatch that constituted Morier's comment on the adjournment, in which he put the principal blame once again on the Colonial Office for "refusing to place confidence" in his judgment, was really off the mark.[30] If Mr. Gladstone, who, before coming into office in April 1880, had denounced the annexation of the Transvaal as dishonorable to the character of his country and therefore to be repudiated, had lived up to his professions, Anglo-Portuguese as well as Anglo-Boer relations might not have reached breaking-point before the century was out.

What had been missed was an opportunity to repair the damage to good relations that the annexation and its corollary treaty had done; in this the British treatment of the Boers and the Portuguese was all of a piece, and it is difficult not to agree with Dr. Leyds, President Kruger's associate, when he puts it down to lack of imagination.[31] As in the case of the bombardment of Alexandria in 1882, which drew from the great Portuguese novelist Eça de Queiroz a splendid piece of anti-Imperialist invective,[32] the British Liberal government might almost have seemed bent on assuring foreign opinion that all that divided them from their Conservative opponents was a coating of Gladstonian unction. They thus gained little credit from the fact that the original railroad treaty with the Transvaal, the basis of so many odious comparisons, was reinstated and, in due course, ratified. The whole episode had strengthened Republican and anti-British feeling among Portuguese politicians and intelligentsia—the latter a group that British diplomatists, perhaps underrating its influence by analogy with the position at home, seldom attempted to cultivate. It thus made the kind of policy contemplated by Corvo harder for Portuguese political leaders to pursue, even had they wished to do so. At the same time, the episode marked the beginning of a new British policy under which relations with Portugal (which, since the restoration of Maria II, had been dominated by measures against the slave trade) became increasingly subordinate to the less obviously philanthropic activities of the Colonial Office in southern Africa.

III

The third panel in Morier's triptych, the Congo Treaty, did not come up for systematic discussion and negotiation until after Morier had been transferred to Madrid and Corvo had refused political office in Fontes' new ministry, established when the Lourenço Marques treaty was safely out of the way (November 1881). How the Congo Treaty was first delayed by the force of British public opinion (stimulated behind the scenes by King Leopold of Belgium) and then given the coup de grâce by Bismarck, has long been familiar in outline, and has

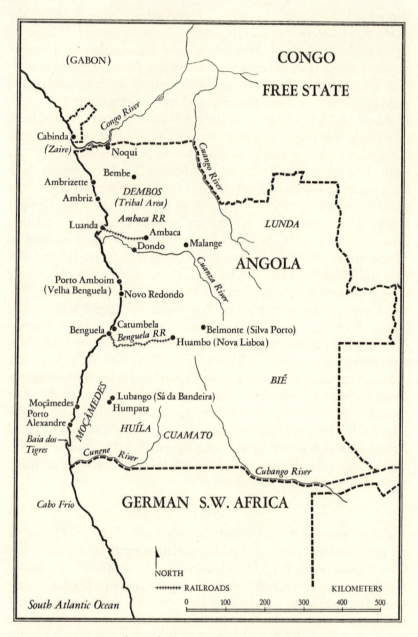

Angola and Surroundings, c. 1850–1900

recently been studied in detail by Dr. Roger Anstey. Likewise familiar is the story of the Berlin West African Conference that grew out of the rejection of the treaty and that brought into being the Congo Free State, formed largely from territories considered by Portugal to be hers by historic right.[33] The indignation of Barbosa du Bocage, the Portuguese Foreign Minister, at these proceedings is understandable—before the conference he wrote of "the unheard-of audacity with which a private company, of uncertain nationality and no known articles of association, seeks by violence and fraud to usurp sovereign rights that it may not exercise in face of the most elementary principles of international law"—words that he was subsequently constrained to eat when Portugal was forced to recognize the new state.[34] The success of Leopold at the conference, it is clear, was a triumph of timing—of being able to present his International Congo Association as being both humanitarian and *not* a great power. It was a part that Portugal would have liked to play but—thanks to a generation of propaganda from the anti-slavery movement—had no hope of playing successfully before a European audience. The failure of the Congo Treaty may likewise be considered a matter of timing. "Between 1879 and mid-1882," writes Dr. Anstey, "a Congo treaty might not only have been negotiated with Portugal but also accepted by the powers. In 1882–84 it was quite another matter."[35] Two implications of that judgment are important: the first, that ratification of the treaty by Portugal herself was a foregone conclusion; the second, that the precise terms of the treaty did not constitute a major stumbling block to its acceptance.

It is, of course, true that Portugal did eventually accede—so far as territorial claims on the West Coast went—to considerably worse terms than she would have obtained under the treaty. Her leaders, however, have never considered it dishonorable to give way under duress, and in the course of the territorial negotiations that accompanied the Berlin Conference the Portuguese delegation specifically requested that duress be applied: "They repeatedly put forward quite impossible demands, which they never expected to be granted, simply in order to provoke an ultimatum of some kind, which they could then show to their government. A somewhat artificial atmosphere of difficulty was in this way imparted to the whole situation."[36] Tactics of this kind, intended for home consumption, could not have been applied in the Anglo-Portuguese Treaty negotiations if only because the

British stipulations were not of a kind that could have been imposed on the Portuguese government by force. Moreover, several of them were exceedingly distasteful to Portuguese opinion. As an Oporto newspaper put it, on March 11, 1884: "It were better to lose the Zaire altogether than keep it subject to such conditions. There is no lack of Portuguese territory in Africa, but the loss of national dignity is irreparable."[37]

As to the terms of the treaty, it is worth while recalling what Dr. Anstey does not mention, namely that Corvo, who had been responsible for reviving the question in 1875, would have been content with the left bank of the Congo as the northern frontier of Angola. He told Morier so when he was out of office temporarily in 1877, and in the first volume of *As Provincias Ultramarinas,* published in 1883 when negotiations were in progress, he repeated that the natural frontier of Angola was on the "Zaire" (Congo estuary), and that rights to Cabinda and Molembo, to the north of it, should be reserved in order to conform with the Charter, "until the matter can be legally resolved."[38] Hence Morier's proposal in 1877 that the British arrange for Portugal to cede them the rights claimed north of the river, in return for recognition of those to the south of it; and the later provision, in his draft treaty of 1881, that the right bank should be ruled by a condominium of powers having trade with the Congo:

The mode I propose [for dealing] ... with the question of the Portuguese claims north of the Congo is the only one which I believe will furnish a satisfactory solution.... Any proposal to formally renounce any territory included in the Charter would be certain to call forth in all its intensity the morbid pseudo-patriotism of which we have seen more than enough during the past few weeks, and to render all agreement impossible....

The joint jurisdiction ... might turn out to furnish an excellent precedent for dealing with many portions of Africa which we do not desire to occupy ourselves, but which we should not like to see occupied by others.[39]

In a dispatch from Madrid (to which he had been transferred), written in December 1882, when negotiations for the treaty were on the point of being opened, Morier again insisted on the importance of this arrangement: "The stipulations respecting the territory north of the Congo would have enabled not us only, but all other civilized nations there commercially represented, to exercise jurisdiction over their nationals." He added that, in common with the other proposals in his draft, it had been accepted at the time by Corvo; and he suggested that France's newly acquired interest in the Upper Congo afforded the opportunity to associate her with it. "She might, therefore, be invited conjointly with us and Portugal, to take a leading part in these arrangements, so long as the question of Portugal's sovereignty up to the Congo, and the conditions on which we would be ready to acknowledge that sovereignty, remained exclusively in our hands and Portugal's."[40]

There is, of course, no knowing whether a workable arrangement of the kind could have been arrived at, or would have been ratified by the Portuguese. But the mere attempt to negotiate it might have disarmed the opposition of France and other interested countries as well as that of the British trading community—the two forces that Morier had tried to reckon with, and that eventually proved fatal to the treaty. It would have avoided the appearance of exclusiveness that clung to the treaty in spite of Granville's professions, and that formed the basis of Bismarck's measured rejection of it in his dispatch of June 1884. In 1882, however, the proposal was not so much rejected by the Foreign Office as lost on it: "The Foreign Office did not seriously consider any alternative means of preserving the freedom of the Congo." The thought Morier had devoted to the whole question largely went for nothing.[41] The Portuguese were entitled to complain of the casual approach of the Foreign Office to the negotiations and its failure to anticipate the opposition that the very proposal to treat with Portugal aroused, so that stipulations that she had promptly accepted were afterwards declared by the British negotiators to be insufficiently precise.* They might also have impugned the logic with which the stiffer British demands were justified in the dispatch which H. Percy Anderson, the new head of the African Department at the Foreign Office, drafted for Granville in March 1883. This insisted that there was no question of Great Britain's recognizing the historic claims of Portugal to the territory between $5°12'$ and $8°$ south latitude: "They [the British government] are not looking back to the past, they are providing for the future ... not ... asking concessions as a favor, but ... attaching them

---

* Roger Anstey, *Britain and the Congo in the Nineteenth Century* (Oxford, 1962), pp. 109–12. Keith's earlier account—"Portugal with singular fatuity persisted in fighting [the British terms] item by item"—is wholly unfair and misleading. See A. Berriedale Keith, *The Belgian Congo and the Berlin Act* (London, 1919), p. 51.

as a condition."* But, as neither Britain nor Portugal was in occupation of the territory, the only way, surely, in which the British could
gain any locus in the question was by reference to the historic claim
to it. It has been argued earlier that a prescriptive right had in fact
been conceded to Portugal by the Treaty of 1817, and that Palmerston's repudiation of this was unhistorical. His argument was, in
effect, that the territory, in form as well as in fact, was a no-man's-land
so far as Europeans were concerned. In that case, however, the British
had no more right than the Portuguese to dispose of it without reference to other interested parties. Exclusive negotiations between the
two made sense only if recognition of the Portuguese claim (the British having none) were presupposed and the conditions, on which
recognition would be publicly afforded, alone remained to be discussed.

That Serpa Pimentel, the Portuguese Foreign Minister to whom the
British assertion was addressed, should not have seen fit to contradict
it may be largely explained by his expressed confidence (which the
British Foreign Office did not share) that other powers would make
no difficulty about the Portuguese claim and had, indeed, already admitted it. This confidence received a blow during the summer of 1883,
when a Portuguese attempt to negotiate with France a settlement of
outstanding boundary questions on the west coast of Africa broke
down on that very issue. It is a mistake to regard this approach by the
Portuguese as an alternative to the treaty with Britain. Their position
could only be secured by treaties with both powers, and in any case
the frontiers of Guiné had also to be settled with France.[42] But the
difficulties with the French doubtless made the Fontes Cabinet more
anxious to secure the British treaty (as well as accounting for the re-
placement of Serpa as Foreign Minister by Barbosa du Bocage, a distinguished zoologist). Even so, it is clear that both sides continued to
underestimate the hostility that the treaty would arouse from other
powers. Otherwise, the Portuguese might not have insisted on, nor
the British acquiesced in, the substitution of an Anglo-Portuguese

---

* Granville–D'Antas, March 15, 1883 (C.P. 4785, No. 119). The drafts by Anderson,
quoted by Anstey, above, did not get into the Confidential Print. A. J. Hanna, *The
Beginnings of Nyasaland and North-Eastern Rhodesia* (Oxford, 1956), p. 124, fairly
describes the British attitude as "candor amounting to insolence," but wrongly implies
that this was their initial response to Portuguese overtures.

commission for the international commission that had been proposed by the British to regulate traffic on the river. Granville indeed made the point, in submitting the Portuguese proposal to the Cabinet, that it would destroy the appearance of disinterestedness that the negotiations had hitherto presented: "Our negotiations have been carried on professedly without any wish to get anything for ourselves which is not open to the whole world. The proposed arrangement would give a different color to what we have done."[43] But the voice of the tempter made itself heard in a minute from his subordinate Villiers Lister:

International Commissions are very troublesome and unmanageable things.... There would be constant combinations to put the British Delegate in a minority. I cannot consider the International Commission as a guarantee for free commerce and navigation; on the contrary, I believe that it would prove to be a great danger to British trade.... The same objections do not apply to the proposed Anglo-Portuguese Commission.[44]

Gladstone and the Cabinet pronounced for the latter, which was, furthermore, to be mandatory instead of permissive as the original proposal had been.[45] It was, of course, taking the line of least resistance at the given moment, and it proved fatal; for the nature of the commission turned out to be the focus of foreign criticism. Even so, the treaty might perhaps have been saved in a modified form but for the opposition of Bismarck. Much speculation has been spent upon his motives, and various reasons adduced why he should have wished to pick a quarrel with Britain in the summer of 1884. There has been less disposition, at least among British writers, to point out that, whatever his motives, he chose his ground well: the objections made in his dispatch of June 7, 1884 are precisely those one would expect of anyone not a party to the treaty. The grant to Portugal of sovereignty was the principal complaint, but the presumption of Great Britain in granting it was hardly less objectionable: "We are ... not in a position to admit that Portugal *or any other nation* [italics mine] [has] a previous right there." A mutual agreement of all the interested powers, such as Bismarck also proposed in the dispatch, was clearly a more appropriate way of dealing with the Congo problem than any bilateral treaty, however enlightened its provisions.[46]

As early as May 11, before Bismarck's views were made known, the Portuguese had suggested to the British that a conference be held, and on May 13 they embodied this suggestion in a circular to the other powers, though without telling their ally. Their motives are not clear, though the idea was not new: it had been mooted by the Belgian Foreign Minister to their minister in Brussels in December 1882. Lavradio describes the move as "a last resort"; perhaps the Fontes government felt that it could not face the next session of the Côrtes without some decisive action to which it might point.[47] The British had demurred to the suggestion on the ground that no agreed basis for a conference existed; but this objection lapsed when Bismarck vetoed the treaty. From then on the initiative lay with Germany and France, and it was they who issued the invitations to the Berlin conference. Territorial questions, which were the only ones of any importance to Portugal, were excluded, at French instance, from its agenda and left to be settled on the sidelines. There the Portuguese negotiators displayed their customary obstinate tenacity, but lacking consistent support from any one power (the British having almost ostentatiously declared that with the collapse of the treaty each party recovered full freedom of action) they were driven to make the best terms they could. The hardest blow was having to recognize the upstart Congo Free State and have it not only occupy the right bank of the Congo, but block their expansion upriver on both banks.

Upon a cool appraisal that should have regard not to historic claims but to effective occupation (actual and potential), the Portuguese might be said to have fared not at all badly. Even the claim to Cabinda and Molembo was reflected in the retention of a coastal enclave north of the Congo, while the boundary of Angola proper was fixed on that river instead of at Ambriz. (As in the Anglo-Portuguese treaty, the inland limit was set at Nokki, leaving Vivi as a river port below the cataracts and outside Portuguese jurisdiction.) Though the new acquisitions were made part of the so-called Conventional Basin of the Congo, and hence were subjected to a special low-tariff regime, the further proposal that they be made neutral in wartime had, with French help, been beaten off. Moreover, certain obnoxious provisions insisted on by the British, which might very well have prevented the Côrtes from ratifying the original treaty, had lapsed with it: freedom of navigation on the Zambezi, the setting of the western frontier of Moçambique at the junction of the rivers Ruo and Shiré, and even the cession of the fort of Ajudá. (This last had not, in the end, been specified in so many words, but only mentioned in an exchange of notes, for the Portuguese had feared that to be explicit about it would cause the king of Dahomey to massacre the garrison.) Nevertheless—and this was important for the future—resentment against Britain remained fierce: the Portuguese could not forgive her for keeping them out of what they considered their heritage until it was too late. Such treatment of an old and faithful ally, Bocage told Petre, the British minister in Lisbon, in October 1884, was without historical precedent, the more so since Britain neither claimed nor could claim any rights there herself.[48]

So far as Portugal was concerned, one important result of the Berlin Conference was the establishment of a formally new basis for colonial claims in Africa—that of "effective occupation" of a coastline—which put an end to the kind of controversy that had arisen over Cabinda and Molembo. Henceforward, it would not be possible for Portugal or any other power to go to the conference table (as Lavradio puts it) "with a beautiful trunk-load of historic claims, but no armed strength to make them tell."[49] The ruling was all but fortuitous, arising from some obscure and ill-conceived machinations of Bismarck that were eventually realized to be inconvenient for Germany's own colonial ambitions. In the watered-down form in which it finally took effect, it merely stated that any signatory power that henceforth might acquire territory on the African coastline should notify the others, so that they might make good their claims, if any. The same rule applied to protectorates; but an attempt to enforce specific obligations to preserve law and order on the protecting power was defeated by the obstinate and at one time lonely insistence of Selborne, the British Lord Chancellor, that a distinction must be preserved in this respect between protectorates and outright annexations.[50] It was this distinction that would allow Portugal, during the years 1885–87, to establish a protectorate over Dahomey, based on the Ajudá fort.

Chapter four

"Effective Occupation" and the Quarrel with Great Britain, 1886–1890

The dropping of the Anglo-Portuguese treaty at the behest of France and Germany, and the dominance of Bismarck over the Berlin conference, made some Portuguese wonder whether British power and influence had not passed its zenith and whether they should not act accordingly. Even before the conference was over, Henrique de Barros Gomes, who had been Finance Minister in Braamcamp's progressista administration of 1879–81, and who had been educated in Germany, presented a motion in the Côrtes regretting that in the course of the negotiations the regenerador government had not shown itself more in touch with the current European political situation. It had, he said, been unduly concerned with maintaining the British alliance, and had ignored Germany, which was nowadays not merely a country of savants, but the foremost military power in the world. He took exception to certain clauses in the treaty as infringements of sovereignty, and quoted Laboulaye, the French Minister in Lisbon, as saying—very fairly—that it constituted, not the recognition of Portugal's rights, but an authorization for her to exercise them.[1] Barros Gomes is not to be written off as a firebrand chauvinist: pious (one critic remarked that he ought to have been, not a politician, but a bishop), high-minded, and with claims to being an intellectual, he was the close friend and literary executor of Oliveira Martins.[2] As Foreign Minister, it was his misfortune to run counter not merely to Great Britain, but to the Marquess of Salisbury, and to be associated forever in Portuguese history with the ultimatum of 1890.

I

The Central African policy of which that national humiliation was the outcome was not, however, the work of Barros Gomes alone, or even of his party. It harked back to the seventeenth century or even earlier, and its modern revival owed something to Corvo, who set on foot the expeditions of Serpa Pinto and of Capello and Ivens. The mixed reception that Serpa Pinto's journey across Africa was given in Portugal, even while he was being lionized in England and France, indicates the hold of the past on the imagination of some of his contemporaries. Manuel Ferreira Ribeiro published in 1880 a 900-page book designed to demonstrate that Serpa Pinto had traversed no ground that was not familiar to Portuguese (and other) travelers, in which he referred to "our Anglo-Moçambiquan province." In an earlier work he had written, "We do not possess there [Africa] merely the coastline to east and west. The whole central territory belongs to us both in law and in fact."[3] Hence the complaint against the new Moçambique tariff introduced by Corvo in 1877, that by providing for transit duties it admitted that the interior, beyond the confluence of the Shiré with the Zambezi, was outside Portuguese jurisdiction. On the point of fact and on the propriety of the admission more than one opinion was indeed possible for a patriotic Portuguese. But on the desirability of taking possession of the interior, which Ferreira Ribeiro urged strongly, there seem to have been few doubts. Oliveira Martins indeed was skeptical about any attempt, even by the British, to do so: "It is not to be believed that England will undertake the conquest of the interior of Southern Africa; but it is more than certain that her missionaries will take with them, along with the Bible, samples of Manchester cottons." But, he added, "the historic domination of the coastline does not give us [the Portuguese] the right to prohibit trading posts in the interior or to harass them with customs duties."[4] Oliveira Martins was conscious, moreover, of the administrative effort, to say nothing of the effort in terms of capital and manpower, that colonial activity required, and for Portuguese colonial administration he had nothing but contempt:

Nature did not cut us out for wise administrators ... the annals of our colonial administration are a web of misery and disgrace. Herculano, discussing the civilizing of our rural population, referred to the parish priest and the schoolmaster as myths created for bureaucratic use; in the colonies there was and is another myth—the governor of the fortress—and all three are to be counted more repugnant and atrocious than any that the imagination of the Phoenicians could invent.[5]

It appears, however, that most of his contemporaries simply did not think in administrative terms: they envisaged a kind of nominal dominion in which the Portuguese mingled with the savage and controlled him through the moral authority and sympathy which they alone among Europeans could command. An extract from a decree following the proclamation of the protectorate over Dahomey, signed by Pinheiro Chagas as the responsible Minister, typifies this belief. After referring to the long neglect of the Ajudá fort, it remarks that the recent closer relationship between the Portuguese and the king of Dahomey

has torn down the mysterious and bloody veil in which the savage court of Dahomey was enwrapped, and has shown that Portuguese influence, so weighty at all points on the African seaboard, exerts itself there also in incomparable fashion. The monarch of Dahomey, the terror of all Europeans, shows himself affable and condescending to the Portuguese alone. It was he who asked urgently that our protectorate should be established upon the coast of his kingdom. . . . It is he who appears disposed to accept at our hands the benefits of European civilization, and to this design he has already borne honorable witness by abolishing human sacrifices.

The Portuguese protectorate in Dahomey is the lighted pathway that links this kingdom of darkness with Europe.[6]

That was in January 1886. About six months earlier Bocage had addressed to Pinheiro Chagas a formal minute outlining the forward policy to be pursued in linking Angola and Moçambique, and enlisting his assistance. It was, he urged, a propitious moment for realizing the dream of their forefathers, now that all eyes were on Africa and powerful nations were seeking there both markets for their superabundant industrial production, and new sources of raw materials. Now was the time to display the new progressive character of Portuguese colonial rule and invite the collaboration of foreign capital (in a word, to extend fontismo overseas), and to confound the calumniators of Portugal. "We must act quickly, and not allow time for others to get ahead and make our task impossible." Bocage went on to stress the importance of fixing the boundaries of the African possessions by a combination of extension of protectorates and agreement with foreign powers, and he outlined the northern and southern frontiers of the proposed Portuguese Central Africa. Its boundaries roughly coincided with those on the "rose-colored map" published in 1887; in particular the whole of Matabeleland and the area of Lake Nyasa were included.* Bocage recognized that they might have to be modified to conform with the claims of others, but did not think it impossible for Portugal to "secure the major part" of the boundaries he had indicated. He suggested to his colleague that two expeditions be undertaken: one to Barotseland from the west, and the other to Matabeleland. He also urged a beginning with the two railroads that had long been projected inland from Luanda and Lourenço Marques, and he was willing to consider "prudent concessions" that would lead to the establishment of foreign capital and foreign settlers in the territory: this would be the best means of getting a trans-African railroad constructed.[7]

An opportunity for putting into effect the diplomatic moves entailed by this program occurred shortly afterward, in September 1885, when the French government proposed boundary negotiations. These began in October, and the chief Portuguese delegate was none other than Corvo, who had become minister in Paris. The principal matter to be discussed was, of course, the frontiers of Guiné. The French gave up their extreme claims on its southern side, but retained both sides of the Casamansa estuary to its north, including the former Portuguese settlement of Zeguichor. They also agreed to the Portuguese proposals for the frontier between the French Congo and the Cabinda enclave. In addition to these strictly practical points, an article (IV) was added to the boundary convention by which France recognized the king of Portugal's "right to exercise his sovereign and civilizing influence in the territories that separate the Portuguese possessions of Angola and Moçambique, subject to the rights previously acquired by other powers." The French had resisted attempts to have the boundaries of the territories in question defined in the treaty, or to have the Portuguese map of 1886, in which they were colored pink, annexed to it, on the ground that France had no claims in them or contiguous with them and hence no locus in the matter. In effect, therefore, the clause was no more than a friendly gesture, and the "rose-colored map,"

* See Map, p. 104.

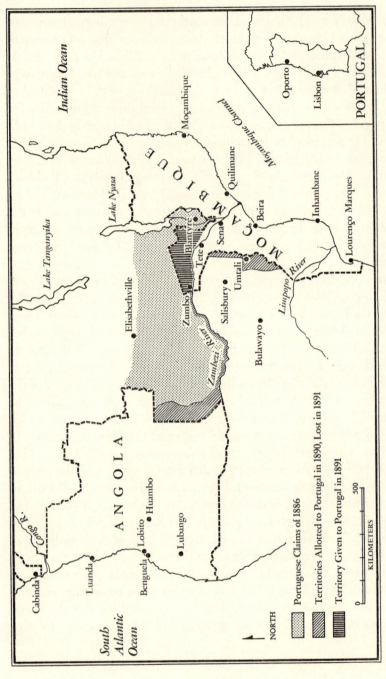

Portuguese Claims in Central Africa, 1886–1891

though published along with the protocols to the Convention, was issued on the authority of Portugal alone. The Convention was dated May 12, 1886.[8]

Negotiations with Germany began toward the end of 1885, but did not get seriously under way until the middle of 1886. In February of that year the Fontes government had been replaced by a progressista ministry headed by José Luciano de Castro, in which the Germanophil Barros Gomes was Foreign Minister. How far this change affected the result, as distinct from the course, of negotiations is not clear. The Germans had quite casually and without warning laid claim to the portion of coastline between Cape Frio and the mouth of the Cunene —a territory which had long been considered as part of Angola and in which a grant of land, with a view to European settlement, had been made by the Portuguese government as recently as mid-August 1885. The German case appears to have been a weak one, and at first Barros Gomes resisted it. But its acceptance was made a quid pro quo for German acquiescence in Portuguese plans for the interior, and the government of Luciano de Castro considered the price worth paying. As Vieira de Castro remarks, Portugal gave a positive benefit, and Germany recompensed her with "a perilous mirage."[9] The relevant article (III) was drafted in substantially the same terms as its counterpart in the convention with France, and the territories in which Portuguese sovereign and civilizing influence was to be exercised were likewise left undefined. The joint declaration was signed in Lisbon on December 30, 1886.[10]

Some later writers have failed to perceive, or at any rate to stress, the continuity of policy between the Fontes and Luciano administrations and hence have tended to exaggerate the importance of Barros Gomes' German proclivities in the period before the ultimatum of 1890. Vieira de Castro even speaks of Germany as "the instigator of Barros Gomes, the accomplice of the *mapa côr de rosa.*"[11] Historically this will not do, like most searches for scapegoats: there seem to have been remarkably few Portuguese critics of the policy until after the ultimatum, which is why that event had such a cataclysmic effect. Nor will it do to say that the policy was faulty in conception, for although it foundered as a result of British opposition, that opposition was slow to crystallize. Barros Gomes himself appears to have summed up the position fairly when he remarked, in a circular dispatch sent to Portuguese missions abroad a few weeks before the ultimatum, that those in Great Britain concerned with Africa were divided into two groups: one in favor of riding roughshod over Portuguese pretensions, and one seeking cooperation. What he failed to realize was the extent to which the proceedings of his government were calculated to ensure that the party hostile to Portugal would prevail: indeed, it had prevailed by the time the circular was sent out.[12]

II

Although Lord Salisbury sent a formal protest to Lisbon against the treaties with France and Germany in August 1887, within a few weeks of their publication in Portuguese "White Books," his government cannot be said to have had at that time any positive policy on the subject, or any firm basis in international law upon which to found one. The protest itself was based on a logical extension of the doctrine of effective occupation laid down in the Berlin Act: if the African coastline had to be occupied by any pretending power in sufficient strength to enable it to "maintain order, protect foreigners, and control the natives," then a fortiori this rule ought to apply to the interior. But this logical step, as Barros Gomes pointed out in reply (and as Salisbury was well aware), was one that the Berlin Conference had quite designedly refused to take; one, moreover, that would have injured the pretensions of the Congo Free State, of Germany, and of Great Britain herself in various parts of the African interior.[13] Salisbury's argument, in effect, was a repetition of that which had led to the original proposal by Granville that the doctrine of effective occupation be extended to the entire continent. Miss S. E. Crowe calls this dense, and a misapprehension of Britain's "true interest"; thus reading back into 1884 (and, incidentally, endorsing) imperialist aims that did not become manifest until some years later. It indicates a want of expansive intentions in Great Britain as late as 1887 that Salisbury, whom no one could call dense, should persist in repudiating Barros Gomes' argument: "The whole spirit of the [Berlin] Act," the Foreign Office told the Colonial Office in December of that year, "implies that powers claiming to exercise a sovereignty or protectorate should be able to fulfill the obligations entailed by the claim."[14] But Salisbury knew better than to pursue the point with the Portuguese.

On another matter of dispute covered by, though not specified in, the two treaties—freedom of navigation on the Zambezi—the British position was equally insecure. Freedom of navigation was wanted partly as a matter of principle, partly to guard the interests of the British missionary settlements on the Upper Shiré. It had been stipulated for in the abortive Lourenço Marques and Congo treaties and had been promised by the Portuguese delegation to the Berlin Conference. But the very fact of its having been a matter of specific treaty provision, and hence the subject of a quid pro quo, suggests that it was legally a concession by Portugal and that the Zambezi was not ex hypothesi an international river. Sir Travers Twiss, the most eminent British jurisconsult of his day, stated that a nation holding both banks of a navigable river, however broad, had an absolute right to exclude all other nations from its use: "The stream, whilst it is included within the territory of a nation, cannot be considered to be destined by the Creator to continue open to the common use of mankind any more than the banks or adjacent lands, which have been appropriated and so withdrawn from common use."

Such a rule might seem to be more than a little hard on upstream riparian nations, and in the view of some international lawyers, at least, it seems to have been qualified by the dictum that the right of navigation should not be withheld from such nations without due cause. The Nyasa settlements, however, hardly came within the definition of a "nation."[15]

The Portuguese refusal to allow freedom of navigation by right, though it may have been impolitic, thus appears to have been justified in international law. Indeed, though they do not seem to have been aware of it, they might have based a claim to the whole Zambezi basin on their control of the coast at its mouth. The locus classicus for this rule appears to be the negotiations over the Louisiana Purchase between Spain and the United States, when it was enunciated that "when any European nation takes possession of any extent of seaboard, that possession is understood as extending into the interior country to the sources of the rivers emptying within that coast, to all their branches and the country they cover, and to give it right, in exclusion of all other nations, to the same."

Sir Travers Twiss stated quite unequivocally that "there is no dispute amongst nations" on this point of law, and that it therefore ruled out an earlier claim, on behalf of the United States, that entrance into and possession of the mouth of a river entitled a nation to claim the whole of its basin: The Law of Nature ... regards rivers as appurtenant to land, and not land as adherent to rivers."[16] The British Foreign Office had earlier shown itself aware of this rule and hence reluctant "to stir the question" of African boundaries with Portugal.[17] In contradistinction to its attitude on the claim to Cabinda and Molembo, it had never disputed Portuguese authority on the east coast between Cape Delgado and Lourenço Marques.[18] One can readily see why (quite apart from the adverse decisions the British had had to accept on previous occasions) Salisbury should have flatly refused to enter into arbitration with Portugal on the occasion of the "ultimatum." But one can see also that so long as Portugal should refrain from provoking the British into exercising their superior strength in despite of international law, it would be difficult to dispose of her Central African claims, however "ridiculous" the Foreign Office might think them.[19]

In the late seventies there had been no disposition on either side to push matters to a conclusion. When Jervoise, the British chargé d'affaires in Lisbon, told Corvo in July 1876 that Lake Nyasa was beyond the territorial jurisdiction of Portugal, the assertion went uncontested;[20] and though O'Neill, the consul at Moçambique, was told by the Foreign Office in January 1880 that he had been injudicious in inquiring of the governor-general, Francisco Maria da Cunha, whether the Blantyre and Livingstonia Missions were regarded as being within Portuguese jurisdiction, the point was not pursued. (The governor-general had confessed his ignorance of their whereabouts, and had asked O'Neill to mark them on the map.)[21] Indeed, as late as November 1881 the opinion was expressed within the Foreign Office that there appeared to be no objection to the Portuguese occupying Blantyre provided they did not harm British subjects or their property there.[22] The abortive Congo treaty, with its provision limiting Portuguese sovereignty on the Shiré at the Ruo, represented a reversal of this opinion; and it was in late 1884, after the treaty had been abandoned, that British officials began to discuss among themselves the possibilities of establishing a protectorate in the Nyasa region, if that were the only way of keeping the Portuguese out. In early 1885 they were more than inclined to regard this as urgent.[23] But by the middle of 1886 their mood had changed, and Petre, the Minister in Lisbon, was so far encouraged by a private talk he had had with Barros Gomes as to suggest that it might be worth while to concede Portugal an exclusive sphere of influence or protectorate north of the Zambezi in return for guarantees safeguarding the position of the British settlers around Nyasa. Barros Gomes, of course, had just taken office and was intent on getting from the British what his predecessor had been in the course of getting from the French and the Germans. Petre argued with considerable force that the immediate advantages of such an agreement would accrue to the British, whereas "this ambitious colonial idea of the Portuguese, if it can ever be realized, can only be realized in the dim and distant future."[24] In February 1887, the Foreign Office was still warning the African Lakes Company and, through it, the missionary interests, of the "suicidal folly of getting up meetings or deputations which would excite the vanity and the hostility of the Portuguese" and so injure Petre's chances of securing substantial concessions from them.[25] Even the British protest against the "rose-colored map" in August 1887 was in part at least inspired by the need to placate what Villiers Lister called "the strong feeling in this country against Portuguese extension in Africa." Salisbury himself minuted that the protest would not be carried out, but "would make them feel uncomfortable." Anderson, the head of the Foreign Office African Department, pointed to the difficulty of proclaiming a protectorate in a territory "harried by slave gangs, where we could not exercise a shred of sovereignty and to which our only access is through the possessions of the power we should be thwarting."[26]

The point of this last statement lay in the fact that no way was then known by which oceangoing ships could traverse the Zambezi delta: everything destined for the upper river had to pass by the so-called Kwakwa Channel and thence by a portage, except in times of flood, from the port of Quilimane to Vicente, the lowest point of navigation. Even if the British should successfully assert, or secure by treaty, the rights they claimed on the Zambezi proper, this would still leave the Portuguese with the right to bar transit over the portage inland from Quilimane. In the last resort, therefore, the Nyasa settlements were at the mercy of Lisbon or the Moçambique authorities, unless and until the British should apply coercion. Hence the feeling of frustration that runs through so many of the Foreign Office papers on the subject and that at times paralyzed even its chief. When, at the end of 1887, the Colonial Office advised against entering into negotiation with the

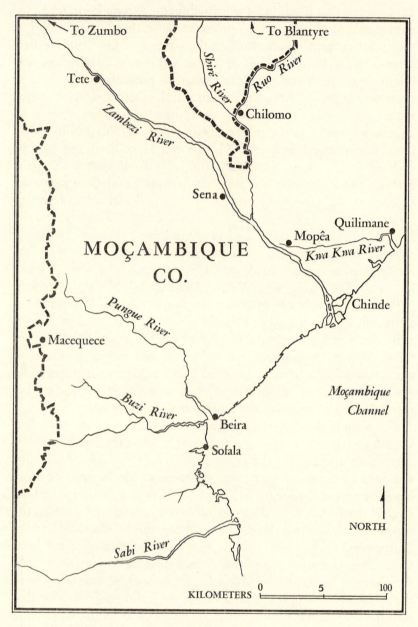

To Zumbo

To Blantyre

Tete

Shiré River

Ruo River

Chilomo

Zambezi River

Sena

MOÇAMBIQUE
CO.

Quilimane

Mopêa

Kwa Kwa River

Chinde

Pungue River

Macequece

*Moçambique
Channel*

Buzi River

Beira

Sofala

NORTH

Sabi River

KILOMETERS   0   5   100

Zambézia, c. 1895

Portuguese on boundaries, Salisbury nonetheless declined a suggestion that the Portuguese be informed that the British were not willing to negotiate: "No—this would be hasty. We have not yet found a lever to influence Portugal and we must not renounce any possible agency as yet."[27]

During the course of 1888 this sense of frustration was enhanced by a long wrangle over the Zambezi navigation and transit. In January the authorities at Quilimane, without reference to Lisbon, attempted to enforce on the African Lakes Company's river steamer *James Stevenson* a regulation of February 1887 that all ships in the coastwise and river trades had to be Portuguese-owned: an action the more vexatious because for a decade previously navigation had been entirely free. Although Barros Gomes, in response to British protests, agreed to suspend action against the steamer, his reaffirmation of Portugal's right to regulate traffic on the river naturally aroused dissent and irritation in the Foreign Office. "The Portuguese are becoming intolerable," declared a minute of March 13.[28] More serious was the question of arms for the Nyasa settlers, who had become involved in war with the Arab slave-raiders who infested the territory.* Although the British government accepted no responsibility for providing the settlers with arms, it used its good offices with the Portuguese government to allow the African Lakes Company to import some on its own account. Lisbon made no difficulty (though it created some delay) about the transit of small-arms ammunition, but demurred to a further request in August that a Hotchkiss quick-firing gun and two mountain guns be let through—on the ground that a private company ought not to be allowed to use artillery in country claimed by Portugal and that there could be no assurance that the guns would not get into the wrong hands and be used against her.[29] The Portuguese themselves were having trouble with the remaining relatives of the rebel Bonga in the Zambezi valley, and a local decree forbidding the importation of arms into Quilimane had been issued in consequence. But this decree was at one point represented to the Foreign Office as being specifically directed to the situation at Lake Nyasa, and naturally evoked indignant minutes about Portuguese rascality.[30] Eventually a way around the

---

* On the Arab war, see A. J. Hanna, *The Beginnings of Nyasaland and North-Eastern Rhodesia* (Oxford, 1956), pp. 79–104.

difficulty was found by stating that the guns were required for use on the northwestern shore of Lake Nyasa, beyond the area claimed by the Portuguese—but not until October, and not until the British had all but threatened to break off diplomatic relations.[31] By the end of the year the British Ambassador in Berlin was writing to the younger Bismarck, apropos of a rumor of negotiations between Germany and Portugal:

> I am to let you know, most confidentially, that our relations with Portugal are somewhat strained. It seems that a powerful expedition has been secretly dispatched to Lake Nyasa, where we have rights.
>
> It would be quite impossible for us to abandon our missionaries there to Portugal, the more so as we are accused of having sacrificed our missionaries further north to Germany.
>
> Lord Salisbury adds that if Portugal interferes with the Lake Nyasa region we should be forced to take some one of the Portuguese possessions in India or the Atlantic coast as a material guarantee.[32]

It is by no means clear what any negotiations between Germany and Portugal could have been about at that particular time, and the Germans immediately denied that any existed. But the sending of the letter indicates a hardening in Salisbury's attitude to the Nyasa question, and an indisposition to be put off, as his officials had been inclined to be, by the local difficulties of dealing with it. Indeed, the Foreign Office had already hinted to the African Lakes Company that it might run its guns up to Nyasa by way of the Kongani mouth of the Zambezi (too shallow for oceangoing ships), and the Admiralty was prepared to assist with a gunboat.[33]

III

A further effort toward a general settlement with Portugal had nonetheless been made by the British in the autumn of 1888. Its occasion was the achievement of another stage in the Cape Colony's drive to the north: the "Moffat Treaty," made at Cecil Rhodes' instigation, by which Lo Bengula, the Matabele king, bound himself not to negotiate with or cede territory to any foreign state without the previous knowledge of the High Commissioner for South Africa. The High Commissioner, Sir Hercules Robinson, had ratified this treaty in April 1888, and it remained to notify the Transvaal Republic that, in effect, its northward expansion was cut off. But any declaration to the Trans-

Preparations for the [Camões] Centenary

Raphael Bordallo Pinheiro, in *O António Maria*, May 20, 1880.

The Congo Treaty

JOHN BULL: *I make you a present of this coffer! Guard it; take care of it; cherish it; dust it; keep it from rotting. Clean it diligently — but only on the outside!*

CITIZEN OF PORTUGAL:—*And the key?*

JOHN BULL: *I will keep the key at the bottom of my strongbox for those occasions when it needs to be cleaned inside!*

Raphael Bordallo Pinheiro, in
O António Maria, March 13, 1884.

Inflammatory poster,
Oporto, January 1890.
"More Dynamite!
More Kerosene!"

AO POVO PORTUGUEZ

DINAMITE E MAIS DINAMITE!!!... PETROLEO E MAIS PETROLEO

Todo o mundo está indignado contra o vil, dispotico e aladroado procedimento da Inglaterra — e consta que

O DRAMA VAE PRINCIPIAR, APENAS CHEGUE A LISBOA

A ESQUADRA INGLEZA?!.....

Nada de sustos, mas cumpre ao nosso governo e ao povo portuguez disporem-se para uma resolução extrema, passando a **VIAS DE FACTO.**

GUERRA DE MORTE AOS PIRATAS BRITANNICOS!!!

Elles tentam roubar-nos, esmagar-nos e aniquilar-nos.

VENDAMOS A VIDA CARA!!!

Ao nosso governo cumpre encher de torpedos **IMMEDIATAMENTE** a foz do Tejo, — collocar ao longo d'elle a melhor artilheria, — pôr em armas a nação, — chamar as reservas — e crear 2.ª e 3.ª linha; — ao povo cumpre secundar o governo e **FAZER O RESTO:**

Apenas esses ladrões disparem o 1.º tiro sobre Lisboa,

MÃO BAIXA EM TODOS OS INGLEZES QUE SE ENCONTREM EM PORTUGAL

e fogo a todos os seus edificios, estabelecimentos e armazens, — principiando pelos armazens de VILLA NOVA DE GAYA, onde aquelles ladrões teem os seus depositos de vinho.

In extremis-extrema!!!...
Nada de contemplações com taes ladrões!!!...
Dinamite e mais dinamite!!!...
Petroleo e mais petroleo!!!...

vaal could hardly be made without involving Portugal: Barros Gomes had formally reserved his country's rights on learning of the Moffat Treaty, and the territories involved lay to the west of, or might even be included in, the district of Sofala. The prospect of an agreement with Portugal, however, appeared brighter because the British Office now seemed disposed to accept the Zambezi as the northern limit of the British sphere of influence, subject to guarantees concerning navigation on, and transit across, that river.[34] Percy Anderson at the Foreign Office welcomed the opportunity thus presented of granting the Portuguese a sphere of influence between Angola and Moçambique:

If our Colonies would be satisfied with the Zambezi frontier, and with getting rid of Portuguese claims in Matabeleland, we should lose nothing by agreeing to the sphere of influence. . . . The northern watershed of the Zambezi is believed to be nearly the most pestilential and inhospitable region in Central Africa, and the more favored country north of it is in the Congo Free State.

The position of the Nyasa settlers, he suggested, could be dealt with by Portugal's promising not to occupy that area without the assent of Great Britain. This would please the traders and missionaries, and at the same time get rid of "the impracticable idea of a British protectorate."[35]

In due course, notice was served on the Transvaal (July 25) and on the Portuguese government (August 1) that the British government considered a territory north of the Bechuanaland Protectorate and the Transvaal, south of the Zambezi, east of the 20th degree of east longitude, and west of the Portuguese province of Sofala, to be within the sphere of British influence. The Cape Colony's endorsement of the proposal to negotiate with Portugal was received at the end of August; but (partly because Petre was home from Lisbon on leave, and partly, perhaps, because the argument over the guns for Nyasa had not yet concluded) it was not until the end of October that the British proposals were tentatively put before Barros Gomes. Their reception, Petre reported, was disappointingly cool: in particular, the Foreign Minister insisted that no agreement which excluded Portuguese sovereignty over the Nyasa territory would have the remotest chance of being ratified by the Côrtes. Barros Gomes even told Petre, by way of aside, that he would much rather leave things as they were than sign any agreement that did not give satisfaction to the territorial claims of Portugal.

It appeared to the British Minister that Portuguese interest in a corridor across Africa had waned and that they were disposed to concentrate on securing their position in Moçambique and the Zambezi basin by direct means rather than diplomacy. All Petre could suggest to his government was that they might think it worth while to waive their objections to a nominal Portuguese sovereignty over Nyasa in view of the immediate practical advantages to be secured thereby.[36] He was not alone in taking this line: no less an expert on the region than John Kirk, onetime companion of Livingstone and consul general at Zanzibar, had told Villiers Lister a few weeks earlier that the best arrangement would be to acknowledge Portuguese sovereignty there, given safeguards; and Lister himself felt that to "neutralize" the territory (Anderson's proposal) would only perpetuate a state of affairs that was "unsatisfactory and untenable." Salisbury's comment on Petre's October dispatches, on the other hand, was simply, "We shall get nothing out of this Portuguese government."[37]

Barros Gomes, defending himself in the Côrtes in June 1891 against a charge that he had slighted Petre's proposals of October 1888 and thereby lost Portugal the chance of getting better terms than she afterward obtained, remarked that they had been not so much proposals as vague overtures whose complete acceptance was made a condition of entering into negotiations. He did not deny that he had received them coldly, but insisted that this had not meant that he was unwilling to negotiate.[38] The doubts he entertained—for instance, on the feasibility of neutralizing the Nyasa area—were clearly not ill-founded or unreasonable, but their unequivocal expression in October 1888 was the reverse of diplomatic. Barros Gomes and his colleagues must have been aware, one would think, of the lengths to which Salisbury was prepared to go in defense of the Nyasa settlers. Portuguese public opinion did not underrate the coherence and comprehensiveness of British imperial aims in Africa: the journalist António Ennes, writing in May 1888, foresaw a linkup between the British East Africa Company and the Cape colonists by way of Lakes Tanganyika and Nyasa. Ennes warned his fellow countrymen against attempting too much: "The present situation, in which one day we are in conflict with the English, another with the Germans and the French, even to the point of picking quarrels with the Sultan of Zanzibar, is an intolerable one for a weak nation.... We ought to prefer more circumscribed, but more secure and less contested, dominions and spheres of influence.... There is a proverb which says, 'Who demands all, loses all.' "[39]

In August of that same year, Ennes' foresight was borne out by an article that H. H. Johnston, under the guise of "An African Explorer," contributed to *The Times* (with the cognizance of Salisbury): an article that Johnston's biographer terms "masterly." "Masterful" would perhaps have been a better term, for the article, as Ennes pointed out, suggested a partition of Africa based on the right of the stronger, and it not only looked forward to a "continuous band of British dominion" between the Sudan and South Africa, but proposed that the British take over Lourenço Marques in spite of the MacMahon award (perhaps Johnston had never heard of it).[40] The article, wrote Ennes,

showed how in the minds of patriotic and ambitious Englishmen, makers of crude cloths and catechisms, propagandists for cotton goods and traders in religion, the greed induced by competition already chafes under the yoke that is called the law of nations. *The Times* publicized the explorer's extraordinary plan, and its readers naturally applauded roundly, regretting only that they had to admit to the leonine partition of Africa a second lion, Germany.

What are we doing to exorcise the dangers, ever growing, ever more imminent, in this situation?[41]

The rebuke to Johnston's imperialism came from one who repeatedly showed himself the most coolheaded of Portuguese imperialists: so coolheaded as to be then under attack from fire-eaters like Serpa Pinto and Pinheiro Chagas, in reply to whom he headed more than one newspaper article, "Less Patriotism!" Ennes' diagnosis was correct and its implications clear: if *The Times* were ready to lend its columns to the kind of kite-flying that Johnston's article represented, it behooved those in charge of Portuguese foreign policy to avoid encouraging the apostles of lawlessness on both sides.* Instead of being cool to Petre's advances, Barros Gomes would have done well to lean over backward in order to get negotiations started. Whether, given the already inflamed state of public opinion in both countries, they would have come to anything is perhaps doubtful.

There was clearly no suspicion in Portugal that Johnston was, in fact, *The Times'* "African Explorer": otherwise, he would not have been persona grata as the new consul in Moçambique, nor would he have been welcomed in Lisbon a few months later (March–April

---

* Think of Geoffrey Dawson and the Munich agreement, just half a century later.

1889) as an "unofficial" envoy to discuss African boundaries on behalf of the British government. The Johnston mission remains an unexplained vagary on Salisbury's part: perhaps, like other informal efforts of the kind, it is to be taken as an indication that the formal resources of diplomacy were already exhausted. No more is known of its origin than that it was proposed almost on the spur of the moment, after a talk between Salisbury and D'Antas, still Portuguese Minister in London. For all Johnston's gifts, which included a knowledge of the Portuguese tongue and of Africa (though not a firsthand knowledge of the territories in dispute), his qualifications for this particular job were not, one would have thought, outstanding. He cannot have been familiar with the peculiar nuances of Lisbon politics, and was clearly inclined to overrate the efficacy of flattery as a diplomatic weapon in dealing with Portuguese politicians, many of them quite clever enough to see through it even while relishing it. By the nature of the case, moreover, he could have no plenipotentiary powers and his mission could be no more than exploratory.[42]

Nevertheless, the attempt by Salisbury, in the House of Lords, to make light of "Mr. Consul Johnston's so-called negotiations" was an evasion; more, he lied to the House in saying that Johnston's proposals were not embodied in a dispatch. As Barros Gomes later pointed out, the mission received plenty of publicity and discussion in the press, and Johnston was sponsored by the British Minister, Petre, who approved the terms of the informal agreement he reached. Barros Gomes went so far as to declare that the talks represented the only serious attempt at an understanding between the two governments during his four years of office as Foreign Minister. This was certainly a handsome tribute to Johnston's powers of persuasion; and indeed it was remarkable that Barros Gomes, who a few months earlier had told Petre that any agreement that excluded Portuguese sovereignty over the whole of the Nyasa district would have no chance of passing the Côrtes, should have been ready, by his own declaration, not merely to accept a western boundary on the Shiré, but to forego altogether the continuous band of territory linking Angola and Moçambique. All that he would have had to offer the Côrtes (and it was the Côrtes, as Morier had learned to his cost, that decided the fate of treaties) would have been some "pestilential and inhospitable" country west of the Upper Zambezi, and the Shiré Highlands—plus, of course, the advantage of an undisputed possession of regions, such as the Zambezi valley below Zumbo and Northern Mozambique east of Lake Nyasa, in which Portuguese claims had not so far been challenged. He would, moreover, have given up all claim to Matabeleland and Mashonaland, and conceded freedom of navigation on the Zambezi.[43]

All this did, indeed, constitute a sufficient answer to those who accused Barros Gomes of intransigence: for although he would have yielded very little of tangible or immediately realizable value to Portugal, the path of British empire builders would have been considerably eased by an agreement on the terms laid down. Small wonder that Johnston should have complimented him on his "frankness and good sense," and that both Petre and Lister should have endorsed the proposals without qualification. But, as the Lourenço Marques treaty had demonstrated, intangibles that transcended or negated the bounds of common sense had to be reckoned with in any Anglo-Portuguese negotiation—and this time they arose on the British side. It is clear from a letter Johnston addressed to Barros Gomes on April 9, 1889, the day after he had drawn up a memorandum of his talks for Petre to forward to London, that he believed, relying on private advices from Lister, that Salisbury was in broad agreement with the proposals. On April 18, after a final interview with Barros Gomes the day before, Johnston again wrote of his, and Petre's, hopes of an early agreement.[44] But Salisbury himself had already expressed, on receipt of a telegraphic summary of the proposals, the view that they did not appear "to be in any considerable degree more conducive to British interests in those regions than the state of affairs at present existing." The rock of offense was, of course, the surrender to Portuguese sovereignty of the missionary settlements in the Shiré highlands, hallowed by the memory of David Livingstone. By any mundane criterion, these were of no account, and their religious significance was not exactly extensive. But their symbolic—and hence their political—importance, particularly for Scotland, was such that from the outset Salisbury ruled out any attempt to impose Portuguese rule on them against their will. He would allow Johnston to persuade the leaders of missionary opinion, if he could; beyond that he would not go. "I do not wish," he wrote on May 7, "to have the appearance of putting pressure on these Scotch people to abandon what they believe to be their rights. . . . Of course," he added drily, "if they come of themselves to the conclusion that their rights will be better secured by the arrangement proposed in Lisbon I will give due consideration to their wishes." It was a singular subterfuge, and one that ought to have deceived nobody: the conduct of foreign relations is a matter for governments, not churches, and there can be little doubt that Salisbury could have secured acquiescence if he had wished.[45]

There is, however, some reason to believe that Salisbury's attitude may have deceived the Portuguese government, or at any rate enabled it to claim that it was deceived. In December 1889 the London newspapers published an account of Johnston's mission to Lisbon and his subsequent encounter with Serpa Pinto on the Shiré, asserting that the rejection of his proposed agreement was due, as Ennes put it, "to Scottish mercantilism and fanaticism." In Ennes' view this could not alter the fact that the proposal to give the Shiré highlands to Portugal had in fact been endorsed by an unofficial agent of Salisbury and that hence their control by England could not be indispensable to her dignity and material interest—the more so since Salisbury had recently declared once again that the Nyasa region was neither British territory nor under British protection.[46]

IV

That declaration, however, had been made on March 25, 1889, and within a few weeks it was out of date. On April 23 news reached the Foreign Office of the discovery of a new mouth to the Zambezi, navigable by oceangoing vessels. In mid-May Johnston met Cecil Rhodes for the first time and promptly secured from him the gift of a sum sufficient to pay the expenses of making treaties with native chiefs in the Nyasa country. Thus the two obstacles to the forward policy there, as set out by the "African Explorer"—Portuguese control of the portage to the Zambezi, and the rooted objection of the British Treasury to providing funds for treaty-making—had been removed or circumvented.[47] Almost simultaneously, the Colonial Office was making up its mind to swallow the "dubious" Rudd Concession* made by Lo Bengula, which was being used as the foundation of a petition for a chartered company that would exploit, in the first place, not Matabeleland proper, but Mashonaland up to the Zambezi. As Ennes declared,

---

* It was so described by Fairfield of the Colonial Office, commenting on a letter from Louis P. Bowler to the Foreign Office dated June 20, 1889 (C.P. 5970, No. 198), ex-

this was as if territorial claims might be based on occasional acts of pillage.[48] Fairfield, whom Johnston considered the best-informed member of the Colonial Office on African questions, would have agreed with Ennes: "I have expressed my view before," he wrote in January 1889, "that this view of the relationship of Mashonaland towards Matabeleland is not well founded; and I think that this cannot fail to become more manifest. . . . But my view has been overruled."[49] A year later Fairfield was to be equally candid about British territorial claims in the region: "I understand F. O. [Foreign Office] to claim right up to the Zambezi on the strength of Mr. Moffat's treaty with Lo Ben: this of course is not evidence against a third party [i.e., Portugal], but no matter."[50]

What Fairfield and Ennes were witnessing, the one with cynicism and the other with indignation, was a progressive shedding of scruple on the part of the British government, and of the Prime Minister in particular. The hint to Germany of direct action against Portugal, at the end of 1888, was another straw in the wind; so was Salisbury's comment in April 1889 on the provision for free navigation of the Zambezi in the Johnston–Barros Gomes proposals: "The free passage along the Zambezi we can take for ourselves whenever the Zambezi becomes physically accessible from the sea; and until it does, the admission of free passage will be of no use." It was left to Lister to offer a gentle reproof to his chief: "That would be an act of war, and it would not be thought justifiable to take by war that which we are offered in peace." Salisbury's only reply was to reiterate that the concessions offered by the Portuguese were "speculative and problematical," and that they had no right to exclude any nation from the Zambezi. The one assertion was tantamount to rejecting any compromise solution of the Nyasa question; the other, a flat contradiction of international law.[51] Again, in August 1889, Fairfield expressed doubts as to whether Rhodes's Chartered Company, once formed, would be able to reach the Zambezi overland: "If we are going to dispute South Central Africa with the Portuguese the matter will have to be settled

---

pressing skepticism about the feasibility of building a railway through Mashonaland to the Zambezi: "I am not sure," wrote Fairfield, "if Mr. Rhodes is really going to drop his five millions in this enterprise. I doubt if his Chartered Company will ever be used by him for any other purpose than that of getting a British ratification for the authenticity of the otherwise dubious Rudd Concession." (C.O. 417/36, file 15938; August 10, 1889.)

in the Tagus and not in Africa itself." "I think," replied his colleague Herbert, "the F.O. has every intention of settling the pretensions of Portugal here."[52]

By the end of 1889, with the British South Africa Company duly chartered and no northern limit placed on its activities, the way was clear for a British move into Mashonaland from the south. Meanwhile, in August 1889, Johnston, after entering the Chinde mouth in H.M.S. *Stork,* had reached the Ruo and begun his preemptive treaty-making expedition to the country west of Lake Nyasa and south of Lake Tanganyika.[53] But to "settle the pretensions of Portugal" by force or the threat of force, a pretext (or, better, a series of pretexts) would be needed which only the Portuguese could provide: not only must British public opinion be excited against them, but there must also be some overt act on their part to serve as casus belli. In the course of 1889, it was to seem almost as if they had set themselves to oblige the British in this respect. In March a British trader who was also unpaid vice-consul at Quilimane was arrested, and subsequently sent for trial at Moçambique, merely for asking permission to clear through customs some war rockets consigned to the African Lakes Company at Nyasa. The case was quashed at the end of May, but only after repeated representations in Lisbon.[54] In April, a request for the passage of further rifles and ammunition for the Lakes Company was refused by Lisbon, on the ground that it would be contrary to an embargo imposed in connection with the anti-slavery blockade of the East African coast, to which Portugal was a party.[55] In June, a decree was issued in Moçambique making the wearing of coats and trousers obligatory: it was clearly aimed at the British Indian traders in the province, whose religious beliefs precluded any "bifid nether garment," and who would have been compelled to leave if the decree had been enforced. Local representations, however, succeeded in getting it modified, perhaps because the authorities came to realize that, as Anderson put it, "if all the unbreeched British Indians leave the colony, it will be ruined."[56] Also in June, the Portuguese government carried out a threat of some months' standing by rescinding the concession given to the American Colonel McMurdo (who had just died) to build a railroad from Lourenço Marques to the Transvaal border, and by confiscating the unfinished line. As most of the capital, and the contractor, were British, there was considerable uproar in London, though official circles, feeling the enterprise was a doubtful one, were wary.*

In November 1889, the Slave Trade Conference at Brussels provided another occasion for the Portuguese to irritate the British government, and, indeed, the other participants. The conference had been called by Belgium on the suggestion of the British Foreign Office, which hoped to divert Cardinal Lavigerie's anti-slavery crusade into channels less visionary and more practical. (It particularly disliked the Cardinal's idea of an international anti-slavery army directed from Brussels: "a dreadful innovation," Lister remarked, "more terrible to its commanders than its enemies." "Not a complete innovation," replied Salisbury. "The Crusades furnish a precedent, but ... not an encouraging one."[57]) The British delegates to the conference were the minister in Brussels, Lord Vivian, and Kirk. Their instructions were guarded: for instance, Great Britain was not to be bound to the provision of money or men for operations at a distance from the coast. As for the more enthusiastic proposals of small powers like Belgium and Portugal for dealing with the slave trade inland, these were regarded with skepticism or downright abhorrence. E. W. Wylde, a member of the Foreign Office sent out to assist the delegation (his father had been head of the Slave Trade department for many years), was cheerfully derisive in a private letter to Anderson: the Belgian government, he said, had circulated "a wondrously compiled Map which puts slave trade routes all over Africa like Chatham [i.e., Clapham] Junction railway lines. It also contains other geographical lines calculated to excite susceptibilities." He went on to say that "the Portugee [sic] ... abused the map ... and finally eulogized the heroic deeds done by Portugal. ... The P. read enough to show that Portugal was prepared to civilize everybody and everything up the Shiré, about Lake Nyasa, up the Zambezi and in Matabeleland, and to run railways with innumerable stations apparently right across Africa. Vivian said he wd. be very glad to see the proposals and perhaps you will too."[58]

When, however, the Portuguese proposals were studied, they were found objectionable, as embodying covert territorial claims: stations being named as established or proposed for the suppression of the

* See below, p. 235.

slave trade at places which the British considered to be within their sphere of influence. After considerable debate, the Portuguese declined to amend or withdraw their statement, and the British had to content themselves with registering an official protest. More adverse comment was caused by a Portuguese memorandum, running to forty printed pages, which rehearsed the whole history of slavery in the overseas territories during four centuries, dwelt tactlessly on the prominent role played by the British in the slave trade, claimed that Portugal had always been in the van of the abolitionists, and represented various recent small annexations on her part, including the seizure of Tunghi Bay on the northern frontier of Moçambique, from the Sultan of Zanzibar (which had annoyed the Sultan's British protectors), as being principally aimed at the suppression of the trade.[59] Moreover, the Portuguese delegation was suspected by all the others of having leaked the conference proceedings to a Paris newspaper, with the object, it was said, of wrecking them—though what advantage Portugal would have gained by this is not clear. The British reaction to the whole of the Portuguese proceedings at the conference can be summed up in a remark by Anderson: "Nothing can exceed the impudence of the Portugese."[60]

Impudence, no matter how much the British might itch to hit out against it, did not constitute a casus belli—but it was calculated to increase their willingness to take advantage of, or even look for, one. A more substantial complaint was found in the armed expeditions that Portugal had been sending into the African interior for some years previously. They could, of course, be readily represented by her as a logical following-up of a policy of pacification, particularly in Zambézia, where it was not until the successive campaigns of 1887 and 1888 that the power of the Cruz family, centered on the stockade at Massangano, had been finally broken. But the British could not fail to note that the effort to make new treaties of vassalage with native chiefs appeared to be concentrated in precisely those inland districts likely to be affected by any advance or assertion of authority on their part, and that they were left to learn of such expeditions, not from Lisbon, but from their consular officers on the spot.[61] It was not, Petre told Barros Gomes in March 1889, a few days before Johnston arrived in Lisbon on his mission, that his government denied the right of the Portuguese to send expeditions into the hinterland, but rather it was "the secrecy, the want of frankness, with which those expeditions had been planned and put in execution, which had so indisposed Her Majesty's Government and precluded concurrent negotiation." Two months earlier, when Barros Gomes had told him that an expedition—one of three—under António Maria Cardoso, which was operating immediately to the east of the Shiré and of Lake Nyasa, was directed against nobody and was solely for purposes of prestige, Petre had retorted: "Then ... why make such a mystery about it?"[62]

In spite of this plain speaking, another expedition, to be led by the famous explorer and colonial zealot Serpa Pinto, was mounted in the spring of 1889. Its original purpose was said to be the relief of António Maria Cardoso, who was reported to be embroiled with hostile chiefs near Lake Nyasa; but before it could set out, Cardoso returned to Quilimane safely—if not in triumph—with a number of treaties.[63] By the time Serpa Pinto himself arrived there, about the third week in May, his primary purpose was stated to be the escort of a survey party for a proposed railroad from Quilimane to Lake Nyasa. Evidently opposition was expected, for the escort was to consist of several hundred native troops and two armed launches recently arrived from Yarrow's London shipyards.* Whether the railroad survey, in itself quite genuine, was a blind concealing an already formed purpose appears uncertain. Vieira de Castro asserts that the real intention was to connect, in the Upper Zambezi, with an expedition headed by Paiva Couceiro, coming from Angola—thus throwing a chain of treaties across Africa to block the British advance. But Paiva Couceiro's expedition, though in line with Bocage's original scheme, was decided on only toward the end of 1889, and his secret instructions from the governor of Angola are dated January 1, 1890. He was to establish Portuguese suzerainty over Barotseland: an "identical expedition," he was told, was leaving from Moçambique but it was to be expected that he would arrive first. If this expedition was one merely contemplated and was not in fact that led by Serpa Pinto, it was forestalled by the British ultimatum. There is nothing to suggest that the British knew of Couceiro's enterprise, but naturally it also had to be called off.[64]

At any rate, whatever Serpa Pinto's ultimate destination, his proxi-

---

* Ross (Quilimane)–Smith, May 26, 1889, in Smith–Salisbury, June 10, No. 30 (received July 24: the transit time of dispatches is something to be kept in mind throughout).

mate objective was the Lower Shiré. There Johnston caught up with him at the beginning of August, was assured that he was conducting "a scientific expedition" (albeit accompanied by over 700 armed men), and tried to persuade him not to force his way through the hostile Makololos—hastening up the Shiré thereafter to make treaties with chiefs who might otherwise do so with the Portuguese.[65] On August 19, John Buchanan, the planter who was Acting Consul for Nyasa, notified Serpa Pinto, at Johnston's direction, that the Makololo country was under Queen Victoria's protection—treaties having been made with four Makololo chiefs a few days before. An exchange of formal protests and counter protests followed, and on September 25 Buchanan, having made treaties with the remaining Makololo chiefs, formally declared a protectorate over their territory and notified Serpa Pinto that any advance into it would be regarded as a hostile act.[66] Such a declaration, even had it been by a regular consul like Johnston, could only have been ad referendum; significantly, when Buchanan's dispatch reporting his earlier notification to Serpa Pinto was received in London at the end of October, Anderson commented (and Salisbury agreed), "We had better wait, before approving, to see what comes of this." A month later, when the formal declaration was received, Anderson remarked that it might have been going too far; but he added, "We now know that the Portuguese are preparing to attack and subjugate tribes under the British flag, and are doing so deliberately and with full knowledge."[67]

In fact, as Barros Gomes did not fail to point out to the British, formal notification of protectorate never was made to Lisbon or to any other foreign capital: it was open to anyone to argue, therefore, that Buchanan's proceedings were not binding on Serpa Pinto. Moreover, an effective protectorate would have restrained the Makololo chiefs from attacking the Portuguese expedition outside their own territory, and this Buchanan was unable to do. There was even cause for doubt about the authenticity of the principal chief's assent to a treaty with the British: according to Buchanan he had a superstitious fear of putting his hand to the paper, and a mark was therefore made by Buchanan on his behalf. Naturally, this explanation evoked derision in Lisbon when the Blue Book containing the treaty was published.[68] Whether these considerations caused the Foreign Office to hesitate over notification, or whether it was simply overtaken by events, one does not know. The decisive—though not the first—clash between the Makololos and Serpa Pinto took place on November 8, after the Portuguese leader had visited Moçambique to confer with the governor-general, Neves Ferreira, and when his reinforced army, even according to Portuguese sources, was about three thousand strong. In the engagement, some distance south of the confluence of the Shiré and the Ruo, a British flag was captured from the Makololos. Earlier, Serpa Pinto seems to have decided on a general advance, but he fell sick and it was his subordinate, the naval lieutenant Azevedo Coutinho, who drove beyond the Ruo as far as Katunga and, on December 8, secured the submission of M'lauri, the superstitious Makololo chief.[69]

News that the Portuguese had crossed the Ruo appears to have reached London in mid-December. Lord Salisbury's daughter and biographer, however, states that in November (she does not give the precise date) the British Cabinet had already decided that Portugal must be taught a lesson: they had first thought of occupying Goa, but the Indian government had objected, and they had therefore decided to seize the island of Moçambique instead.[70] Salisbury himself had clearly evinced an intention to coerce the Portuguese at least as early as December 1888. Presumably the Cabinet's decision arose less from what it vaguely knew might be happening along the Shiré than from the issue in Lisbon of a decree, dated November 7, creating a new district of Zumbo around the village of that name on the Upper Zambezi.* The boundaries allotted to this new district took in considerable territory in Mashonaland that was claimed to be under the suzerainty of Lo Bengula and hence destined for the activities of Rhodes' Chartered Company: its formation was therefore a direct challenge to the British, but one which they might have had some embarrassment about meeting with force. Not so the challenge represented by Serpa Pinto: his expedition was not only disturbing a state of affairs whose maintenance had long been a keystone of British policy in central Africa, but was arousing the *odium theologicum* and causing the ghost of David Livingstone to walk. The clamor of the English newspapers when news of the "Serpa Pinto raid" arrived (as if, António Ennes observed, Serpa Pinto were a second Genghis Khan) may well

---

* See above, p. 112. The decree is summarized in Petre–Salisbury, November 11, 1889, No. 148 Africa (C.P. 5970, No. 326).

have been music in Salisbury's ears.[71] Here was a chance to pin the label "aggressor" unequivocally upon the Portuguese, and to act accordingly; and Salisbury, even though stricken by an epidemic of "Russian" influenza, took the chance without hesitation. As good luck would have it, Parliament, which might have asked awkward questions, was not sitting: for some reason there had been no autumn session in 1889.

In March 1889 Petre had told Barros Gomes, at a time when Serpa Pinto was about to leave for Moçambique, that he hoped the Portuguese government would not allow him a free hand, or he would "infallibly get them into a mess or embroilment"; and Barros Gomes, in reply, had assured him that clear and most stringent instructions would take care of this.[72] It was now to appear that Lisbon, or at any rate the Ministry of Foreign Affairs, had not been really aware of what Serpa Pinto and Neves Ferreira were up to, much less in control of it. As late as December 20, Barros Gomes was still professing unawareness of any later engagement between Serpa Pinto and the Makololos than that of November 8, on the Portuguese side of the Ruo. Telegraphic inquiry from Lisbon to Moçambique evoked only vague statements that the Makololos had been subdued and the Shiré occupied—and these were of less assistance to Barros Gomes than they were to Salisbury. He promptly demanded (January 2, 1890) an immediate declaration that the Portuguese government would make no attempt to settle territorial questions by force—pointing out that if Serpa Pinto dissented from Buchanan's declaration of protectorate, he should have caused his objection to be raised through diplomatic channels.[73] A time limit was set for the reply, which coupled acceptance in principle with the suggestion of an international conference to resolve all matters in dispute. Salisbury now demanded to know (January 9th) whether explicit instructions had been sent to Moçambique for, inter alia, Portuguese withdrawal from the Makololo country, Matabeleland, and Mashonaland. In reply, Barros Gomes told Petre that not only had Serpa Pinto returned to Moçambique, but that his forces, recruited at Inhambane, had returned thither. This was not in accordance with a telegram that William Churchill, the acting vice-consul at Moçambique, had sent his government six days earlier: Serpa Pinto himself had told Churchill that the Shiré was still occupied, and was to be fortified and garrisoned. Without more ado, this conflict was taken by Salisbury as evidence of bad faith on the part of the Portuguese government, and Petre was told to withdraw his legation (*i.e.*, to break off diplomatic relations) unless proof were furnished that appropriate instructions had been sent.[74] It is evidence of the inadequate liaison existing within the Portuguese administration that on January 11, the very day this ultimatum was delivered in Lisbon, the Moçambique official gazette was publishing a formal Act whereby the Shiré region was annexed to Portugal.[75]

v

"I am convinced," Villiers Lister had written in April 1889, in a vain effort to convert Salisbury to an approval of the Johnston–Barros Gomes proposals,

> that the terms offered are far more favorable than we had any right to expect, or that any Arbitration would give us, and that the rejection of them will lead to a long enmity between England and Portugal, to the ruin of present and prospective British interests in South-East Africa, and to the closing up of that northern outlet for our Cape Colonies, which is already a matter of importance.[76]

It is clear from his pessimistic conclusion that Lister, at any rate, did not contemplate using force against Portugal; it is also clear that he was making the very large assumption that what would pass the Portuguese Ministers would also pass the Côrtes. He was, therefore, asking Salisbury to incur certain odium in Scotland for the sake of concessions which were "speculative and problematical"—not, as Salisbury was perversely inclined to argue, per se, but because of the provisions of the Constitution of Portugal and the state of public opinion there.[77] These difficulties, however, were inherent in any attempt to negotiate with her at all, and the Johnston mission was pointless unless they were recognized. The secret of success in such negotiations was the application of an agreed amount of duress, such as could be represented to the Côrtes as *force majeure* without loss of face: it was in this way that the Congo question had been settled in 1885. But that matter had seemed, and indeed was, more urgent of settlement than the Anglo-Portuguese question appeared to be four years later.

Lister's views were somewhat colored, perhaps, by his having no use for missionaries, especially the Scotch variety; but his prophecy of a long enmity between England and Portugal proved well-founded. "Men of my generation," wrote Lavradio in a book published under official auspices nearly half a century later, "still feel their faces reddening at the brutal blow of January 11, 1890, and even today recall the injustice and bad faith of the British action, and boil with indignation at the affront." In another such book, published in 1959, Professor José Gonçalo Santa-Rita describes Portuguese criticism of Serpa Pinto's rashness as "a revolting injustice" and puts the blame on Johnston and the "other agents of the Chartered [Company]" for inciting the Makololos against the Portuguese.[78] In Portugal, that is to say, the ultimatum is still a live issue—as is shown by the fact that all the documents about it known to exist in Lisbon have yet to be thrown open for scholarly inspection.* Even allowing for the fact that it is easier to forget an injury inflicted than one received, the lasting influence of this particular action on the Portuguese public mind is something that would have surprised its perpetrators—something, moreover, that no one who wishes to understand Portugal can afford to ignore.

How much is there in the accusation of injustice and bad faith, bearing in mind that it can properly be leveled only at a particular British government or individual, not at the nation? An attitude of injured innocence befits neither party: if the use made of the Rudd Concession and the treaty-making activities of Johnston and his associates constitute sharp practice, so did the secret expeditions of the Portuguese government; if there was little legal merit in the claim for free navigation of the Zambezi, there was little good sense in the refusal of passage for the African Lakes Company's handful of arms and ammunition. If the Makololos' attack on Serpa Pinto was instigated by the British (and though no solid evidence appears to have been adduced that would point to this, some of the Lakes Company's people would not have been above it), he had no occasion, no evident military necessity, to respond by sending troops across the Ruo (an action, moreover, which seems to have been taken quite deliberately, in consultation with Neves Ferreira but not with Lisbon). This was the one act of provocation, above all, that common prudence dictated avoidance of: if the governor-general of Moçambique authorized it

* See the bibliographical note in P. R. Warhurst, *Anglo-Portuguese Relations in South-Central Africa, 1890–1900* (London, 1962), p. 159.

without reference home, on his shoulders rests the greatest share of personal responsibility for what ensued. Leaving aside, as unconfirmed, Buchanan's declaration of protectorate, the Makololo country was nonetheless an area in dispute, in that the British had maintained it should be treated as a European no-man's land; and even though the Portuguese might consider themselves entitled to ignore their ally's known objection and occupy it, the decision to do so would be plainly a Cabinet matter, not one for even the highest provincial official to determine. Given the relative strength of the parties and the possibility that the British might be looking for an opening for direct action, the Portuguese government was asking for trouble if it failed to enforce its authority on subordinates. The ultimatum may be considered as the penalty for the administrative and political incompetence that allowed the British to put the Portuguese ostensibly in the wrong.

On the other side, it must be said that Salisbury's actions, at the end, were more precipitate than obvious necessity required, and his language to an independent nation peremptory to the point of insult. Granted his right to satisfy himself that the Portuguese government was in fact complying with the British demand (to which it agreed on January 8) that it withdraw its forces from the territories in dispute, there seems no reason why he should not have allowed it a few days' grace in which to do so: no urgent or vital British interest could thereby have been affected. Unless one attributes both haste and language to the Russian influenza, one is forced to conclude that Salisbury wanted to humiliate the Portuguese, or was determined to have done with them before Parliament reassembled (or perhaps both). One of the most noteworthy aspects of the whole crisis is that it is scarcely reflected in British Foreign Office documents other than the bare dispatches. This is doubtless due in part to Salisbury's having conducted the business from his sickbed at Hatfield House. But the fact remains that he appears to have consulted no one, unless verbally: he is not known, for instance, to have sought Petre's advice on what the effect of sending an ultimatum might be (he may well have suspected that Petre might advise against it). There is in existence a print of a memorandum by Anderson, of which it has been impossible to discover either the original or any papers related thereto, dated January 6, 1890.[79] It constitutes a sustained indictment of the Portuguese as having, ever since the spring of 1885, pursued a consistent policy of aggression in Africa at the expense of British interests: the case is well argued even though a cynic might say that the document (of which no use appears to have been made) is just the kind of paper that a power contemplating aggression would be at pains to have prepared beforehand. Its clear implication is that the Portuguese had forfeited all claims to consideration on Great Britain's part—and certainly Salisbury acted as if he thought so. He might otherwise, for instance, have shown some compunction about the position of the new king of Portugal, Carlos I, who had succeeded his father less than three months earlier.

Even if Salisbury had refrained from making the final turns of the screw, the fact of pressure having been applied and been yielded to would not, of course, have been altered: the threat to break off relations and the naval measures lying behind it would simply have been less brutally explicit. That no effort was made to save the face of an ally was an additional cause of recrimination in Portugal. There is no evidence that Barros Gomes and his colleagues preferred to be bullied openly: on the contrary, Petre thought that up to the last minute they had not realized that they faced a rupture with Great Britain.[80] Lavradio, seeking to vindicate the Portuguese Ministers from the charge of incompetence leveled against them by contemporaries, notably Pinheiro Chagas, argues that the very fact of Salisbury's resort to the ultimatum is a tribute to the tenacity with which they had defended Portuguese interests.[81] In a sense this is true: though to incur an ultimatum, more especially by possible inadvertence, is not generally counted as proof of diplomatic skill. It was indeed tenacity rather than skill which had characterized Portuguese policy since Corvo, and the limitations of this tenacity now stood plainly exposed. Possessed in several respects of a better case than the British, the Portuguese had not only been outgunned, but also outmaneuvered, by a master of his craft. Barros Gomes, it appears, had counted on German moral, and perhaps even material, backing in a dispute with Britain; but it was Salisbury who had achieved rapprochement with Germany, and it was Germany that later on, as successor to the Sultan of Zanzibar on the African mainland, was to avenge Portugal's seizure of Tunghi Bay in 1887. The German annexation of the Kionga triangle, between Cape Delgado and the mouth of the Rovuma, to which Portugal was forced to agree by an additional convention in August 1894, furnishes a wry epitaph on the policy of which the original Convention of 1886 had been the symbol.[82]

That policy, as the original Tunghi Bay annexation, if not the crossing of the Ruo, demonstrates, no more eschewed the use of force than the policies of other countries: it differed only in having less force at its disposal. Barros Gomes' Portugal was trying to play the game of power politics, without having the equipment to do so. Without military strength to back it; operating amid the clamor of a militant patriotism of which the politicians were at once the creators and the creatures, and which hamstrung any attempt at a negotiated settlement; reposing on a ramshackle governmental structure in which a colleague or powerful subordinate might at any time choose to pursue his own line of action or inaction; not always well informed by its representatives abroad, and perhaps unwilling to listen to them—Portuguese diplomacy was unequal to the strain an independent foreign policy imposed. Even the British, after all, were finding that splendid isolation could no longer be afforded. Though Salisbury's conduct of the affair seems to have had a distinctly willful and arbitrary tinge throughout, this gives the Portuguese no moral right to complain of methods which differed from their own only in being successful. As Henry Labouchère said in the Commons debate on the ultimatum, there was little to choose between Buchanan and Serpa Pinto; but, as he went on to say, the case was really one for arbitration.[83]

With that judgment it seems difficult to quarrel, for all that it flew in the face of jingo sentiment aroused by Serpa Pinto's supposed insult to the Union Jack.* One looks in vain for something at stake on either side worth the life of a single soldier—something as rational, if as sinister, as a sizeable economic motive. The gold supposed to exist in Mashonaland cannot be counted a major influence on policy, nor, in the light of the British attitude at the Brussels Conference, can the suppression of the Nyasa slave-raids—the one unequivocal advantage that may be said to have come out of the ultimatum. Essentially

---

* Hanna reprints a *Punch* cartoon whose caption expresses this sentiment in typically patronizing fashion, but at least it does not, like a cartoon in *Moonshine,* represent a Portuguese general as a monkey. A. J. Hanna, *The Story of the Rhodesias and Nyasaland* (London, 1960), p. 113; Luiz de Montalvor, comp., *História do Regimen Republicano em Portugal* (Lisbon, 1930), Vol. I, facing p. 329.

the conflict was between two dreams, nourished on the modern equivalent of Don Quixote's chivalric romances: small-scale maps of Africa colored in rival shades of red. Of the two, that of Rhodes and Johnston had less to commend it from an economic point of view: a Cape-to-Cairo railroad, unlike that projected from west to east by the Portuguese, would certainly have been unsuccessfully competitive with merchant shipping, instead of ancillary to it, as a carrier of freight.

The south-to-north drive of the British prevailed not because of its superior rationality but because they carried bigger guns and because an eccentric and idealist multimillionaire was at hand to give it a forward push at a critical time—a time when common sense, personified by Goschen, Salisbury's Chancellor of the Exchequer, was unwilling to find a mere two thousand pounds for its incidental expenses. The poverty-stricken, all but bankrupt kingdom of Portugal, having no Goschen, was far more ready than he to spend public money on imperial projects. It was, in an ironical kind of way, fitting that Rhodes, the embodiment of capitalist enterprise, who made his fortune out of mining diamonds—the emblem par excellence of Veblenian conspicuous waste—should outdo the state in expenditure on another such (unrecognized) emblem—African imperialism—and that his dividendless Chartered Company should prove Goschen's point. Less fitting, if no less ironical, was the part played by the Scottish missionaries, servants of One whose Kingdom was not of this world, as a stumbling block (or was it a stalking-horse?) in the path of a boundary settlement with Portugal—talking, as Lister once remarked, "as if the Portuguese were Mahdists."[84] The missionaries furnished one Portuguese commentator with this reflection—ironic because almost certainly well-founded: "If, at the time the Scotch missions established themselves in Blantyre, where in 1874 they recognized our right to exercise sovereignty [a doubtful contention], we had stationed there a Portuguese authority with a sufficient force to guarantee the security of those missions, that region would belong to us today, and we should have avoided the ultimatum."[85]

Chapter five

Moçambique: the Aftermath of the Ultimatum, 1890–1893

In the House of Lords debate on the ultimatum of January 1890, Salisbury explained that one of his motives in pressing the Portuguese government so hard and so fast had been to prevent its reply from being decided, not in the council chamber, but in the streets of Lisbon: in other words, to avoid the government's being goaded by public opinion into a futile resistance which could do Portugal only harm.[1] The decision to yield was, in fact, made not by the Cabinet but by a non-partisan advisory body, the *Conselho do Estado,* and the principal motive which weighed with it was the fear that once the British were in occupation of some portions of Portuguese territory it might be difficult to get them out again. So little time, however, was given to prepare the public for what was coming, that news of the fait accompli burst on it like a thunderclap. Recovery from the initial stunning shock took the form of a wave of patriotic anger that swept the country, or at least the towns.* In Lisbon, the British consulate was stoned, and, for good measure, so was Barros Gomes' house—at which he is said to have remarked, "Happily, the insult has been felt!"; and the statue of Camões was wreathed in black crape. In Oporto, the gentleman-traders of the English colony were insulted in the street, and their ladies were said to be afraid to walk abroad; Oswald Crawfurd, the British Consul, took it upon himself to reprove clamorous students,

---

* A lively account of the episode, from the Republican point of view, is that of F. Reis dos Santos, in Luiz de Montalvor, comp., *História do Regimen Republicano em Portugal* (Lisbon, 1930), Vol. I, pp. 316–36.

and a demand went up for the withdrawal of his *exequatur*. (A few months later, he was sent quietly on leave by his government.) Posters were put up in Oporto exhorting the multitude to set fire to British property there.* Students at the University of Coimbra were equally fervent in their protests. A boycott of British goods was proposed, and a national subscription to buy a warship was opened: little, however, was heard of the first after a few months, and as for the second, after a year it had reached the paltry amount of 400 contos—less than one hundred thousand pounds sterling.[2]

I

A good deal of the excitement was doubtless ignorant or factitious: as one of Lord Salisbury's unsolicited correspondents observed later, a great many of those protesting had doubtless no idea of the whereabouts of the territories in dispute.[3] In March the very government excited derision by admitting that it did not know where Chilomo (Chiromo) was. (It is at the junction of the Shiré and the Ruo.) The government had, at any rate, the excuse that it was a new one: José Luciano de Castro and his progressista colleagues had resigned on the morrow of the ultimatum and had been replaced by a regenerador ministry, which was bent on a prompt settlement with Great Britain even though its head, Serpa Pimentel, had been the one member of the *Conselho do Estado* to hold out to the end against unconditional submission.[4] Barros Gomes' place had been taken by Hintze Ribeiro, a younger man inexperienced in foreign affairs; but as an earnest of the government's intentions, Barjona de Freitas, a politician of long experience and great shrewdness, and the leader of a dissident group in the regenerador party, was sent to London as Minister in place of the old career diplomatist Miguel D'Antas.**

Barjona's welcome in London was in many respects warmer than he had expected, for as Salisbury had told Queen Victoria on February 24, British policy was "to make the fall as soft for Portugal as possible." "Let bygones be bygones" had been his words to the new Portuguese

* For Crawfurd's attitude, see above, p. 29. One such poster is reproduced facing p. 112.
** Barjona was notorious for his amours, and there was some acid press comment in Portugal when it was learned that Queen Victoria had asked him and the lady currently passing as his wife to dinner at Windsor Castle. See "O Anno Terrivel," *A Republica Portugueza*, December 31, 1890 (entry under February 27); reproduced in Montalvor, *História do Regimen Republicano*, facing p. 313.

envoy at their first official interview, a few days earlier.[5] But Salisbury, intent above all at this time on completing his African settlement with Germany, was in no haste to come to terms with Portugal or even to propose terms to her. He was content to refuse all appeals to mediation or arbitration by third parties, to throw the onus of making territorial proposals on Portugal, and to leave any personal negotiations with Barjona to Currie, the Permanent Under-Secretary at the Foreign Office. It is difficult not to see in all this a determination to teach the insubordinate junior partner in the alliance a never-to-be-forgotten lesson. The task of the Portuguese negotiator was, of course, appallingly difficult: in view of public opinion at home he dared not put forward any proposals likely to be acceptable to the British, and the most he might expect to be able to do would be to whittle down, in some small degree, their more extreme demands.

Any exchanges between the two sides in the first half of 1890, therefore, may be dismissed as shadowboxing, intended to give the Portuguese public the illusion of negotiation and to enable the regeneradores to organize the elections. These were held on March 30, with the customary result—overwhelming victory for the government. But the city of Lisbon returned several Republican deputies for the first time, and the growing strength of anti-monarchist sentiment (as if the new king had been in some way responsible for the national humiliation) became henceforth a major preoccupation of successive ministries. With it came the recourse, new for constitutional Portugal, to suspension of the rights of free speech and of the press from time to time.* The effect of the ultimatum had not been to unite all politically minded Portuguese in face of a common danger, but rather to exacerbate the divisions that already existed among them—for all that those divisions were within a small and socially homogeneous ruling class and did not reflect any underlying clash of social forces. The new king was never able to make himself into an embodiment of national unity. Moreover, the regeneradores were as incapable as their predecessors had been of controlling the warlike impulses of their men on the spot. Azevedo Coutinho, the firebrand of the Shiré, became involved in a variety of incidents with the British during March and April, in one of which the African Lakes Company's river steamer,

* By a press law of April, described by Raphael Bordallo Pinheiro as "infamous," in *Pontos nos ii,* April 10, 1890, p. 113.

the *James Stevenson,* was fired upon. Reports of these incidents were, naturally, conflicting, but their very occurrence played into the hands of Salisbury and Rhodes by exciting public opinion in Great Britain.[6] As Salisbury was to remark in May 1891, when there were rumors that another foray, this time by the Goanese prazo holder Manuel António de Sousa ("Gouveia"), might be pending: "If they commit one good open flagrant outrage on our international rights, we shall shake free of much criticism in this country, and some pressure from friendly Courts. Once armed with a solid grievance, we can recognize Gungunhana [as independent of Portugal] and hand over Sofala and Gaza to the South African Company."[7]

In essence, the terms of the Anglo-Portuguese Convention, signed by Salisbury and Barjona on August 20, 1890, constituted a British *diktat,* inasmuch as the Portuguese had nothing with which to bargain. An American historian has called them "not flagrantly unjust," and in terms of the territory effectively occupied by Portugal before 1886 or so, this seems a fair judgment.[8] The boundaries of the British and Portuguese spheres of influence were set in a fashion roughly corresponding to the present political boundaries, with but two major exceptions: the western boundary of the province of Sofala, north of the River Sabi (Save), ran considerably farther west than the present line, more or less along the 32nd meridian of east longitude; and the Portuguese were excluded from the north bank of the Zambezi between Zumbo and the point where the river turns southeast toward Tete, thus bringing under British control a number of the Zambezi prazos.* West of Zumbo, which was to remain Portuguese, a strip of land twenty miles wide north of the Zambezi and parallel to it as far west as the eastern frontier of Angola was to be regarded as common to both countries for purposes of communication—a kind of ghostly legatee of the *mapa côr de rosa* of 1886. Freedom of religion, and of navigation on the Zambezi for the ships of all nations, was provided for. At the suggestion of H. H. Johnston, Portugal was obliged to grant a 100-year lease of ten acres of land at the Chinde mouth of the Zambezi for the purpose of transshipping to river steamers persons and goods destined for Nyasaland. She also agreed to build, or to allow to be built, a railway and a telegraph line from the mouth

---

* See map, p. 110.

of the Pungué river, where Beira now stands, to the Rhodesian border. Lastly, Portugal undertook not to dispose of Zumbo, or any of her territories south of the Zambezi, to any other power without the consent of Great Britain.[9]

It was this last proviso, adding insult to injury, which aroused the greatest anger in Portugal when the terms were published. "We were resigned to sacrifice material interests, but not dignity," wrote António Ennes:

The consent of England! But the right of disposal is inherent in full proprietorship: *our* Africa no longer remains *ours*, even though robbed in extent and subject to all kinds of onerous burdens! In public law, the requirement of such a consent constitutes a state of dependence, of subjection, such as is customarily imposed only on savage potentates in the treaties they accept in exchange for bales of cotton or barrels of rum. England treated us like the chief of the Matabele or the sultan of Zanzibar, and our Government is still doing obeisance to her for her grace and favor—the mere grace and favor of not despoiling and humiliating us in greater degree![10]

The analogy, drawn by supporters of the agreement, with a similar proviso in the treaty with China under which Portugal held Macau, was, declared Ennes, invalid, inasmuch as Macau was in form a concession from the Chinese—who might reasonably claim the reversion of what had been, and perhaps still was, a part of their territory. The Portuguese title to the African dominions was in no sense attributable to the British, who were simply neighbors with no more rights than the Germans or the Boers. Moreover, the wording of the new agreement—*"consentimento"* (consent) instead of *"acordo"* (accord)— was peremptory: "Either the arrogant Briton was unwilling to compromise with the Portuguese negotiators even on *a matter of wording,* or those negotiators did not seek to save, at any rate, the most obvious appearances of national dignity!" Petre's comment on Ennes' views (which he attributed to Barros Gomes) was that the distinction between words was "a distinction without a difference" which would suggest that his diplomacy, like that of Salisbury and Morier, was a trifle coarse-grained.[11] It is precisely in such nuances that the true diplomatist deals.

Ennes did not deny that, questions of amour-propre apart, the terms might well have been the best that were to be had.[12] But he was exasperated by the claim that they were advantageous to Portugal, and he subjected it to scornful analysis. Apart from a tiny section of Amaton-galand south of the territory awarded to Portugal by MacMahon in 1875, Great Britain had yielded nothing: she had merely recognized Portuguese rights in places—like Eastern Angola—where they had never been disputed, or where she herself had no pretensions. As for the communication zone, what probability existed that the terrain would be found suitable for a coast-to-coast railway? The whole thing appeared to be "a jest, got up between Lord Salisbury and Senhor Barjona, to impose upon the Portuguese aspiration of linking the two sides of Africa. And it was the Portuguese [negotiator] who imagined that a railroad link would do duty for a link comprised of a continuous stretch of national territory!" For all his indignation, however, Ennes was no more a firebrand than his friend Barros Gomes: he disapproved of those who were making political capital out of the treaty, "converting its seals into bullets to kill a government, and inditing on its paper the doom of a dynasty," and he wanted it rejected only with "the greatest tact, prudence, and especially dignity.... Our true strength must lie in moderation." He refused to be alarmed by the professed fears of the government about the results of the rejection:

England is not a veritable wild beast, free of all international obligations and moral scruples. No doubt the very shadow of a pretext would suffice her to attack us—but she has to have at least that shadow. Before the ultimatum she had it on her side, for she was able to exploit the incidents on the Shiré, albeit provoked by her subjects, so as to make out that her flag had been insulted, her prestige wounded, and her protegés maltreated; even so, she judged it necessary to excuse the brutality of Lord Salisbury in the eyes of European opinion by making believe ... that it was we who compelled her to go to such lengths by taking the law into our own hands. But the mere rejection of the treaty, *in itself,* does not give her the least right or even the appearance of right to retaliate.[13]

If Portugal, Ennes added, were to proffer, of her own volition, substantial concessions to foreign interests in Africa, she might still retain substantial rights of sovereignty there, disarm British aggressiveness, and above all, preserve the national dignity. Oliveira Martins, whose views on the treaty have already been quoted, would doubtless have agreed with Ennes.[14] So would Eça de Queiroz, for all that he had no patience with the more frothy patriotic manifestations that had followed the ultimatum. "I know," he wrote to Oliveira Martins in January 1890, what one ought to think of this renaissance of patriotism—these cries, these crapes on the forehead of Camões, these appeals to the academies of the world, these heroic renunciations of cashmeres and wrought iron, these jewels offered to the motherland by ladies . . . all this sentimental and windy conglomeration in which high school students and petty tradesmen seem suddenly to have taken the helm of the ancient Portuguese galleon. . . .

Carlos Valbom, who wrote to me a few days ago, says that all this is frightening and dangerous. I don't know why, but it seems to me that it is inescapably comic as well. The intelligent patriotism that leads newspapers to want to do without *English periodicals* any more (!!), teachers not to teach English, impresarios to want no English people in their theatres, hotelkeepers not to welcome English guests—appears to me an invention out of the English Dickens. . . . The Nation was affected by a strong and lively sentiment, and . . . as it is in a state of complete intellectual anarchy, this sentiment was in general unsuitably expressed.[15]

II

Even though the affronted national pride, the *brio,* of the Portuguese might take ridiculous public form, the sentiment itself was no more selfish or ignoble than were those of Don Quixote. The reaction to the ultimatum and to the August treaty was yet another example of uneconomic imperialism, for it could never be said of most of those concerned that they wanted colonial territories for what could be got out of them. Eça de Queiroz, a few years earlier, had hit off his countrymen's attitude very well in a comment on a characteristically pompous remark by *The Times* that, "whatever Portugal's errors may have been, it cannot be said that she has ever been content with the mere number of her possessions, without endeavoring to extract profit therefrom. . . ." On the contrary, said Eça:

Precisely what absorbs us, what gratifies us, what consoles us is to contemplate *simply the number* of our possessions; to put a finger on the map here and there; to say in ringing tones, "We have eight; we have nine: we are a colonizing nation, we are a maritime people!" While as for *extracting profits* . . . neither the praetor nor the descendants of Alfonso de Albuquerque care a fig for such sordid details![16]

Ennes' diagnosis of the situation, though shrewd and statesmanlike, omitted one factor in it. There *was* a wild beast abroad—namely, Rhodes' Chartered Company, which in May 1890 had begun its trek into Mashonaland under the doubtful aegis of the Rudd Concession, and which seems to have been not so much indifferent to as unaware of the rules of civilized international behavior. Rhodes himself seems to have been under the impression that the Charter and the ultimatum combined entitled the company to seize all it could lay hands on; and his fury at the August Convention was equal to that of the Portuguese.[17] In particular he wanted the whole of Barotseland and a free hand in Gazaland, the country immediately north of the Limpopo, in which Gungunhana, whom the Portuguese claimed as a vassal, was the paramount chief. The Chartered Company's directors in London were in constant touch with the Foreign Office and must have been aware that the Gaza claim was out of the question;[18] as for the Lochner concession, secured by the company's agent in Barotseland, news of it arrived after the agreement was signed and while it was still uncertain whether the Portuguese would ratify.[19] There could be no question, the company was told, of reopening the matter in the meantime. In Cape Town, however, a simpler mode of life prevailed: thus Rhodes cabled the London office in mid-September, "Cannot too strongly urge upon you you [presumably H.M.G.] must abandon the Agreement." "The Co. seems to have very loose ideas about agreements and signatures," was Lister's comment.[20]

As a result of one of his rare personal interviews with Barjona, at Dieppe, on September 9, Salisbury had agreed to modify the treaty in certain details that had given offense in Portugal: in particular, the "consent" proviso was to be altered to one giving Great Britain a first refusal of any of the territories in question. These changes came too late to appease the opposition in Portugal. Oliveira Martins, for one, greeted them with contempt, and went on to add: "The legatee is England, the deceased is Portugal, the grave-digger is the government."[21] On the day his article appeared (September 16), Hintze Ribeiro, the Foreign Minister, resigned: the reception of the treaty in the Côrtes the day before had been so hostile and tumultuous that his colleagues were unwilling to proceed with the ratification immediately. The resignation of the whole Serpa ministry followed the next day.[22] The leaders of both principal parties having now been driven from office, King Carlos cast about for a nonpartisan Prime Minister, and after three weeks discovered one in the aged General João Chrysóstomo, a respected figure who was known to have been opposed, in the Conselho do Estado, to an unconditional capitulation to the British ultimatum. The new Foreign Minister was, ironically,

Bocage, the originator of the rose-colored map; the new Minister of Marine and Colonies, none other than António Ennes himself.

To Ennes was due the next diplomatic move, designed to hold the Chartered Company in check pending negotiation of a fresh treaty: the signing of a temporary modus vivendi with Great Britain, which should provide for freedom of communication with the interior and temporarily freeze the boundaries agreed on in the abortive August Convention.[23] Luíz de Soveral, who, as chargé d'affaires in London, had taken over from the luckless Barjona, secured Salisbury's agreement on November 4 and his signature on November 14, although with one significant qualification: the boundaries were to be those in existence at that date, not at the date of the convention.[24] A Republican writer has called the modus vivendi "prestidigitation" intended to deceive the public at home, but even if it were that, it was something more besides, for it impelled Salisbury to call a halt to the buccaneering exploits of Rhodes' men, which, had they continued for a few months more, might have left Portugal with very little of Moçambique south of the Zambezi.[25] As things were, news of the modus vivendi reached Africa too late to prevent the "Manica incident" of November 15, when a handful of Chartered Company "police" seized the kraal of the minor chief Mutasa, near Umtali, in gold-bearing territory that, under the terms of the August Convention, was clearly within the Portuguese sphere of influence.* In the process, which was bloodless, they captured Colonel Paiva d'Andrada, one of the foremost Portuguese colonialists and a former military attaché in Paris, and the famous *capitão-mor* Manuel António de Sousa (described by his captors as a "common black man"), and sent them to Cape Town under escort.[26]

The skill of the operation is undeniable; the thought of the disconcerted Portuguese leaders, and of the drunken chief Mutasa as *tertius gaudens,* is, one must confess, diverting. Nevertheless, the Manica incident was simply the piratical culmination of a piece of sharp practice: the making of a "treaty" with Mutasa on September 14, when it was not yet certain that the convention would not be ratified. The

---

* There is a good short account of the Manica incident in R. I. Lovell, *The Struggle for South Africa, 1875–1899* (New York, 1934), pp. 222–29, and a good longer one in P. R. Warhurst, *Anglo-Portuguese Relations in South-Central Africa, 1890–1900* (London, 1962), pp. 14–44.

Chartered Company had simply jumped the gun: quite apart from the unwitting infraction of the modus vivendi, fair play required that the territory be acknowledged as within the Portuguese sphere of influence.* If Ennes' original form of the modus vivendi had been accepted, there would have been no room for argument on this score; Salisbury's subsequent insistence on retaining a not very important piece of territory was due as much, perhaps, to the desire to give the Portuguese yet another lesson, as to Chartered Company pressure. On the whole, however, the effect of the incident in London was probably favorable to them rather than to the company, which was rapidly acquiring the character of an "over-mighty subject." A company letter laying claim to Manicaland and Barotseland on the basis of "effective occupation," received at the Foreign Office a week before the signing of the modus vivendi, was described by Anderson as "aggressive" and by Salisbury himself as "insolent."[27] By contrast, Paiva d'Andrada's report on the incident made a good impression: it was "admirably" written. "The Portuguese case has never been stated so well," was Anderson's comment.[28]

The Chartered Company's attempt to put Gungunhana in its pocket, though lacking any incident as spectacular as the seizure of Mutasa's kraal, had the same quality of shady melodrama, not incompatible with a considerable display of personal courage and endurance by the company's agents. The "agreement in principle" (if such a term is appropriate) made with Gungunhana in October 1890, by which a mineral concession was to be traded for £500 a year plus 1000 rifles and 20,000 rounds of ammunition, was, as Salisbury later told the company, an evident breach of the August Convention.[29] The sending of the steamer *Countess of Carnarvon* up the Limpopo in February 1891 with the rifles—and, moreover, armed with the false papers with which she had cleared the ports of Lourenço Marques and Port Elizabeth—was an equally evident breach of the modus vivendi (although the Portuguese officer on the Limpopo made the mistake of granting customs clearance), and the subsequent arrest of the steamer was justified, inasmuch as the duties had not been paid. Dr. Starr Jameson's

* See Salisbury's repudiation of the treaty made in similar circumstances with Gungunhana, and the conclusive arguments on behalf of Portugal in Bocage–Soveral, March 24, 1891, *Livro Branco,* "Negociacões do Tratado com a Inglaterra, IV" (Lisbon, Imprensa Nacional, 1891), No. 168.

feat, in March, of actually persuading Gungunhana to sign the concession, under the very noses of a Portuguese mission led by the experienced José d'Almeida, was only less remarkable than it was impertinent—in every sense of that term. Looked at from Gungunhana's point of view, it was a piece of deceit, pretence that the British were his friends at a time when London, if not Cape Town, had already determined to side with the Portuguese against him. Sir Henry Loch, the High Commissioner at Cape Town, had been warned in December 1890, three months earlier, against giving encouragement to Gungunhana to resist the Portuguese government or hinting that he place himself under British protection.[30] Only in the improbable event of the modus vivendi with Portugal not leading to a lasting settlement would this policy have been modified. "The Company seems to have been wrong on every point," minuted Salisbury on the whole episode.[31] Two weeks earlier he had written:

It is imposs[ible] to ask Portugal to stipulate that G[ungunhana]'s territory shall not be P'guese. Our interest in such a decision would be small—it would be resisted to the utmost by the PGse—and it is so contrary to what has been usually accepted as to this coast, that we should have the opinion of all Europe and most of the disinterested part of England against us. Though probably, in strict right, Gungunhana *is* independent, we are not called upon to incur an infinite amount of embarrassment and difficulty in order to fight his battles.[32]

Less important than the foregoing, but equally indicative of the Chartered Company's disregard for legality, was what it called the "Beira outrage." Beira, at this time a sandbank, liable to flooding, on which a small settlement had been established, was at the mouth of the Pungué River, and was the nearest seaport to Manicaland, where the Chartered Company's pioneers had established themselves; and one of the stipulations of the August Convention had been that the Portuguese should build a railway to the boundary of the British sphere of influence inland. The modus vivendi had likewise provided for freedom of transit: Rhodes and his associates professed to interpret this as entitling them to build a road, without permission from the Portuguese, inland from the head of navigation; and Colonel Sir John Willoughby, Bart., who was noted for his offensive manner, was sent from Durban to Beira, where he arrived on April 14, in charge of a road-building expedition consisting, in part, of one hundred native laborers.[33] A further one hundred and fifty men would have been sent but for the intervention of the Foreign Office, which appears to have learned of the expedition from the company's London office only on April 6, four days after Bocage, acting on a telegram from the governor-general of Moçambique, had told Petre about it.[34] "At my suggestion," wrote Currie the same day, "Colonial Office has telegraphed Loch to stop them. He ought to have let us know before. It is a deliberate attempt of Rhodes to force hand of H.M.G."[35]

Had Petre thought Bocage's communication worth a telegram as well as a dispatch (which did not arrive until April 7), Willoughby, too, might have been stopped, but Loch, who had authorized the expedition, reported that he had already left and could not be reached. However, as his native roadbuilders were unarmed, his capacity for mischief was limited. The governor-general (the well-known army engineer Joaquim Machado, who had surveyed the railroad from Lourenço Marques to Pretoria), was ready for him, courteous but firm. Willoughby was told that he might not go up the river unless he would formally promise not to incite the natives against Portugal. When he refused to do so, and announced his intention of proceeding with the whole expedition, he was warned that he would be fired on, first with blank and then with ball. As it happened, blank was all that was necessary: "They will hit him in the leg," Rhodes had forecast, but, as Lovell puts it, "Willoughby did not expose even his uniform breeches to ball. Instead, he promptly hove to."[36] That was the "outrage" and the end of the expedition; characteristically, Loch, on receiving Willoughby's report, cabled Salisbury that he "appeared to have been fired upon without notice." Salisbury later wrote privately that (as Soveral had pointed out to him) Willoughby was in the wrong in taking the law into his own hands instead of complaining to the government about noncompliance of the Portuguese with the modus vivendi—a course that would in no way have suited Rhodes, who seems even at that late date to have hoped that by arousing public opinion at the Cape, if not in Great Britain, he could gain territory at Portugal's expense.[37] If Salisbury nonetheless sent a remonstrance to Portugal about the episode, it was no more than window dressing for a Blue Book.*

When Salisbury, apropos of Gungunhana and the Portuguese, used

---

* A necessity from which modern Foreign Secretaries have managed to free themselves.

Raphael Bordallo Pinheiro, in
Pontos nos ii, August 3, 1889.

Noble John Bull

"Obsequiousness toward the great.
Arrogance toward the weak."

Retrato de Brejeirona de Freitas

Portrait of the Rascal Barjona de Freitas
This is what he is made of—a mess of pottage.

Raphael Bordallo Pinheiro, in *Pontos nos ii,* October 2, 1890.

the words "embarrassment" and "difficulty," he may well have been thinking of the persistent concern shown by other European powers lest his terms be such as to endanger the Portuguese dynasty. On January 31, 1891, a Republican insurrection had broken out among the Oporto garrison. Badly organized and set off prematurely, it was crushed in a matter of hours: nonetheless, it was a straw in the wind. What troubled the European chancelleries was not so much solicitude for the Saxe-Coburg branch that styled itself the House of Bragança, as fear that Spain might go the same way as Portugal.[38] Hence the representations by Hatzfeldt, the German ambassador in London, to Salisbury, at the end of March and again a few weeks later, in which he proposed (and indeed secured) minor modifications that would make the draft convention then under discussion with Portugal more palatable to her.[39] Hatzfeldt also undertook, at his own suggestion, unofficially to advise the Portuguese government to accept the terms, in order that they might be able to say to their critics at home that they had acted in accordance with German advice and not merely on their own responsibility. The intervention was evidently one that Salisbury, equally unofficially, was willing to countenance, and perhaps even welcome, though an official dispatch he wrote on the subject was suitably guarded in tone.*

Negotiations for a new Anglo-Portuguese treaty followed roughly the same pattern as on the previous occasion: a certain amount of shadowboxing for the benefit of Portuguese public opinion, followed by the presentation of a text drafted by the Permanent Under-Secretary, Currie. The Portuguese had little ground on which to maneuver, for Salisbury had made it clear when the August Convention lapsed that he would not countenance any treaty that gave them generally better terms; and, in fact, the one major change was one that they had by no means sought—the retention of virtually the whole of the so-called Manica plateau by the Chartered Company, with the exception of Massi-Kessi (Macequece). As an act of grace (as well as a sign of grace, constituting an admission that the company's title to Manica was not good), Salisbury offered compensation in the form of a size-

---

* Salisbury–Malet, May 1, 1891, No. 107 Africa (C.P. 6227, No. 202). For the unofficial submission of the draft treaty to Hatzfeldt, see F.O. 84/2190. The French ambassador in London, Waddington, also made representations: Salisbury–Lytton, May 11, 1891, No. 76A Africa (C.P. 6227, No. 249).

able territory on the left bank of the Zambezi, north of Tete and east of Zumbo.* At a time when Rhodes was declaring that the Manica goldfields were "infinitely richer" than the Witwatersrand, this looked almost derisory, though the offer did have the result of restoring a number of prazos to Portuguese control.[40] A few years later, when the gold bubble had burst, and with it had gone the last chance of the Chartered Company's ever paying a dividend, the Portuguese might have ventured to think that for once they had the better of the bargain.[41] A suggestion from the British that Gungunhana's independence might be jointly recognized by Great Britain and Portugal was not well received and was not pressed. Johnston's proposal for a Chinde concession was, by agreement, excluded from the treaty and made the subject of a separate exchange of notes: a reciprocal concession was to be made to Portugal on the shores of Lake Nyasa. The right of first refusal to territory proposed to be alienated was likewise made reciprocal, south of the Zambezi. Portugal still undertook to construct a railroad inland from the Pungué River to the British sphere of influence, but was no longer obliged to accept as consultant an engineer chosen by the British government, nor to hand over the task of building the railroad to an Anglo-Portuguese company if she could not carry it out herself; and provision was made for a neutral arbitrator in the event of disagreement over the railroad. Provision was also made for arbitration should the mixed commission charged with delimiting the western boundary of Barotseland fail to reach agreement; no such provision was made for the boundary of Moçambique. The relic of the rose-colored map, the transit strip across Central Africa, quietly vanished.[42]

In order to avoid a repetition of the fiasco of 1890, Salisbury had stipulated that the new treaty should be submitted to the Côrtes after initialing and before signature—a course for which precedents existed. But the state of public feeling in Portugal was now very different from what it had been a year earlier, and there was no longer either hope of getting better terms or disposition to blame the former government for not doing so. Ennes, its most formidable critic, had, as a modern commentator puts it, "realized from harsh experience the gulf be-

* This was perhaps a sop to conscience. Soveral declared that Salisbury had promised him to give up Manica if it were proven to be on the Portuguese side of the line established by the August Convention, but Salisbury afterward denied this. See Soveral-

tween directing a journalistic campaign, bent over the editorial desk, and confronting events with the heavy cross of public administration on one's shoulders.... Hintze Ribeiro began to be vindicated."[43]

If resentment against the British was no less, its indulgence was a luxury that Portugal, beset by financial difficulties, could not afford: a settlement was urgently necessary. Hence approval of the treaty came with the minimum of discussion and recrimination and with a display of dignity which was at the opposite pole from the angry scenes of September 1890.[44] Hintze Ribeiro and Barjona de Freitas not unnaturally took occasion to remark that the terms were worse than than those that could have been obtained earlier, and Barros Gomes, to vindicate, not unskillfully, his past policies; but these were funeral orations rather than a display of opposition to accomplished facts.[45] When all was said, it remained true that the treaty of 1891 was free, as its predecessor had not been, from provisions derogatory to Portuguese national dignity: if Salisbury's conditions, at any rate in intention, were somewhat harder, his manners had been improved. Considering how little of real substance the Portuguese had at stake in the argument about boundaries, they might well consider the price of courtesy worth paying.

III

One new factor had emerged, during the eighteen months between the crisis of 1889–90 and its resolution in June 1891, which, though it sharpened the edge of the conflict in Africa, nevertheless strengthened the Portuguese government's hand. This was the reorganized *Companhia de Moçambique,* the Portuguese answer to Rhodes' Chartered Company. Its origins went back a dozen years, to a concession given by the Fontes government to Paiva d'Andrada, at that time military attaché in Paris, to exploit a large area in Zambézia.[46] Morier, reporting on the concession at the time, referred to Andrada as "an enthusiast . . . stung by the sorry figure which Portugal . . . cuts in the field of African enterprise . . . the direct product of the invectives of Captain [Lovett] Cameron and Mr. Young." Andrada's idea at that time was to build a railroad between Tete and the Shiré,

Bocage, telegram, December 18, 1890, *Livro Branco,* "Negociaçoes . . . IV (1891)," No. 77; Soveral–Salisbury, January 29, 1891 (C.P. 6086, No. 82); Salisbury–Soveral, February 5, 1891 (*ibid.,* No. 101).

so as to provide an outlet for the coal deposits known to exist between that river and the Zambezi. "It would certainly be gratifying," Morier continued,

to think that these dreams had any chance of being realized, for certainly a railway between Tete and the Shiré would very effectually put down the interior Slave Trade in that important quarter, and a large population of wage-earning Negroes would offer a promising field for the disposal of cotton prints. But I fear it is more probable that Captain Andrada will fall a victim to fever or the bullets of the Makololo, that model tribe whose children are being educated at the Nyasa Free Kirk Mission, and whose young men, as Mr. Young and Dr. Kirk inform us, have stockaded themselves on the Lower Shiré with the determination of shooting every Portuguese whose avocations may take him along the course of that river.[47]

The supporters of Andrada's proposed company were mainly personal friends he had made while in France: neither then nor at any later date was he able to attract any sizeable investment from Portugal, and so long as the Bonga and his relatives dominated the Zambezi from Massangano any development plan for the valley was out of the question. The history of the next few years is one of repeated unsuccessful flotations and abortive expeditions into the interior, but in March 1888, after the final defeat of the lords of Massangano (in which Andrada himself had played a leading part), the Companhia de Moçambique was at length founded with the aim of taking over the legacy. As late as April 1889, however, those associated with it were complaining of lack of support both from the government and from the investing public, and in August 1889 the subconcessions it had granted to mining enterprises in the Manica area, most of them British, were declared void. In November, however, the right to subcontract was explicitly granted, and existing subconcessions reinstated, and the company bound itself to build a light railway from the coast to Manica within two years. In December, free entry was granted for its railway material.[48]

The British Foreign Office might be forgiven if it took these activities as so much paper. But the Manica incident, in which were involved not only Paiva d'Andrada and Manuel António de Sousa, but also the Baron de Rezende, resident representative of the Companhia de Moçambique at Macequece, disabused it of any such belief. Letters began to arrive from addresses in the City of London denouncing the usurpations of the Chartered Company in the name of various companies: the Ophir Concessions Company Limited, the Zambezi Concessions Company Limited, the Zambezi Gaza Company Limited, and several others. At about the same time a French financier named Bartissol, a member of the Chamber of Deputies, was reported to be actively promoting an increase in the capital of, and a revised charter for, the Moçambique Company—and an agreement, if possible, between it and the Chartered Company. In February 1891, one of the aggrieved subconcessionaires sent the Treaty of Vassalage, claimed to have been made by Gungunhana with Portugal, for publication in *The Times*. By March the Chartered Company was obliged to announce that the rights of any people who had actually begun prospecting in Manica would be respected regardless of the territorial settlement. Negotiations between the two companies were by this time at an impasse, for the Moçambique Company was still trying to insist on the boundaries of the August Convention—though inasmuch as the British South Africa Company was to have acquired a substantial minority holding in the Moçambique Company, its reasons for objecting to this do not appear strong.[49] An effort was made by Sir Donald Currie, the shipowner, to mediate between the parties, and signatures to an agreement were actually in course of exchange when the Chartered Company's London board abruptly broke off negotiations: their pretext was the news that Willoughby and his party of roadbuilders were not to be permitted to go inland from Beira (which they had not yet reached). Rhodes, who had recently returned to the Cape and who, while in London, had shown no interest in coming to terms with the Moçambique Company, had played the rogue elephant once again.[50]

Negotiations between the companies about the railroad were nevertheless resumed in the summer of 1891, when the Anglo-Portuguese Treaty was an accomplished fact; and an agreement was drawn up under which the Moçambique Company would build a narrow-gauge Decauville line, to be completed through the "fly country" not later than May 21, 1892, and the British company would subscribe for half of the debentures that would be issued to finance the project. But partly because of Portuguese dislike and mistrust of Rhodes and partly because the British company insisted on a penalty of £250 a day for any delay in completing the line beyond the appointed date, this arrangement fell through.[51] Instead, the Moçambique Company gave a concession for the railroad to one H. T. van Laun, a (presumably) Dutch company promoter operating from London. About the same time, it was learned that the company had found a counter to the Chartered Company's Dukes of Abercorn and Fife in the person of the Duke of Marlborough, who, reported the Chartered Company's Paris correspondent, "appears to have married a rich American lady who will put money into this affair."[52] The Foreign Office, however, made it its business (presumably under pressure from Rhodes, who was worried about the fate of the Mashonaland pioneers) to bring van Laun and the Chartered Company together, and on December 7, 1891, an agreement was made by which van Laun's rights were transferred to the company in consideration of £2,000 cash down, a further £8,000 as first charge on a debenture issue by the railway company to be formed, and shares to the value of £295,000 in that company. Like every one else connected with the Mashonaland venture, van Laun was evidently sanguine about its prospects.[53] The difficulties of constructing the line—which may be summarized as floods, lions, tsetse fly, and fever—proved immense.* By October 1893, only 75 miles had been built; by the end of 1896, only 113. Not till 1898 was the frontier at Umtali reached—on the lightest of rails and with a 2-foot gauge necessitating transshipment to the 3 ft. 6 in. gauge of the Rhodesian and South African lines. By that time it was clear, moreover, that Fontesvilla, the original starting point on the Pungué, was an impracticable place for a port, because of the shifting currents; a further line had had to be built thence to Beira by a separate though related company—the original company being virtually bankrupt. Baron d'Erlanger, who placed the shares of the "Beira Junction Railway Company," later described the operation as "the craziest piece of finance with which I have ever been associated." The burden of debt carried by the whole line, as a result of the heavy discounts at which the shares had had to be issued, averaged over £6,500 a mile.[54]

---

* According to Freire de Andrade, the renewal of the Moçambique Company's concession was intended by the Royal Commissioner, António Ennes, solely as a means of unloading Portugal's treaty responsibility for the line to Umtali, and would have been canceled as soon as this object was achieved, "but unfortunately he did not have time to arrange things as he wished." Some pretext would have had to be found for canceling the concession: presumably the failure to promote land settlement by Portuguese would have served this purpose. See *Relatório sobre Moçambique*, Vol. III (Lourenço Marques, Imprensa Nacional, 1908†), p. 50n.

IV

António Ennes, who had been appointed Royal Commissioner in Moçambique to oversee the carrying out of the treaty of 1891, described the "goldrush days" of Beira in a report of 1893, in a passage that must rank with the most vivid ever included in a government document:

Look what happened and is still happening at Beira, that most sad of places, which inspired in our compatriots stationed there the view that Africa was good only . . . for blacks and naval officers. Prudent foreigners, who visited it when the harbor first came into use, quailed at the spectacle of mudbanks and sand. But capital, which among us is a symbol of timidity, neither quailed nor was afraid! No sooner was it put about that there was gold in Manica and that a railway would be constructed to transport it, than pounds sterling appeared by the ten thousand—opening stores, establishing steamship lines, setting up land transport services, starting industries, selling liquor, attempting to exploit in a thousand ways not so much the gold as the future exploiters of the gold.

What fantastic and bold schemes this inrush of sterling promoted! Even before a road was made into the interior, there were already at Mapanda fine mail-coaches, varnished like bridal carriages, bearing gold-lettered signs: "The River Pungué to Manica." It was known that the country was infested by tsetse, but here came British and Boers with team upon team of draft oxen. The sandbanks of the Pungué grew and sprang up beneath the very keels of the ships; nevertheless, the *Agnes* and the [*Countess of*] *Carnarvon* crept above them, stopping here, taking soundings there, competing for passengers. Likewise at Mapanda, in the midst of the swamps, two enterprising fellows set up a comfortable hotel, with polished metal beds clothed with diaphanous mosquito nets, where one could eat buffalo steaks and loin of zebra baked with spices. For the parties bound for Massi-Kessi and Umtali, bungalows were improvised to await tenants, heaps of canned goods were piled up to await consumers, demijohns of alcohol to await the drinkers—and these alone were awaited but a short time. In Beira a few square inches of sand fetched as much as if it were mixed with gold dust; the village spread its rows of multicolored, wood-and-galvanized-iron houses out along the beach as far as the Gea bridge; the Decauville wagons of the expeditionary force circulated hour by hour, transporting to the markets boxes, bales, and barrels of the most varied merchandise, and every drink under the sun, to await likewise an uncertain future. All these premises cost rivers of money. Ten or twelve pounds a month was paid in order to live baked by slow heat between sheets of galvanized iron. A carpenter would earn four and a half milréis [one pound] per day putting up hut frames. And men incurred all these expenses, made all these sacrifices, ran all these risks, tied up contos and contos of réis, suffered the weather, were devoured by fever, died forsaken in the bush, merely out of hope: the whole creation was motivated by sellers, and buyers were wanting. The shop-keepers did business with one another, and the innkeepers let rooms to themselves. All this was done in order to take advantage of the gold and the railway; however, no one knew whether the gold was a reality or whether the railway was not a deception. "Is there or isn't there? Will it be made or will it not?" were the endless themes of the talk of the speculators, standing in knots at the doors of the empty stores. Some came to me seeking my confidential opinion on these vital questions, asking me not to give it to their neighbors. If the word got abroad that a vein had been discovered or that an engineer was arriving, champagne corks popped all over the camp and choirs of tipplers cried, "Hurrah!"

Beira should rather have been called Esperança [Hope]. No contretemps could dispel hope, nor any disaster frighten away those funds.

The shining mail-coaches were devoured by white ants while still in a perfect state of virginity. The hapless oxen, bitten by the fly, attacked by lions, killed by thirst, were left as carcasses scattered along the tracks into the interior, to be stripped by the vultures and the Zulus, greedy for rotting flesh. The hotel at Mapanda confirmed the judgment of its chef, who so many times said to me, "*Sale affaire, monsieur, sale affaire!*" and closed, for the hyenas alone were guests within its elegant rooms. The *Agnes* ran aground on the Pungué sands, and crocodiles now sun themselves upon her bridge. In the interior, some huts floated away in the floods; the inhabitants of others were forced to eat the canned goods and drain the demijohns, and none knows whether they died from fever or drink. As the railway delayed and the gold failed to appear, there came a period of anguish. Already no man went up to Manica; those that had already gone thither returned. And how did these wretched adventurers return? After selling the blacks their rifles, their tools, and their clothing, for handfuls of maize or manioc roots, they took to the bush on foot, asking alms of Nature or of the occasional traveler. I have seen a letter in which an Englishwoman, who had been to Fort Salisbury, told how her unlucky compatriots would seek succor from the Portuguese by the roadside; and our authorities, our doctors, and our officers many times came to the help of those in grievous straits. In the evening, a visitor to the taverns of Beira could hear veritable concerts of curses and blasphemies from the disillusioned, calling down fire from Heaven upon those who had deceived them with false hopes of wealth; the innkeepers, however, were ordering more liquor with which to stupefy the despair of more and yet more obstinate victims of the same hopes.

But not even in this period, with all these reverses, did capital and effort draw back. Gold persisted in not appearing: well, then, the railway would go in search of it. When an English ship loaded with secondhand material appeared in port, the whole of Beira went mad! For the starting point of the project some flats at the edge of the Pungué were chosen, which in time of rain or flood were under a considerable depth of water; this waterlogged ground, to which the hybrid name of Fontesvilla was given, was leased at exorbitant prices, the influx of would-be lessees being such that the offices of the Moçambique Company had to be guarded by police.

The buildings of Beira spread themselves day by day over the sand. Nothing is solid and firm, not even the ground one treads; everyone knows that over the whole area hangs doubt—of life or death, of fortune or ruin, a formidable "to be or not to be"—whether or not payable gold exists. Nevertheless, upon the shifting sand and with a question mark for the future, are already established innumerable businesses whose shares are quoted on bourses; and funds press themselves on the company that directs this land of adventure and mirage, either for direct investment, or for making embankments, constructing docks and quays, undertaking plantations, or attempting any business that might recommend itself to the credulity of shareholders![55]

The evident enjoyment with which the foregoing was written was not its sole justification; Ennes was primarily interested in showing that foreign capitalists, given the proper opportunities, could indeed be made to interest themselves in developing Moçambique. He continued his account with a derisive description of the bureaucratic restrictions that discouraged investment in land. The land itself was cheap to rent—a mere ten réis a hectare—but possession would be granted a lessee only after the property had been officially surveyed and a plan drawn, and not only was the scale fee for these services out of all proportion to the value of the land, but so great was the shortage of official surveyors that a delay of years might occur before the matter was concluded.[56] Even then the tenant enjoyed no legal security. Ennes proposed to get over these difficulties by allowing tenants to undertake their own mensuration work and by providing for the outright sale of Crown lands.[57]

However desirable these and other reforms may have been, the question that principally arises is why the value of land—much of it, as along the Limpopo, admirably suited to plantation agriculture—was so low that development could be effectively checked by the impediments Ennes described. The reasons, as he saw, were partly political—the weaknesses of the provincial administration, the absence of any security outside the coast settlements—but only partly. The social and economic, to say nothing of the climatic, obstacles to development were more profound and harder to remedy. One was the absence in Portugal of what one may call a colonizing class. As one of those would-be helpful letter-writers whom the British Foreign Office habitually rewarded with a bare acknowledgment wrote in November 1890:

I am applied to by some of these Portuguese Banks and trading establishments to know if I can find them men who have some means and position and who have worked in India or Ceylon, because they would like to give them concessions and advance capital to get them out into Portuguese territory; they state that they have no class of people in Portugal who will go out as colonists or who understands plantation and factory work. . . . Mr. Hornung [founder of a sugar company in Zambézia]* . . . has had entirely to depend on English and Scotch labor for engineers and managers for the sugar factories.[58]

Ennes would have agreed: the Portuguese emigrants to Moçambique, he remarks, were, and would be, rarely other than "hands . . . possessed neither of capital . . . nor of the energy and aptitudes that can do duty for it . . . individuals already defeated in life's struggle . . . useless people without a trade, led astray by the belief that in Africa one digs gold with one's fingernails."[59] Those who did not succumb to climate or disease within months, or return to Lisbon at government expense, almost all became innkeepers or government employees; few went into trade, and none into agriculture.

There was nothing new about all this, nor was it at bottom a matter of the immigrants' qualifications, for even had they been ready and willing to go into trade or agriculture, no incentive existed for them to do so. In the eighteen-nineties it was still true, as it had been a century earlier, that no obvious, large, unexploited market existed for the produce of the soil of Moçambique. In becoming innkeepers, the immigrants were taking the line of least resistance and exploiting the one exception to this rule, for the demand of the natives for liquor was, for all practical purposes, unlimited. "The measure of the state of trade is the importation of intoxicants. The crop year is reckoned good or bad according to the birth and ripening of the cashew nut. The worst calamity to befall Lourenço Marques was not so much the reduction in the public works budget as the stoppage of sales of alcohol in Gazaland." When Ennes asked landowners why they did not grow coffee or cocoa, rice or sugarcane, their answer was everywhere the same: "The coconut palm is far better; there is nothing to equal the cashew!" Even where, as around Inhambane, sugarcane was beginning to be grown, it was not for sugar but for rum or *sôpe*, a fermented drink beloved of the natives. The only industry in the province, apart from the making of bricks and lime, was distilling: "Everyone distils; in some areas every native hut has a still devised from a clay pot, a gun barrel, and a cover of dried mud."

In this alcohol-based economy it was the whites and Asiatics who

* Now Sena Sugar Estates, Limited.

produced or imported liquor and the blacks whose primitive agriculture (or produce-gathering) furnished the means of purchasing it. No sizeable export trade could be built on such a foundation, which indeed was wholly precarious. For if the terms of trade turned against native drinkers, they could become self-suppliers or seek more remunerative work in the Transvaal or Natal. Both these things were already happening in the district of Inhambane, whose trade was therefore in marked decline. Ennes saw no immediate remedy for this state of affairs: plantation agriculture was the ultimate solution, but its introduction would take time. Nor could unaided private enterprise bring about improvement: the state must step in, both in the name of economy and in that of morality.

I have not joined the Salvation Army, and I have always considered as chimerical the canons of the Council of Brussels, in which the holy fathers of European temperance prohibited, in the vastness of Africa, drunkenness irrepressible in London and St. Petersburg.

Europeans can rest assured that the black race will not shame their intemperance by its sobriety, even though the great powers should combine to impose it. The Negro drank, drinks, and will continue to drink. If all the fleets of the signatories of the General Act of Brussels were to blockade African ports, and their armies were to patrol the bush, they could not stop him. . . . It is a calumny to say that the whites incited him to this madness. . . . Nature made the African a toper . . . civilization only cultivated his palate. Children in arms leave their mothers' breasts to put their tongues into cups of *aguardente,* and do not burn them. The blacks have, indeed, a special trait which, I judge, not even the European drinking fraternity would think trivial: they do not get drunk because they enjoy drinking, but they drink in order to get drunk.

In the district of Inhambane the situation was especially bad, even though the import of spirits was tiny and production by big landowners not extensive. "The natives have learned to distil sugarcane, pineapples, mangoes, cassava, every fruit, every plant, and every root that allows of the operation, and thus possessed of their own means for drunkenness, . . . so abuse them that . . . their reason and manhood evaporate." Delirium tremens was becoming general among the elders. Elsewhere in the province, drunkenness was not so much endemic as seasonally epidemic, depending on the ripening fruit of the cashew, that "tree of vice and ruin." Ennes wrote:

In Moçambique and in Quilimane, in the season of this accursed fruit and of its products (which happily do not suffice for the needs of the whole year), when the atmosphere is poisoned by the resinous odors of the fat jugs displayed in the markets and in the taverns, native laborers leave the hoe, carriers abandon their loads, servants flee their masters, soldiers and sailors desert; the drumming of *batuques* is heard on every side; vagrancy and saturnalia continue so long as the supplies of drink last; when they begin to be scarce, they command higher prices than that of the best port wine![60]

V

The picture of patriarchal innocence conjured up by this passage was not one that appealed to Ennes. Rather did it epitomize the sense of frustration felt by so many Europeans, bent on promoting the development of Africa, who found the African reluctant to accept the curse of Adam. Portuguese administrators, thinking of their countrymen at home sweating from dawn to dusk under the powerful Lusitanian sun, chafed at the liberal legislation that—they declared—allowed the black man to live by the labor of his women. Abolishing slavery was all very well, but this was overdoing it. "The regulations treat the masters as scoundrels against whose misdeeds no precaution can be too great, and consider work as a punishment applied to the helpless Negro. Whoever hires servants is more vexed than a robber put on probation by a judge." Favorable conditions of diet and housing were insisted on, such as were enjoyed neither by Negroes in their tribal existence, nor by workers in Portugal itself. Moreover, the *serviçal,* for his part, could not be disciplined: the worst that could happen to him was to be committed to prison, where he was fed and housed better than he would have been outside, and had no obligation to work.

The worst jail is a better shelter from the weather than a native hut . . . , the plank bed less harsh than the bare ground, the rations more appetizing and varied than maize porridge. To spend one's life recumbent, telling tales of fetishes and hyenas (interspersed with crude ditties), does not tire the body or make calloused the skin as does the pole of the litter or the handle of an oar, and it frees one from the severities of the chief, the attacks of enemies, the claws of the tiger, and the teeth of the crocodile. True, prisoners are supposed to be deprived of women and drink; but jail discipline at times is indulgent toward human weakness.[61]

Ennes had no doubt but that the African should be given work and compelled to do it: not, indeed, as the chattel of a private owner, but through the philanthropic compulsion of the state. What this compulsion might amount to in practice can be inferred from the remarks of Lord Salisbury's correspondent, who has already been quoted:

One inducement held out to his [Mr. Hornung's] company was that having the labor under control, which really means slave labor, they can command the actual work for their sugar plantations from the chiefs living in the neighborhood. They tax these chiefs and receive payment in the shape of labor, the chiefs sending their slaves to do what is necessary on the plantations and for making the roads.[62]

This account is borne out by a report to the British Admiralty from Lieutenant Commander Keane, the officer in command of the armed stern-wheelers that had been sent to the Zambezi in the autumn of 1890. Writing in March 1891, he referred to the sugar company in question as having taken over from a defunct opium company the possession of a prazo in the Mopéa district and as having the right, in consideration of having farmed the native taxes due from the area, to compel the inhabitants to work for it. Though H. H. Johnston, to whom the question was referred, discounted this report, it appears to have been substantially correct.[63] By a decree of 1880, the former system of holding prazos by emphyteusis (copyhold), abolished on paper in 1832 by Mousinho da Silveira and again abolished in 1854, had been replaced by a simple lease; subsequent provincial regulations laid down that all *colonos* (native inhabitants) were obliged to work for the lessee or the government at a standard wage of 400 réis per week. The *mussoco*, or head-tax, amounted to 800 réis, payable in money or exportable commodities, so that two weeks' work a year would suffice to discharge it. Whether, in fact, the obligation to compulsory labor stopped at this point is uncertain, for it is hard to see how a colono could be expected to enforce his rights against a lessee or an official determined to override them. In this, as in many other instances, it is hazardous to infer the actual practice from the letter of the law.[64] One would, for instance, never guess from Ennes' account that the palmatória was still being used as a disciplinary measure for native servants or as a punishment for evildoers. Yet in April 1894, Lieutenant Commander Carr, commanding the British naval vessels on the Zambezi, reported that his native pilot had been arrested and given two dozen strokes for refusing to leave British service. He forwarded a drawing of the instrument along with his report, adding, "Though the Palmatória is forbidden by the Portuguese laws, its use is a matter of daily occurrence in this port [Chinde]." Presumably officials felt that no other effective discipline was open to them.[65]

In the Moçambique of the early nineties, of course, the Portuguese writ still did not run very far beyond the limits of the coast settlements, and neither Ennes' description of economic and social conditions nor, a fortiori, his voluminous legislative proposals, could be taken as applying to the interior. The one exception was, of course, Zambézia, with its prazos, though not all of these were now securely in Portuguese control; and it was still on Zambézia, rather than on the districts farther south, that hopes of developing a plantation agriculture were primarily fixed. In November 1888 Barros Gomes had appointed a committee, of which Ennes was a member and Oliveira Martins the relator and leading spirit, to examine the prazo system and put forward measures for its reform. The committee took but three months to prepare its report, so that there was no time for it to make any investigation on the spot; and though several of its members had served in Moçambique, and it took evidence from one or two prazo holders, the main influences on it were clearly the historical and economic theories of Oliveira Martins himself.[66] The report was at once brilliantly convincing and fundamentally misconceived, in a way that no lesser man could have contrived. The misconception, as Alexandre Lobato has shown,[67] lay in the belief that the prazo had been in essence designed to ensure cultivation of the soil, instead of being quasi-military in purpose, and that the colono was a kind of medieval serf. The belief had arisen at a time—the mid-eighteenth century—when the institution was already in decline; it had inspired the abortive attempt to limit the size of prazos, and had been perpetuated by such descriptive writers as Sebastião Xavier Botelho (1835).[68] The liberals' failure to eradicate the prazos was now to give the belief, and hence the institution, a new lease on life.

In the eighties, particularly under the energetic governor-general Augusto de Castilho (1885-1888), attempts had been made to convert the mussoco of Zambézia into an ordinary hut-tax (*imposto de palhota*), and have it collected directly by the government. The intention was to break the political power that indirect collection gave to the prazo holders (*muzungos*), which was held to be the cause of the numerous native revolts that had plagued Zambézia; but since this political power was at the same time the base of such Portuguese authority as existed in the interior, its destruction would have called for direct military intervention there on a scale never previously envisaged. Any benefits to the provincial treasury that might accrue from official collection would, in a sense, be pledged in advance—

given the doubtful assumption that the troops and equipment could be procured. In any case, the policy aroused the hostility of the muzungos, and it had been applied only to a handful of prazos around Quilimane by the time Barros Gomes, apparently in response to their complaints, set up the Committee of Inquiry.*

A few months earlier, Major Caldas Xavier, who had been associated with the opium company at Mopéa, had published a pamphlet advocating that the mussoco, far from being taken out of the hands of the prazo holders, should be turned into an engine of economic development. He pointed to what had been done by the opium company, by agreement with the local chiefs, to remedy the shortage of labor on its prazo. Briefly, it had allowed colonos to discharge their tax obligations by working, or by sending a proxy to work, on the company's land for two weeks. Alternatively, where conditions permitted, minors and even small children might act as substitutes— working, of course, a longer period of time. Food and shelter were provided by the company. According to Caldas Xavier, this arrangement had been welcomed by a majority of the natives, who had flocked to take advantage of it; but certain headmen had lost followers thereby, and it was they who, in August 1884, had raised a revolt and attacked the company's headquarters.[69] This revolt had been defeated, mainly by the efforts of a contingent of foreigners led by Frederick Moir of the African Lakes Company.[70] The implication was that if public order could be guaranteed, as it had not been at Mopéa, means lay ready at hand to promote plantation agriculture on a large scale.

This not very solid argument made a strong impression on the majority of the Committee of Inquiry, who were prepared to apply it, not only to Zambézia, but to the remainder of the province. Their report made, in effect, only one distinction between prazos: whether or not they were subject to incursions by "rebel peoples," and for that reason unsuited to agricultural development. For those prazos so subject, the existing system of leases might be continued, though military administration would be preferable; but as reconquest proceeded, all should be brought under a new régime based largely on Caldas Xavier's proposals. Leases of prazos should be granted for thirty years to the highest bidder at public auction, the minimum rent to be half the

* See above, p. 39.

mussoco multiplied by the number of inhabitants. In addition, the prazo holder should be obliged to take on lease a portion of the land, not already in use, with a view to its cultivation. To this end, at least half the mussoco, equal to a week's work for adults or two weeks for children, should be made payable in labor on the land, the employer to furnish food, water, fuel, and shelter. This obligation should be freely transferable, so that it would, in fact, fall collectively on the inhabitants of the prazo, and not on each and every individual. The amount of land to be so designated for cultivation should likewise be fixed in terms of the population of the prazo. The report envisaged a splitting-up of prazos deemed to be excessive in size, and the eventual extinction of the whole system when a sufficient proportion of the land was brought under private ownership or cultivation. It also made a number of miscellaneous recommendations, such as the establishment of a system of inspection, the regulation of private armies, the establishment of markets at fixed places within each prazo, and the consequent prohibition of itinerant traders.[71]

These recommendations, with some changes in detail, were embodied in a decree issued by Ennes as Royal Commissioner in November 1890, which, however, applied only to the area in which prazos already existed. Detailed regulations issued in July 1892 not only spelled out the recommendations—making, for instance, the area to be cultivated equal to one hectare for every ten inhabitants—but added at least one provision clearly traceable to Ennes' personal views. This was the extension of the vagrancy law of metropolitan Portugal to black colonos without fixed abode or occupation. Such men, if they were not cultivators of one hectare of crops or its equivalent in fruit trees, or were not domestic servants, or were not employed for wages on the land for at least twelve weeks in the year, might be compelled to work for others or allotted land to cultivate on their own account. In any such enforcement proceedings the native authorities on the prazo were to participate.[72]

VI

It would be beside the point to consider whether a regulation such as this was an enlightened means of compelling the native, willy-nilly, to take part in economic development or whether, on the contrary, it was, at least potentially, a piece of oppression. It must rather be regarded as a sign that the national penchant for paper legislation on a vast scale, without regard to its suitability or the means of administering it, was too strong even for men of the calibre of Oliveira Martins and António Ennes. Like its eighteenth-century analogue, the legislation could be said to ignore the social and economic realities of Zambézia, such as the practice of shifting cultivation and the consequent migration of populations to and fro: it treated the black colono as though he were a peasant, holding an identifiable piece of land in servile tenure, and it assumed that the population of a prazo could be accurately ascertained quinquennially and used as the base of rental calculations. Caldas Xavier had indeed indicated a variety of ways in which the natives evaded the count (and the tax), and had remarked that the extent of this and other evasions varied with the extent of abuses by the lord of the prazo; but this realistic passage had counted for nothing compared with the attractions of his positive proposals.[73]

The fact, which became apparent as soon as the authorities began to take census, that the population of the prazos, even those nearest to Quilimane, displayed wide fluctuations from year to year meant that the very basis for determining the prazo holders' annual dues (and the land they were to cultivate) could never be other than conventional. This was, however, by no means the most serious weakness of the scheme. What was more damaging was the assumption that each and every prazo, regardless of size and geographical location, was capable of development in a degree governed largely by the number of its native inhabitants, and that rent might be charged for it accordingly. Such an assumption ignored the most elementary economic factors governing the value of land. There could be no comparison in this respect between the long-established prazos adjoining Quilimane—which, of course, differed among themselves—and those far up the Zambezi and dependent on its uncertain navigation. Caldas Xavier had seen the point, in a way, for he had called for the building of railways, even by foreign capital, in Zambézia: "What are the Zambezi, Shiré, Nyasa, and Cafué worth without the benefit of railways? Nothing!"[74] But the efforts of Barros Gomes and others in this direction had come to naught. Quite apart from transport considerations, it was idle for the provincial government to fix a minimum rent for prazos unless it wanted them left on its hands, just as it was idle for it to determine their proper extent by some a priori rule of thumb. In the last analysis, these questions would have to be decided by circumstances, such as the economic expectations of prospective lessees. So, too, with the proviso that unless a minimum area of land were devoted to plantation crops, the whole lease of a prazo would be, ipso facto, void. A lessee could not reasonably be expected to pay native labor, at a statutory wage, to cultivate such crops unless there was a prospect of selling them profitably; and it would be useless to confiscate his lease for default unless another lessee could be found. Ennes once wrote that knowledge of economics and finance was essential for one who would govern Moçambique as it should be governed.[75] His regulations for prazos constitute an eloquent if curious commentary on this dictum. They can only escape economic and administrative reproach by pleading guilty to the charge—often leveled at the Portuguese by foreign critics—of being mere window dressing. But this charge at least must fail in the light of overwhelming evidence that they were meant —and taken—seriously.

The subsequent history of the prazo régime followed a course which, in its main features, was predictable at the outset. The elaborate provisions of Ennes' legislation were either openly whittled down or allowed to fall into disuse. The independent inspectorate, which might have been a thorn in the side of the prazo holder, was weakened in 1896 and virtually abolished in 1901. The fixed but free markets within prazos failed to establish themselves: instead, the prazo holder tended to acquire a trading monopoly. Ernesto de Vilhena remarks that the very attempt to establish *feiras* (markets) within the prazo was a piece of inappropriate archaism.[76] The original seventeenth-century feiras had been successful precisely because they were meeting-grounds outside a single territorial authority. Although a law of 1901 not only reiterated the principle that leases of prazos should be bestowed by auction but also extended this principle to renewals, in 1907 renewals were decreed to be at the discretion of the governor-general. The minimum rent laid down by Ennes with reference to the population of the prazo became a maximum, attained only on a handful of prazos close to Quilimane. The requirement to cultivate was likewise complied with only on a small minority of prazos, and even there not to the extent prescribed. Governor-General Freire de Andrade, writing in 1906, remarked that if the law were to be strictly enforced, all the leases would have to be revoked.[77] This would have been impracticable, and, in the majority of cases, unfair to the lessee: as an acute if somewhat belated critic, Pedro A. Alvares, remarked in 1916, "In the present state of communications in the province of Moçambique, the greater part of the area of Zambézia and virtually the whole of the rest of the province are incapable of being brought under plantation agriculture." Alvares added that Oliveira Martins ought not to have failed to take this aspect of the problem into account, and therefore was much to blame for the situation that had arisen.[78]

R. N. Lyne, an Englishman who served for some time as Director of Agriculture for Moçambique, afterwards wrote flatly that "the prazo companies . . . are, in the main, organizations for the exploitation of the natives: this exploitation taking the form of imposing on them taxes to be paid in kind."* He regarded the system as one of exclusive monopoly, acting in hindrance of development, though he added that the district of Quilimane was the most progressive in the province, and what progress there had been was the work of the prazo holders. He also praised the prazo companies for their work in teaching the natives handicrafts: "No missionary station that I have ever visited in East Africa could provide such an object-lesson in native industry and application as one of these large prazo stations, for example, Porto Bello."[79] Alvares likewise referred to the abuse by which the prazo holders insisted on receiving payment in kind or in money at their option (which by law was the right of the colono) and how they exploited the difference between the official price of produce and its market price. He noted a number of other malpractices: listing adults as youths, whereby the holder forwent the mussoco but more than recouped himself by paying for their labor at half rate; paying wages in kind, and overvaluing the goods so paid; failing to provide food and shelter for workers fulfilling their statutory obligations; monopolizing trade on the prazo; failing to provide education as prescribed for prazos having more than two thousand inhabitants; cutting wood and quarrying without license; avoiding liquor duties on spirits sold or given to natives.[80]

One does not know the extent of these abuses. Alvares himself re-

---

* In private, Lyne was more emphatic. In a letter of April 12, 1912, to Errol MacDonell, Consul General at Lourenço Marques, he referred to the "tyranny and oppression of natives . . . principally in the district of Quelimane. . . . The 'palmatoria' is the chief weapon by which these local administrators maintain their authority. . . . Its use is illegal, yet it is openly displayed at Government and prazo stations, and I myself have seen it used." (C.P. 10242, No. 25, enclosure.) He went on to relate a number of atrocities of which he had been told (but which he had not seen). Hence, perhaps, Sir Edward Grey's description of the prazo system as "abominable."

marked that though not all appeared on every prazo, they were all carried on with impunity somewhere or other. Mousinho de Albuquerque, Ennes' successor as Royal Commissioner between 1896 and 1898, regarded the existence of abuses as inevitable but unimportant in comparison with the civilizing influence of the system in general, and was in particular prepared to condone and even encourage trading monopoly as an alternative to the baneful Indian trader whom he (unlike Ennes) wished to expel from Moçambique. Mousinho already noted "the facility with which the colono can pass from one prazo to another, and the competition between lessees ever desirous of increasing the population of their prazos."[81] R. C. F. Maugham, who served as a British consular officer in Moçambique for many years, concluded that this stultified the whole purpose of the system:

So long as the remote prazo holder is satisfied with the amount of income he derives from the proportion of the native hut-tax [i.e., poll tax] which he is allowed to retain, and makes no attempt to employ the people residing upon his concession, an assured income is his; but from the moment that he insists upon utilizing their labor, in no matter what branch of industry or agriculture, his taxpayers immediately cast about for a prazo where life flows more peacefully, and in a short time the man of action finds his native locations deserted.... The present generation of the remoter prazo proprietors, profiting by the bitter experience of those who have gone before, seek first of all to attract as large a native population as possible by dint of indulgent treatment, and by making it quite understood that labor will not be required of them to any execessive degree. This once done ... the happy proprietor will assuredly see his undeveloped prazo densely populated, and his coffers overflowing with easily collected hut-taxes.[82]

Maugham added that the prazos near the sea consisted almost exclusively of coconut plantations, the maintenance of which made no great demands on native labor. Even so, the Companhia de Moçambique, whose territory included the right bank of the Zambezi, was said to have attracted natives from across the river because it did not oblige them to work.[83]

Lyne remarked of the system: "It belongs to a back era and must go."[84] Alvares demonstrated in detail that not a single objective of the Committee of 1888 had been accomplished. Far from being abolished, the *prazos fiscais,* serving only as a means of tax collection, constituted the majority; and far from escaping land monopoly, virtually the whole of Zambézia was in the hands of five large companies. The carefully specified conditions to be imposed on the initial lease and retention of prazos were not being carried out. Monopolies of trade flourished. No supervision was exercised over lessees' proceedings, particularly the compiling of tax rolls, and no protection was given to the native. In sum: "The regime ... as it functions today in Zambézia, has nothing in common, whether financially, economically, or politically, with what Oliveira Martins visualized in his report or A. Ennes attempted to carry out in his legislation; neither the State, nor the lessee, nor the colono has achieved the brilliant results those statesmen expected."

Alvares held that the reason for this failure was in some degree inherent in the very legislation itself, and that the abuses were secondary. He dismissed any notion of administrative foul play: "I have the clear impression that it [Portugal] has suffered far more from incompetent administration on the part of its public men than from their dishonesty."[85] He attributed the hasty and ill-thought-out modifications that had been made over the years to insufficient study and want of local knowledge. That more might have been done in Lower Zambézia is beyond doubt: Freire de Andrade, writing in 1909, admitted as much, putting the blame partly on inexperience, partly on overambitious ideas on the part of the lessees, and partly on the government for tolerating abuses and making positive mistakes of policy. In particular, he believed that the Companhia de Zambézia—the inheritor, on the left bank, of Paiva de Andrada's original concession of 1877—had been allowed to rent far more prazos than its limited capital justified.[86]

As late as 1914, the total amount of land under cultivation by lessees of prazos in the district of Quilimane was less than 25,000 hectares, of which nearly half were in coconut groves. In the district of Tete, the amount was 2,500 hectares, more or less equally divided between cotton and rubber. These figures, amounting to less than one fifth of one per cent of the total area of Zambézia, afford a derisive comment on the hopes that the prazo system would bring about its own extinction through economic development. Alvares made some calculations intended to constitute a reductio ad absurdum of these hopes, arguing that Ennes' requirement that half the area be brought under cultivation before the system could be abolished would entail production of crops, and hence the use of resources of all kinds, on an altogether impossible scale. His point was well taken, despite the fact that he based his calculations on the total area rather than on a cultivable area that must have been considerably less.[87] It indicates the inherent misapprehension of scale underlying the original proposals—a misapprehension greater than that of Rhodes about Manica, in that the discovery of mineral wealth might, whereas the practice of plantation agriculture might not, plausibly be expected to bring about a dramatic transformation of a whole economy. As in neighboring territories, these false hopes were based on ignorance of the terrain, coupled with disregard of the economic limitations on development. Of these, the restricted outlet for produce, rather than shortage of capital or native labor was (and indeed still is) overriding; and after it, inadequacy of transport. It is hard to believe that the wisest of policies could have substantially overcome these limitations. The experiences of the British South Africa Company and of the Moçambique Company suggest, on the contrary, that here was another case of involuntary uneconomic imperialism.

Chapter six

António Ennes in Moçambique, 1893–1895

The detailed settlement of the western boundary of Moçambique in accordance with the treaty of 1891 proved to be both lengthy and contentious. It had been entrusted to a mixed commission of which António Ennes himself was the Portuguese member, though the work in the field was undertaken by his assistant, Captain Freire de Andrade, conjointly with the British commissioner, Major Julian Leverson, R.E. Had these two professional military engineers been left to themselves, everything would have gone smoothly, though slowly—for the frontier district had never been properly surveyed and mapped, and work was possible only in the dry season. By the end of 1892, they had covered almost all the ground south of the Zambezi. Then, however, Ennes quite unexpectedly rejected a line—to which Freire de Andrade had agreed—proposed by Leverson in the Manica region. His motives are by no means clear, but the area was still thought to be rich in gold, and it was suspected by the Chartered Company (which thought Leverson's line unduly favorable to the Portuguese) that the British directors of the Moçambique Company had instigated Ennes' move.[1] What had made the move practicable was an ambiguity in the Portuguese text of the treaty of 1891, referring to the plateau of Manica, coupled with the discovery that the plateau had no clearly defined eastern rim to form a boundary between the English and Portuguese spheres, but only broken country crossed by several deep river valleys. Leverson had proposed, in effect, to ignore these valleys, and to draw the boundary—with due regard to practicability—in the way it would have run had the terrain been what the makers of the treaty had anticipated. This would have meant giving the Chartered Company some heads of valleys above 2,000 feet altitude. Ennes, on the other hand, sought a line that would run on high ground—and therefore farther west—throughout; and he defended his position by reference to the Portuguese text, according to which the line was to run along "the crest of the eastern slope of the Manica plateau" (*a crista da vertente oriental do planalto de Manica*). He argued that this rule ought to apply even if the crest of the eastern face were also that of the western face: that is, even if it coincided with the water parting.

It must be said at once that Ennes' view was not one that could be sustained. Not only had Salisbury, in the negotiations for the Treaty of 1891, specifically rejected the suggestion that the water parting be the boundary, but the English text of the treaty had merely referred to "the upper part of the eastern slope": phrasing less specific than that of the Portuguese text, which was clearly a mistranslation. Moreover, it so happened that in this instance the drafting of the treaty had been in English throughout—a Portuguese translation having been prepared for formal purposes only after the initialing of the substantive agreement in London on May 28, 1891. But though Ennes' interpretation of the treaty might be rejected as impossibly strained, this would not suffice to establish the Leverson line in the absence of any obvious topographical feature corresponding to "the upper part of the eastern slope."[2] As Anderson of the Foreign Office at length admitted in the face of repeated Portuguese requests, there was clearly ground for arbitration, and the result would be uncertain.[3] It was the more difficult to resist arbitration because the Portuguese had offered in November 1893 to accept the remainder of the line agreed upon by Leverson and Ennes; but it was known that Rhodes would object, and both Currie and Rosebery, the Foreign Secretary, favored postponing arbitration as long as possible. Soveral had candidly explained that the Portuguese government desired it, not because they minded what line was drawn, but because it would be easier politically for them to accept even an unfavorable award at the hands of an arbitrator than to agree to the Leverson line of their own volition.

I

In February 1894, an incident occurred which enabled London to over-come the obstacle at Cape Town. Among the provisions of the treaty of 1891 had been one guaranteeing, inter alia, the right of the British to telegraphic communication across the long tongue of Portuguese territory between Nyasaland and Southern Rhodesia. H. H. Johnston, representing Rhodes, had therefore made a provisional agreement in June 1893 with Captain Andrea, the governor of Tete, under which a subsidiary to the Chartered Company would be allowed to construct a line. Rhodes had himself adhered to this agreement in July and had sought the assent of the British government. But when news of it reached Lisbon early in September, Andrea was disowned by his government for acting without authority, and was recalled in disgrace. In point of fact, a telegraph concession had been granted by the Portuguese several months previously to the Companhia da Zambézia, in which the explorer Lovett Cameron held a leading interest. The Foreign Office learned only in March 1894 that the Chartered Company had been made aware of this concession as early as May 1893, and that in consequence, the Johnston-Andrea agreement—whether or not the immediate parties were aware of it—constituted an attempt to circumvent Cameron.[4] The Portuguese government professed to maintain that if the line to be constructed by Cameron's company were linked with the British lines (as he himself had proposed to the Chartered Company), this would constitute a sufficient fulfillment of its treaty obligations; and that, moreover, it was precluded from granting a second concession. But the Chartered Company was understandably reluctant to rely for its communications on a telegraph line controlled by a foreign company that was a commercial rival, and that it regarded as financially shaky. Failing local instructions to the contrary, work on the line across Portuguese territory was actually started toward the end of 1893.

Early in February 1894, Anderson suggested informally to Rochfort Maguire, the Parnellite member of Parliament and right-hand man of Rhodes, that if the Portuguese were persuaded to give way on the telegraph, the Chartered Company should accept arbitration on the

Manica boundary as a quid pro quo. Early in March, Maguire indicated that Rhodes would reluctantly agree, but wanted to stipulate in addition for some kind of preemption right over the Delagoa Bay railway.[5] By that time, however, news had reached London, via Lisbon, of an incident at Tete between the would-be telegraph builders and the Portuguese authorities, in which two British gunboats of the Zambezi stern-wheel flotilla were somehow involved: their commander, the Portuguese complained, had threatened to use force. Johnston, who, as commissioner at Zomba (Nyasaland), was overseeing the telegraph construction, had already been told by cable on February 17 that he "would not be justified, in opposition to the Portuguese authorities, in proceeding with telegraph works on Portuguese territory." The Foreign Office, therefore, could and did tell Lisbon that any threat of force was "completely unauthorized." The Portuguese government, for its part, had sent instructions that force was not to be met with force—and so the only real danger was from disobedience by the men on the spot.[6]

It was, however, some months before London and Lisbon would find out what happened—or—perhaps it should be said in view of the conflicting nature of some of the local testimony—devise an agreed version of what had happened. Johnston's dispatches from Zomba seldom took less than two months on the journey, and he had as yet no telegraph. It is not clear how or when the instruction of February 17 reached him, or even that it reached him at all, for he never acknowledged it in set terms: a later, more urgent telegram of March 6, warning him against trying to enforce his own personal interpretation of the treaty of 1891, and ending "You must at once return to explain," was answered from Moçambique on April 26 by a telegram denying that any clash had occurred at Tete.[7]

By that time, dispatches had arrived making it clear that Johnston had pressed on with the telegraph work (as he had told the Foreign Office he intended to do) until February 15, when the local Portuguese authorities indicated that they had instructions from Quilimane to stop it, and in particular, to prevent him from setting up a pole on an island in the Zambezi. Some of the telegraph material had apparently been brought up on board the British gunboats *Herald* and *Mosquito,* whose commander, Lieutenant Commander Carr, R.N., told Johnston's subordinate Bowhill, who was supervising the construction, that he had orders to use force if necessary. Commander Carr, in fact, told the Portuguese that he proposed to erect the pole in dispute, and to defy them to remove it—but the pole did not arrive in time for the intended showdown. Johnston, on hearing of this, advised Carr (and instructed Bowhill) to yield to force. Meanwhile, the Portuguese commandant who had talked of calling up the prazo holders' black troops to oust the English, found his own people averse to a clash and decided to await events.[8]

Prudence having prevailed locally on both sides at the eleventh hour, time was given for the orders of higher authority to take effect, and it became possible for the two governments to deny that any incident had taken place, despite reports to the contrary in British newspapers. Johnston blamed the Portuguese *volte-face*—for such, locally, it appeared to be—on the intrigues of one Machado, representing the Companhia da Zambézia, and he referred bitterly to "the tortuous policy pursued by Captain Cameron." It hardly lay with anyone connected with the Chartered Company to complain on a score of that kind: even if, for want of proof, one absolve Johnston from deliberately scheming against Cameron's concession, it cannot be denied that his treatment of the Portuguese contained at least a modicum of bluff and effrontery. Maguire, on being questioned by Anderson early in March, denied knowledge of any orders to proceed with the telegraph in spite of opposition, and did not think Rhodes had been in communication with Johnston recently—a view that is the more plausible since the two had not long before quarreled irreconcilably over the future of Nyasaland. Maguire could not have known that on the very day Anderson reported this to Rosebery, Rhodes was telegraphing Johnston urging him to "hold the fort"; but this action seems to have been an unpremeditated response to newspaper reports of a clash.[9] If Rhodes did not inspire the instructions to Commander Carr to use force, which had very nearly led to hostilities, the question remains who did: for it is inherently unlikely that the officer in command at Simonstown would have issued them on his own responsibility. Loch, the High Commissioner, was certainly capable of it: in a dispatch described by Rosebery as "amazing" and by Anderson as language that would not have been surprising from Rhodes, he had spoken of the risks the Portuguese would be running by forcibly opposing the construction of the telegraph line "which has been guaranteed by treaty."

This, as the Foreign Office realized, was to prejudge the point at issue.[10]

As it turned out, what was thought to have occurred rather than what actually occurred was decisive. Anderson told Maguire on March 9th that, in consequence of the Tete collision, Rhodes had lost his opportunity for a bargain, and that arbitration on the Manica boundary was now unavoidable. A few days earlier, Rosebery had observed that he had no further arguments with which to oppose it: "Delay has been carried to an extreme length, and should the matter be raised, we have no parliamentary case." On March 15, Kimberley, who had taken over from Rosebery as Foreign Secretary, told Soveral that the British government accepted arbitration in principle.[11]

As the Portuguese government's partial default on its foreign debt, in June 1892, had embroiled it with the French and German bond-holders who were the principal creditors, it was deemed wise that the chosen arbitrator should be an Italian; and after some little searching, the choice fell upon Paul Vigliani, a retired judge of great age and high reputation. Thereafter, matters hung fire until the middle of 1896: Ennes had unexpectedly been obliged to return to Africa for a second term as High Commissioner, and though the preparation of the Portuguese case went on in his absence, its presentation could, apparently, be entrusted only to him. When he did return, in the spring of that year, he found the case as prepared unsatisfactory and set himself to rewrite it.[12] The arbitration proceedings eventually began in Florence in June 1896, and it immediately became evident that Vigliani was bent on compromise and would have liked Ennes and Leverson to agree on a line which he could then adopt as his award. Leverson was willing to attempt this, for it was clear to him, as to Ennes and Freire de Andrade, that the arbitrator was incapable, by reason of age, of grasping the technicalities at issue. Moreover, he thought that Ennes, though quarrelsome and difficult (Leverson had to make peace on one occasion between him and Vigliani), was anxious for a settlement. The Foreign Office and the Colonial Office were agreeable, provided the appearance of an arbitration was adhered to: Ennes, on the other hand, thought that the compromise, if it were reached, should be avowed, and this Lisbon would not hear of.[13] In the end, Vigliani agreed to go on with the arbitration, with the aid of a technical assessor from the Military-Geographical Institute at

Florence. His award was given on January 30, 1897, and was decidedly favorable to the British, awarding them more than four-fifths of the territory in dispute. The principal benefit to the Portuguese was that the frontier was drawn less tightly, and on higher ground, around Macequece. It was thus ridiculous, though foreseeable, that the Chartered Company should complain that the award gave them "the husk" and Portugal "the kernel": Leverson was firmly of the opinion that the Portuguese would have done better to compromise.[14]

II

Ennes' return to Moçambique at the end of 1894 was the Portuguese government's response to some months of unrest among the native inhabitants of the crown lands (*terras da corôa*) immediately north of Lourenço Marques—unrest which had kept the town in an intermittent state of alarm, not to say panic, and had bid fair to bring about international complications. The unrest had been occasioned by a succession dispute among the local chiefs which the Portuguese authorities had attempted to adjudicate without due regard to Kaffir custom, and had been compounded by sundry grievances, including a rumor that the hut tax was to be increased. The chief principally aggrieved, Mahazul, had refused to appear before the local commandant at Angoane unless accompanied by two thousand armed warriors; and an attempt to arrest ten of his *indunas* (councilors), at the end of August 1894, had been frustrated in a skirmish in which shots had been exchanged.[15] After this incident, it began to be put about that the natives intended attacking Lourenço Marques, which was virtually undefended. On September 1, Bernal, the British consul, took it upon himself to cable Simonstown for a gunboat. Later in the month the rumors gained force, and Bernal incurred odium with the governor-general (and a reproof from London) for neglecting to ask Portuguese permission before having twenty-five bluejackets landed from H.M.S. *Thrush* to guard the consulate.[16]

Thus far, the alarm seems to have been mainly among the inhabitants; the authorities, although they issued arms to European civilians and set up barricades and blockhouses in the surrounding areas, professed to make light of the threat; but by mid-October, outgoing telegrams indicated that the position had deteriorated, with exchanges of fire and sporadic looting occurring in the outskirts. Cecil Rhodes arrived, en route for Beira, and offered to use his influence to persuade the chiefs not to attack—an offer which prompted the suspicion, apparently quite baseless, that he was behind the insurrection.[17] (It was also, even more implausibly, blamed on the Swiss missionaries, who had several stations in the area.)* The Portuguese called upon the services of several thousand Amatongan warriors from the area immediately south of Lourenço Marques, but they objected to the make of rifle they were offered and retired after doing a little looting on their own account. On October 14, some 1,500 insurgents attacked the town, causing "indescribable panic," but were driven off after an hour by the rifle and machine gun fire from the improvised defenses.[18] No further attacks were made, and by the end of the first week in November the barricades in the streets were removed and the town reverted to normal. With the arrival of troops from Angola and Lisbon, the resources of the defense were said to be "more than sufficient." Captain Campbell, of H.M.S. *Philomel,* who reported this to the British naval authorities, was disposed to dismiss the whole affair: "The whole scare seems to me to have been one of the greatest farces I have ever been witness to, and has probably been instigated by interested persons, British, colonial, or foreign." Kimberley, the Foreign Secretary, disagreed: "The naval authorities," he wrote, ". . . do not comprehend the situation."[19]

What Kimberley presumably meant was that the potential dangers in the situation at Lourenço Marques were not the less great because on a particular occasion they had failed to become actual. The weakness of Portuguese military authority there was no less palpable because the blacks had attacked in insufficient force; and this weakness afforded not merely the prospect of further attacks from them, but of interference from without. Imperial Germany, always ready for an excuse to show the flag, had ordered two warships to Lourenço Marques. Worse still, the Transvaal Republic had offered assistance to the Portuguese, and when this was declined, had offered to facilitate the recruitment of volunteers. An agitated Whitehall conjured up the specter of Surtees' Mr. Jorrocks—"Where I dines, I sleeps"—and wondered if such volunteers, once arrived in the town, could ever be made

* For the accusation against the missionaries, see Marquês de Lavradio, *Portugal em Africa depois de 1851* (Lisbon, 1936†), p. 206. Ennes, it should be noted, gives no countenance to it.

to leave. The Colonial Secretary, Lord Ripon, invoked the Convention of London, which, he claimed, prohibited the Boers from dispatching volunteers without the British government's permission, and was promptly told, not only by the Boers but by his own Acting High Commissioner in Cape Town, that he was in error—the Convention could not be held to apply to recruitment by a civilized state.[20] However, no volunteers were recruited, for the objection of the Portuguese Foreign Minister was as strenuous as that of the British ally, and for identical reasons. The Portuguese minister in London (Soveral) should perhaps be allowed the last word on the incident, as reported by the French chargé d'affaires to Hanotaux: "The day the German newspapers began to make it known that their government would oppose the English intrigues at Delagoa Bay was the day on which alarming news ceased, as if by miracle—the blacks suddenly became peaceful. You would think that they read the *Cologne Gazette*!"[21]

The prime task before Ennes, therefore, was to reestablish Portuguese authority in the Lourenço Marques district. In one important respect, his hand was strengthened by an event that arose directly from the troubles: on November 21, Rhodes had met Soveral at the Foreign Office in London and had given categorical assurances that the Chartered Company and the Cape Colony were concerned to maintain the authority of Portugal in Africa, and the integrity of her colonial possessions there. He had gone further, and spontaneously offered to forgo the company's claims under its concession with Gungunhana, so far as Portuguese territory was concerned. In respect of the part of Gungunhana's country that fell within the British sphere, Rhodes would be prepared to pay the subsidy to the chief through the Portuguese government. Direct contact between Gungunhana and the company, which for the past two years had been maintained by its agent Longden, would therefore cease. When Soveral subsequently wrote to Rhodes that the Portuguese government was looking forward to a new era in their relations with the British South Africa Company, he was uttering no more than the strict truth. What Rhodes had done was to give the Portuguese a free hand in dealing with Gungunhana—though doubtless he was as surprised as anyone else to find out what they did with that free hand.[22]

There is not a shred of evidence to show that Gungunhana had any direct hand in the goings-on at Lourenço Marques. Indeed, consider-

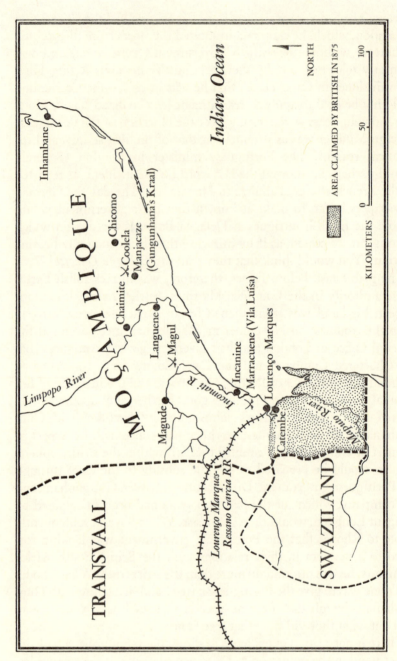

TRANSVAAL

MOÇAMBIQUE

Indian Ocean

Limpopo River

Inhambane

Chicomo
Coolela
✕Chaimite ●Manjacaze
(Gungunhana's Kraal)

Languene
✕Magul

Magude

Incomati R.

Incanine
Marracuene (Vila Luísa)
Lourenço Marques

*Lourenço Marques–
Resano Garcia RR*

Catembe

Maputo River

SWAZILAND

NORTH

AREA CLAIMED BY BRITISH IN 1875

0   50   100

KILOMETERS

Southern Moçambique, c. 1895

ing his formidable reputation, he was remarkably averse to overt acts of violence against white men: he had talked in mid-1892 of making war on the Portuguese, but had readily yielded to contrary advice, sent by the British through Smith-De La Cour (Bernal's predecessor as consul) together with a Portuguese promise of redress of grievances.[23] For that matter, the actual extent of his oppressive activities among the native population of Gazaland may well have been much less than one might suppose from the awe in which his name was held. Gungunhana, like a great many other rulers, had contrived to be taken at his own valuation by white and black alike; and he had hitherto been helped in this by his ability to play the British and Portuguese off against each other. But with the appearance of power went the odium that power excites, and any disturbance of the peace in Moçambique south of the Zambezi was bound to be laid at Gungunhana's door. If it became at any time evident that the legend of his invincibility was hollow, his position would be precarious.

Before the treaty of 1891, it had of necessity been Portuguese policy to keep on good terms with Gungunhana, and since 1886 they had maintained a "resident" at his kraal, to which, in addition, various envoys had gone from time to time. In his earlier report on Moçambique, written, of course, after the treaty, Ennes had flatly condemned this policy, holding that the resident was no more than a tool in the hands of the chief; and that his very presence served to deceive the Portuguese, by leading them to believe that they knew what was going on at the kraal. "I judge the services of a resident neither necessary, useful, nor becoming—at least at present." The resident had not, Ennes noted, been able to prevent the rifles from the *Countess of Carnarvon* from reaching Gungunhana: he had, indeed, handed them over to him. Any influence a resident might exercise over the chief had been more than counterbalanced by the influence of the chief on the resident:

Anyone reading the official correspondence of the *intendencia* of Gaza would suppose that he was reading notes from Gungunhana's Foreign Minister to the Moçambique Government; he will find virtually nothing there except complaints, invocations of promises made and agreements entered into by Portugal, requests for presents, memoranda about the chief's rights to land and vassals, ... often accompanied by threats of war.[24]

In Ennes' view, supervision of Gungunhana's activities were better exercised by the military commandant of the Limpopo district—that is to say, at a respectable but convenient distance, rather than on the spot. His low opinion of the resident's usefulness may have been influenced to some extent by antipathy toward the most conspicuous and able to the officers who had held that post, José d'Almeida. Almeida had been secretary-general of the province of Moçambique at one time —hence, apparently, the fact, with which Ennes made derisive play, that Gungunhana referred to him as "the secretary"—and had returned to Africa in 1892 as secretary-general of the Companhia de Moçambique, which operated in the northern part of Gungunhana's nominal dominion. He had evidently gained considerable, if intermittent, influence over the chief—he had, for instance, persuaded him to store most of the Chartered Company's rifles and ammunition in a hut, instead of issuing them to his followers—and he was in consequence naturally inclined to what Ennes might have termed "appeasement."* Moreover, he had apparently criticized certain of Ennes' policies privately and publicly; and Ennes, as Leverson was to note a few years later, was hypersensitive.[25]

In 1893, Ennes had been inclined to think that the problem of Gungunhana was one that the government of the province could live with—that a policy of firm though friendly containment would serve to prevent him from becoming a serious nuisance. "For the rest, time will tell. Gungunhana may not live long and he has many sons." However, he returned to Moçambique convinced (presumably by the events of 1894) that Gungunhana ought to be broken, if it were possible. He was, therefore, all the more vexed to find that Almeida, acting on behalf of the Moçambique Company, had visited Gungunhana's kraal toward the end of 1893 and had concluded with him a modus vivendi by which, in effect, a kind of joint native administration was set up in the company's territory, under which Gungunhana was to receive half of the hut tax levied therein, and one-third of a tax to be levied on all native marriages involving polygamy. Gungunhana also had undertaken to furnish troops with which the natives of such areas as Barué, which had not yet been subdued, might be brought under the company's effective jurisdiction. Almeida was acknowl-

* The hut was subsequently destroyed by fire, along with its contents. Whether Almeida had arranged this, or whether it was an accident, remains uncertain.

edged to be intelligent as well as experienced; and he, better than any of his colleagues, knew Gungunhana—whom Ennes, incidentally, never dealt with face to face. Clearly, he made this agreement in the belief that it would be kept, inasmuch as it had been formally entered into in council (*banja*) before numerous witnesses. He and Gungunhana appear to have trusted each other, and this virtually disqualified Almeida from advising Ennes, who was disinclined to trust his own countrymen, much less a "savage."*

To Ennes, for whom Gungunhana was a sanguinary and capricious autocrat, Almeida's modus vivendi, presupposing as it did a system of native law and custom that imposed obligations on a chief no less than on his subjects, must have appeared to be not merely mistaken but unintelligible. He did not, indeed, seek to annul the agreement, but there had been some incidents in the company's territory suggesting that Gungunhana himself had thought better of it; and in February 1895, Ennes told Almeida that if this were true the agreement should be allowed to lapse. It had not, he pointed out, had the prior consent of the provincial government, and must therefore be considered to have been made ad referendum—an impracticable proceeding, "inasmuch as native potentates are not familiar with the casuistical legal habits of Europeans," and it would, therefore, be virtually impossible to repudiate an agreement once concluded.[26] Almeida was even then on his way to the kraal, principally to clear up the status of the agreement, but also to convey the official reply to certain requests Gungunhana had made. One of these was that the Portuguese should supply him with a thousand rifles similar to those sent him by the Chartered Company and subsequently lost or destroyed, in order that he might repay the company and so be relieved of his obligations under the concession granted to Aurel Schulz. The request was taken, rightly or wrongly, as not being in good faith, and was refused. The

---

* Two works are indispensable for the study of Ennes' dealings with Gungunhana: his own account, *A Guerra de Africa em 1895* (Lisbon, 1898), henceforward cited as Ennes II, and that published by friends of José d'Almeida and written by Trinidade Coelho—*Dezoito Annos em Africa* (Lisbon, 1898)—which reprints much of the contemporary correspondence verbatim. A second edition of *A Guerra de Africa* that appeared in Lisbon in 1945 contained some additional contemporary material; except for this material, however, I have preferred to cite the first edition for ease of cross reference with other works of the period. For the incident of the rifles, see *Dezoito Annos,* p. 388. For the modus vivendi, see *ibid.,* pp. 374–76, and Ennes II, p. 141.

company's sole concern, however, was with the agreement, and Almeida not unnaturally felt that, in view of Ennes' objections, there was now no reason why he should visit the kraal at their expense. Ennes was willing, indeed anxious, that Almeida should go, even at government expense, to deal with the other outstanding business, and he proposed that a fresh agreement be made by which Gungunhana, in return for a subsidy, would turn over the right of collecting hut tax to the company's agents exclusively. Almeida, however, thought that this solution, though it might be accepted, would be impracticable, since the company would encounter the same difficulties of collection that the government itself, though "infinitely more powerful," had encountered in the interior districts of Cape Delgado, Moçambique, and Angoche. He declined, therefore, to put it forward, adding dryly that he would "prefer to leave the glory of so important a service to someone else more competent in dealing with savages." He did agree, however, to carry out the other missions, inasmuch as the requests had been made to him in the first place.[27]

That Ennes should have been willing to allow a man he mistrusted (and who mistrusted him) to go to Gungunhana's kraal is explained by the paramount need to prevent the chief from taking the initiative. He himself was not yet ready for the decisive step that would mean peace or war, and felt it might be fatal if his hand were forced. Gungunhana had requested a visit from Almeida, and, if he failed to appear, might construe this as an act of hostility. Moreover, Ennes proposed to employ the commandant of the Limpopo district, Judice Biker, as a watchdog. Almeida, for his part, took the precaution of asking Ennes to supply him with an official interpreter whose competence and credentials could not thereafter be questioned. On March 4, his expedition, amounting to more than one hundred persons, set off from Inhambane, and reached the "residency" at Manguanhana, close by the kraal at Manjacaze, twelve days later. On March 20, a banja was solemnly held—significantly, at the residency and not at the kraal—at which the replies of the king of Portugal to Gungunhana's requests were duly read out. The proceedings were enlivened by an incident involving Gungunhana and Judice Biker, who had previously reported that the chief had told him that he had secret matters to discuss with Almeida. On being taxed with this in open council by Almeida, Gungunhana flatly denied it; and he maintained this denial in face of Biker's reassertion. Biker thereupon withdrew from the banja, to the chief's manifest surprise—"How can the king's man," he is reported to have asked, "leave the council while the king's justice is being done?"—and refused to have any further dealings with him. Biker furthermore asked Almeida, who had been intending to return to Inhambane immediately after the banja, to remain in charge at the residency, since Gungunhana had made it impossible for him to do so.[28] Ennes, when he heard the news at the beginning of April, evidently thought Biker had fallen into a trap set by Almeida: "I know how to applaud a well-organized coup, even when directed against myself, and this one was masterly!"[29] But he resolved to connive at the irregularity of Almeida's appointment, since he had no one with whom to replace him—certainly no one so competent at keeping Gungunhana quiet, nor having so much interest in doing so.

III

As yet, Ennes was not committed to attacking Gungunhana; but the task of restoring Portuguese authority in the terras da corôa had gone surprisingly well in the first three months of 1895, and so had confirmed Ennes' view that the larger undertaking was not nearly so formidable as those who thought in terms of the *impis* (regiments) supposedly at Gungunhana's call were inclined to maintain. In particular, it had become evident that even in the immediate environs of Lourenço Marques the chiefs were incapable of making common cause against the Portuguese. On January 7, a few days before Ennes' arrival there, close to three thousand insurgents had attacked a point on the railway line two kilometers from the town, killing two European foremen and some seventy native women who were harvesting crops. These women belonged to the Matolla tribe, and some were said to be the chief's own concubines. The chief, who had hitherto been neutral, thereupon joined with a neighbor who had hitherto been hostile, and offered armed assistance to the authorities in their pursuit of the rebels. Ennes accepted this offer, and it was decided to make a demonstration in force against Marracuene, some twenty miles north of Lourenço Marques, in the midst of the disaffected area. Marracuene was chosen partly on political grounds, but mainly because it was on the right bank of the Incomati estuary—which afforded the Portuguese the possibility of maintaining communications by sea rather than through the bush, which in 1895 extended right up to the houses of Lorenço Marques itself. "At two paces from the capital," wrote Ennes, "the country is the same as it is two, or two hundred, kilometers away: a country of savages. The only difference is, perhaps, that its inhabitants know more vices—and also more Portuguese words."[30]

To say that sea communications with a force occupying Marracuene were possible is not to say that they were easy. In the first place, Ennes had no naval vessels, strictly speaking, that were suitable for the purpose. There was one coasting steamer, the *Neves Ferreira,* bought secondhand in Natal, which was in poor condition, and which drew so much water (eleven feet) that she could only get over the Incomati bar at the fortnightly spring tides. There was a secondhand steam launch, the *Bacamarte,* which was armed with a machine gun and provided with some improvised protection for the crew of four. On her very first trip to the Incomati, her commander was killed by a shot fired from the mangroves on its banks; but thereafter, though often hit by bullets, she performed invaluable service.* A third launch, the *Xefina,* was awaiting new boilers from England and could not be relied on in the meantime. These three lame ducks constituted the "Incomati squadron," which operated in support of the advance on land.

A mixed column of white and Angolan troops, totaling some 700 in all, set out from Lourenço Marques on the morning of January 28, and reached Marracuene the following afternoon without incident. Naval support arrived shortly afterward; the native auxiliaries that had been promised, however, did not appear. Six hours after the march began, the weather, which throughout January had been dry, broke —and torrential rain fell thereafter without stint. At Marracuene, the already sodden troops were forced to bivouac in the open, and it was clear that, whatever the enemy might do, they would have to retire on Lourenço Marques if the weather did not improve, and that their retreat might well be perilous. Ennes himself at this time regarded

---

* Not all the bullets came from tribesmen: there was a native trader, known by the English nickname "Finish," who lived at the mouth of the Incomati and had instructed his adherents to fire on ships entering the river. It was they, so it was thought, who had killed the *Bacamarte*'s commander; but their activities were more akin to highway robbery than to rebellion.

the expedition as a dead loss, and was thinking (he tells us) only of how to mitigate the consequences. "Seeing it rain as I never supposed it could rain, I thought that only amphibians could live for days and nights in such a deluge, and that there could be no cohesion, no discipline, no habits of obedience, no sense of pride, that would not be dissolved, extinguished, chilled, by so much water."[31] Communication with Marracuene was maintained only by the *Bacamarte,* for the *Xefina* had broken down as expected, and the *Neves Ferreira* was shut up in the Incomati river. Moreover, the troops' rations were thought to be running out, and there was no means of sending more.

In point of fact, things at Marracuene had not been going at all badly, in spite of the rain: improvised shelters had been constructed and rations supplemented by raids on the deserted native habitations in the neighborhood. On February 1, the rain stopped: Caldas Xavier, nominally the second in command but in effect the leader, made plans to cross the Incomati in search of the enemy as soon as naval support should be available. Early the following morning, when the troops were already alerted, the bivouac, which was in the customary form of a hollow square, was attacked by the vanguard of a force of some two thousand natives armed with rifles and assegais. The side of the square manned by Angolan troops was actually breached, but the white officers succeeded in rallying and reforming them, and the remainder stood firm. "The terrible fire of the Kropatschek [rifle] did the rest, and by six in the morning the enemy was in flight."* The losses of the defenders were all but negligible. But the rain returned next day, and with it disappeared all hope of advancing further. On February 5, Caldas Xavier, now nominally as well as actually in command, retired, on Ennes' instructions, burning villages as he went; next day, his force entered Lourenço Marques, muddy, soaked, fever-ridden, exhausted, but triumphant: "Remember," he had told them, "that you will be seen by foreigners!"[32]

In terms of scale, Marracuene was little more than a skirmish; yet it must rank as a decisive battle in the history of Moçambique. Its im-

---

* A firsthand account of the skirmish at Marracuene is given by Ayres d'Ornellas in "Combate de Marracuene," reprinted in Aires de Ornelas, *Colectânea das Suas Principais Obras Militares e Coloniais* (Lisbon, 1934†), Vol. II, pp. 7–28, and also in a letter to his mother, dated February 8, 1895 (*ibid.,* Vol. I, pp. 84–92). The quotation cited here is from p. 88. Compare with Ennes II, pp. 92–99.

mediate results were not negligible, for the native auxiliaries had, after all, been in the neighborhood, apparently waiting on events, and had taken advantage of the outcome to avenge Chief Segaul's concubines many times over. Even so, the physical losses suffered by the insurgents were probably less important than their loss of face, at the hands not only of the white men but of rival tribes. The Portuguese, for their part, had demonstrated that they were not "hens," to be dispersed merely by the cries of the enemy. The complete pacification of the terras da corôa had indeed to await an improvement in the weather, and the resting and refreshment of the troops, but it was already secured. Early in March, two islands commanding the mouth of the Incomati were occupied, and later Marracuene. In May, army engineers under Freire de Andrade completed a bridge of boats higher up the river, at Incanine, enabling a punitive expedition to reach and destroy the centers of insurgent activity (including that of "Finish") on the left bank as far as the mouth. The way was thus open for a push into Gungunhana's territory.[33]

A short account of successful military operations inevitably makes them seem easier of accomplishment than they actually were. Ennes had as yet no cause to be confident that he could launch the major campaign, let alone bring it to a successful outcome. Climate and disease were, for both men and horses, more formidable and persistent enemies than the hosts of Gungunhana. Supplies of many kinds were short in quantity or deficient in quality, and called for improvisation on all sides: the anchors for Freire de Andrade's bridge of boats, for instance, were taken from disused torpedo boats lying at Lourenço Marques. Ayres d'Ornellas, Ennes' aide-de-camp, had to be sent off, as the only cavalry officer with a command of English, to buy remounts in Natal. Ennes' personal position was in some respects equivocal. As Royal Commissioner, he was commander-in-chief; but as a civilian he was bound to rely heavily on his military advisers, and the staff officers detailed for this purpose were apt to proffer advice that to him smacked too much of the military academy. Of the competence of Eduardo da Costa and Ayres d'Ornellas there was indeed no doubt; but they lacked African experience, and therefore, the confidence to improvise campaigns at short notice. The Marracuene expedition, in the preparation of which, as Ayres d'Ornellas observed, they were asked to do in six days what had not been done in the previous two and a half months, had been mainly planned, therefore, by Caldas Xavier, a supernumerary regimental officer with African experience; and it was on similar officers, like Paiva Couceiro and his aide of long standing, Freire de Andrade, that Ennes preferred to rely for advice. His plan for the campaign against Gungunhana, submitted informally to the Minister of Marine and Colonies in April, was drafted, not by the staff officers, both of whom were away on mission, but by Couceiro.[34] Costa, the senior of the two, seems not to have resented the fact, but Ornellas' references to Ennes thereafter, especially in private correspondence, took on a decidedly critical tinge.[35]

These personal frictions did not diminish as time went on. At the end of March, Ennes, writing to his wife, referred to the "*má vontade*" (unwillingness to cooperate) of many people, especially officers."[36] Three months later he told his favorite daughter, Luísa, that he was utterly weary in spirit and his patience was exhausted; that he had to content with everything and everyone; and that Lisbon failed to appreciate his services and sacrifices:

When I get out of here I shall finish completely with public life. I don't want to be anybody in a nation that is in decomposition! . . . Only yesterday I discovered a piece of infamy such, and of such extent, that it made me positively weep with shame and disgust. The whole thing is rotten . . . the few men who stand out from the mass . . . like Couceiro and Freire d'Andrade, are considered *crazy*. One cannot govern with such people. . . . If I suceeded in avoiding shame and disaster, I shall have performed a true miracle, such as to make one believe in Providence. . . .[37]

Ennes, the dramatist, excelled at dramatizing himself: before leaving for Moçambique he had sworn before Queen Amélia that he would bring Gungunhana as a prisoner to the king's feet, or never return; he slept at this time with a revolver under the bolster and let it be known that he would commit suicide in case of defeat. (Couceiro, hearing of this, secretly removed the ammunition.)[38] An easygoing man, however, would have accomplished nothing in the Moçambique of 1895, or under a minister (Ferreira d'Almeida) who was so frankly skeptical of Portuguese imperial capacity that he had, at one time, proposed in the Côrtes that Moçambique and Goa be sold and the proceeds used to develop Angola. Moreover, informed opinion abroad, as well as a strong and vocal, if partisan, opinion in Portugal itself, still held that the conquest of Gungunhana was beyond the country's powers. MacDonell, the British minister in Lisbon, warned Portuguese ministers that an expedition against the chief would almost certainly entail disaster.[39] F. C. Selous, on being told by Ayres d'Ornellas the size of the force with which the Portuguese intended to invade Gaza ("... and I exaggerated," Ornellas adds), "made a highly significant grimace."[40] On Ennes, therefore, as on no other man concerned, rested the burden of potential failure; and the numbers of those on whom he felt able to rely—and who had confidence in him—diminished rather than increased as time went on.

Although from the very outset Ennes had been bent on nothing short of the capture of Gungunhana, he had been careful not to commit himself publicly to the attempt, and had even tendered his resignation on receiving, in June, a telegram from the home government to the effect that "anything less than the total annihilation of Gungunhana would not be in conformity with the heavy sacrifices that the nation had made."[41] His plan of campaign against the chief amounted, in fact, to a demonstration of force such as might persuade him to submit to effective Portuguese control without a fight, or, alternatively—and perhaps, in Ennes' mind, preferably—force him to give battle in circumstances where he could not hope to win. An essential part of the plan, in either case, would be to detach from allegiance to Gungunhana—an allegiance that for the most part rested on nothing but fear—as many of the petty chiefs as possible. The strategy would be offensive: two columns, one based on Lourenço Marques and the other on Inhambane, would converge on the kraal from the south and from the east. The tactics, on the other hand, would be defensive, as befitted forces greatly inferior in numbers but superior in armament: stockades, blockhouses, and barbed wire would be established on the line of march, and the column in movement would be so drawn up as to be able to form a defensive square at short notice. The objective, of course, would be kept from Gungunhana as long as possible.

During April and May, further reinforcements had arrived from Europe, together with a senior army officer—Colonel Rodrigues Galhardo—to take command of the army in the field, and the dashing cavalry captain Mousinho de Albuquerque. Mousinho had served in Africa before, having been governor of Lourenço Marques at the time of the *Countess of Carnarvon* incident; not so Galhardo, who, though competent and resolute, and always correct in his regulations with Ennes, was inclined to be a stickler for military rules and regulations. In mid-June, the southern column started off, partly overland and partly by river; by mid-July it had established a series of small bases along the great bend of the Incomati, and it had only to cross the river to move into territory considered tributary to Gungunhana. The northern column, with Galhardo himself in command, naturally took longer to organize, since all its supplies had first to be assembled at Inhambane, from which the column set out on July 5. Four weeks later, its main body was established at Chicomo, about eighty miles from the starting point, and twenty-five miles from Gungunhana's kraal. It had met with no opposition, but there was already much disease among the troops—by August 7, a hundred and twenty (or a seventh of the total) were reported sick, while the cavalry arm was all but incapacitated by horse-sickness. There was a risk that the whole enterprise would fall victim to the climate before battle could be joined.*

Meanwhile, specific negotiations had begun with Gungunhana for, inter alia, the surrender of the two leaders of the insurrection in the terras da corôa who had placed themselves under his protection. In the last week of May, Almeida had left the kraal and returned via Inhambane to Lourenço Marques; the chief, he reported, was fearful of war, and he brought with him two indunas, who asked the Portuguese not to start hostilities. Ennes, of course, was little disposed to trust either Gungunhana or his informant, but saw that he might be able to enforce sincerity on the chief's peaceful professions: "While the negotiations were in train, the troops would be on the march."[42] He therefore refused to see the indunas or to receive their gifts, inasmuch as their master was conniving at rebellious acts. Instead, he drew up a series of stiff conditions upon which he would accept Gungunhana's submission, and he prevailed upon a reluctant Almeida to return to the kraal—this time accompanied by Ayres d'Ornellas—to place them before the chief. The departure of the envoys was delayed because Almeida was ill with fever, but they finally left Inhambane on July 15.[43]

In a lengthy and extremely revealing passage in his war memoirs,

---

* A short account of the whole campaign, evidently based on Ennes' account, is in Teixeira Botelho, *História Militar (1833–   )*, pp. 469–96.

published in 1898, Ennes explains his motives for using as his agent a man whom he did not trust and who did not trust him. He likens Almeida to a lion tamer, whose value depends on the lion's being neither too weak to render him unnecessary, nor too strong to be under his control. Thus, Ennes argues, Almeida was bound to put peace with Gungunhana above all else, but there was no danger that he would encourage him to resist Portuguese demands: "If patriotism did not forbid this course, self-interest would." In any case, the position would be secured by the military preparations already in train. Ayres d'Ornellas was sent with Almeida "not to spy upon him, not to hinder him, but to ensure that the army had voice and ears."[44] The impropriety of this whole passage can only be fully savored in the light of Almeida's long and unblemished colonial record, dating back to 1878. His friends, in a lengthy and closely documented rebuttal, were able to show that at no time after 1891, when he resigned his post in Gaza, had he evinced any desire to return to the kraal; he had done so only at the earnest request, first of the Companhia de Moçambique, and then of Ennes himself.[45] If it be replied that one cannot prove a negative from documents, one must rejoin that any public servant is entitled to the benefit of the doubt. On his own showing, Ennes' treatment of Almeida, however patriotic its motives, was completely without scruple: it goes far to show why he came to be distrusted by subordinates like Ayres d'Ornellas and Mousinho de Albuquerque (though Mousinho distrusted Almeida even more, at the time).[46] Almeida, indeed, knew how to take care of himself: he arranged, for instance, that Ornellas draft all the correspondence relating to their joint mission. But he also—which was not easy—won Ornellas' confidence and respect: "Almeida," wrote Ornellas to his mother on August 14," is the *only* Portuguese who has been able to contrive that he [Gungunhana] always pays the first call on him; he is naturally, therefore, one of the colonial officials of whom the others speak ill and on whom Marianno [de Carvalho] has made so many attacks; but of all those known to me, he has the most good sense and the most knowledge of affairs here [at the kraal]."

In the same letter, Ornellas described the banja at which Ennes' ultimatum was discussed:

From the beginning, one great difficulty confronted us: that of convincing Gungunhana that submission to our demands would free him from war. "If there are so many troops sitting on my frontiers, it is not simply so that you can tell me this. If I had already said no, their presence would be understandable." It would take too long to set out the arguments on one side or the other in three *banjas,* each lasting about four hours. I will only say that I admired the man, holding forth for that length of time in lucid and logical terms.*

The difficulty was all the greater because Couceiro, on July 17, had stretched his instructions and—without opposition—had occupied Magude, on the left bank of the Incomati, within what Gungunhana considered his rightful dominion. This was contrary to an undertaking Ennes had given Almeida, but he did not see fit to order one of his few trusted subordinates to retire.[47] In the end, it was the natural dislike of the chief for negotiating under duress that provoked a breach. Gungunhana professed willingness to accept all of Ennes' terms, and he offered two of his indunas as hostages against the capture of the two rebel chiefs, along with £1000 in gold and three large tusks of ivory, on condition that the mass of Portuguese troops were withdrawn. Both Ornellas and Almeida felt that this was the most that could be obtained; Ennes, on the other hand, felt that Almeida was now speaking through the mouth of Gungunhana, and was responsible for his doubts of Portuguese good faith. Ornellas, who had protested to Ennes as early as July 30 that he did not wish to be the party to deceiving "even a black," later wrote that "Ennes, naturally, destined the negotiations to fail, so that Almeida should not have the glory of winding up the question." This may oversimplify Ennes' motives, but he was certainly reluctant then to give his envoys time in which to succeed: they did not arrive at the kraal until August 8, and already a week's deadline had been set for "decisive news" to be received in Lourenço Marques, which was four days away by runner and telegraph.[48]

The reason for this, as Ennes frankly explained, was that the southern column was getting restive, and was anxious to make a move against Matibejana, one of the two original rebel chiefs, who had recently returned from Gaza to the farther side of the Incomati. His return gave cause for suspicion that Gungunhana's willingness to treat was insincere. On learning that the negotiations had been held up by court mourning for one of the chief's relatives, Ennes did give Almeida permission, on August 14, to remain at the kraal; but two days

---

* Ornellas, letter, August 14, 1895, in Ornelas, *Colectânea*, Vol. I, pp. 135, 137. Presumably, "the man" denotes Almeida, but Gungunhana may have been meant.

later he changed his mind and ordered the mission to withdraw immediately.[49] At this point, Gungunhana disclosed his hand: if the king of Portugal did not want him as a subject, he would seek the protection of other white men. Three of his indunas had, in fact, presented themselves to the resident commissioner at Eshowe (Zululand) on July 16, carrying a tusk as a present for Queen Victoria. Consul Bernal had warned Gungunhana, through the chief's adviser Fels, that the British authorities would not accept tribute, but the warning had not been heeded and the inevitable rebuff followed. The indunas endeavored to take ship from Cape Town to England, but instead were sent back home by sea, Lisbon having granted them a safe conduct. They passed through Lourenço Marques on September 26, so that it could have been only at the beginning of October that Gungunhana knew definitely that all hope of playing one set of white men off against the other had gone. His adversary, of course, had known this from the beginning, but Almeida and Ornellas evidently did not.[50]

Meanwhile, the military situation had moved in favor of the Portuguese. A detachment from the southern column, led by Freire de Andrade and Couceiro, and accompanied by a sizeable force of native auxiliaries, crossed the Incomati on August 30 and marched on Magul, headquarters of the rebel Matibejana. There it encountered a force of natives, and a parley ensued in which the enemy were granted three days to surrender the chief. Freire de Andrade used this space to summon reinforcements from the advanced post at Magude, and when his terms were not complied with, set out again for Magul. There, on September 8, the column was attacked by a force estimated at 6,500 men, armed with rifles and assegais. As at Marracuene, superiority of armament and discipline were decisive: the attackers were unable to get to close quarters, where their superiority in numbers would have told. They fled in disorder, pursued by the auxiliaries with assegais. Five European soldiers were killed and twenty-six wounded. The column retired, exhausted, to base; but thereafter only mopping-up operations were required south of the Limpopo. They were assisted by two naval vessels that Ennes sent up the river. A small post was established at Languene, on the right bank, at the end of November 1895.*

* A firsthand account of the Magul campaign, by Paiva Couceiro, is reprinted, oddly enough, in Eduardo da Costa, *Colectânea das Suas Principais Obras Militares e Coloniais* (Lisbon, 1939†), Vol. II, pp. 27–102; discussion at pp. 35–36.

In the first weeks of September, Ennes had still not resolved on the next move on the northern front. Almeida and Ornellas had returned to Chicomo, the advanced base of the column, on August 26. But though only twenty-five miles separated Chicomo from the kraal at Manjacaze, Galhardo reported that, for want of transport and supplies, an immediate advance was out of the question. Nor was this mere excess of caution on his part: Mousinho de Albuquerque, a very different type of officer, was no less discouraging. In a letter to Ennes he listed the difficulties: hatchets more suited to a butcher's shop than to cutting a way through the bush; lack of mules to haul the artillery; poor quality of cavalry mounts. It were better, he thought, to regroup forces and put off direct attack till next year. The best, he was saying, was the enemy of the good. "I looked at Mousinho's letter over and over again," wrote Ennes later. It placed on him, the civilian, the responsibility for giving orders to the military against their advice—of crying "Forward," when Mousinho, of all people, was crying "Back!" In conference with Galhardo, on September 1st, a compromise was reached. The idea of a march on the kraal was not yet given up; but plans were concerted for the alternative favored by Mousinho, in order to consolidate the occupation of Gungunhana's frontiers. Almeida, much against his will, was obliged to remain at Chicomo in case his services were needed again:

I asked Galhardo to tell him that I was convinced that he ... had suggested ... that the troops retire before the rebels were given up ... in order to frustrate the plan he attributed to me of attacking the chief after he had been weakened and humiliated by the conditions of submission; but that I hoped that he would see that his doubts of my good faith had been groundless, and that he would atone for the disservice he had done his country.[51]

Desultory exchanges of messages, in which Gungunhana continued to protest his peaceful intentions toward the Portuguese, and to promise the handing over of the rebel chiefs if only he could lay hands on them, continued during the first part of September. On the 13th, news of the victory of Magul reached Ennes at Inhambane, and he immediately decided that the time for negotiations with Gungunhana was past. If Galhardo could not march on the kraal immediately, he should at any rate begin raids into enemy territory. Ennes himself prepared to return to Lourenço Marques; but before he could sail, messages reached him from the governor there to the effect that rebel hordes had crossed the Sabi River, were on their way to attack the town, and were asking for reinforcements. The news appeared serious, but Ennes kept his head. Far from weakening the forces based on In-hambane, he urged Galhardo to attack from Chicomo. His judgment proved better than he could have hoped, for on reaching Lourenço Marques he found the panic over. It had been solely the result of rumors brought by friendly but frightened natives to a Portuguese outpost near the Sabi: rumors perhaps arising from the movements of the host defeated at Magul. Clearly, the general level of morale was even now not high.[52]

The northern column, moreover, was still bogged down at Chicomo for want of transport, particularly draft oxen for the Boer wagons. Galhardo's paper requirements for these were impossible to meet: only half of those ordered from Durban had so far arrived. The short-age of oxen for the troops' meat ration was no less serious. The num-ber of sick at one time reached 350; and the only consoling news was that Gungunhana's forces remained inactive, that they were said to be short of food, and that desertion was rife among them. But the rainy season—to say nothing of the cashew season—was now ap-proaching, and before long there would be no choice but to advance from Chicomo or to retreat on Inhambane. There Ennes and his new district governor, Macedo e Couto, worked incessantly to procure oxen, arms, and ammunition, and native carriers with which to get the force on the move. At the same time, Ennes took a long, searching look at the stated transport requirements for the column, and found clear evidence of over-insurance: in rations, in ammunition (it was proposed to take ten times the amount of cartridges used at Magul and Marracuene together), and in miscellaneous baggage (upward of 200 pounds for every officer). He appealed to Galhardo in the name of patriotism to delay his march no longer, but still (as Ornellas acidly and perhaps rather unfairly noted) refrained from giving him orders to do so.[53] Some weeks earlier, Ennes had told his daughter that the column was doing nothing on account of the incapacity of its com-mander, and that Freire de Andrade and Couceiro were "fed up." (They were indeed: the one wrote to the other at this time that he wished Ennes would transfer the command to Caldas Xavier and send them up there to get things moving.) At length, on October 31, Ennes definitely ordered Galhardo to proceed immediately.[54]

Accordingly, the column set out from Chicomo on November 4. It made slow progress, being limited by the pulling power and endurance of the draft oxen on a mainly sandy terrain under tropical sun; on the third day out, it could cover only about four miles and was forced to halt at Coolela, about that much short of its destination. Opposition there had been none, and Galhardo proposed to cover the remaining distance to Manjacaze without the baggage train. Next morning, November 7, when the force was drawn up ready to start, it was attacked by Gungunhana's army, estimated at eight to ten thousand strong. The experience of Magul—"What it is to have discipline and armament!"—was repeated: "It is not possible," wrote Ornellas, "to break a square armed with Kropatschek [rifles] and mountain guns at the corners." In forty minutes, all was over and the enemy in flight.[55] Galhardo, however, did not march at once on Manjacaze: his reason was that the lives of his wounded might be endangered if they had to be moved. (It is characteristic of Ennes that he should find this explanation inadequate, and that he should say so.) Four days later, sustained by the arrival of fresh food supplies fetched from Chicomo, the whole column set off for the kraal, which it reached the same day and found recently deserted: Gungunhana had waited for the sound of artillery close by before leaving.*

The battle of Coolela represented the denouement of Ennes' real-life play: for Gungunhana there remained only a pathetic epilogue. The task of hunting him down was entrusted by Ennes (who set sail for Portugal in mid-December) to Mousinho de Albuquerque, who was appointed governor of a military district established ad hoc (Gaza) so that he might be free from bureaucratic constraints. Mousinho's headquarters were fixed at Languene on the Limpopo, the site of the advanced base just established by the southern column. When he arrived there on December 16, he found that Lieutenant Sanches de Miranda, in command of the post, had what appeared to be recent and reliable news of Gungunhana's whereabouts. Moreover, on December 13, Matibejana, one of the original two rebel chiefs, had surrendered himself to Miranda on Gungunhana's instructions. Mousinho acted immediately. He endeavored to raise a sufficient force of

---

* Ennes II, pp. 524–28, 531. Among the effects abandoned by the chief was "a large box almost full of bottles of [Eno's] fruit salts."

cavalry for a raid, but none were forthcoming: the unit still at Chicomo was suffering from fever and shortage of rations. Rather than give the chief respite, Mousinho determined to use infantry. With some fifty white troops from the Languene garrison and a force of auxiliaries that increased, en route, to as many as two thousand, he crossed the Limpopo and marched toward Chaimite, where Gungunhana was reported to be. Undeterred by messengers from the chief bearing presents and promising peace, Mousinho pressed on, and on the third morning of the march reached the kraal. Leaving the auxiliaries to surround it, the small force of white troops entered, whereupon Gungunhana surrendered without offering any resistance. Two of his indunas, indicated by him as anti-Portuguese, were summarily shot; he himself was humiliated by being made to sit on the ground before his followers. With a few chosen companions, the fallen "Lion of Gaza" was marched to the Limpopo, and then shipped on board a gunboat to Lourenço Marques, where he arrived on January 4, 1896. En route, he must have passed another vessel—none other than the *Countess of Carnarvon*—carrying categorical orders to Mousinho that he was on no account to attempt to capture Gungunhana.[56]

The exploit of Chaimite turned Mousinho into a national hero overnight. It is no reflection on his memory—for no man is obliged to be more heroic than the occasion warrants—to say that, for all its boldness and resolution, the feat lacked heroic stature: the element of risk was insufficient. At Coolela, where his horse was killed under him, Mousinho had been exposed to danger far more evident and imminent, though in circumstances making less appeal to the public imagination. He earned his rewards—promotion honoris causa to the rank of major, appointment as Governor-General and, later, Royal Commissioner—for a piece of successful exorcism: for ridding Portugal of an incubus that had become a national obsession. By ironical chance, the political effect of Chaimite was to be enhanced, at any rate in Portugal, through its coincidence with the humiliation (by the fiasco of the Jameson Raid) of Cecil Rhodes—an adversary far more fearsome than Gungunhana. MacDonell noted the influence of the combination of the two events in a dispatch of February 25, 1896:

The stock approach leveled at this Government by the Opposition and Republican press is that they follow subserviently in the footsteps of England. Though they themselves make no public attempt to deny the charge, and lose no opportunity to assure me in private that such is in fact their policy, the unconscious bent of their mind appears to me at present to lie in the following direction, viz., first, an exaggerated idea of the predominant part which their late success in ridding themselves of Gungunhana will henceforth authorize them to play; secondly, a conviction that, by the discomfiture of the Chartered Company ... they have recovered their freedom to devote whole attention to the development of their African possessions. . . .

These, and other considerations of the same kind, would seem to have combined to create in their minds the general impression that no immediate necessity remains for courting the good offices of England, and that the study of her interests in colonial matters may now be safely subordinated to that of the wishes of other and rival nations whom it may be politic to humor.[57]

MacDonell was referring mainly, of course, to Imperial Germany, which had caused some embarrassment at the time of the Jameson Raid not only because of the notorious telegram of congratulation sent by the Kaiser to Kruger but also because of the request that German sailors be allowed to land at Lourenço Marques en route for Pretoria "to defend German interests."[58] It was believed that only the prompt defeat of Jameson had prevented this request from being pressed.

MacDonell's analysis does more, perhaps, to explain British policy over Moçambique—obsessed as it had become by thoughts of sinister combination between Germany and the Transvaal—than it does to explain the Portuguese attitude. What the events of 1895 had done was to restore their military self-respect—quite justifiably, inasmuch as, for all the small scale of the operations against Gungunhana, they represented a level of professional competence that had probably not been attained in Portugal since the time of Beresford. True, this competence would have gone for little but for the driving force of one whom a political opponent once dubbed "Africanus without being Scipio." Mousinho himself was singularly ungrateful when he alluded to Ennes scornfully as "one who . . . attains the rank of general without enlisting." For if it was Chaimite that alone gave credence to the reports of Magul and Coolela, even in Portugal, it was Magul and Coolela that made Chaimite possible.[59] Ennes gave Mousinho his opportunity for glory, even though Mousinho, in taking it, vindicated Ennes in the eyes of the skeptics. A high British officer, who knew Gaza at first hand, had warned Soveral that the Royal Commissioner "was either deceiving the government or was himself deceived: the

Vátuas could not have been defeated by 300 men at Magul or 600 at Coolela." After Chaimite, he apologized for his error, and added that the Portuguese victory was the most notable yet gained in Africa. Overestimation of native armies was common to professional soldiers at the time, perhaps as a result of the Zulu War: the Matabele were likewise overrated, and were quite readily overthrown by European amateurs armed with machine guns and magazine rifles. This profitable example, of which Ennes was fully aware, was not the least important help that the British gave him in his campaign; but there were others, such as the furnishing of remounts and oxen and the hire of ships, which were indispensable. Without the British colony of Natal as a supply base, an offensive against Gungunhana could not have been mounted.

The Portuguese campaign, then, was a triumph but not a miracle, though Ennes might be forgiven, considering the difficulties that he had had to overcome, if he regarded it as providential.[60] It would be in the highest degree anachronistic to regard it as a triumph of Europeans over "Africans"; in the long-standing tradition of Portuguese colonial policy, Ennes had exploited, to a much greater degree than the British against the Matabele, tribal and personal resentment against a hegemony based on fear. Even before Marracuene, some support from native auxiliaries had been proffered him, though it did not manifest itself until after the event; and thereafter, each victory added to his active sympathizers, till, at the end, Gungunhana's supporters were plainly outnumbered as well as outgunned. It is for his grasp of the inherent weakness of the chief's *political* position, as much as for his direction of the military side of the campaign, that Ennes must be given credit for being the organizer of victory. One may, indeed, legitimately doubt whether he could not have gained his ends by negotiation and pressure. Almeida and Ornellas felt that it was sheer willfulness to acquiesce in the occupation of Magude before negotiations had started, as well as to allow so little time for their completion. One must recall that they were withdrawn from the kraal before Gungunhana's envoys to Queen Victoria had at length returned from their fruitless errand and (as it appears) convinced him that if he fought the Portuguese, he fought alone.

Of course, if Ennes had not been successful, the charge that he forced war upon an adversary who wished for peace would have resounded through the opposition press in Lisbon. One of the useful results of Chaimite was that it silenced criticism. At first sight, it would seem unlikely that the war against Gungunhana was an imperative political necessity: as Ennes himself had written earlier, the chief represented a problem the provincial administration could live with, and it was more than likely that his realm would be fragmented on his death. On the other hand, it is understandable that, having assembled forces that seemed capable of dealing with the chief once and for all, and having, with great difficulty, got them within striking distance, Ennes should have been reluctant to settle for anything less than total victory: for if Gungunhana had later repudiated any agreement he entered into, the campaign against him would have had to start again virtually from scratch. Given the political climate of Portugal and the financial straits the country was in, there could be no assurance that a second chance would ever occur. In this respect, Ennes' position differed *toto caelo* from that of a contemporary British colonial governor with a punitive operation on his hands, who would know within reasonable limits what forces and supplies were at his disposal, and what his terms of reference were. The weakness of Portuguese colonial cadres, the necessity of improvising from the ground upward, and the uncertainty of financial suport, all precluded the kind of superior routine that, over the long run, constitutes good administration: they constituted a state of affairs in which the normal, run-of-the-mill official shrugs his shoulders and the exceptional one resorts to gambles and improvisations. The victories of 1895 were, in a sense, victories for routine on the battlefield; but the organization that lay behind them, though it owed something to military method, transcended mere method at all points. It was the work of dedicated men undertaking more than a strict assessment of official obligation would require. This is as true of Almeida, returning to the kraal when not fully recovered from fever, as of Mousinho at Chaimite, or of Ennes himself.[61]

When Ennes became Minister of Marine and Colonies in November 1890, Raphael Bordallo Pinheiro had marked the occasion with a sardonic cartoon for All Souls' Day, depicting a tomb: "Here lies the great journalist . . . defender of the national liberties."[62] Five years later, Ennes might claim the last word, for he had not only concluded a triumphant military campaign, but could write about it in vivid prose such as few men of action can command. It had, he claimed, cost incredibly little in men and money: one hundred or so lives lost in combat or from disease, and much less than two thousand contos (about half a million pounds sterling). Moreover, it had been fought with a want of material resources almost unprecedented in modern colonial warfare:

Today colonial wars, even more than wars in Europe, are carried on with materiel well-chosen . . . even luxurious, satisfying all requirements and minimizing inconveniences. The Portuguese of 1895, however, encamped and fought . . . with scanty materiel almost as primitive as that which their rude ancestors employed in the conquest of the Indies and the exploration of Africa in the fifteenth and sixteenth centuries.

Ennes goes on to list these conditions:

Transport, alike of food and of munitions, of ambulances and of wounded, was by means of wattle-and-mud carts drawn by slow-moving oxen; for tent or shelter, there was the starry sky, or a hut in the bush—or, if the ground were damp, one found a bed of branches, a stretcher, or a hammock; for carrying rations, the iron pots used by the Kaffirs, and in place of sanitary and comfortable mobile infirmaries, huts made of straw and banana leaves. . . . The very engineers had only crude mattocks . . . while as for the rations . . . their principal features, for soldiers subjected to temperatures in excess of fifty degrees centigrade, were the classic macaroni and chick-peas, seasoned with paprika! . . .

Nowadays, no one makes wars in this way except ourselves and, perhaps, the Spaniards.[63]

Ennes went on to compare officers like Couceiro and Mousinho to the paladins of the heroic age of Portuguese history. The comparison is not merely fanciful: the notion of anachronism seems alien to Portugal, where present and past are all of one piece.* Ayres d'Ornellas set store on his descent from a noble family, one of whose members was knighted for valor on the field of Aljubarrota (1385) by King João I.[64] Both he and Couceiro were to go into voluntary exile with King Manuel II in 1910, and were to lead vain attempts to restore the monarchy by force of arms. The ultimate fate of Gungunhana, too, might have been the same at any time within the last five hundred years: imprisoned with some companions in the fortress at Angra do Heroismo,

---

* Others have noted this: Frank Huggett, *South of Lisbon* (London, 1960), p. 110, says, "The steady progression of time in the northern sense just does not exist [in Portugal]."

in the Azores—the same that had held out for Maria da Gloria in 1828–29—he was baptized amid pomp in the cathedral by the local bishop, in April 1899, and thereafter went by the names Reinaldo Frederico Gungunhana.[65] He died at the fortress in December 1906; the last of his companions survived until 1927. They had been freed from close captivity after the first few years, and seem to have been on good terms with the local population. Ennes himself, for all his bourgeois origin and want of illusion about the existing state of public affairs, partook of the same chivalric spirit as his aristocratic subordinates and—like Oliveira Martins before his death—came to see in an enlightened monarch the only hope for Portugal.[66] Oliveira Martins' own writings, indeed, afforded little ground for supposing that a national savior would spring from the House of Bragança, even though it had received a powerful, indeed predominant, admixture of the blood of German princelings: such a belief can only be termed a rationalized form of sebastianismo, an earnest of political despair. In 1895 it was, nevertheless, something to sustain Ennes and his subordinates through times of discouragement: the personal interest of Queen Amélia in particular meant much to him.*

Certainly it could not be said that there was anything mercenary about the campaign of 1895. When Ennes wrote to his daughter, "All that I have done, all that I yet seek to do, is only for the honor of it. I have never thought of rewards, advantages, or plaudits: these things I count for nothing . . . ,"[67] he was not writing for a public, and the protest rings true, even though it recall the mocking phrase of Eça de Queiroz: " As for extracting profits, . . . neither the praetor nor the descendants of Alfonso de Albuquerque concern themselves with such sordid details."[68] That—a utilitarian might remark—was precisely what was the matter with Portuguese imperialism. It was all very well to say that the war with Gungunhana had cost a paltry two thousand contos, but her foreign bondholders, if not her taxpayers, might be pardoned for claiming that this was two thousand contos too much. Moreover, if the former were to gain the power of foreclosure over Portugal's colonial possessions, the triumphs of Ennes

* The letters of King Carlos I to the political leaders of his time—many, if not all of them, in the king's own hand—are engaging in their friendly informality and utter freedom from condescension.

and Mousinho would be barren. Jubilation in Lisbon over the defeat of Gungunhana and the humbling of Rhodes the Antichrist was thus not unalloyed with misgiving. The soldiers had exceeded all expectations in Africa, but the decisive battle for continued African dominion would be fought in the diplomatic quarters and money markets of London, Paris, and Berlin.

Chapter seven

Concessions and Concession Hunters

In November 1894, Graham Bower, the Imperial Secretary at Cape Town, reported to his chief, Loch, a casual conversation he had had in the street with the German consul-general about the disturbances at Lourenço Marques: "He said that there was a feeling in Germany that countries that could not pay their debts had no right to colonies. I said, 'We have never been disloyal to Portugal, and are not going to begin now.'"[1] The propriety of Bower's reply is evident, though it might have carried more conviction if the partition of Moçambique between Great Britain and Germany had not been currently under discussion in a section of the British press.[2] The German official line at that time, like that of the British, was in favor of preserving things as they were: not only political sovereignty, but the control of the port and railway of Lourenço Marques, should remain in Portuguese hands. But, as Dr. Kayzer of the German Foreign Office told the British chargé d'affaires in the course of a general discussion on colonial issues, sooner or later the question would arise of the inheritance of the Portuguese possessions in southeast Africa. Why, he asked, could not all these matters be settled by another Anglo-German agreement, on the model of that made by Salisbury in 1890? A few weeks earlier, Hatzfeldt, the German ambassador in London, had spoken in similar, if less explicit, terms to Kimberley, the Foreign Secretary.[3]

It is easy to dismiss these exchanges of view as self-interested and cynical. Certainly the disappearance of Portugal from Africa was something few British or German men of affairs would have shed other than crocodile tears over, and that many would have cheerfully helped to bring about. But it was equally, in the prevailing circumstances, something that a completely detached observer might reasonably have predicted, and that it was the duty of diplomacy, therefore, to provide against. Indeed, there were many in Portugal who doubted her ability to stay in Africa, even though few were prepared to follow Ferreira d'Almeida and advocate that she voluntarily give up some territory in order to retain the rest. One can, of course, attribute these doubts in part to an ingrained pessimism among Portuguese public men—not for nothing did Oliveira Martins and Soveral, among others, belong to a group styling itself *Vencidos da Vida* ("those defeated by life")—but the state of Portugal in the nineties would have made Dr. Pangloss himself less than sanguine.

I

The British ultimatum and its consequences, though wounding to national pride and damaging to the stability of the monarchy, did, at any rate, clear the air, disperse illusions of long standing, and lead to a definite territorial settlement. The economic and financial crisis that followed shortly upon the ultimatum appeared a far greater challenge to Portuguese statesmanship, since it could not be resolved by simply yielding to *force majeure,* nor was it brought about by mistakes of policy that could be set right without touching the administrative weakness that lay beneath. Indeed, it was precipitated by events outside the control of any Portuguese government: events that for an economy less precarious and more self-sustaining (to use a fashionable expression) than that of Portugal might have amounted to no more than temporary inconveniences. At first sight, it might seem surprising that a country predominantly composed of peasant proprietors should have been so vulnerable to external circumstance: in such a country one thinks of poor harvests rather than balance-of-payments difficulties as a cause of possible distress. There must indeed have been a great many Portuguese, probably a majority, who, by reason of poverty or economic isolation, did not feel the direct impact of the crisis any more than they shared substantially in the economic benefits conferred by fontismo. Their relation to the kind of economy represented by Lisbon and Oporto was, as it always had been, peripheral, like their relation to the Portuguese polity. But the fact that the crisis was, like the policy of which it constituted the nemesis, less than truly national in impact did not make it any less serious or less difficult of remedy for those involved.

If, as contemporaries conspicuously failed to do, one separates the essentials of the situation from the incidental errors and ineptitudes of government policy at the time, the crisis is seen to emerge from a failure to adapt economic and financial institutions—and, in the last analysis, social institutions also—to the requirements of a policy of economic growth. Fontes and his associates had been correct in thinking that the modernization of Portugal could not be undertaken without foreign loans. But successive governments over forty years had acted as if the mere securing of foreign loans were enough, and as if the rate at which they were secured and the use to which they were put were matters more or less indifferent. Between 1862 and 1884, for instance, 3 per cent bonds to the nominal value of £50 million were floated on the London market, for which the Portuguese treasury received less than £21 million—so that the actual rate of interest was, on the average, over 7 per cent.[4] From 1853 through 1860, the service of the consolidated debt absorbed three and a quarter thousand contos annually; from 1879 through 1890, it absorbed fourteen and three-quarter thousand contos. Government receipts, though rising, could not keep pace: the percentage of receipts devoted to debt service (excluding the short-term floating debt) almost doubled over the period, reaching nearly 45 per cent of the total. The very fact that budget deficits were the invariable rule from 1857 onward would indicate that they constituted, not a forecast of Keynesian economics-for-growth, but simple ineptitude. True, no less than 191,000 contos were officially stated to have been spent on public improvements during the forty years ending with 1890/91; but during the same period, over 526,000 contos were added to the national debt. The wonder is that the crash did not come earlier, for, as the young Fontes himself had written in 1852:

So long as there is a deficit, small or great, that constantly burdens the treasury, the country will inevitably move toward an abyss, from which it can only be saved by energetic and suitable measures; the worse the evil becomes, and the more delay there is in tackling it, the more difficult and ineffective [such measures are likely to be].[5]

The older Fontes had singularly failed to act on his own prophecy, and forty years later it was to be borne out in full measure. Two conditions were requisite if *fontismo* were not to lead to national bankruptcy: a more rigorous control of expenditure, and a reform of taxation. Both of these would necessarily have involved the Portuguese ruling class in an unwonted exhibition of self-abnegation: the former because it would have reduced the opportunities to eat at the public trough, and the political advantages to be gained by a judicious use of patronage; the latter because any sizeable increases in revenue could only have come from taxing the rich.* Even when, as in Fontes' case, a leader sought no monetary advantage for himself, the temptation to exploit for political ends the weakness of others was too strong to be resisted. In the hands of less scrupulous men like José Luciano de Castro, matters were worse: Augusto Fuschini, whose memoirs carry the stamp of honesty on their face, described Luciano's administration of 1886–90—the same that was brought to an abrupt end by the British ultimatum—as displaying the

ultimate degree of moral decadence, disorderly administration, and political cynicism. The acts of this administration in themselves explain the current crisis: they constitute, so to speak, a synthesis, over a short time, of the immoral acts, follies, and prodigalities with public funds perpetrated by previous governments in the long run.[6]

Fuschini was writing as one who—for a short time as Minister of Finance in 1893—had striven for radical reform and had found the political traditions of Portugal too strong for him. The picture he draws of the contemporary scene, in which faction and personal ambition reign supreme and principle goes for nothing, is depressing—though hardly more so than that conveyed by António Ennes. Perhaps both were too intolerant, like Adam Smith, of the craft and insidiousness that seems almost indispensable to success in politics. At any rate, the crisis of the nineties can be sufficiently accounted for in terms of the impact of external events on a situation that was chronically unstable, without bringing in the specific acts of extravagance, favoritism, inefficiency, and corruption of which Fuschini and other critics complained. Even though the José Luciano–Barros Gomes administration may have been—through its spending on African expeditions, for example—riding for a fall, it would have taken a miracle to save the country from a fall sooner or later. There were many, both in

* This was pointed out by a member of the British legation staff, Dudley E. Saurin, in a report to his government on the finances of Portugal, in January 1880 (B.B.P. [1880], Vol. LXXII, pp. 38–58).

Portugal and abroad, who recognized this. As a foreign banker once remarked to Fuschini: "With Portuguese bonds one eats well but sleeps badly; with English and French, one sleeps peacefully, and all but dies of hunger."[7] British investors apparently disliked insomnia, for in the years after 1885 they took advantage of a rise in Portuguese funds, brought about by their admission to the French and German money markets, to unload the greater part of holdings that had once constituted a monopoly in foreign lending. At the time of the arbitrary reduction of interest payments by Portugal in June 1892, British holdings of her 3 per cent consolidated funds amounted to but one-fifth of the total nominal value; French holdings amounted to three-fifths. As for amortizable bonds, half the total was held in France, a third in Germany, and only one-fortieth in Great Britain. Moreover, the British holdings (on the average) had been acquired at about 40 per cent of par value, compared with the 50 per cent at which they had been sold.[8] The relatively small amount at stake reinforced the Foreign Office's traditional policy of not intervening in support of British holders of foreign bonds, and it was the French and German governments who tried to put the screws on Portugal during the prolonged negotiations that preceded and followed the 1892 interest reduction, and that only reached settlement ten years later.

What actually set off the crisis was an economic collapse in South America during 1890, which affected both the Portuguese balance of payments and the current demands on the treasury. On the one hand, Brazilian remittances, which the previous year had amounted to almost one million sterling, fell to less than one-fifth of that sum; on the other, the great London financial house of Baring Brothers, which was heavily committed in Latin America, failed in November 1890, and its short-term advances to Portugal, amounting to £700,000, were called in.[9] Attempts to arrange fresh short-term credits on the London market failed: the Bank of Portugal was forced to use the gold reserves backing its notes in payment of outstanding commitments. On May 7, 1891, the bank was authorized to redeem its notes in silver instead of gold for a period of three months; on May 10, a sixty-day moratorium was decreed; and on July 9, the inconvertibility of the note issue was made permanent. Opportunity was taken at the same time to abolish the right of note issue belonging to a number of small banks in Oporto. The disturbance caused by these measures was considerable, the more so as the use of checks and bank credit was in its infancy, and the country's business was customarily transacted in British gold sovereigns, which were legal tender at the fixed rate of 4.5 milreis to the pound. During 1891, these either disappeared into hoards (as did the silver coins that were issued to replace them) or were exported: the net export of gold coins and bullion in that year amounted to nearly 26,000 contos (five and three-quarter million pounds), though Portugal, if only by reason of her foreign loans, had been accustomed to be a net importer of gold.[10] The authorities were somewhat slow to recognize that this withdrawal of metallic currency called for an increase in the note issue (and for the issue of notes in small denominations). While the total currency in existence just before the crisis may have amounted to 100,000 contos—of which 70,000 was in active circulation and the rest in bank reserves and deposits or private hoards—the fiduciary issue that replaced it was initially fixed at less than 20,000 contos, and only raised by stages to 54,000 contos (May 1892).[11]

One must suppose that the temptation to hoard inconvertible paper was considerably less than that to hoard precious metal, particularly in the circumstances of 1891, and that increased velocity of circulation would do something to make up for the sharp shrinkage in the quantity of money that accompanied the departure from the gold standard. Nevertheless, although the paper milreis promptly depreciated against sterling by some fifteen to twenty per cent, wholesale prices of goods entering into international trade *fell* in Portugal from 1891 to 1894 inclusive, roughly in accordance with world price trends at that time —and this despite the introduction of a new protective tariff in 1892. At the same time, the excess of imports over exports was reduced roughly *pro tanto* with the fall in the value of the milreis. Other economic indicators for the period show a marked improvement: from 1892 to 1896, for instance, passengers carried by rail increased from 5.7 million to 8.3 million (which would have delighted Fontes); shipping entering and leaving Portuguese ports increased from 13.1 to 17 million tons; employment of workers in manufacturing industry, though very small, rose by fifteen per cent, and the use of steam power was almost doubled; imports of raw materials and machinery rose by more than one-quarter. A comparatively recent writer refers to the period as constituting convalescence from the crisis of 1891, and to the policies pursued—notably the introduction of a protective tariff—as highly successful. One is all but called upon to believe that the crisis itself, by shaking the country out of its economic lethargy, was a blessing in disguise.[12]

That, however, is not how contemporaries saw it. Partly, perhaps, because the comforting statistical picture, under Portuguese conditions, only emerged several years after the events it portrayed; partly because the improving situation of the economy was not matched by a lessening of the financial difficulties of the government or a reduction in the gold premium that contributed to them; partly because a variety of proposals for radical reform, arising out of the crisis, made political shipwreck, so that the burden of recovery was seen to fall mainly on the poor—for all these reasons, the symptoms of convalescence went unnoticed and earned successive governments, deservedly or not, little political credit. The years 1890–1893 were, in any event, politically confused, for the temporary eclipse of the two great rotativist parties that followed on the British ultimatum had led to a kind of twilight period in which prime ministers were chosen largely on grounds of personal prestige, and cabinets were made up of men having varying or weak party affiliations. It was a period, also, in which the young king appeared to be taking a degree of initiative in the choice of ministers that went beyond the customary bounds of the prerogative. Changes of government were virtually annual events, and finance ministers averaged two a year. Continuity at the Ministry of Finance was restored only with the full return of party government at the end of 1893, when the regenerador Prime Minister, Hintze Ribeiro, got rid of the last of a series of would-be financial saviors and himself took over the post of Minister of Finance. That event was a sign that the impulse toward reform had spent itself, and that politicians might return with relief to the familiar routine.

II

At a time when the economic crisis seemed imminent, the non-party ministry headed by General João Chrysóstomo, which had taken office after the rejection of the first treaty with Great Britain, had revived the expedient, last used in 1844, of granting a monopoly of tobacco manufacture in return for a loan. A state *régie* had been established by the Luciano de Castro ministry a few years earlier (it was headed,

from 1889 to 1891, by none other than Oliveira Martins). Now it was
proposed to transfer the monopoly to a syndicate of Portuguese,
French, and German bankers, in return for floating a loan that should
be the first charge on its profits. A contract to this effect was signed
in February 1891; the nominal amount of the bond issue was to be
45,000 contos (10 million pounds sterling) at 4½ per cent, amortizable
over thirty-five years. But in the first place, the Portuguese group,
which was responsible for 30 per cent of the total, made it a condition of subscribing that the government should repurchase, at the
issue price, its holdings of a previous four per cent loan that the public
had failed to take up; and in the second place, the flotation, whether
in Portugal, France, or Germany, was a failure. By the time various
other conditions had been met and creditors satisfied, there was
virtually nothing to show for the loan, which had been granted on
humiliating terms: the Côrtes was to be called into special session to
give its approval, and any attempt at modification was to be forbidden on pain of being forced into bankruptcy. The terms were approved in March: but when Marianno de Carvalho became Minister
of Finance of the reconstructed government in May, he found (according to his own account) 15,000 contos in outstanding commitments
and only 600 contos of prospective loan income with which to meet
them. No Portuguese political leader was more familiar with the
realms of high finance than Marianno, unless it were his former rival
—now his colleague in the second Chrysóstomo ministry—Lopo Vaz
de Sampaio. But in the second half of 1891, all that was open to him
was a series of short-term expedients, such as borrowing privately
from Paris bankers to pay debts falling due. In January 1892, he was
forced from office, when his ministerial colleagues refused to endorse
certain advances he had made from public funds to the privately
owned Royal Portuguese Railway Company, then in financial difficulties. (He said he had been given to understand in Paris that a failure of the company to pay its dividends and foreign debts as they
fell due would be a fatal blow to the national credit.)[13]

The resignation of Marianno de Carvalho brought down the second
Chrysóstomo ministry, which was succeeded by a completely non-
party administration headed by José Dias Ferreira, an eminent jurisconsult who had been Minister of Finance for a short time in the early
seventies, and had been a persistent critic of successive ministries ever

since. King Carlos would have willingly done without Dias Ferreira, but he wanted above all to secure Oliveira Martins, whom he admired, as Minister of Finance, and Oliveira Martins refused to serve under the king's choice, the Conde de Valbom, on the grounds that the Marianno episode had discredited him (as a member of the retiring ministry).[14] Whereas his predecessor had sought, at any rate, an interim solution to the financial problem through jugglery and temporizing, Oliveiro Martins was convinced that absolute frankness coupled with rigorous retrenchment was essential, and that an agreement with Portugal's foreign creditors ought to be made promptly. "We must do penance for our past errors and resolve to sin no more!" he told a cynical Chamber. Dias Ferreira later remarked that Oliveira Martins "conducted business on his knees"—not the most effective posture for negotiations with one's banker. The discussions with the creditors were entrusted to the experienced Serpa Pimentel, but his bargaining position was weakened not merely by the finance minister's all-too-candid disclosures, but by the fact that prior parliamentary sanction had been secured for the negotiations, and thus they could not be represented as ad referendum.[15]

The bondholders, for their part, tried to strike too hard a bargain. They insisted that interest payments equal to at least half the nominal amounts due should be made weekly in gold to an agency of their choosing in Lisbon, and that these payments should be made a prior charge against Portugal's customs revenues. Serpa was prepared to recommend these terms, and Oliveira Martins to accept them; and an agreement to that effect was actually signed in Paris on May 25, 1892. But the terms were too much for Dias Ferreira, who by this time was anxious to be rid of Oliveira Martins anyhow. On May 27, he tendered the resignation of the whole Cabinet: "I have emerged from the minsterial sewer," wrote Oliveira Martins to Eça de Queiroz.[16] In the reconstructed government, Dias Ferreira became his own Minister of Finance. On June 7, it was decided to reject the agreement with the creditors and forgo the foreign loan that would have gone with it; on June 13, a decree was issued reducing interest payments on the foreign debt to a third of their nominal value. (Holders might convert into the internal debt, which was less harshly treated, but on which interest was paid in paper milreis.) Naturally, the bondholders were furious, and invoked the aid of their governments: Ribot, the

French Prime Minister, called for collective intervention by all the interested powers, and French commentators spoke of international control of Portuguese finances, on the model of Egypt. In Berlin, there was talk of taking over Moçambique by way of satisfaction. But Dias Ferreira was unmoved: to a German note containing a more or less veiled threat to withdraw the minister from Lisbon, he dispatched a laconic acknowledgment. "Is your government making fun of us?" remarked an indignant Baron Marschall to the Portuguese minister in Berlin.[17] Questions of tact apart—and the overweening behavior of certain German ministers to Lisbon was such that the temptation to take them down a peg must have at times been almost irresistible— Dias Ferreira may be said to have adjudged the situation shrewdly, for the imposition of foreign financial control on Portugal would only have been feasible with British agreement, and this was never forthcoming. The degree of June 13 constituted, of course, a declaration of national bankruptcy; but as this appeared inevitable anyway, there was much to be said for negotiating with creditors on the basis of a fait accompli.

Oliveira Martins' prescription for national salvation had included a sharp increase in direct taxes. Those on real property, on house rents, on industrial enterprises, and on income from government bonds, had been raised by amounts varying from ten to thirty per cent; and a special tax was levied on all government-paid salaries and pensions above 300 milreis annually—an expedient to be repeated by Dr. Salazar some forty years later. When Dias Ferreira came to draw up his own budget, early in 1893, he proposed to take the "war taxation"— as the public called it—a stage further, and to increase the already onerous excise duties on foodstuffs and other articles of common consumption. But his parliamentary position had been undermined by a general election the previous October, in which the regeneradores had secured a majority: one of the weaknesses of a non-party administration being management of elections. His proposals were defeated in committee; and when the king refused his request that the Côrtes be adjourned, he resigned (February 1893). He was succeeded by a predominantly regenerador ministry headed by Hintze Ribeiro, in which, however, the portfolio of finance went to another prospective savior, the independent Augusto Fuschini, who was Dias Ferreira's particular bête noire, and a trenchant critic of previous administrations. To Fuschini fell the task of dealing with the foreign creditors, who by this time were clamorous; and by what appears to have been skillful negotiation, he brought about an informal settlement, which was embodied in a decree of May 19. In effect, the terms of Dias Ferreira's decree were confirmed, subject to an arrangement by which the holders of the external debt took half of any increase in the customs revenues above a specified sum (11,400 contos) and half of any advantage that might accrue to the Portuguese treasury by reason of a reduction in the gold premium. The debt was to be administered by a board (the reconstituted Junta de Credito Publico) composed of five members, all Portuguese citizens, of whom two would be chosen by the bondholders.[18]

Having thus relieved the external pressure, the cabinet seems to have felt that it might relax its efforts. Fuschini had in view a series of radical administrative reforms that would have got rid of the deficit without hardship to the general body of taxpayers, by abolishing the inequities of assessment and the possibilities of evasion. The manner in which the tax on real property, in particular, was assessed and collected was a crying scandal. There was no land register, and hence no base for equitable assessment. Instead, the amount desired to be levied was apportioned among the twenty-one districts into which Portugal was divided, and thereafter assessed on individual proprietors by a combination of whim and political pressure—a system under which wealthy supporters of the government of the day were likely to come off best.[19] As a result, the tax combined the maximum oppression of individuals with the minimum yield to the exchequer. Fuschini estimated that the traditional ten per cent tax could be made to yield half as much again if a proper register were compiled, and that this task would take eight years. Preliminary steps were taken to set the work on foot. But parliamentary time was too short to admit the passage of Fuschini's complex and contentious tax proposals, and the Côrtes adjourned on July 15 without voting on the property tax reform or its corollary, the abolition of the ancient *réal d'agua,* a tax on food and other essentials of life which was expensive to collect and which was borne almost entirely by the poor. What an English observer had remarked over a decade earlier was now to be borne out: "Let the taxes fall equally on the rich as on the poor. Only for this it would need the iron hand of another Marquis de Pombal."[20] Opposition to each and every proposal of Fuschini had been fierce, and his colleagues were unwilling to support him. Before another session of the Côrtes came around, they had decided on a dissolution; and though it seems probable that the king would have liked to retain Fuschini's services, he was powerless to do so—to have refused a dissolution to Hintze would have been to deliver himself into the hands of José Luciano and the progressistas. On December 9, the dissolution was announced, and a few days later Fuschini resigned.[21] (Oliveira Martins' untimely death occurred a few months later.)

So the inertia of rotativismo reasserted itself, and the hope of a reforming monarchy which would beat the Republicans at their own game visibly faded. There was remarkably little to show, so far as internal politics was concerned, for the non-party interregnum that had now ended in anticlimax (the protective tariff of 1892 was per-haps the most important measure). New taxes, coupled with the re-duction in debt interest, had reduced the deficit almost—but not quite —to vanishing point in the year 1893/94; but even so, the reduction in debt charges had not been commensurate with the amount of in-terest of which the foreign bondholders were deprived, for the govern-ment had greatly increased its debt to the Bank of Portugal as con-sideration for increasing the fiduciary issue and abolishing the North-ern banks' right to issue notes. In 1889/90 this debt had amounted to 10,000 contos; by the end of 1892 it had reached well over three times that amount, and by 1898, five times. By way of collateral, the bank was given unissued 3 per cent domestic bonds of equivalent mar-ket (and of course much higher nominal) value, which, as Fuschini pointed out, it would have had difficulty in realizing in time of trou-ble.[22] (This may explain why a modern writer has stated that there was no recourse to credit operations in the years 1890–96 inclusive.)[23] Other net economies in expenditure had never been achieved; and in the years after 1893 budget deficits reasserted themselves, though never, at least in appearance, on the same scale as in the eighties and early nineties. What happened was that revenues and expenditures rose more or less *pari passu,* with the first always lagging behind the second: "The constant increase in receipts," wrote Roque da Costa in 1912, "has been the chief reason for an increasing [he should rather have said persisting] deficit."[24]

To contemporaries, of course, the very fact of deficit was reprehensible, and successive Ministers of Finance were at one in apologizing for it and promising amendment. There is no evidence, however, that the moderate deficits between 1895 and the fall of the monarchy in 1910 did any harm to the economy of Portugal. As Soares Branco, writing in 1950, puts it:

There was followed in the metropolitan country the system that some recommend for colonies: ... public expenditure was not restricted to the corresponding receipts; the deficits were paid out of floating debt that was subsequently converted by the issue of loans into consolidated debt; all these operations were taken up on the internal [bond] market, which also allowed the repatriation of a considerable part of the foreign debt.[25]

In effect, raising these loans was a substitute for taxing the wealthier classes, and had the same effect, *pro tanto,* on the economy. The recourse to credit was not, apparently, carried so far as to become inflationary: at no time between 1895 and 1914 did the trend of wholesale prices in Portugal diverge from that of world prices, despite fluctuations in the rate of exchange. Indices of economic activity showed an almost uninterrupted upward trend: the volume of rail and shipping traffics in 1914 was treble what it had been in 1891. "As for the much abused gold premium (*agio do ouro*), it was, in effect, a tax levied for the benefit of production upon all those with fixed incomes, helping our exports and making it easier for us to substitute home-produced articles for those we were formerly obliged to import."[26]

Looked at in this retrospective way, the economic policy of Portugal before 1914 appears exemplary, and the contemporary outcry against it due to nothing more than vulgar prejudice. If so, it was a prejudice fully shared by the very ministers who were criticized. For instance, Ressano Garcia, the *progressista* who became Minister of Finance in 1897, budgeted for a small paper surplus and promised reductions in expenditure; he professed hopes of reducing the floating debt to the Bank of Portugal, and hence the size of the fiduciary issue—which would have been tantamount to increasing the gold reserve and so reducing the gold premium. In 1898 he again budgeted for a surplus, but as it turned out, both 1897/98 and 1898/99 ended with substantial deficits.[27] The latter year, moreover, marked the lowest point to which the milreis fell in terms of sterling, and the highest yet reached by the note circulation. Ressano would doubtless have claimed that this was his misfortune rather than his fault: he was a professed disciple of Goschen, not an intentional forerunner of Keynes. The Bank of Portugal, for its part, protested against the increase in the permitted fiduciary issue to 72,000 contos, in 1898—and did so justifiably, in the opinion of Anselmo de Andrade, writing as much as twenty years later.[28]

It is easy to argue, in the light of what actually happened and of the economic doctrine now generally accepted, that the proponents of "sound finance" were mistaken, and that their policies would have been so deflationary as to hinder economic expansion. The point appears well taken; yet it by no means follows that a policy of allowing limited deficits ought to have been advocated or consciously pursued. Portuguese administration was incapable of the firm control and fine adjustments such a policy requires, as well as being innately biased toward deficit: this had been made abundantly clear before 1890. It was only by aiming at equilibrium that the deficit stood some chance of being kept within bounds; and only in retrospect does the economic history of this period look like the result of wise policy, unless one argues that the path of wisdom is identical with that of short-term expediency. To contemporary observers, and even to the Ministers of Finance themselves, the situation was one of perpetual embarrassment, of continual shifts aimed at satisfying the most pressing duns. If economic and financial calamity did not overtake the country, it was because Adam Smith's "invisible hand" is not altogether mythical— not because statesmen exhibited conspicuously superior wisdom. Apprehension of calamity was, however, the predominant political emotion in Portugal around the turn of the century: not only were the bailiffs lurking around the corner, but certain creditors seemed indecently anxious to use their services. The property on which it was desired to distrain was, of course, the African colonies, especially Moçambique.

III

The bankruptcy of the Portuguese state and its consequent exclusion from the international money market came just when its political need to raise funds for colonial development was greater than ever before; and this accounts for both the extent and character of the concession hunting that became rampant in Lisbon during the last decade of the nineteenth century, when, as MacDonell put it in a dispatch to his government, "the system took root . . . of granting concessions in Africa to any applicants, without inquiry into their substance or respectability," and the spectacle became common "of Portuguese Peers, Deputies, and members of the Royal Household hawking Concessions about the money markets of Europe, and joining hands with doubtful speculators to organize unblushing swindles."[29] This remark was occasioned by the scandalous history of the Nyassa Company, in which the Portuguese government had been constrained to intervene. In September 1891, a concession covering the district of Cabo Delgado, the northernmost area of Moçambique, had been granted to certain Portuguese citizens for the organization of a chartered company on the lines of the Moçambique Company.[30] The administration and economic exploitation of the district were to be turned over to the concessionaires, subject to the reservation of ultimate sovereign rights and certain rights of appointment (as of judges), and of certain powers of general regulation. The concessionaires bound themselves, inter alia, to build a railway from the coast inland to Lake Nyasa, and to establish not more than one thousand Portuguese families in the territory within five years—transport thither to be furnished by the government. In consideration of taxes forgone, the government was to receive seven and a half per cent of the company's annual profits, or the amount of the tax revenues for the year 1889/90, whichever was the greater.

As usual in such cases, the grant was conditional on the formation of a company and the deposit of caution money within a limited time, and it is no matter for surprise that the concessionaires found difficulty in raising the wind. Within months, the required deposit had to be reduced almost to one-fifth, from 10,000 pounds to 10,000 milreis, and a light Decauville railway substituted for the full-gauge one. Even so, it was not until the middle of 1893 that the Nyassa Company at length came into being, the period of its concession having, in the meantime, been extended from twenty-five to thirty-five years, beginning in September 1891. By that time the original concessionaire, Daupias, was described as "bankrupt"; but this, apparently, did not prevent him from serving as a director of the company. Among the other directors were a former Minister of Public Works; two peers who were members of the Queen-Dowager's household; Baron Merck, a Bavarian living in Lisbon and described as an insolvent banker and merchant; another bankrupt merchant named Mitchell;

and George Wilson of London, described as a concession broker of dubious reputation. Wilson, who appears to have been the leading spirit in the new company, was made managing director, in spite of his being a British subject and therefore ineligible for the position under the terms of the concession.[31]

It seems clear that directors of this calibre could at no time have had serious hopes of raising, unassisted, a million sterling (the authorized capital of the company) on the stock markets of Europe, nor could the prospects of the company have been plausibly represented as justifying an issue of that size. The financial difficulties of the promoters continued: even the bill of exchange that had been lodged with the government as caution money was dishonored. Meetings required by statute, whether of shareholders or directors, were apparently not held, nor was any proper office established in Lisbon. The business of the company appears to have been conducted principally by the London committee, which at first consisted of Wilson and Merck, and then of Wilson alone.* However, the chief preoccupation was the raising of capital, primarily to provide remuneration for the promoters; and on this score Wilson and some of the Portuguese directors fell out. The matter in dispute was whether control should pass to an English or a French syndicate. The majority of the Portuguese directors seem to have been inclined to the latter, on the grounds that the parties chiefly interested in the British firm—the Ibo Syndicate, Limited—were already mixed up with the Moçambique Company, and had a hand in various activities in Zambézia; and that French predominance in the district of Cape Delgado would neutralize both British pressure from the south and German pressure from

---

* One act for which Wilson—who appears throughout to have disregarded Portuguese company law—was responsible was the printing of unauthorized postage stamps, which were immediately unloaded on British philatelists through an exclusive arrangement with a stamp dealer in Salisbury. When the dealer found out, he protested to the Foreign Office, which declined to intervene. W. Brown, stamp dealer, to Foreign Office, March 20, 1895 (F.O. 63/1302).

Wilson was also alleged to have had coins minted without authority (by the Salisbury dealer). *Sobre Negocios da Companhia do Nyassa,* III (Lisbon, September 1895), pp. 7, 13–16. This was one of a series of pamphlets put out by the anti-Wilson group. From the papers printed therein it would appear that Merck ordered the money paid for the stamps in England to be refunded, and that the governor of the territory was alert enough to prevent either stamps or coins being put into circulation there.

the north. Wilson appears to have tried to play one side off against the other; and he finished by making incompatible contracts with both. By mid-1895, the split between the English and French parties was wide open: two offices, each claiming to be the one and only genuine center of the Nyassa Company, were open in Lisbon, and the government decided that the only course to pursue was to turn the whole matter over for criminal investigation. MacDonell, who was consulted, agreed with this course: the undertaking, he thought, had been tainted with fraud from the very beginning.[32]

Legal proceedings in Portugal, however, were and are leisurely. These were still stated to be pending in September 1896, when the Portuguese government caused a warning to prospective investors in the company's shares to be published abroad. In March 1897, presumably in face of impending danger, the rival groups in the company settled their differences: henceforward the controlling interest was to be British and, apparently, respectable. (Wilson had disappeared from the scene, and of the five members of the new London committee two were baronets and one a knight.)[33] No doubt this was a relief to the Portuguese government, which had never wanted to rescind a concession for which there were no other takers. But if the company could no longer be called fraudulent, it remained all but inert—"living," as Ayres d'Ornellas put it, "on the customs revenues of Ibo." No more than a beginning appears to have been made with the railway, or with the settlement scheme.[34] The scandal, however, had one important result: the law of Portugal was altered so that ratification by the Côrtes was indispensable before any concession could come into force. The claws of the concession hunters were drawn, though they—and still more the investors on whom they sought to prey—were slow to realize the fact.

The Moçambique Company, though more reputable than the Nyassa Company, could only be called active in its early years by comparison with the latter. The most onerous of its charter obligations, the construction of the railway to Umtali, had, of course, been turned over to the associates of Rhodes via the Van Laun concession. The requirement that a thousand Portuguese families be established on the land within five years remained a dead letter—not surprisingly, in view of the climate of Beira and its environs. To imperialists like Mousinho de

Albuquerque, the foreignness of the company was a rock of offense: not merely was most of the capital held abroad, but most of the managerial staff on the spot were French or British.[35] Ayres d'Ornellas wrote in August 1896 that the company's territory was Portuguese only in name:

> Until now, British subjects have been at the head of almost all the public departments, and it is perhaps for this reason that saints' days and Portuguese days of festivity are not observed in Beira.... The orders of the Company's administration are posted in English.... The very Negroes speak English, all the way to the frontier; the units of measurement—miles, feet, acres—are English; the landed property is English.*

Ornellas was inclined to blame the incumbent governor, Joaquim Machado, for subservience to the British; and it is true that Machado was later awarded a knighthood by the British government. But so was Mousinho de Albuquerque, who was subservient to nobody. Mousinho himself complained that the home government was too indulgent toward the company, particularly in the revised charter of 1897, which he, as Royal Commissioner in Moçambique, was not consulted about in advance, and first learned of from a newspaper. He objected especially to provisions whereby the cost of suppressing disorders in the company's territory fell upon the government:

> This article would make it advantageous for the Company to have a war in some part of its territory annually. The auxiliaries it raises are paid by the Government, and the Company furnishes rations for all the troops at Government expense. All this represents money spent in the territory, and might allow the Company to do a very profitable business.[36]

Mousinho held that direct administration could have achieved all that the Company had achieved, and more, but he added a proviso that some might think nullified the assertion: "It would be sufficient for this purpose to put aside the bureaucratic formalism, the narrow-mindedness and the centralization in Lisbon that have hitherto

---

* Ornelas, "O Caminho de Ferro de Beira..." (report, August 1896, *Colectânea,* Vol. II), p. 77. Unfortunately the "minute and truthful report... from which one will see how perilous is the administration of the Company, which in consequence is turning the region into a British possession," which Ornellas told his mother he had written (letter, September 6, 1896, *Colectânea,* Vol. I, pp. 232–33), was omitted from his collected writings.

brought to naught efforts made officially and under the direct aegis of Government." It seems at least possible that the administration in Beira was tolerably free from these vices, and yet achieved little on account of adverse circumstances. Certainly its pursuit of profit, like that of the rival concern across the Rhodesian border, was not conspicuously successful.[37]

The spheres of activity of the Moçambique and Nyassa Companies, like that of the Companhia da Zambézia (which did not enjoy semi-sovereign powers), were sufficiently far north to remove them, once the territorial settlement with the British was accomplished in 1891, from the forefront of the international scene. There were, however, other concessions in Moçambique, some of them economically unimportant or even abortive, which continued to be the subject of the liveliest speculation—diplomatic, financial, or both—for several years around the turn of the century. The basis of this speculation was the rivalry between the great powers in Africa and, more important, the enmity between the British and the Boer Republics, in which the Portuguese could not but be involved. It was an enmity that seems, on the part of many British politicians and officials, to have been almost pathological in character, considering the disparity in force between the two sides. That each should have disliked the other and that the Boers should resent British suzerainty and economic domination was natural in the light of past history. But running through many of the British dispatches and memoranda of the time is a kind of obsessive fear and suspicion of Boer motives that goes beyond reason. Some officials—notably Fairfield and Meade of the Colonial Office—were free from it: Meade, in a minute of August 1894, wrote its epitaph in advance:

Every nerve should be strained to prevent such a disgrace as another South African war. History would have a terrible tale to tell. We annexed the Transvaal, misgoverned it until the Boers took up arms and inflicted a crushing defeat upon us. We then gave up the country to them for a time till the influx of an English population enabled us to compass by intrigue what we had lost by political and military ineptitude. History will go on to show that we stirred up an insurrection against the Boer govt. and supported the rebels by pouring in troops and in this way regained the country.[38]

Meade, however, was no more successful in restraining the new Colonial Secretary, Joseph Chamberlain, than Lister had been with

Salisbury in 1889. The Jameson Raid was the abortive outcome of just such a conspiracy as this minute described; and Chamberlain was in it up to the hilt.* Official successors to Meade and Fairfield, both of whom retired from the Colonial Office in 1896, showed no qualms about adopting an anti-Boer line fully in accordance with that of their political chiefs, Chamberlain and Selborne. For them, the Boers were the enemy long before their declaration of war in October 1890. As such, they had to be regarded as at once strong, menacing, and capable of being readily defeated—for if they were weak, one need not go to war with them, and if they were strong without qualification, it would be dangerous to do so.

Such a picture of the Boers would have been implausible had it not been possible to represent them as in league with sinister foreign influences directed against the paramountcy of Great Britain in South Africa. There was a sense, of course, in which this was true: as has been said, "All states are predatory and the Transvaal was no exception."[39] The Boers had lost their independence once, even before the discovery of gold and diamonds had turned their country into a Naboth's vineyard. Formal and binding alliances they were debarred from making, so that Great Britain really held them in the hollow of her imperial hand: their domestic policies were outside her control, but in the diplomatic sphere all they could do was wriggle.[40] Small wonder that they should welcome a variety of foreign capital, and seek to buttress their position in such other ways as were open to them. Hemmed in on the south and southeast by the Cape Colony and Natal, on the west by the Bechuanaland Protectorate, and on the north by the Chartered Company, their feeling of claustrophobia is understandable. Their only line of communication not under British control was that running to Lourenço Marques; but the hold of Portugal on the place appeared precarious. Consequently, it was on Lourenço Marques that Boer hopes and fears were fixed and what British official papers all but invariably termed "Transvaal intrigues" were centered. From such papers one would seldom gain the impression that any legitimate economic enterprise, untainted by subversive

---

* It seems sufficient to cite the discussion in J. S. Marais, *The Fall of Kruger's Republic* (Oxford, 1961), pp. 79–95, 136.

political motives, could be undertaken there by non-British subjects. An innocuous concession for a wharf for landing timber for the Rand mines, for instance, secured by one Lingham, was an object of British suspicion until it was discovered that he was not an American but a Canadian; then it became a pawn in the British game directed against the Catembe (Katembe) concession, across the river Espirito Santo from Lourenço Marques proper.[41]

The Catembe concession had been granted by Augusto de Castilho in 1887 to a group of local residents for a variety of business purposes —agriculture, lime burning, brickmaking, and the processing of sea-salt were mentioned. In June 1895, Ennes, as Royal Commissioner, had granted the concessionaires permission to build piers adjoining the concession, subject to approval of the port authorities, for any works extending below high water mark. This permission, coming as it did after the 1894 change in the concession law, was subject to ratification by the Côrtes; but its very existence transformed a simple commercial enterprise into a matter of such high political import that the concession became the object of a clause all to itself in a secret treaty. In November 1895, the concession (after being offered to the Natal government without success) was bought by a Hamburg merchant named Eiffe, with money said to be supplied by a Transvaal bank; Eiffe's firm was in alliance with the Woermann shipping line, and on good terms with Dr. Leyds, the Hollander who was President Kruger's secretary of state and (no doubt because of his formidable ability) a kind of pantomime Demon King to British ministers and officials. All sorts of schemes at once began to fill the dispatches from Pretoria, Lourenço Marques, and Lisbon: there was talk of building a railway through Swaziland to terminate in Catembe, and of turning the concession into a coaling station for the German Navy. The palpable weakness of Portugal, the hazy notions entertained by most British officials about the geography of the region, and a general Boer-phobia combined to make these projects seem a great deal more practical and imminent than they really could have been. The Catembe site had the fatal disadvantage of being on the far side of the estuary, and so not readily accessible from the existing railway inland: it could never have competed with proper harbor works such as the Portuguese government was contemplating building. However, it had a certain speculative and nuisance value of which the most was to be made in the years preceding the Second Boer War.*

Even more speculative was the proposal, first mooted in 1890, of putting the District of Inhambane, between the Save and Incomati rivers, under a chartered company. The original grant had been made to two Portuguese subjects, who turned it over to a London syndicate; but although the legal formalities for forming a company were gone through, the caution money was apparently not forthcoming, and the concession lapsed. The government then decided to split it into three separate concessions, which were awarded to separate individuals, but were, it seems, hawked abroad as a single entity. One L. P. Ford, the attorney-general of the Transvaal before its retrocession, endeavored, early in 1896, to enlist the support of the Foreign Office in an attempt to secure them; but cautious neutrality on its part turned to covert hostility when it began to suspect that Ford was maintaining Transvaal connections that he professed to have abandoned. Ford's interest was taken over by another British subject, G. P. Witt, who sought the support of the Colonial Office; Mr. Chamberlain, however, was inclined to regard the scheme as "simply a device to extract money from the British, German, or Transvaal Governments."[42] At about the same time, the British agent in the Transvaal claimed to have information of a secret meeting of the Republican government at which it was decided to attempt to get the original Inhambane port and railway concession revived "regardless of expense."[43] Whether or not the report was correct, nothing came of it, though the question of the concessions continued to crop up from time to time. In January 1898, Barros Gomes, now once again Minister for Foreign Affairs, and Mousinho de Albuquerque jointly assured MacDonell that the concessions would not be proceeded with in their present form.** Nevertheless, at the very end of 1898 private advices were reaching the

---

* Translations of the relevant documents are annexed to MacDonell–Salisbury, April 16, 1898, No. 34 Africa (C.P. 7213, No. 70). Mousinho de Albuquerque remarked on the inefficacy of Ennes' measures in promoting development of the site. J. Mouzinho de Albuquerque, *Moçambique, 1896–1898* (Lisbon, 1899), pp. 349–51. The offer of the concession to Natal came from one Henry Milne, who talked of submitting it to Kruger. Anderson minuted Salisbury: "I do not think this is to be neglected though Mr. Milne may be blackmailing." (July 12, 1895; F.O. 63/1304.)
** MacDonell–Salisbury, January 8, 1898, No. 1 Africa (C.P. 7213, No. 2). Mousinho, unlike Ennes, disliked all foreign concessions on principle.

Colonial Office that Dr. Leyds was engaged in "intrigues" in Lisbon to promote a scheme to build a railway from Inhambane to Spelonken: "President Kruger is delighted, and considers the scheme a final check on that murderer Rhodes." The Lisbon government, however, categorically denied having been approached by either private or public sources about any such scheme.[44] A line that linked Inhambane, an inferior port with a poor hinterland, to the principal centers of the Transvaal by a circuitous route could never have competed commercially with the direct line from Lourenço Marques; it would have been a gratuitous addition to a railway network that, in terms of current and prospective traffic, was already outsize. Only a desire to guard against the alarming possibility that Lourenço Marques might fall into the hands of a great power, which would then have the republic at its mercy, could have brought the Transvaal to take a serious view of the scheme—if indeed it did. Had a line to Inhambane been constructed, it would have been an early example of a genre that is nowadays familiar: a work of uneconomic anti-imperialism.

Chapter eight

The McMurdo Concession and the Delagoa Bay Arbitration

All these concessions granted or proposed were as nothing, however, compared with the one that was rescinded: that of the Delagoa Bay railway. After the retrocession of the Transvaal had finally disposed of the Morier-Corvo scheme for a British-built railway to Lourenço Marques, the question lay fallow for some little time; but during 1883, the engineer Joaquim Machado completed a survey of the route up the Incomati valley, and in December 1883, the Portuguese government granted a concession to a "Kentucky colonel," Edward McMurdo, for the building of the line to the frontier. The particular attraction of McMurdo's proposal was that it dispensed with the government subsidy which was commonly necessary for African railroads at this time and which was to make the Ambaca line in Angola so expensive to the Portuguese treasury. Instead, grants of land adjoining the line were to be made to the concessionaire, on the American model. McMurdo must have been possessed of plausible manners and the willingness (if not the wherewithal) to spend money on sweetening politicians, for he appears to have had no other credentials worth mentioning. It was said that the New York Stock Exchange had become too hot for him some years previously, and that he had therefore transferred his company-promoting activities to London, where also he was not considered reputable. Probably, like so many of the concession hunters at Lisbon, he was chiefly concerned, not to build a railroad, but to make money. At any rate, his actions immediately after signing the contract were such as to arouse suspicion. One Alprovidge, who called himself an engineer, was sent out from London in January 1884 to inspect the terrain: he later told Machado that he had been furnished neither with drawings, letters, nor instructions, and that he did not know what McMurdo wished him to do. In June 1884, the pretense of making further studies of the route was abandoned, and there began a series of attempts, a few of which the government agreed to, to whittle down the provisions of the contract: for instance, it was suggested that the gauge might be reduced from three feet six inches to three feet, the rails reduced in weight, and the viaducts and retaining walls constructed of wood instead of brick or stone.[1] In the meantime, the statutes of a company to be registered in Lisbon had been elaborated, and permission sought to issue bonds to the nominal value of £425,000. The share capital of the company was to be £500,000. On May 26, 1884, a contract was entered into between McMurdo and the company, by which he surrendered his concession to it in return for all but 1,060 of the 500,000 shares. The company undertook to employ him to construct the line, in return for which he was to be given the whole of the bond issue.[2] Machado had estimated that the cost of construction, without the simplifications now agreed upon, would amount to £281,000. If McMurdo could have unloaded the paper thus authorized upon the public at anywhere near the nominal value he put on it, he would have made a sizeable fortune.[3] It is no matter for surprise that the terms of this contract were not disclosed to the Portuguese government for nearly three years.*

* Many of the documents cited are contained in a Portuguese Green Book, *Documentos Relativos ao Caminho de Ferro de Lourenço Marques (Contrato de 14 Dezembro de 1883)* (Lisbon, Imprensa Nacional, 1889). Though this states on its title page that its publication was ordered by the Ministry of Marine, it was apparently never issued officially. Petre, the British minister in Lisbon, was given a copy by a confidential informant, on condition that it was not to be quoted either in writing or conversation (Petre–Salisbury, April 8, 1890, No. 99 Africa [C.P. 6058, No. 55]). According to this informant, the book was ordered to be prepared by a progressista minister (Ressano Garcia), partly with the object of discrediting his political opponents. These unexpectedly came to power as a result of the ultimatum of January 1890 and so were enabled to suppress it. It was cited, nevertheless, by Mario Simões dos Reis in his study of the arbitration *Arbitragens de Lourenço Marques* (Lisbon, 1936), Segunda Parte, at, for example, pp. 301, 318, and 327, but was omitted from the bibliography. The copy now in the possession of Stanford University was bought from a bookseller in the ordinary way of business.

I

It is hard to see how, a year before the Rand goldfield was discovered, McMurdo could have had serious hopes of raising that amount of capital for a line little more than fifty miles long. His strongest card was the belief that he was at liberty to charge what the traffic would bear, without reference to the Portuguese government—a belief that appeared justified by the existence of a written assurance to that effect, given on behalf of the Minister of Colonies in May 1885, and incorporated into the company's revised articles of association. But this freedom to fix rates was not included in the original concession, and with good reason: it would have been contrary to the law, as embodied in decrees of 1864 and 1868, under which railway companies might themselves formulate or revise their tariffs, but not introduce them without government approval.[4] In any case, there had never been any lasting intention of allowing the company a free hand: on May 17, 1884, a few days before McMurdo entered into his leonine contract with it, the Portuguese government had, under pressure, agreed with the Transvaal that, if the line to be built by McMurdo were not finished with due dispatch, it would allow the construction of a "tramway" over Portuguese territory for the conveyance of the material for the Transvaal section of the line to Pretoria; and that this tramway might be used to convey passengers and merchandise if McMurdo and the Transvaal's concessionaires failed to reach agreement on rates. But this last undertaking was not made fully public till April 1889—a misleading statement to the effect that the government would do no such thing having appeared in the official White Book of 1885.[5]

This equivocation was harmful to McMurdo only because his enterprise already bore a dubious aspect. Machado had already reported from Moçambique that McMurdo was well known in the Transvaal: "Nobody there supposes that such a fellow could carry out the contract of December 14." Expert advice within the Ministry of Colonies had cast doubt on the company's statutes: in particular, the authority for a bond issue amounting to £425,000 at a time when the genuinely paid-up capital amounted to no more than £25,000. Pinheiro Chagas, as minister, had nonetheless approved the bonds, perhaps because he wished to afford McMurdo no further excuse for delay (or because his political ally Serpa Pimentel was chairman of the Board.[6] Thus, the Portuguese government could be said to be aiding and abetting with one hand any financial malpractices resorted to by McMurdo, while with the other it was hindering his chances of raising capital— for of course the fact of the tramway concession leaked out in the Transvaal and, though wholly contingent, was used by McMurdo's enemies for more than it was worth.

For the remainder of 1884 and the whole of 1885 nothing was done. The Lourenço Marques and Transvaal Railway Company remained what it had been from the beginning: in the words of a Portuguese official, the company law of Portugal "allows the organization of phantasmagoric companies," and this term precisely describes Mc-Murdo's creation.[7] Its capital consisted of the concession, upon which an arbitrary valuation had been put, and which was thereupon deemed to be paid-up shares: on the strength of these, the company proposed to issue loan capital to cover the cost of construction (and more). Its future profitability depended entirely on the completion of the line within the Transvaal by another company, and this was still in doubt: some burghers wanted no railway at all; others wanted no dealings with McMurdo. Even in the hands of a reputable promoter, it would evidently have been a speculative venture. Moreover, the cost of railway construction in South Africa was well known, and the amount of water in the nominal capitalization plain to see (at least one British contractor was to refuse the work on this ground).[8] It hardly needed Transvaal "intrigues" to explain why McMurdo should have been unable to dispose of his shares and bonds and why, in November 1885, the company should have asked the government to extend the time limit for the completion of the line from three years to four, ending in October 1888, on condition that work be begun by June 1886. This request was agreed to, but was soon followed by another: that the land grant to the company be doubled, from 100,000 to 200,000 hectares, as this would make it easier to raise capital. Even for a minister as well-disposed toward the company as Pinheiro Chagas, this was "completely impossible": amounting, as he said, to rewriting the original contract.[9]

Early in 1886, Pinheiro Chagas had formally assured the Transvaal government that work on the line would begin by June; but by mid-March there was still no sign of anything happening, and the question of how the assurance—which the new progressista minister,

Henrique de Macedo, renewed—was to be honored began to be venti-lated in Lisbon. The original contract had omitted to specify a time limit within which the works were to be begun, so that even though the company should fail to fulfill the condition upon which an exten-sion of time had been granted, no grounds for rescinding the con-cession existed—at any rate, until the lawyers' "reasonable man" could aver that there was no chance of completing the work before the end of October 1887.[10] Failing a voluntary and swift surrender of the con-cession by the company, only one way out seemed possible, and this was taken: the government itself began constructing the line on the company's behalf. The board of directors in Lisbon agreed to this course, though McMurdo objected, claiming that he had just suc-ceeded in raising a loan in Brussels and was prepared to begin the line immediately. But the Belgian lenders had second thoughts—professedly because of rumors about the conditional tramway con-cession—and asked the Portuguese government for a guarantee of in-terest at six and a quarter per cent on the loan, as well as for other modifications in the terms of the concession.[11] Some of these—though not the proposal for a guarantee—had already been embodied in a contract between McMurdo and a Belgian banker. But McMurdo, though the chief shareholder and sole bondholder of the company, was not empowered to act on its behalf: so that the government might properly, and did, refuse to take cognizance of his doings. If, as he truly said, he had been put in a difficult position, it was nonetheless absurd for him to say that this was because the tramway agreement had "virtually annulled" his concession; and to write to *The Times* alleging bad faith on the part of the Portuguese government.[12] Nor was there justification for the claim of a group of English sharehold-ers, made at the end of 1886, that the value of their shares had been depreciated and that they were entitled to compensation.[13] At about the same time, the English directors of the company proposed—again basing themselves on the damage alleged to have been done the com-pany by the government—that a guarantee of interest should be pro-vided, or that the concession should be transferred to an English company on more favorable terms. McMurdo, for his part, proposed that the transfer of the concession to the company should be nullified; a resolution to that effect was carried by the weight of his votes, against the opposition of the Portuguese directors, at an extraordinary general meeting on February 1, 1887.

The English company in question was already in course of formation, and its prospectus was issued on February 14. Doubtless because
the prospects of the line had improved, McMurdo had managed to
secure some persons of repute to act as directors, including the indispensable peer of the realm (if only, in this case, an Irish one—Lord
Castletown of Upper Ossory). The government, being unwilling to
see the concession pass back to McMurdo, decided to annul it—on the
ground that less than eight months remained for the completion of
the line—and a decree to that effect was actually signed. But Serpa
Pimentel prevailed on the Minister of Marine to hold up publication,
inasmuch as funds were at last being secured. The decision was doubtless helped by favorable reports from Costa Ricci, the government's
financial agent in London. Even so, the government made it clear that
it could have no direct dealings with the English company. It did not
object, however, to what seems to have been a last-minute proposal
to get over the difficulty: namely, that the English company should, in
fact, take the place of McMurdo in his contractual relations with the
Portuguese company, becoming at once the latter's principal shareholder and its agent for the construction of the line.[14] The English
company had already agreed with Sir Thomas Tancred, a well-known
public works contractor, that his firm would undertake the work.

Though the company was thus enabled to begin construction, the
financial condition of the enterprise and the dubious nature of its
operations remained virtually unchanged. The initial prospectus had
forecast the issue of £500,000 of debentures at seven per cent: presumably insufficient were applied for, for three weeks later the issue was
replaced by one of £400,000, which, it was announced, had been completely underwritten for a commission of seven and a half per cent.
On March 19, however, *The Times* announced that this issue, too,
had been withdrawn, since no more than one-quarter of it had been
subscribed for, and the underwriters had had the rest left on their
hands. It was, said *The Times*, an undertaking "which never ought
to have been offered to the public at all."[15] The relations of McMurdo
with the English company evoked such sharp criticism that the London Stock Exchange refused permission to deal in the debentures.[16]
What he had done was to hand over his original ordinary shares in the
Portuguese company for an equivalent number of shares in the English company, plus £117,500 in cash—this last presumably the redemption price of the Portuguese company's debentures that Mc-

Murdo had originally been given in his capacity as contractor for the line. At a later date, the articles of association of the English company were amended to provide for a gift by McMurdo to the directors ("or some of them") of £200,000 worth of ordinary shares; and for an unspecified cash payment by way of commission to the directors and others for placing the debentures. No public explanation appears to have been given of these maneuvers. Furthermore, there was inserted in the articles of association an extraordinary proviso (Article 66) which formed the majority shareholders, McMurdo and his wife, into a consultative committee, which controlled the company's voting rights in the Portuguese company and had both mandatory and veto powers over the actions of the English company's directors. As *The Statist* remarked in September 1888, "A more remarkable article probably never was inserted in any articles of association. . . . The vendor has therefore sold the concession for a large sum of money, but controls the concession as entirely now as he did before the sale took place." The paper added: "It is instructive to find that gentlemen of considerable commercial standing in the City of London are found willing to continue to remain directors of a company in which apparently they can only act in accordance with the concessionaire, who occupies no seat on the board."[17]

As *The Statist* had earlier remarked, it was strange that in these circumstances some shares in the company had changed hands at over twice the nominal price. It was not merely that the connecting line within the Transvaal, without which the traffic returns were bound to be insignificant, had not been built. By the summer of 1888, if not earlier, it must have been plain that the enterprise was short of money. Its ordinary shares were a liability pure and simple. Of the proceeds of its first issue of debentures—which had yielded in cash considerably less than their £400,000 nominal value—at least one-third had gone straight into McMurdo's pocket. A further £100,000 worth of debentures had been offered in February 1888, and apparently were placed successfully; but "£500,000 in 7 per cent debentures is a heavy charge on the revenue of a railway only 52 miles in length."[18] The high value placed on the ordinary shares could only be accounted for, therefore, by politics—by the hope that some interested government would take over the line at a fancy price. But in August 1888, the Parliamentary Undersecretary for Foreign Affairs, Sir James Fergusson, had publicly poured cold water on the notion that either the British or the Cape or Natal government would do any such thing.[19]

Sir Thomas Tancred had completed his contract with considerable dispatch: by the beginning of November 1887, the line was declared to be ready for business; and it was actually inaugurated in December. A good deal of the construction work, however, had been scamped, with the intention, it later appeared, of making improvements the following year; and this contributed to the heavy damage the line suffered in the early months of 1888, when several bridges were swept away by floods. Moreover, since the date of the original concession of 1883 and Machado's original survey, it had been discovered that the inland terminal point provided for in the plans approved in October 1884 (and embodied in Tancred's contract) was five miles or so short of the Transvaal frontier—a frontier that had been fixed by treaty, but never marked out on the ground. Machado later claimed that the company had known about this extra mileage almost from the beginning: that he had mentioned it to Alprovidge in Lourenço Marques in March 1884. In the *portaria* (official pronouncement) approving the plans, it was noted that this approval was "without prejudice to the presentation of a project for the last part of the railway near the frontier."[20] The length of this last part, however, was not specified; and although Machado furnished a trace for it in August 1885, nothing appears to have been transmitted to the company officially at that time—perhaps because the concession was considered moribund through the inaction of McMurdo. Only in July 1887 was the trace supplied by Machado to the contractor and the company's engineer on the spot (to their professed surprise). Complications, Machado told his government, might ensue because the building contract had not been based on a sum per kilometer, but on a lump sum to cover the whole 82 kilometers that it had been supposed were to be constructed.[21] Not until November was Pinheiro Chagas, who had succeeded Serpa as chairman of the Portuguese company, formally notified that the government did not consider the line to have been completed. This was not merely because of the outstanding length to be constructed, but also because the works were incomplete in a number of particulars. Pinheiro Chagas—better aware than any other could have been of all the questions surrounding the line—thereupon retorted that the company could not submit its proposals for the remainder for approval until the position of the frontier had been given to it.[22] While this made a good debating point, the fact remained that the company had been singularly incurious about a contingent liability that had been in existence for more than three years. Moreover, as the Minister of Marine pointed out in reply, although the exact position of the frontier was still under discussion with the Transvaal, it was already known that seven of the outstanding nine kilometers would be required in any event, and the company could proceed with those. A few months later, however, the minister seems to have changed his mind on the point: it would be unreasonable, he told his colleague Barros Gomes, who was under pressure from the Transvaal to do something about McMurdo's continued refusal either to finish the line or to come to an agreement about rates, to ask the company to fulfill its obligations by installments at uncertain intervals.[23] (There was no technical reason, however, why a contractor to the Transvaal line should not have completed any outstanding stretch for the concessionaire's account.)

In effect, therefore, the company had been presented with a valid excuse for inactivity: an excuse that it badly needed, for it was still in financial low water, despite the issue of debentures in February 1888. Far from beginning work on the remainder of the line, it was unable to pay its existing contractor's bills.[24] This was eventually to occasion an action by Tancred in the English High Court; in the meantime, it caused further delays in the repair of flood damage. Tancred was apparently uninterested in building the extra nine kilometers unless he could get a contract from the Transvaal company for a further twenty-four kilometers on its side of the frontier; and as McMurdo quite frankly put it, the existing terminus was as good as any that could be found for transferring freight to oxcarts for transport further inland.[25] In sum, so long as the Portuguese government would tolerate the existing position, so long could the nuisance value of the unfinished line be exploited to the possible profit of the concessionaire. As Beelaerts van Blokland, the Transvaal's minister at The Hague, who was intimately concerned with the railway negotiations, later observed:

An agreement on tariffs ... might be injurious to the speculative operations that were Mr. McMurdo's chief concern. He wanted to sell his shares, whether to the British government, to the government of the South African Republic, to the

Cape government, to the government of Natal, to the British interests represented by Sir Donald Currie, or to the colonial interests represented by Mr. Cecil
Rhodes. He was constantly in negotiation with one or more of these groups . . .
seeking at the same time to whet the appetite of one by means of another. Most
of these people were anxious that the Lourenço Marques railway should not become a reality. They might be brought to buy McMurdo's shares in order to slow
up the progress of a competitive railway, or to make it unworkable by excessive
rates. The speculative value of McMurdo's shares would thus be diminished by
an advance agreement on tariffs.[26]

Hence President Kruger's decision, which was subsequently confirmed by the Volksraad in July 1888, that work on the Transvaal
section of the line should be postponed pending an agreement on
rates; and hence the Portuguese government's decision, shortly afterward, to put renewed pressure on McMurdo.

This pressure was applied in two stages. In the first place, the government took legal advice on the question of its right to regulate the
tariff. It was advised that, though the company had the initiative in
proposing rates and charges, it might not bring them into force without the assent of the government: "The right of approval implies the
right to modify and to reject."[27] Though undoubtedly correct, this advice was, of course, at variance with the assurances that had been given
to the company in earlier years. Fortified with it, the government sent
the company, with its endorsement, a draft agreement on tariffs that
had been put forward by the Transvaal in combination with *its* con-
cessionary company. At the same time, the company was asked to say
how soon it could begin work on the extension after agreement on
the frontier was reached, and how long the works would take: to
which it returned an evasive reply, referring, however, to the impossi-
bility of working in the rainy season. It also professed that the very
proposal to extend the line was a novelty for which it ought to be
compensated, and talked of going to arbitration on the terms.[28] The
government thereupon decided to apply further pressure: it resolved
that, for the purposes of the concession, it would set the frontier at
a specified point, regardless of any subsequent agreement with the
Transvaal, and it decided, on Machado's expert advice, to fix a time
limit of eight months, ending on June 24, 1889, for the submission
of plans and the completion of the remaining nine kilometers of
track.[29]

"The Company, which, it seems, asked nothing more than that the negotiations with the Transvaal should become perpetual, so as to have a plausible motive for not going on with the works, appears to have got no more than middling satisfaction from this way of overcoming the difficulty." Such was the comment of the Swiss arbitrators later.[30] The reaction of the concessionaire and his English company seems to have been that they would comply, but only in their own good time. Thus, though McMurdo wrote to Barros Gomes, the Minister of Marine and Colonies ad interim, blaming the other side for all the difficulties over the tariff, his general tone was conciliatory, and he did not refuse to consider the Transvaal's latest proposal.[31] As for the fixing of a time limit, the London board protested that the eight months set included the rainy season, during which it would be unwise to start work; but they did not, as they might have done, object to the actual fact of a time limit having been set without prior consultation. Instead, they proceeded as if no such limit existed. In December 1888, they issued another £250,000 worth of debentures, ranking after the first £500,000. In February 1889, they submitted the plans for approval, in a form so rough as to evoke adverse comment from the Public Works Consultative Committee: the plans were approved, subject to more detailed submissions being made to the government engineer in Lourenço Marques. At the end of March, they at length reached agreement with a new contractor, Ernest Sawyer, on terms eloquent of the distrust in which he held them: the construction expenses were to be deposited to his credit in advance, and he was to account for them thereafter. "The principle on which my agreement with the company was based," he later wrote, "was that of a bankrupt: first, the money was placed to my personal credit *before* spending it; second, I could spend it as I pleased and it did not matter what the work cost no responsibility attached to me on that account."[*] Company spokesmen, both in London and Lourenço Marques, made it abundantly clear that they had no intention of starting work before May, and pooh-poohed the notion that the concession might be canceled and the railway confiscated if it were not ready in time: "I do not think we need trouble ourselves on that point in the very least," the vice-chairman had told a meeting of shareholders in January.[32]

The English company had, in fact, troubled itself to the extent of

* Quoted (in English), Araujo–Ressano Garcia, July 31, 1889 (*ibid.*, No. 831). This is a verbatim transcription from the original Portuguese document.

soliciting help from the British and United States governments in October 1888; but for some months neither government appears to have done more than institute unofficial inquiries and watch the position. At the end of April, the whole question was debated in the Côrtes, at the instance of Augusto Fuschini, and both Barros Gomes and Ressano Garcia, who from being a director of the Portuguese company had become Minister of Marine, reiterated that the time limit set the previous October would not be extended—a statement which was received with cheers.[33] Matters had now reached a point where it was virtually impossible for the Portuguese government to change its mind, even supposing it had wanted to. The only circumstances that would have afforded justification for such a change were two: an acceptable plea of force majeure on the part of the company, or an agreement on the tariff. If work on the extension had been started before the rainy season, a fair case could have been made for delay in completion, for the rains that winter did even more damage than those of the previous year; but the company had put itself out of court on that score by making no attempt to begin work until May 1889, when there was obviously no chance that it could be finished in time. As for the tariff, in April the company had submitted counterproposals which, inter alia, stipulated that the Transvaal government should not build any line toward the coast that might compete with the Lourenço Marques line, under penalty of £2,000,000—a proviso calculated to make any negotiations impossible. (These counterproposals were not, apparently, made known to the British or American governments at the time.)[34] On May 8, McMurdo died—too late to affect the attitude of the English directors, who, in any case, seem to have been as inflexible as he. Diplomatic representations in Lisbon came to nothing: on June 25 a decree was issued declaring the contract to be rescinded and the line was taken over by the government. A staff had sailed for Lourenço Marques some weeks earlier to effect the changeover.*

It was typical of the attitude of the London directors of the company that they should have told the Foreign Office that they would resist the seizure by force, and had instructed their employees to arm them-

---

* The negotiations from this point onward can be followed in C.P. 5988, *passim*. For the decree taking over the line, see Green Book, No. 713; Petre–Salisbury, June 26, 1889, No. 95 Africa (C.P. 5988, No. 83).

selves. One of them, wrote Sanderson on June 11, "was in that emphatic state . . . rather characteristic of him. . . . He is himself in favor of taking Delagoa Bay straight off. I am afraid that my assurance that the case was going to the Law Officers sounded rather tame."[35] The takeover at Lourenço Marques was, in fact, enlivened by some foolish heroics on the part of the resident general manager, Knee, who happened for the moment to be acting vice-consul, and who telegraphed for a gunboat. No less than three were sent, but on the arrival of the first, all was found to be quiet. The governor of Lourenço Marques turned out to be an old shipmate of her commander, and the conduct of acting vice-consul Knee was subsequently castigated by the commanding officer at Simonstown as "absurd and grossly improper."[36] This view was supported by the construction engineer, Sawyer, who seems to have been mainly instrumental in putting an end to the useless and illegal resistance ordered by the London office. The only result of the incident was to precipitate the resignation of Pinheiro Chagas and the other directors of the Portuguese company, who held that they could not countenance an appeal by their employees for the protection of a foreign government.[37] Otherwise, the changeover at Lourenço Marques went smoothly: the Portuguese promptly entered into a contract with Sawyer to finish the line and to repair the previous winter's damage; most important of all, in September an agreement on the tariff was signed with the Transvaal. The way was at last clear for carrying out the treaty of 1875: the economic future of Lourenço Marques was secured.

II

"Portugal was absolutely within its rights in seizing the railway," wrote Fairfield in September 1892, ". . . but it is affirmed very generally that the Am. govt. will somehow hypnotize the negotiators into giving a corrupt and cowardly decision."[38] In an earlier comment, he had remarked, apropos of a Portuguese Yellow Book published early in 1891:

If the F.O. think that this is anything novel, they have discovered a mare's nest. . . . It was because the Company stood on its rights to fix a tariff uncontrolled that the Portuguese Government took action against it in 1889, and this Yellow Book makes it a little more clear than before that the T.V. [Transvaal] were inciting it to do what it did. But we are to a certain extent partakers in the iniquity.

... This Office was never friendly to McMurdo in his lifetime; but in his latter days he induced some Englishmen of name and position to associate themselves in his East African project; and they are now protected by the F.O. Whatever Kruger could do to force the adoption of a moderate tariff was in accordance with general trade and shipping interests in South Africa and good for English interests at Johannesburg—hence our benevolent attitude in 1888. The F.O. did not agree to Kruger receiving the amount of encouragement that we and Sir H[ercules] R[obinson] desired to give him, but still the *effect* of the whole correspondence was not discouraging to him in his action against McMurdo.[39]

Fairfield was referring to the reply given to President Kruger in July 1888, when he asked for an assurance that the British government had no intention of acquiring the Delagoa Bay railway or a controlling interest in it: a reply which had been followed in August by Sir James Fergusson's statement in the Commons.* The avowed purpose of the request had been to weaken McMurdo's opposition to an agreement over tariffs; so that in fact, if not in form, the British had conceded the Transvaal argument that a monopoly right given to McMurdo was not in anyone's interest but his own. (It is evident that in conceding it in the first place, the Portuguese government had been acting contrary to the spirit of the treaty of 1875, under which the line was being built; but from some contemporary comments one would never gain the impression that the Transvaal had any special locus standi in the matter.) A year later, however, the Foreign Office seems almost to have forgotten its part in the episode—Anderson going so far as to remark that "the Portuguese Govt. connived at the raising of money in England, meaning all along to break the Co. unless they would give way on the tariff." Lister, on the other hand, expressed "great misgivings about the Co[mpany]s case and the accuracy of their statements"; but even he does not appear to have felt that the British government was in any way inhibited by its own past conduct from taking up that case strongly with the Portuguese.[40] Salisbury's dispatch to Petre on September 10, instructing him to demand compensation for the wrongs done the company by the seizure of the line, made the case seem stronger than it actually was by ignoring the express reservation in the *portaria* (directive) of October 1884 approving

* Kruger's request was embodied in identic telegrams to the governor of Natal and the High Commissioner at Cape Town, dated May 26, 1888. These, and the subsequent exchanges, are annexed to Robinson–Knutsford, June 27, 1888, No. 266 (File 14292, C.O. 417/21).

the plans about the part of the line for which plans remained to be presented. Secretary of State Blaine, in a dispatch of November 9, 1889 to the American minister in Lisbon, did the same. Both, of course, were relying on ex parte statements by the company.[41]

The British government's willingness to endorse the company's claim at no time extended to the amount of it—set at £750,000 in respect of the par value of the debentures, and £1,000,000 for the equity shareholders. The Treasury had hastened to point out that a prerequisite of any such endorsement would be a full investigation of the company's affairs, and had noted that its memorial of complaint gave no information about the circumstances in which the latest issue of debentures had been required, or the use to which the proceeds had been put. The disclosures that were made during the years that followed were not calculated to make the Treasury easier in its mind: a private letter to Lister in October 1891 stated that the Chancellor of the Exchequer was "rather anxious" lest the government make itself responsible for the "*justice* of the claim. . . . There appears to have been extraordinary financing on the part of the Co."[42] The position was complicated by the existence of a coplaintiff against Portugal—the United States claim on behalf of McMurdo's widow being inseparable from but not identical with that of the company's British bondholders, who ranked before her in any claim on the assets. If the British government did not display due zeal in pressing the company's case, it might be accused by the Americans of sacrificing *their* client; and at one point, Secretary Blaine did threaten to withdraw from the arbitration if the company were to be allowed to distribute the proceeds of an award at its discretion.[43]

It does not seem to have occurred to the directors in London that the frequently expressed willingness of the Portuguese government to accept arbitration might be a warning that the company's claim was less strong than they supposed, and that the balance of advantage might lie in a negotiated settlement. Although they sent negotiators to Lisbon immediately after the seizure of the line, and again early in 1890, the basis of their offers to treat was invariably, not the cost of construction plus something for the land grant, but the nominal value of the shares and bonds that had been issued—about five times as much.[44] There was thus no incentive for the Portuguese to come to terms rather than to go to arbitration—quite apart from the fact that the British ultimatum of January 1890 had supervened and made it all but impossible for any Portuguese government to concede any-thing to the British except under duress. In fact, the question of terms was never reached, for successive Portuguese governments remained obdurate in their refusal to treat with the English company, and in their insistence that the original Portuguese company, in limbo since the resignation of its directors in July 1889, was the only duly consti-tuted entity with which they could deal. Any arbitration would, there-fore, be a matter for the Portuguese courts, and the British and Ameri-can governments would enjoy no locus standi whatever.

One wonders whether this argument was not adopted precisely in order that those governments—for whom, one must suppose, the words "Portuguese justice" embodied a contradiction in terms—might reject it. For there was one provision in the original contract that any Portuguese court could hardly have failed to enforce. A subsection of Article 42 provided that in case of default by the company leading to a rescission of the contract, the right of construction, together with such works and materials as were already in existence, should be auctioned on the same terms to the highest bidder within six months —the proceeds, less any expenses incurred by the government, to be returned to the company. It seems pretty clear that the draftsman of the subsection did not contemplate a situation in which the original concessionaire might be ready and able to bid, and so to recover the concession at no cost beyond out-of-pocket expenses. But that such a situation might arise had been pointed out by Fuschini in the Côrtes, in May 1889, when he warned the government of the difficulties that might result from rescission. Moreover, by making its rates agreement with the Transvaal after rescission, the government had varied a con-dition implicit in the original contract and thus made it impossible that Article 42 could be complied with in full.[45] On the other hand, it could be argued that, given the attitude of the Transvaal, the line would have been valueless without an agreement on rates.

Now, if the government were to yield to force majeure and accept the demand of the British and American governments that the matter go to international arbitration, it could argue that those governments had ruled an auction out of court, and hence avoid any reopening of the rates question. It could also put on the British and Americans the odium of having bullied a small power into forgoing its legal rights.

These considerations would explain why, early in April 1890, Hintze Ribeiro should have asked the United States, through its minister in Lisbon, to send him an ultimatum on the subject of the American claims—a request that was not repeated to the British, presumably because an unsolicited ultimatum on another matter had recently been received from them. The request was promptly complied with by both British and American governments, and early in May international arbitration was accepted in principle: after some discussion, the Swiss Federal Council was approached, and agreed to nominate three leading jurists to form an independent tribunal. The tribunal, which was to sit at Berne, was duly constituted in mid-September.*

Thus were set on foot proceedings that were to last the best part of ten years and to provide what must have seemed an eternal backdrop to Portuguese diplomacy. Their protracted character occasioned from time to time expressions of impatience, not to mention accusations of sinister influence, on the part of the plaintiffs.[46] However, it was almost inevitable that the proceedings should be leisurely. They were conducted primarily in writing, so that all three parties had to be given time in which to prepare claim and counterclaim; they were written in French, involving massive translation of arguments and evidence; and they involved much previous history and expert advice on African railway building. The amount of paper generated was enormous, in keeping with the inflated character of the enterprise.** On the whole, the proceedings were uneventful, though a small storm arose early in 1899 when the tribunal proposed to take evidence from President Kruger—a proposal that it abandoned in view of British and American protests.[47]

The mastery of the evidence shown in the 200-page document embodying the final award, handed down in March 1900, is clear even on a casual reading, and clearer still if the material is studied closely:

---

* Salisbury–Pauncefote (Washington), April 10, 1890, No. 9A Africa; see Blaine–Lincoln, October 13 (C.P. 6058, Nos. 45, 233). This Portuguese maneuver deceived Simões dos Reis, as it doubtless deceived contemporaries, into blaming the British and U.S. governments for exerting undue pressure. Simões dos Reis, *Arbitragens,* pp. 184–85.

** There is a useful list in Simões dos Reis, *Arbitragens,* pp. 121–24. Most, if not all, the papers in the proceedings have been given asterisks in the F.O. Confidential Prints. As they are supernumerary to the regular series, there is no way of checking the completeness of current holdings by reference to that series. When I inspected them in 1960 these papers were still in the Foreign Office Library and had not been transferred to the Public Record Office.

the lucidity of its presentation is beyond praise.[48] The greater part of the document was, naturally, taken up with a recital of the history of the concession, the circumstances of its rescission, and the claims of the respective parties to the arbitration, together with a summary of the reports made by the experts the tribunal itself had employed. In passing, the tribunal dismissed the claim that the tramway concession had injured the concessionaire's interests: "No causal relationship, direct or indirect, has been established between the memorandum [of April 17, 1884] and the damage now alleged." Perhaps the most salient point brought out by the experts' investigation was the slovenly way in which the line had been constructed. It was, reported the Swiss railway engineer Nicole after an investigation on the spot, a line easy to build, but little trouble had been taken over it: the curves were unnecessarily sharp, and the grades unnecessarily frequent and steep. The ballast put down by the company was unworthy of the name; the sleepers were weak, and the rails out of alignment. Some of these faults were being corrected, but before the line could carry heavy traffic at high speed (which it would need to do as the Transvaal developed) extensive remodeling would be required. "In general the [original] works were badly carried out, whether constructed by the Company or by the Government; the works made subsequently ... without being admirable, appear at least to be solidly constructed."

Passing at length from the facts of the case to the law, the tribunal began by accepting the Portuguese contention that the company registered in Lisbon was, and from its inception had been, the true concessionaire, and was therefore subject to Portuguese law; but it added that this point was only of academic interest, inasmuch as Portuguese law contained no special provisions differing from those of other nations. The tribunal then went on to ask whether the rescission had been in accordance with the terms of the original contract—bearing in mind that the Portuguese government had not, at the time, invoked (as it might have done) a clause providing against failure to repair the line within a reasonable period. The Portuguese had contended that the setting of eight months' grace by unilateral decree was not in breach of the concession, inasmuch as the period of three years for the completion of the line had long since expired; the company contended that a fresh period of three years began in February 1889, when the final part of the plans was approved. The tribunal rejected both these views. It held that—contrary to the argument of the company—the Portuguese government was within its rights in unilaterally fixing the frontier for the purpose of the concession: "The international relations of Portugal were not the plaintiffs' business." The government was not, however, within the terms of the concession in fixing the eight months' period arbitrarily: not because an eight months' grace, even in the rainy season, was unreasonable but because the action was unilateral, and because any period of grace could only run from the time the plans were approved. The original article providing for three years' grace would have been applicable, the tribunal thought, only by analogy; it would have been the responsibility of the parties to fix a shorter period (or to seek arbitration).

On the capital point at issue, therefore, the Portuguese government was legally in the wrong, and the plaintiffs were entitled to damages in respect of *damnum emergens* and *lucrum cessans*. But—the tribunal went on—the wrong lay rather in the form than in the substance of the government's action: the line could have been finished within eight months if the works of the earlier part had been solidly built and if the English company had been soundly based financially. Moreover, the Portuguese company had failed to reply when asked how long it needed to finish the line, and had not at first objected when the eight months' grace was fixed. These mitigating circumstances were such as to rule out any penal or exemplary assessment of damages. In effect, it appears, the tribunal considered the Portuguese government justified in terms of *raison d'état*—"to which any railway concession must be subordinate"—and incorrect merely in its procedure. It was ironic that the government should incur damages for a technical wrong done, after it had more than once refrained from canceling the concession—for instance, in the spring of 1887—in circumstances when it would have been immune.

As for the basis on which damages should be assessed, the tribunal rejected outright that of the issued share and loan capital of the English company. This was something with which the true plaintiff, the Portuguese company, had nothing to do. In any case, the share capital of the English company was purely nominal. As for the £750,000 worth of debentures, less than £600,000, even on the company's own showing, had been spent directly or indirectly on the railway (including the £117,500 paid to McMurdo); and the remaining £150,000 had gone "one knows not whither." The tribunal conceded that when the arbitration started there was no way of knowing what the profits of the line would be, and that the basis now rejected might be said to have been put forward for want of a better. But the passage of time —the members remarked, with perhaps a trace of self-satisfaction— had remedied this difficulty: the connecting line was open and expert analysis of the returns was available. The Portuguese government would, in any case, have been entitled to recover the line after thirty-five years, on payment of an amount equal to twenty times the average annual receipts for the seven years immediately preceding recovery. The tribunal therefore proposed to estimate what this figure would have been, add to it the real or estimated net profits aggregated over the thirty-five years, and apply a time discount, so as to get the value of the line in June 1889. The details of this arbitrary but not unreasonable procedure do not need to be gone into; but the matter did not end there. The value of the line so determined did not represent the indemnity to which the plaintiffs were entitled, for not all the capital that had been put into it was theirs. The Portuguese government, up to 1897, had had to spend on repairs and improvements rather more than the company's total expenditure, and would have to find almost twice as much again over the next ten years. It had virtually come to the rescue of a bankrupt enterprise. "For the Company, the *lucrum cessans* resulting from the rescission is far from equaling the advantages that have resulted from the Portuguese intervention.[49] It followed that the value of the line ought to be adjusted to take account of the prospective expenditure, and thereafter apportioned between the company and the Portuguese government in accordance with their respective capital investments. The amount due to the company, as of June 25, 1889, was put at 13,890,000 Swiss francs, to which was added a more or less arbitrary figure of 2,000,000 Swiss francs for the value of the land. At just over twenty-five francs to the pound sterling, the award amounted to rather less than £640,000, or a little more than the company claimed to have spent in the first place. To it, of course, had to be added interest at the rate of five per cent per year for more than ten years, making a total of about £1 million.[50]

Nogueira Soares, who was Portuguese minister in Berne for the whole period of the arbitration, thought that the award was essentially a "judgment of Solomon"—arbitrators being naturally inclined against coming out wholly in favor of either side. Support is given to this view by the tribunal's own remark that it had given the plaintiffs one-third of what they had asked for and made the defendant government pay three times what it had offered. But the further insinuation, repeated by a later Portuguese writer, that the tribunal had been influenced by American threats to reject the award if it were too favorable to Portugal (which threat, if in fact made, could have been no more than bluff, since all the litigants had bound themselves to accept the tribunal's judgment), or by fears for the Swiss tourist trade, seems to be no more than the remark of a bad loser.[51] The award was, in any case, a moral victory for Portugal, and an exposure of the company: apart from calculating the indemnity differently—and any such calculation was clearly a matter of rival expert opinion—it is hard to see how the tribunal could have awarded less, once it had decided that the Portuguese government was technically at fault. This it was bound to do, unless it accepted the view that the rescission was an act of sovereignty and that it was for the government alone to judge whether or not the company was in breach of contract.[52] Despite the fact that this view appears to coincide with that of the Swiss Supreme Court—among other legal authorities—it does not appear consistent with a contract that provided safeguards for the concessionaire against arbitrary action, not only in the form of an arbitration clause, but by stipulating that the period of grace for construction should run from the time the plans were approved. This proviso had been clearly broken by the government, and however undeserving the concessionaire, he was clearly entitled to the benefit of it. In sum, it would seem difficult for one not an interested party to find fault with the award on the ground of equity. The British government, at any rate, had reasons of its own for not complaining about it. As Francis Bertie, Anderson's successor as head of the African Department at the Foreign Office, remarked, in a minute that was a curious combination of legal misapprehension and political acumen: "It is not to our interest to reopen the case. We do not want to increase the indemnity to an extent which might force Portugal to borrow under the Anglo-German agreement [of 1898]."[53]

Chapter nine

The Anglo-German Treaties of 1898

The case of the Delagoa Bay railway is interesting as a locus classicus of international arbitration, as an example of the workings of the demimonde of international investment, and as a salient feature in the history of Anglo-Boer relations. Above all, it is important on account of its bearing on the Portuguese financial crisis. Solicitude lest the Portuguese should not be able to pay the award and helpful proposals designed to get them out of the difficulty were common currency throughout the nineties. Fairfield, as usual, had an apt description for them. Of a proposal put forward in September 1892 by one Trehane, an American attorney resident in London who represented the McMurdo interests, he wrote: "These vast schemes of purchase and guarantee are being constantly pressed on us by all sorts of people—generally moneyless themselves—ex-tobacconists, Irish Militia majors, men-milliners, and suchlike."[1] Not all the projectors, of course, were of this character. Even before the seizure of the line, the Foreign and Colonial Offices had discouraged a scheme for its purchase, propounded at the end of 1887 by Sir Charles Mills, the agent-general in London of the government of Cape Colony;[2] and neither Sir John Pender, Sir Donald Currie, nor Cecil Rhodes—all of whom at one time or another were concerned with such schemes—could have been described as "moneyless."[3] But the characteristic figure in most of these projects is not the rich principal but the shadowy, if not shady, intermediary. There was Baron Merck, sometime director of the Nyassa Company, who worked on behalf of Rhodes for a time in

1894. There was one Davis, who claimed to represent a Portuguese syndicate in Paris with an extensive concession from the Portuguese government. A man named Henderson was brought to the Foreign Office by Sir Sidney Shippard in May 1897 with another such scheme: "Mr. Henderson," wrote Bertie, "seemed to think that a word of approval from H.M.'s Govt. would insure the requisite money being produced in the City.... I told him that in the City people are not influenced by the benevolent wishes of the Government."[4] Of another projector, named Wallach, who appeared in July 1897, the Colonial Secretary (Chamberlain) remarked: "He must be a knave or a lunatic."[5] The Moçambique Company's directors—"not very recommendable" people, as Soveral is said to have remarked—likewise entertained notions of securing the railway through an extension to the company's concession. Having failed to interest Leyds in mid-1897, they turned next year to the British government, but found it equally unenthusiastic.*

This was not because the British government would not have liked to secure control of the port and railway of Lourenço Marques, but because it was more aware of the difficulties than most of the projectors. The chief obstacle—other than Portuguese unwillingness to surrender control to any foreign interest—was the attitude of Germany. At the time of the so-called "native revolt" of 1894, the Germans had reiterated earlier objections to Lourenço Marques passing into British hands, and had asserted that all they wanted was a maintenance of the status quo; but this was not long after a German-Dutch syndicate, in which the Bank of Darmstadt was interested, had failed to get a concession there—the British having previously made it clear that any concession to a third party would be, in their view, contrary to the right of preemption over the territory that had been granted in the Treaty of 1891. In essence, there was deadlock, with the British holding the stronger cards on account of their treaty rights; but the Germans had evinced willingness to make a deal. Portugal, meanwhile, with British assent, maintained in and out of season that noth-

* Warhurst, *Anglo-Portuguese Relations,* p. 139; Bertie, minute on interviews with R. W. Murray and Soveral, February 2, 1898; memorandum on interview with representatives of the Moçambique Company, June 27, 1898 (C.P. 7213, No. 84). Wingfield, minute, February 18, 1898: "We cannot allow Lourenço Marques and the Railway to fall into the hands of a Company controlled by French Directors" (File 433S, C.O. 537/134).

ing could be done pending the award of the Berne tribunal.* But what thereafter? What may be called the forward party in British governmental circles mistrusted Portugal and was willing to risk any German displeasure. In October 1895, G. V. Fiddes of the Colonial Office drew up a scheme under which the British government would purchase the Delagoa Bay railway and hand it over for joint administration by the Cape and Natal: so that neither could use it against the other and there would be no object in the Transvaal's boycotting it. Fiddes was ready to pay a "fancy price" (£2,000,000 or more) for the line: "From an imperial point of view, it seems absolutely necessary that we should acquire the railway (and hereafter the Bay) at any cost."⁶ His colleague Fairfield, on the other hand, had suggested "a cooperative transaction confined to them [the Germans] and ourselves." "Will H.M.G.," he wrote, "face an estrangement with Germany, with all its far-reaching consequences in Egypt and elsewhere, by bidding for the line?"⁷

I

The atmosphere created by the Jameson Raid and the Kaiser's telegram to Kruger made an immediate Anglo-German deal out of the question; but it was not long before the idea recurred to British officials. On March 15, 1897, apropos of a grandiose scheme hatched by Herbert Magniac (a director of the Delagoa Bay railway) and the Lisbon financier Count Moser, for leasing the whole province of Moçambique for no less than £900,000 annually, Sanderson of the Foreign Office remarked that:

The Germans wd violently object to our acquiring D[elagoa] B[ay] without any kind of agreement as to freedom of transit through it. If they had the reversion of the Province of Mozambique [that is, north of the Zambezi] they would not so much mind our getting that of Lorenzo Marques provided that we gave an assurance that Delagoa Bay would be an open port with full facilities for transit subject to some moderate rate of duty. Anything less than this would bring us to the verge of an open quarrel.**

---

* G. V. Fiddes, memorandum on the question of the Delagoa Bay railway, October 11, 1895 (C.O. Confidential Print, African [South], No. 508), is a tendentious but useful summary of the position. Anderson of the Foreign Office described it as "excellent" in a letter of March 25, 1896 (File 130S, in C.O. 537/129).

** Sanderson, minute, March 15, 1897 (F.O. 64/1466). In the light of this minute and that of Fairfield it is odd that the latest writer on the subject, J. A. S. Grenville, *Lord*

It was at this time that MacDonell was putting forward another scheme, propounded by an English director of the Moçambique Company who had discussed it with Ressano Garcia, the newly appointed Portuguese Minister of Finance. As elaborated by Bertie of the Foreign Office, after consultation with his friend Alfred de Rothschild, it would have involved a loan to Portugal for colonial development (and payment to her continental creditors), and the creation of one or more Anglo-Portuguese companies to pay off the Berne award and run the port and railway of Lourenço Marques. The Rothschilds were of the opinion that a British government guarantee of the interest on any loan would be indispensable, but it does not appear that the Treasury was consulted on this point.[8] Part of the bait for Portugal was a renewed British guarantee of the integrity of their possessions: neither Bertie nor Soveral, to whom the proposal was to be put, seems to have been aware that the guarantee was already in force, being a quid pro quo under a treaty of 1661 for the cession of Bombay as part of Catherine of Bragança's dowry, and having been reaffirmed as late as 1873, when the Portuguese government was fearful of aggression by the short-lived republican government of Spain.* Nor was Joseph Chamberlain, who thought the MacDonell-Bertie scheme "very vague." He went on, "*We* are to have control of Port and Railway through a *bona-fide Portuguese* undertaking. To a plain man this appears contradictory.... I assume that Lord Salisbury will never guarantee their possessions except in return for some substantial recognition of our paramount interest in Delagoa Bay."[9] Chamberlain took this line in subsequent discussions that he—contrary to normal protocol—had with Soveral during the spring and summer of 1897; and

---

Salisbury and Foreign Policy: the Close of the Nineteenth Century (London, 1964), p. 182, should observe: "In 1897, neither Chamberlain nor anyone else in the Cabinet gave much thought to the possibility that the Germans might demand compensation for allowing Britain control of Delagoa Bay. It seemed to the British ministers a purely Anglo-Portuguese affair."

* The relevant correspondence, with treaty clauses, was reprinted and circulated to the British Cabinet on June 17, 1898 (F.O. 63/1359), and will be found in C.P. 7303 (enclosures, Salisbury–MacDonell, June 23, 1898, No. 70 Africa). Some of it was reprinted in Gooch and Temperley, eds., *British Documents on the Origins of the War, 1898–1914*, Vol. I, No. 69 (London, 1927), but without noting that it had been circulated to the Cabinet. Grenville, *Lord Salisbury*, p. 261, is thus wrong in saying that "no one at the Foreign Office was quite sure what the treaties had said since their full texts were not known."

it was clearly too strong for success, inasmuch as both the French and the Germans appeared willing to offer Portugal a loan without insisting on any change in the status quo at Lourenço Marques. By the end of June, the discussions had petered out.[10]

In January 1898, however, they appeared to be reviving: Soveral told Bertie that he was anxious about French and German designs and that if he could get the Goa railway question—another outstanding issue between Great Britain and Portugal—settled on reasonable terms, he would try to persuade his government to give the British "practical but not territorial control of Delagoa Bay in return for a guarantee of the African possessions of Portugal."[11] In March, Mousinho de Albuquerque visited London and was told about the loan scheme in a talk with A. J. Balfour and Chamberlain. In May, the Portuguese government appealed for the good offices of the British government: it required a short-term credit of £200,000 to pay off a maturing debt to the Crédit Lyonnais. Rothschilds would find the money only if the British government would stand security for it, and Bertie urged that this be done: it would be a useful handle to keep the French out of Delagoa Bay. But Chamberlain and Salisbury, while agreeing in principle, wanted further undertakings; and in the end, the Portuguese had recourse to the Bank of Portugal instead.[12] Early in June, Soveral returned from a visit to Lisbon, having found out that the British guarantee of Portuguese territory was already operative and hence could not be part of the quid pro quo for any concessions at Lourenço Marques.[13] He nevertheless proposed its reiteration in an interview with Salisbury two days later, when he asked also for a loan to pay off the floating debt and (presumably) the Berne award, and to provide funds for developing the port and railway at Lourenço Marques under the aegis of an Anglo-Portuguese company. In essence, the scheme was that drafted by Bertie the previous year, but with one significant addition: the interest on that part of the loan relating to Lourenço Marques was to be guaranteed by pledging the customs revenues of the province of Moçambique. This proviso may have been suggested to Soveral by Bertie, for such a pledge had been incorporated by him in a comprehensive memorandum containing, inter alia, proposals for preventing Portugal and her colonies from "falling under the influence, if not into the power, of other nations— that is, France or Germany. The total amount of money required was later given by Soveral as £8 million, of which £2 million were intended for Lourenço Marques.[14]

It was at this point that the German government decided to intervene, and though the intervention had about it a characteristic element of bad melodrama, it should have caused no surprise to any informed person. Hatzfeldt, the ambassador in London, had lost little time in pointing out to Salisbury, on June 17, that if the customs duties of a particular territory were pledged to a given power, "it would amount to a declaration of future ownership" on that power's part; and he had gone on to suggest common action by Germany and Great Britain in the matter of the loan to Portugal. Salisbury had professed ignorance of the details of the Portuguese proposals and repudiated any link between the pledging of customs duties and the future of a territory; however, he admitted that if there were any question of alienation, the Germans would have every right to be consulted.[15] On June 21, King Carlos received the German minister in Lisbon, at the urgent personal request of the Kaiser. Count Tattenbach, who appeared in military uniform the better to emphasize his point, told the king that his master would not continue on good terms with Portugal if Soveral's current negotiations disregarded Germany's legitimate interests.[16] The French minister entered a similar protest, presumably at German instigation: a few days earlier Von Bülow had suggested to the French Foreign Minister, Hanotaux, that the two countries take joint action in the matter. As Hanotaux was on the point of being replaced by Delcassé, nothing more came of this move; but its very possibility was exploited by the Germans to bring pressure on both British and Portuguese.[17]

The Portuguese, as the weaker power, were naturally the first to give. "My private opinion," wrote MacDonell sourly to Bertie on June 30, "is that, after all, nothing very advantageous will come out of these pourparlers. The German Govt. has succeeded in establishing a regular state of 'funk' in the mind of this imbecile Govt."[18] But Chamberlain, who had once again taken over the negotiations with Soveral, appeared equally willing to make an agreement with Germany, despite the rebuffs he had had from her earlier in the year in unofficial proposals for an alliance. He told Soveral on June 22, and again on July 6, that he thought "there would be no difficulty in coming to an arrangement with Germany to divide the loan and the responsibility. This could be done by separating the spheres over which preemptive rights were to be given and which were to be mortgaged for the payment of interest and sinking fund. I could not admit that France had any interest...as her possessions were not coterminous with those of P'gal, but...we should certainly try to come to an amicable agreement with Germany."[19] Such views must have been the reverse of welcome to Soveral, indicating as they did the possibility of a loan only on the very kind of terms the Portuguese government was anxious to avoid. It is not surprising that a week later he should have told Salisbury that his government had decided to abandon the idea of a loan from the British or any other government. Instead, it was endeavoring, in accordance with its announced policy, to reach an understanding with the French bondholders, on whose behalf a detailed proposal was presented on July 31.*

If Soveral thought that by removing the occasion of the German intervention he could prevent an Anglo-German deal on the question of the Portuguese colonies, he was very shortly to find himself mistaken. All that happened was that the occasion became the principal hypothesis on which a deal was to be based. What the Germans wanted was, in essence, simple—and to Chamberlain, at any rate, acceptable—namely, that any loan to Germany should be part German and part British, and that the customs duties securing each part should indicate the territorial claims of each power should Portugal go to pieces. "The difficulty," commented Salisbury, "will be a form of note which shall not look like cutting up Portugal while still alive."[20] However, the difficulty lay not in the form but in the substance, since the German territorial demands were considerably greater than the British expected: they began by asking for the reversion, not merely of that part of Moçambique not already reserved for Great Britain, but of the whole of Angola; for Blantyre (as if, Chamberlain remarked, the British had asked for Wittenberg), and for Portuguese Timor. Such demands caused even Chamberlain to talk of German "blackmail"—blackmail that he was none the less ready to allow, for, as Soveral remarked to Sir Edward Grey many years

---

* Salisbury–MacDonell, July 13, 1898, Africa No. 83 (C.P. 7303, No. 12; B.D., Vol. I, No. 76). A copy of the French proposals is appended to Augusto Fuschini, *O Convenio sobre a Divida Externa: discurso proferido na Camara dos Senhores Deputados na sessão de 21 de maio de 1901* (Lisbon, Imprensa Nacional, 1901), pp. 51–54.

later, "he thought only of the Transvaal and Delagoa Bay."[21] What could be more satisfactory than the Germans should sacrifice the Boers in return for hypothetical gains at Portuguese expense? The Germans, for their part, were quite willing to be paid to do something they had apparently decided to do some time before—write the Boers off: the Kruger telegram of January 1896 had marked the end, not the beginning, of a chapter.[22] As Von Bülow had told the French ambassador in Berlin, German interests were now greater in China than in Africa.[23]

The course of the negotiations has long been familiar to scholars, inasmuch as the main documents, on the side of Germany and Great Britain, were published in 1924 and 1927 respectively.* They reveal a bargaining process pure and simple, in which the territories concerned might have been on another planet, for all the interest that was taken in their nature, inhabitants, and prospects. It is the cold-blooded haste with which the thing was done that accounts, one feels, for much of the moral obloquy that has clung to it ever since: Salisbury salved his conscience by not actually signing the agreements; Sir Arthur Nicolson described them as a "supremely cynical maneuver"; and Sir Edward Grey, even though he renewed them in 1913, insisted that they must not remain secret. It is pleasant to record that the Foreign Office came to regard them as inconvenient and embarrassing. What Eyre Crowe remarked in June 1912 of "the existing undoubtedly unsatisfactory arrangement about Timor" was true, mutatis mutandis, of much of the rest:

That arrangement... would never have been made at the time if the departments concerned had been duly consulted. It is very much to be hoped that future governments may not again find themselves tied by treaty stipulations of grave inconvenience because they were entered into without proper and exhaustive study of the issues involved.[24]

It was fitting that an agreement jointly negotiated, on the British side, by the forceful amateur Chamberlain and the skeptical amateur Balfour should come in for such thorough professional condemnation.

---

* The best account is still that of the Portuguese Luís Vieira de Castro in *D. Carlos I* (Lisbon, 1936), pp. 138–55. Grenville's 1964 account (*Lord Salisbury*, pp. 177–98) is most notable for its attempt to whitewash the behavior of the British. I think this is an unprofitable task.

II

As signed by Balfour (Acting Foreign Secretary in Salisbury's absence) and Hatzfeldt, on August 30, 1898, the Anglo-German agreement took a tripartite form. There was first a Convention providing for joint action in the matter of *any loan to Portugal that might be secured by the customs revenues of Moçambique, Angola, and Portuguese Timor.** The British part of any such loan would be secured on the revenues of Moçambique south of the Zambezi, and of a central strip of Angola which included the port of Luanda; the German part would be secured on the remainder. Each side agreed not to seek concessions in the other's bailiwick. Secondly, there was a Secret Convention, by which the British and Germans agreed to oppose jointly any intervention by a "third power" (that is, France) in the territories concerned, whether by way of loan secured on the customs revenues or by acquisition of territory; and each agreed not to seek "possession, occupation, control, or exercise of political influence" in the territories allocated to the other. These provisions, along with another allowing for equal treatment of each other's nationals in economic matters, were necessary, the preamble explained, in case it might "unfortunately not be found possible to maintain the integrity" of the possessions in question—this maintenance, together with the obviation of international complications, having been the stated object of the first convention. The Secret Convention also contained an article by which the British government undertook to adopt a friendly attitude in respect to the "so-called Katembe Concession." Lastly, a Secret Note provided that, in the meantime, no cession of territory, or other concession, granted by Portugal to one of the signatory powers should be valid until an analogous grant of approximately equal value should have been given the other; and that the town and port of Ambriz, the precise latitude of which was not known, should in any event fall to Germany. The implied difference in status of these three documents was not observed in practice, since all were officially kept secret: the first two, however, became known in informed circles almost immediately in all but trivial details. Several later claimed to have known all about the agreements from the beginning, adding

* The texts of the agreements are printed in B.D., Vol. I, Nos. 90–92. The words I have italicized constitute an important qualification, overlooked by Grenville (*Lord Salisbury*, p. 198).

that they were settled between Eckardstein and Chamberlain, at Alfred Rothschild's house.* As early as September 14, Bertie wrote privately to Salisbury that Mensdorff, the First Secretary at the Austrian embassy, had told him: "I have heard all about it from Vienna. At Berlin they are not so mysterious as the English F. O. and Count Hatzfeldt."[25]

It was, of course, inevitable that the first convention, covering the loan, should become known if it were to be implemented; and this seems to have been the original intention of both the British and German governments. Conway Thornton, the chargé d'affaires in Lisbon, was enjoined to keep in touch with his German colleague, Tattenbach, with a view to preventing Portugal from raising a loan in France on the strength of colonial customs revenues; and the two acted together in pressing the Portuguese government to seek a loan from Great Britain and Germany instead. Thornton even represented to the Portuguese Foreign Minister, Veiga Beirão, that the proposal for a joint loan was British in origin, and that Tattenbach's instructions confirmed this.[26] But with Salisbury's return to the Foreign Office, collaboration with the Germans became increasingly reserved; and though as late as September 28 Salisbury approved Thornton's activities earlier in the month, he does not seem to have been pained by reports that the Portuguese government was objecting to any proposal for a government-to-government loan and that José Luciano de Castro, now once again Prime Minister, was absenting himself from Lisbon and "playing hide-and-seek" with them.[27] When Thornton reported, on September 30, that José Luciano had virtually rejected the joint loan proposal "before having mastered its most elementary details," and that he himself had asked the Prime Minister "if he did not consider that there was an element of danger in the hesitation of his government to take advantage of such a weighty and favorable proffer of assistance," Salisbury sent word that "these expressions" went somewhat beyond Thornton's instructions.** There-

---

* Grey, note of January 25, 1911, in B.D., Vol. X, Part II, p. 427. Soveral also gave a circumstantial account to Rouvier, the French minister in Lisbon, in October 1902 (Rouvier–Delcassé, October 5, 1902, D.D.F., Série II, Tom. 2, No. 423).

** Thornton–Salisbury, September 30, 1898, No. 93 Africa; Salisbury–MacDonell, October 19, No. 112 Africa (C.P. 7303, Nos. 58, 64). MacDonell told Rouvier that he had been instructed to correct Thornton (Rouvier–Delcassé, April 12, 1899, D.D.F., Série I, com. 15, No. 139).

after, all pressure from the British on Portugal to conclude a loan ceased—Salisbury contenting himself with assurances that the proposed loan from France would not involve foreign administration of Portuguese finances, and would not be secured on the revenues of the Azores as well as those of continental Portugal. The Germans were thus constrained to relax their pressure also.

In J. L. Garvin's smug and prolix *Life of Joseph Chamberlain* there is, as Langer says, a tendency to gloat over the way in which the Germans were at once bilked by the British and outwitted by the Portuguese in the matter of the 1898 agreements. It is understandable that the Germans should have been vexed by the British insistence on taking at their face value the words in the preamble to the convention about preserving the integrity and independence of Portugal, when they were so much at variance with the spirit of the rest. Even if one agrees with Garvin that the Germans deserved to be taken in, the element of sharp practice in British conduct is undeniable.[28] It will not do to plead in mitigation that they were negotiating under duress, because the quid pro quo they were given—a free hand to deal with the Boers—was, except in the eyes of dyed-in-the-wool imperialists, something that could have been dispensed with. They were not bullied, but rather tempted into a bargain that could neither be carried out nor evaded without discredit.* Salisbury, along with

---

* In the Foreword to Volumes I and II of *British Documents on the Origin of the War* the editors say: "It was decided to begin with the year 1898, in view of the fact that certain influential members of the British Cabinet, alarmed by the hostility of France and Russia, then desired to substitute a policy of alliances for the traditional principle of 'splendid isolation.' It was felt, however, that the years covered in the first two volumes could be treated in a more summary fashion than would be desirable after 1904."

It would be difficult to quarrel with this statement of policy on general grounds. But so far as the Anglo-German secret treaties are concerned, the principles of selection have resulted in creating a misleading impression of British policy. Every document of evident major importance, beginning with Bertie's memorandum of May 1, 1898, was included. However, as the foregoing narrative shows, the following significant details do not emerge from the selection:

(1) The earlier hints at a deal with Germany, in particular Sanderson's minute of March 15, 1897.

(2) The anti-French motive behind such a deal.

(3) The cooperation between Thornton and Tattenbach in Lisbon immediately after the signature of the secret agreements.

(4) The statement in Tattenbach's instructions that the initiative in the negotiations came from Great Britain.

(5) The fact that until Soveral pointed out Great Britain's existing treaty obligations

a number of others, had the grace to be ashamed of the deal, though this did not prevent his government from taking advantage of it. As MacDonell, who had been privy to the negotiations while on leave, later put it to Rouvier, the French Minister in Lisbon, they had wanted to get rid of German opposition in the Transvaal and Lourenço Marques, but not pull Germany's chestnuts out of the fire. Salisbury's attitude in this instance, like his attitude toward the Boer War, was that of a slightly detached observer—as if, though Prime Minister and Foreign Secretary, he was not really responsible for what his Cabinet colleagues did, and need not resign if they overruled him on a major point of principle.[29]

The equivocal position into which the British had got themselves was emphasized by Portuguese ownership of the key to the Transvaal —the port of Lourenço Marques. For if Chamberlain and Milner were considering the use of armed force against the Boers—as by this time they undoubtedly were—the acquiescence of Portugal could not be dispensed with; and it was, therefore, decidedly tactless to have bought that of Germany—which was desirable rather than necessary —at Portuguese expense.[30] Soveral, who regarded the whole British dissension with the Transvaal as something got up by Chamberlain at the instigation of Rhodes and his Chartered Company, saw in it a way of nullifying the Anglo-German agreements by putting the British under obligation to the Portuguese for help against the Boers.[31] His opportunity came when, in the summer of 1899, the British forcefully raised the question of the transit of arms and ammunition through Lourenço Marques to the Transvaal. The right of such transit was guaranteed by the Transvaal-Portuguese treaty of 1875, which the British government as suzerain had ratified in 1882; it had not been contemplated, of course, that arms for possible use against the suzerain might be covered by it. But the Portuguese government pointed out that it would be difficult for them to impose restrictions on the trade in time of peace. If war were to break out between Great Britain and the Transvaal, that would be a different matter; and on

---

to Portugal, the Foreign Office, and still more the Colonial Office, appeared to suppose that a territorial guarantee could be made a *quid pro quo* for virtual control of Delagoa Bay.

The result is an inadvertent presentation of the British as much less willing to enter an agreement than they seemingly were—Salisbury himself excepted.

September 12, 1899, Soveral went so far as to propose—with, he said, the authority of his government—an Anglo-Portuguese "engagement" that "would enable England to attack the Transvaal by the Delagoa Bay Railway, and to make Lourenço Marques our base of operations."[32] This seemingly cynical proposal—for unless the Transvaal should attempt to seize Lourenço Marques, Portugal could have no direct quarrel with her—rested at bottom on a reciprocal obligation to defend each other's territory, embodied in the earliest Anglo-Portuguese treaties of alliance, dating from the fourteenth century. To revive this obligation would have provided Portugal with an answer to any charges of bad faith coming from the Transvaal, and with the means of enforcing its corollary on the British. King Carlos, with a view to silencing doubters in the Portuguese government itself, wrote to José Luciano in support of Soveral's proposal:

Any doubts raised at this moment can only serve to delay a decision, and such *occasions* are so few that it is necessary to grab them by the hair: if we let this one pass, we shall certainly not soon have another; and it is necessary for our peace of mind that we do not let it escape by any means.[33]

Nevertheless, Lisbon boggled at an out-and-out obligation to declare war at British request; and Salisbury, for his part, felt that the fourteenth century was "going very far back" and that it would be better to rely, so far as British obligations were concerned, on the ipsissima verba of the treaties of 1642 and 1661. The first precluded a declaration of neutrality by Portugal, which might have prevented British ships from coaling at Lourenço Marques; the second bound the British "to defend and protect all conquests or Colonies belonging to the Crown of Portugal against all his enemies as well future as present." The Anglo-Portuguese Secret Declaration,* signed by Salisbury and Soveral on October 14, consisted, in effect, of a recital of the relevant clauses of the treaties of 1642 and 1661, with two up-to-date glosses forbidding the passage of arms through Lourenço Marques and precluding a Portuguese declaration of neutrality.[34] By the time it was signed, the second Boer War had already broken out.

Von Bülow, who first heard of the declaration unofficially about a year later, referred to it in his *Memoirs* as a piece of "perfidious duplicity ... in flagrant contradiction to the spirit of the Anglo-German

* This is often referred to mistakenly as the Treaty of Windsor.

agreement ... [and] above all, an encouragement [to Portugal] not to pledge her colonies."[35] One sees what he means—yet the declaration contained no new undertaking not implicit in existing treaties, and for that reason required no ratification (unlike the Anglo-German conventions). Sir Edward Grey evidently saw no incompatibility between the undertakings to Germany and to Portugal, for he not only entered into a revised version of the former in October 1913, but proposed to publish all.[36] It was not until the new agreement with them had been initialed that the general terms of the Anglo-Portuguese Declaration were conveyed to the Germans officially.[37] The German government, however, professed to think that public opinion would accuse them of having made a fool's bargain if the treaties were published: properly so, one might add, for if the Wilhelmstrasse had done its homework in 1898, instead of forcing the pace out of greed for territory, it could have found out the precise extent of British commitments to Portugal.* The amateurishness condemned by Eyre Crowe was not unilateral. As publication was, for Grey, a sine qua non of entrance into any further agreement, the matter was allowed to rest by mutual consent in the spring of 1914. Something might have come of it if World War I had not supervened, for Grey made no bones about his dislike of having his hands tied: "I wish," he wrote in January 1913, "to get the Portuguese Alliance subsequently made for a term of years instead of for eternity."[38] The explicit anti-Boer and anti-French aspects of the original agreements had, indeed, become obsolete with the passage of time—and only the implicit betrayal of an ally remained.

---

* Grenville, *Lord Salisbury,* pp. 262–63, errs in supposing that the Portuguese government had had an unqualified objection to the text of the declaration of 1899 being communicated to the German government. According to Lansdowne himself, Soveral said that this might be embarrassing *unless* [my italics] Portugal were simultaneously informed of the Anglo-German agreements, and the German government gave an undertaking not to communicate the Anglo-Portuguese Declaration to any other power. He further pointed out that the latter did not affect German territory or interests, whereas the former did affect Portuguese territory and interests. "I told M. de Soveral," Lansdowne continues, "that in my opinion it would be much better that the Portuguese Declaration should not be communicated to the German Government nor the Anglo-German Agreement to Portugal." Lansdowne–MacDonell, February 19, 1901, No. 15 Africa (C.P. 7537, No. 40; not in B.D.).

The Boer War, expectation of which had been the motive for the 1898 and 1899 agreements alike, has often been regarded as the archetype of economic imperialism as expounded in the work of J. A. Hobson and his successors.[39] Such an interpretation of history presupposes conscious calculation in considerable degree—and of this, at any rate, the agreements must be pronounced innocent. Instead of getting a long-term economic advantage—control of the port of Lourenço Marques—in return for reiterating their treaty obligations to Portugal, the British got a short-term military one; for the hypothetical reversion of a fragmented African dominion, both British and Germans sacrificed what, in appearance at least, were promising openings for capital investment. Though the agreements of 1898 had no proximate economic motive, they, together with the Boer War, had quite marked economic consequences for the affected territories. The political motive for concession hunting disappeared, with the opportunity for playing off one designing power against another. The British and the Germans had not merely agreed each to refrain from seeking concessions in the territory of which the other had the reversion: they had gone further and agreed that any concession to one must be matched by an equivalent concession to the other. In these circumstances, there was no incentive for either to seek additional concessions, nor for the Portuguese government to grant any. It is true—the more so since their existence was not officially admitted—that the treaties did not bind private individuals. But the British government, at any rate, felt bound to discourage any of its nationals from making fresh investments in the territories assigned to Germany. When Grey remarked, as he did more than once in 1912 and 1913, on the need for the Portuguese colonies to be developed, he was seemingly unaware that the treaties had been drafted as if with the deliberate intent of discouraging development—a feature which was preserved in the revised Anglo-German agreement of 1913.[40]

The subsequent history of the Catembe (Eiffe) concession shows, however, that those responsible for the treaties of 1898 had only a hazy idea of what they were doing. The importance attached to the concession on both sides seems to have been due to topographical ignorance. In November 1898, Bertie drew up a solemn memorandum about it, in the light of the Portuguese reluctance to contract an Anglo-German loan—a fact, he concluded, that did not relieve the British from their obligation to adopt a friendly attitude toward the request for the Catembe concession to be confirmed.[41] He suggested, however, that the Germans might be forestalled if a British syndicate acquired the Lingham concession (which, though Bertie may not have been aware of it, was on the same side of the Espirito Santo river as Lourenço Marques and capable, as Catembe was not, of ready connection with the existing railway inland). MacDonell, for his part, pointed out that any objections raised against Eiffe could be turned against Lingham.[42] Nevertheless, the Colonial Office continued to make difficulties about the statutes of the proposed company that was to work the Eiffe concession—a matter that lay entirely within the province of the Portuguese government; and neither MacDonell nor Chamberlain was wholly satisfied with Salisbury's acceptance of assurances by Soveral, in March 1899, that the company to be formed by Eiffe was and would remain Portuguese and that the Catembe foreshore would not be alienated.* The concession was at length confirmed, as was that to Lingham; but the Boer War cut it down to size at long last. In 1902, Eiffe threw his hand in and actually offered the concession to the British government, which in turn referred the question to the new government of the conquered Transvaal. After that, it seems to have disappeared from political history.[43]

Any importance the Catembe concession ever had was political rather than economic; but there were more ambitious enterprises that were likewise affected by the Anglo-German treaty. One of these was the Mossamedes Company, which had been established in 1894 by José Pereira do Nascimento, an enthusiastic promoter of white settlement in southern Angola. Its area of operations comprised a broad strip of land immediately north of the frontier with German Southwest Africa, running behind, but not including, the coastal strip south from Porto Alexandre to the mouth of the Cunene River, and extending inland as far as the yet undelimited eastern frontier of Angola with Barotseland. It was well south of the port of Moçâmedes and the existing settlements on the Huíla plateau. The total area of the concession

---

* MacDonell even referred, in a private letter to Bertie, to "His Lordship's [Salisbury's] apparent infatuation and 'complaisance' to Soveral." MacDonell–Bertie, private, March 9, 1899 (F.O. 63/1440).

was twenty-three million hectares; the initial capital wholly or mainly French.* Clearly, any chance of development on a large scale depended on building a railway inland from Porto Alexandre or Baia dos Tigres, the harbor farther south. In May 1898, Count Blücher, the grandson of the co-victor of Waterloo, approached the Foreign and Colonial Offices in London with a scheme for taking over the concession and building the railway. Alfred Beit and other associates of Rhodes were also said to be fishing for the concession, and there was talk—which Chamberlain and Selborne pronounced inopportune— of bringing them and Blücher's group together. Monson, the British ambassador in Paris, took soundings and reported that this group did not want to have anything to do with Rhodes: "Naturally . . . [they] apprehend that the ogre Rhodes would devour them." There followed an episode worthy of one of Hilaire Belloc's satirical novels of Edwardian politics: an unsigned letter was produced by Blücher to the effect that "Mr. Cassell [presumably Ernest Cassel, the financier and friend of King Edward VII] would be willing to put up the money to buy the concession in return for a K.C.M.G." This caused a good deal of hilarity among ministers and high officials, but some answer had to be returned, and eventually an unsigned reply went back to the effect that Her Majesty's government could not bind Her Majesty in advance, but that in the past it had never been chary of rewarding services to the Empire. Even before the Anglo-German treaty was signed, however, Salisbury gave instructions that the business not be pursued: to do so would be to court "the suspicion of bad faith," inasmuch as there was no likelihood that the area in question would ever come into British hands. Later, it was rumored that the German government had bought a large block of shares in the Mossamedes Company.[44]

More embarrassing to the British were new proposals for acquisition or development that arose after the treaties came into force, and had to be discouraged without adequate explanation. The most important of these concerned the Benguela railway, the entire length of which was to run through a part of Angola of which Germany had the

---

* Arthur de Moraes Carvalho, *Companhias de Colonização* (Coimbra, 1903), pp. 106–8; J. Darcy, *La Conquête de l'Afrique* (Paris, 1900), pp. 164–66. The French Admiralty would have liked a coaling station at Moçâmedes; see Note for the Minister [of Foreign Affairs], May 15, 1899 (D.D.F., Série I, Tom. 15, No. 176).

reversion. Its promoter, Robert Williams, who intended to exploit the Katanga copper belt and needed a rail outlet thence to the Atlantic, was, fortunately for his project, given a private introduction to Soveral. Soveral had long been aware of the possibilities of the line—he had talked to Salisbury about it in 1898, by way of reproach for the Anglo-German treaties—and in October 1902, he himself introduced Williams (telling him on no account to inform the Foreign Office) to Teixeira de Sousa, the Portuguese Minister of Marine and Colonies.[45] It so happened that Teixeira de Sousa was even then seeking bids for the first section of a railway inland from Benguela, to be built at state expense under a law passed in 1899, and he rapidly fell in with Williams' proposal when he found, to his surprise, that caution money of no less than £100,000, which he had stipulated by way of deterrent, was forthcoming. A contract for the whole of the line was signed at the end of November. There was to be no subsidy: indeed, the Portuguese government was to receive shares in the proposed company to the value of £300,000, one-tenth of the nominal capital. There can be no doubt that one of the strongest motives for granting the concession was the desire to frustrate the Anglo-German treaty, and it was therefore inept of Teixeira de Sousa's critics to carry on an extended press campaign against the "Williams concession" on the ground that it meant the loss of Angola to Portugal.[46]

The concession was to prove an act of faith on the part of all concerned, for the difficulties of construction and of finance were far greater than had been foreseen: work was not begun until two years after the contract was signed, and a year later only forty miles of the line had been even partly completed. Virtually no local labor was available, so that East Indian coolies had to be brought from Natal; the climb from sea level up onto the Angolan plateau was through absolutely waterless country and the gradient so steep in one place that the expensive rack-rail system had to be adopted over two and a half miles of track. Finally, at the end of 1908, construction was held up completely through lack of funds.[47] There were political difficulties besides: the Germans were "furious" (King Edward VII's word) about the very grant of the concession, and opposition to the scheme in South Africa was steady and persistent.* The Foreign Office, debarred from

* For King Edward VII's observation, see minute (unsigned), November 30, 1902, on Gosselin–Lansdowne, telegram, November 29, 1902, No. 29 (F.O. 2/638), reporting the grant of the concession.

doing anything for the promoters and unable to tell them why, had recourse to a kind of despairing skepticism: "If the scheme is really impracticable," ran a minute of November 1903, "it would be better for it to be abandoned now, rather than later on . . . the less the amount of capital lost, the less the injury to British financial and engineering prestige."[48] Nearly ten years later, when the line was yet again in need of money, the Foreign Office went so far as to advise Williams to seek it in Germany. That an enterprise in territory under Portuguese sovereignty should be hindered in raising capital by reason of a restrictive secret agreement made with ulterior motives by two foreign powers was no less indefensible because it was implicit in the original Anglo-German treaties.*

Another equally unforeseen result of the treaties was to appear in the subsequent history of the Moçambique Company. In the first years of its existence, that concern had been predominantly French, and for that reason the British Colonial Office had been strongly opposed to the suggestion, put forward in 1897, that its concession should be extended to take in the district of Lourenço Marques. The leading influence on the company's London committee, which shared the effective control with its Paris committee, was one Ochs, who was connected with other African enterprises, including the Djibouti–Addis Ababa railway, and whose principal concern seems to have been to get rid of his shares at a profit. In the autumn of 1898, he was said to have been approaching Rochfort Maguire and Alfred Beit in the hope that the Chartered Company would buy him out. In 1897, he had apparently been in touch with Leyds, and had proposed a covert sale to the Transvaal.[49] French influence at the European end of the company had never been matched by a comparable influence at Beira, which was, for most practical purposes, a British colonial settlement (as Ayres d'Ornellas had noted) and where the key individual was a certain Colonel Arnold, a protégé of Sir George Goldie, who, since 1899, had been "Director-General of Exploitation" for the territory.

After the Boer War, Ochs and his party made a sustained attempt to gain control of the company, and enlisted the support of the Foreign Office to ensure benevolent neutrality on the part of the Portuguese government, which had a considerable number of sharehold-

---

* See, for example, Vansittart, minute, July 2, 1914 (B.D., Vol. X, Part II, p. 574). Nicolson, somewhat earlier, had referred to the proviso in the treaty as "an arbitrary and unusual act" (minute, December 28, 1912, *ibid.*, p. 498).

ing votes ex officio, but had never used them. In November 1902, a compromise between British and French interests was reached under which the Belgian Colonel Thys, King Leopold's associate, became chairman of the united London and Paris committees, and the British nominee, the Marqués de Fontes Pereira de Mello (son of the creator of fontismo) became managing director in Lisbon. In January 1903, Arnold discussed the whole question with Chamberlain and Milner, apparently on the assumption (which was said to be shared by Thys) that complete British control of the territory was simply a matter of time; and that the only question was how best to achieve that end. As Arnold put it, in October of the same year: "The London Directorate have . . . arrived at a point beyond which it becomes difficult if not dangerous for private financiers to advance. It thus becomes necessary to turn round and see upon what lines the amplification and increase of British control of the Territory can best advance."[50]

According to Arnold, Chamberlain and Milner were at one with him in agreeing that the Chartered Company, or a group backed by it, would be the most suitable vehicle. The Foreign Office, remembering Portuguese hostility to the Chartered Company, counseled caution: "I spoke . . . to Ld [Albert] Grey," wrote Lansdowne in August 1903. "He quite understands the necessity of keeping the Chartered Company out of the affair. If any Mozambique shares are bought, they will be acquired by persons wholly unconnected with the Co."[51]

Nothing more was done at that time, but at the end of 1904, the question of control arose again: a further appeal was made for Foreign Office assistance in getting rid of Thys, and again Portuguese neutrality was secured by "unofficial" representations. Sir Thomas Holditch now became chairman of the London and Paris committees in place of Thys. Nothing more was done openly till July 1908, when Arnold wrote to the Colonial Office suggesting that the Moçambique Company's territory be leased to the British. It appears that the Colonial Office had never been informed officially of the Anglo-German treaties—and Chamberlain had by that time retired from politics.[52] Even Selborne, who had been Colonial Undersecretary in 1898 and who now, in accordance with what in Portugal would have been termed rotativismo, was High Commissioner in South Africa in succession to Milner, was ignorant of (or had forgotten) them, for he expressed sympathy with Arnold's scheme. But the Foreign Office, to whom it was submitted, at once pointed out that it would bring the Secret Note of 1898 into operation, under which the Germans might demand a quid pro quo before such a lease could be effective. On Arnold's comment to Selborne that "much spadework must be done" before the matter could be broached between governments, the Foreign Office observed that the sooner such spadework was put a stop to, the better.[53] A proposal, about this same time, by the new Transvaal colonial government to lease the port and railway of Lourenço Marques was discouraged on the same ground.[54]

Yet another instance of the shortsightedness of the British negotiators of 1898 had come to light a few years earlier. In 1899–1900, the British Major Spilsbury had led an expedition, on behalf of the Nyassa Company, which had established the settlement known as Porto Amélia on Pemba Bay, and had penetrated some distance inland. In January 1900, he wrote to the Foreign Office giving an account of the country and of the splendid harbor: referring to the rumor that it might revert to Germany, he urged that the British should not agree to this in ignorance of its true value. A few months later, the Admiralty wrote officially to the Foreign Office that it considered it of great importance that Pemba Bay should not fall into the hands of Germany or any strong maritime power. In each case, the most the Foreign Office could do was to register a secret comment: "Too late."[55]

IV

The Portuguese financial crisis, which had been the pretext for the treaties of 1898, was at length resolved in 1902 by an agreement with the foreign creditors.[56] During the first part of 1899, the government and various national bondholders' committees had reached agreement in principle on a scheme whereby the interest to be paid on the various classes of external bonds would be gradually increased, beginning July 1, 1903, from one-third to two-thirds of its nominal amount (that is, to twice the rate currently being paid), and fresh arrangements would be made for their redemption. Thereupon the bondholders would forgo their shares in excess customs receipts and in the profits arising from a fall in the exchange rates provided for in Fuschini's decree of May 1893. As before, the interest would be secured on the customs receipts. Two stumbling blocks, however, arose at the last moment: the German and French bondholders' committees attempted to insist on a positive control of Portuguese revenues beyond that secured by bondholders' representation on the Junta do Credito Publico; and the rumors, resulting from the Anglo-German agreements, that Portugal intended to sell or lease one or more of the colonies, caused all the bondholders to wonder whether they should not attempt to secure a share in the proceeds of any such transaction. Negotiations with the German and French committees continued into 1900, and they were still not concluded by June, when the Luciano de Castro government fell and was replaced by the regeneradores under Hintze Ribeiro. Hintze, of course, had been Prime Minister when the decree of May 1893 was passed, and he now declared that it represented the most that the Portuguese treasury could afford for the present. He may have been influenced by the immediate need to find a million sterling for the Berne award ("no small matter," as King Carlos remarked, adding that it was less than he had expected, but that "abroad it appeared very little and was a great disillusionment to many.")[57]

Nevertheless, in November 1900 Hintze sent a high official of the Ministry of Finance to reopen negotiations in Paris. These did not go well, and both French and German governments appeared to be making menacing noises on the part of their constituents—so much so that the Portuguese appealed to the British, who had already made it clear to all concerned that they would not accept foreign control of Portugal's finances. Any attempt to forestall discussion in the French Parliament was ruled out in London, for this would only have irritated Delcassé, the French Foreign Minister, to no purpose: in February 1901, such a discussion did take place in the Senate, and Delcassé spoke with some force on the financial misdeeds of Portugal. Meanwhile, the Germans had also been moving: Tattenbach, their minister in Lisbon, called on MacDonell early in January and expressed the view—for which he can hardly have expected sympathy by that time—that it was time to act up to the spirit of the secret arrangement of 1898 and "bring the Portuguese to their senses." It was as a result of this interview that Soveral was sounded by Lansdowne about the publication of the Anglo-Portuguese declaration. It had, however, been noted in London that Delcassé had refrained from demanding any foreign control of Portuguese finances; and Lansdowne, in conjunction with Soveral, used his good offices to restart the negotiations between France and Portugal.[58] The French treasury official Louis Lhomme, who had been consultant to the French bondholders since 1897, and had throughout acted in the closest collaboration with the Quai d'Orsay, went to Lisbon in June and at once concluded an agreement which his government was prepared to recommend and the French bondholders to accept.[59]

The new agreement was decidedly less favorable to the bondholder than that which had fallen through, thanks largely to French opposition, the previous year: and it was now the turn of the English bondholders to protest. They objected that the rate of interest on the three per cent loan (the only one held in Great Britain), instead of gradually rising to two-thirds of its nominal value, would be pegged in perpetuity at less than half that value by a means that was in itself objectionable, namely the arbitrary reduction of the nominal capital of the loan by 52.62256 per cent.* But they got scant sympathy from the Foreign Office, partly because of its traditional policy of non-intervention on behalf of private investors, and partly because it would do nothing in furtherance of the designs of Germany upon Portuguese territory. As Bertie wrote to Lansdowne at Christmas, 1901, the London bondholders' committee was "playing the game of the German Govt. and bondholders, which is opposed to British political interests."[60] Because the British and French governments were agreed in refusing to exercise diplomatic pressure on Portugal to improve its offer to the bondholders, and the German government was not, apparently, disposed to take a dissenting line, the result was a foregone conclusion: the offer was accepted in March 1902 after only minor amendments. The agreement provided that if the governments concerned wished it, a formal exchange of notes confirming the pact might take place; and the French and German governments acted accordingly, though the British, at Portugal's request, declined to do so on the ground that it might encourage interference by foreign powers in the administration of the Portuguese customs.

The agreement, for all that it ended years of anxiety, aroused great controversy in Portugal. There were student demonstrations at Coim-

---

* This monstrous decimal fraction was eventually rounded off to 50 per cent.

bra; the windows of the train bringing the Portuguese negotiator home from Paris were stoned (at the instigation, it was said, of Fuschini, who had been an inveterate opponent of any revision of his decree of 1893 so long as the finances of the country were unreformed), and the parliamentary debate before ratification was long and heated. Moreover, in the course of debate the government was constrained to admit that the customs receipts might prove inadequate to pay the increased rate of interest, that the rate might prove an excessive burden on the economy, and that financial reform was essential—or, in other words, that the debt agreement was a gamble taken for political motives.[61] In fact, things turned out better than either the government or its critics would have found reason to hope or expect. Indices of economic activity rose steadily during the first decade of the twentieth century. Revenues remained buoyant, lagging only slightly behind expenditures; and, thanks to a renewed influx of capital from the emigrants in Brazil, the exchange value of the paper milreis rose until, between 1905 and 1907, the premium on gold that had obsessed and embarrassed governments in the nineties was all but eliminated.[62] In short, a measure of financial and economic recovery was attained without the drastic medicine prescribed by Fuschini and other reformers—medicine that, by shrinking the note issue for instance, might have brought about economic depression. It is noteworthy that contemporary discussions of the Portuguese currency problem centered on the inadequate gold backing held by the Bank of Portugal for so large a note issue, and overlooked altogether the adequacy of the note issue for the business needs of the economy.

In the eyes of the reformers, these facts, had they realized them, would have been repugnant to political morality: like Dr. Salazar a generation later, they believed that the therapeutic effect of economic medicine was more or less proportionate to its unpleasantness. Moreover, they would have said, and said correctly, that the very smallness of the budgetary deficits after 1900 was proof that they were unnecessary—nothing more than evidence of corruption and maladministration. One reputable writer, Roque da Costa, even went so far as to condemn the original partial default of 1892 as unnecessary, the result of excessive pessimism about the country's economic prospects: "It is enough to recall that, notwithstanding all the upsets to which the régime of bankruptcy gave rise, the public receipts have risen between then and now by the colossal amount of 30,000 contos annually, in order to understand how easy it would have been to clean up Portuguese finances without recourse to undesirable means . . . compromising the nation's credit irremediably."[63]

This argument was valid up to a point, for taxable capacity had increased very considerably over the previous twenty years. But in one important respect it rested on a misapprehension: far from the national credit having been compromised by the events of 1892, they had been discounted in advance in the issue price of bonds. Successive governments had, in fact, borrowed at seven per cent, but had been deemed to have borrowed proportionately larger sums at lower rates, and hence were precluded from taking advantage of any improvement in the terms of borrowing that might have occurred in the interim. The chief incentive to balance the budget—the prospect of an advantageous debt conversion—was thus wholly absent: the fact that the country was expected to go bankrupt virtually forced it to do so.

An agreement whereby the bondholders conceded not merely a reduction in real interest rates but a reduction of capital indebtedness in return for a guarantee of payment was thus an indispensable preliminary to any reform of Portuguese finances. Contemporaries tended to think of such a reform in terms of a balanced budget; but this, as Afonso Costa was to show in the first years of the Republic (and Oliveira Salazar in the years after 1928), required no more than determination to bring about and was certainly not a cure-all. To quote Roque da Costa again:

It is not difficult to balance budgets by seizing from the taxpayer the greater part or the whole of his resources. Such a policy may gain applause for public men who seek easy publicity among [political] illiterates; but politicians of that sort are anything but statesmen. Your true statesman knows, above all, how to promote the national welfare by encouraging the creation of wealth, not atrophying it by fixed notions of budgetary equilibrium without regard to consequences.[64]

Roque da Costa was not, of course, arguing in favor of unbalanced budgets so much as in opposition to excessive taxation: he would have agreed with Dias Ferreira's principle that the way to bring the finances into equilibrium was to reduce expenditure. There is little to suggest that this way of doing things would have been conspicuously more advantageous, economically speaking, than the other, or than the course of moderate deficits that had been customarily pursued in the last years of the monarchy. In any case, the trouble with Portuguese taxation was not its weight per capita so much as its unfair incidence and bad administration. For this to have been changed in short order would have required the combined talents of Pombal and Mousinho da Silveira: it was certainly beyond those of the shaky régimes that preceded and followed the fall of the monarchy in 1910.

The fact that the settlement with the bondholders became in practice a substitute for financial reform rather than a preliminary to reform did not make it a bad thing in itself. But though it was initially thought of as a means of reducing the actual debt burden and the gold premium that had made that burden so onerous—and was, in fact, followed in 1903 by the floating of a fresh loan of £4 million in London with which to redeem the floating debt—its principal significance turned out to be political.[65] By setting off, in effect, the negotiations that led to the Anglo-German treaties of 1898, Ressano Garcia had caused to be raised the whole question of the relation of Portugal to the great powers, as well as the future of her African colonies. Distracted by their obsession with the Transvaal, the British had been led into a false—though immediately profitable—step which only World War I enabled them completely to retrace, but which they were at pains in the meantime to nullify. Having made a treaty which in part was directed against the French (MacDonell's Lisbon dispatches were for a time filled with denunciations of French "concession-mongers"[66]) they found themselves, eventually, at one with the French government in urging moderation on their own bondholders lest the power with whom they had made the treaty should be enabled to exploit it. The Portuguese, for their part, had learned that resentment makes a bad counselor, and that it was time to forgive, if not to forget, the ultimatum of 1890. As Wenceslau de Lima, Foreign Minister in 1906, claimed to have told Tattenbach, the embroilment with Britain at that time had been due to German instigation, and when the critical moment arrived, the support the Portuguese had expected from Germany had not been forthcoming. Whether this reproach was altogether justified is perhaps doubtful, though the British Foreign Office seized on it as an example of Germany's "want of scruples as to underhand dealings."[67] But it was indicative of the degree of rapprochement that by then had been attained between the British and Portuguese governments, and hence of the greater security of the Portuguese possessions. Whether that rapprochement extended to the majority of politically conscious Portuguese is doubtful—for the traditionally anti-British Republican party was growing in strength year by year.

Chapter ten

The Last Years of the Monarchy

In November 1901, Eduardo da Costa, Ennes' onetime chief of staff, gave an address to the Lisbon Geographical Society entitled "Military Occupation and Effective Dominion in Our Colonies."[1] He was concerned, he declared, to combat two false, though opposing notions that were prevalent: a majority opinion holding that, inasmuch as the soldiers in the colonies were accustomed to win their battles, there was no need for any special public concern with military matters; and a minority opinion that battles and punitive expeditions were no more than manifestations of a warlike itch, not founded on any real need to affirm and consolidate Portuguese rule. Though Costa did not say so, both opinions appear to have drawn strength and reinforcement from the meteoric career of his colleague Mousinho de Albuquerque, already in honorable eclipse as tutor to the heir apparent and within months of taking his own life. Later writers have made Mousinho into a martyr for the cause of empire, a part for which, indeed, he may well have cast himself on discovering that he might play no other.[2] Contemporaries were more skeptical, even in the aftermath of his coup at Chaimite. King Carlos himself told MacDonell, less than a month after Mousinho was made Royal Commissioner in Moçambique, that he was a first-rate officer but no administrator; and the British consul in Lourenço Marques reported later that Mousinho's well-intentioned activities had made a change in administration indispensable.[3]

I

In common with other officers of his generation, Mousinho was markedly articulate. His own account of his stewardship is persuasively and brilliantly written, and shows both breadth and depth of view; and it is not until one goes behind his policies to his modus operandi that his failure can be accounted for.* It is clear that from the time of his appointment as governor-general in March 1896—even before the special powers that Ennes had enjoyed were conferred upon him—he was prepared to act in defiance both of the Constitution and the Ministry of Marine in Lisbon. His friend and admirer Ayres d' Ornellas, who served as his chief of staff, clearly spoke for them both when he wrote home that:

[Our] astounding colonial legislation, for the most part enacted *à contre sens,* stands as a monument to the fatal effects of theories even on superior minds. To go no further, the most inapplicable of all are the financial law of Barros Gomes and the administrative law of Júlio de Vilhena. Both are literally incapable of application; and as attempts have been made to carry them out more or less literally, complete confusion has resulted.

It would take two or three years, Ornellas went on, to ascertain what was practicable in each district and what could be incorporated in laws of general application. Only then would it be possible to present a complete reform of the provincial organization:

Shall we be granted time for this? Shall we be allowed to remain here, when at every step we have to struggle against the ineptitude of the Ministry of Marine and its complete ignorance of the Overseas Territories? I don't know; but what I do know is that we are going ahead as if success were possible; and [I know too] that if Mousinho could be, was given time to be, the Faidherbe of this colony, we should have already done more for the Nation than all the Ministers of Marine in the last fifty years.**

---

* See Mousinho de Albuquerque, *Moçambique, 1896–98, passim.* A characteristically pointed criticism of this and similar appointments was made later by Ernesto de Vilhena, instancing the case of De Brazza in the French Congo, "Apuramento," *Diario Popular,* November 12–13, 1909; reprinted in Vilhena, *Questões Coloniais,* Vol. I (Lisbon, 1910), p. 400.

** Louis Léon César Faidherbe (1818–89) was a famous French administrator and military commander. He served two terms as governor of Sénégal, from 1854 to 1861 and from 1863 to 1865.

OCCUPATION IN 1906

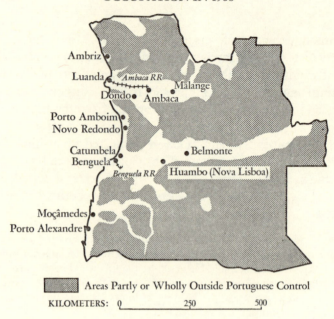

Areas Partly or Wholly Outside Portuguese Control

KILOMETERS: 0   250   500

OCCUPATION IN 1911

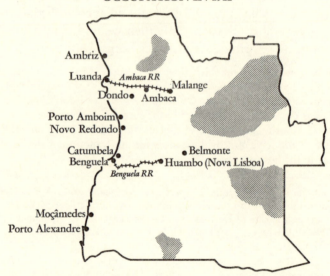

Angola: Extent of Occupation in 1906 and 1911

Ornellas was equally contemptuous of the Portuguese parliament: "when a man embodies, as Mousinho does, what popular feeling ranks highest—the love of glory and the need for authority—the miserable intrigues of the chattering lawyers who make up our bourgeois parliamentary system cannot cope with such a force."[4]

In the authoritarian atmosphere of Salazar's Portugal, such sentiments find a ready response: "The medieval paladin Mousinho," writes João Ameal, "was incompatible with the sorry parade of vanity and hypocrisy that marked the liberalism of 1900."[5] When one considers that a major achievement of the European Middle Ages was the enforcement of the rule of law, that judgment appears facile and partial. What exposed Mousinho to attack was precisely his evident willingness to suspend the rule of law in favor of military dictatorship—and not only in Moçambique, if rumor were to be trusted.[6] His unconstitutional raising of the hut tax in May 1896 (even though with the consent of the Minister of Marine), his arbitrary proclamation of a state of siege in the Moçambique district as a preliminary to punitive operations against certain chiefs on the mainland (the *namarraes*), and his subsequent court-martialling of five civilian inhabitants of the town of Moçambique on charges of giving aid and comfort to these chiefs were all actions impossible to defend by a plea, however justified, of good faith.[7] Such behavior played into the hands of critics who declared that the whole campaign against the namarraes was a put-up job to gain glory—and certainly there seems to have been no overt provocation on their part, but simply a want of submissiveness in general. Moreover, the first expedition against them was a failure—though not, apparently, an ignominious one—and the court-martial consequently bore the appearance of a hunt for scapegoats.

Mousinho's judgment in attacking the namarraes at all was further impugned when, early in 1897, a serious insurrection broke out in that very Gaza country that the capture of Gungunhana was thought to have made safe. Mousinho left the new district governor, Eduardo da Costa, to deal with the namarraes and organized a new expedition. At Macontene it routed five thousand ill-armed insurgents; their leader, Maguiguana, was later hunted down and slain.[8] As on previous occasions, a small column of trained troops—some 300 in number—was assisted by a force of African auxiliaries perhaps ten times as large, who served to crown the enemy discomfiture that overwhelming fire-power and a cavalry charge had begun. The outcome of any campaign fought in open country (as distinct from the denser brush in which the namarraes operated) was never really open to doubt: the Gaza insurrection presented no threat to Portuguese domination. Nevertheless, its very occurrence so soon after the glorious campaign of 1895 was calculated to provoke what Eduardo da Costa has called "malicious wonderment."[9]

It is one thing to hold the class of professional politicians in contempt; it is quite another to suppose that in consequence one can govern without regard to political, let alone legal, considerations. A man of Mousinho's opinions required a greater, rather than a lesser, degree of common prudence, since he could command no indulgence such as politicians commonly allow to one another. They were unlikely to feel the same way about allowing exceptional powers to him as they had in the case of Ennes, a civilian and one of themselves. Moreover, in February 1897 the regeneradores fell from power and José Luciano's progressistas took their place. It was not to be expected that any of the new ministers (and particularly the Minister of Marine) should feel a sense of personal obligation to a subordinate he had not chosen and who, moreover, did not regard himself as such; yet Mousinho persisted in behaving as if ministers were morally bound to support him in everything he chose to do. Every adverse or overriding decision, every delay in acceding to requests, was attributed to bad faith or want of moral courage. The blistering letter of resignation he addressed to José Luciano would convince all but the most partisan admirer that the writer was an impossible colleague: "My superiority consists in *having only one face* . . . . Your excellency, being a politician, *does not have only one*." [Italics in original.][10]

That Mousinho was riding for a fall does not, of course, alter the fact that he was got rid of in shabby and underhand fashion. Having encouraged him, in the winter of 1897–98, to go on a triumphal tour not only of Portugal but of western Europe (whence he returned with British, French, and German decorations), and having allowed him to return to Moçambique in the belief that his main proposals, including the raising of a loan for harbor works at Lourenço Marques, were acceptable, the government, without warning, issued a decree in July 1898 stripping Royal Commissioners of all exceptional powers—an action which could have had no other purpose than to force Mousinho's resignation.* That decree was, of course, signed by King Carlos, whose personal goodwill toward Mousinho is beyond doubt, but who was bound to have some regard for political realities. Mousinho's tragedy lay in the fact that he not only had no such regard but gloried in the fact; and it was this, as much as the malevolence of his political enemies, that brought about his untimely downfall and death.

To men of Mousinho's stamp, praise and blame are equally apt to be meted out in excess; and he would doubtless have agreed that the conclusions that had been drawn from his career were too sweeping. Costa argued that it was wrong to suppose that the role of the military in Portuguese Africa could henceforth be reduced to that of an armed police force responsible for keeping order. True, there were virtually ungarrisoned areas, like the district of Inhambane, where Portuguese dominion appeared firmly established; but these were exceptional. The experience of other colonial powers, like that of Portugal, demonstrated that complete military occupation was a prerequisite of political domination; and this was even more the case for Angola and Moçambique, with their powerful neighbors. Even though their boundaries were now recognized by treaty, and the powers appeared well disposed toward Portugal, it would clearly be unwise to count on a continuation of this state of affairs. "Let us beware *the doctrine of the fait accompli* and the *pressure of public opinion* in those great countries, where the strongest governments have to take it into account."[11] The time had gone by when Portugal could rely on men like the Goanese Manuel António de Sousa to sustain her influence; indeed, it was because she relied on his irregulars, rather than an organized force such as had triumphed in 1895, that she had lost the Manica plateau. (For Mousinho, Manuel António was no more than a potential Bonga, and his predominant part in the capture of Massangano was an index of Portuguese decadence.)** Neither the trader

---

* There was good constitutional warrant for it nevertheless. See *Administração Financeira das Províncias Ultramarinas: Proposta de Lei Orgánica e Relatorio Apresentados ao Congresso pelo Ministro das Colonias Artur R. de Almeida Ribeiro* (Coimbra, 1917†), p. 133. (This work is hereinafter cited as Almeida Ribeiro, *Administração Financeira*.)

** See pp. 141–42.

nor the missionary, valuable means of penetration though they were, could replace the soldier—and for that matter, did not the family of the Bonga claim to be Christians?[12]

The unsubdued areas of Angola and Moçambique, Costa urged, though they might be peaceful for the present, constituted a potential danger which should be dealt with before it could become actual. Two kinds of measures were required. Lines of penetration, fortified at intervals, should be established between the seaboard and the inland frontiers, thus covering the whole country with a network of fortified posts, which would be maintained regardless of the disposition of the inhabitants. In addition, any areas inhabited by recalcitrant tribesmen should be systematically subdued, not merely by destroying any armed resistance but by the seizure of crops and cattle and the internment (*pondo a bom recato*) of captured women and children. One should, Costa declared, follow the example given by Hoche in dealing with the counterrevolutionaries of the Vendée: show benignity to those who submit and extreme severity to those who resist. A forward policy of this kind would, he conceded, cost money, which the government did not have and the colonies could not produce. But there was no alternative: "Either we organize our colonial dominion *rapidly and solidly,* or we shall see it, very shortly, reduced to fragments of territory without value and ports without trade."[13]

II

The proposal to take the military initiative presupposed the creation of a civil administration for the territories that would likewise play a positive part, different from anything already existing there. The frustration endured by Mousinho and his colleagues at the hands of the *Terreiro do Paço* indicated clearly that the attempt to treat the colonies as if they were integral with the kingdom was absurd in principle and inefficient in practice.* For primitive Africans to have legal and political rights equal to those of the white inhabitants, whether of Portugal in Europe or overseas, was not only an affront to civilized men but pragmatically wrong as well. Mousinho had, for instance, poured scorn on the notion that penalties for crime be uniform:

* Terreiro do Paço is the location of the government offices in Lisbon, and the name is used in the same sense as "Whitehall" or "the Quai d'Orsay."

To apply to savages the penalties of a civilized country, in which men's moral sensibilities and conscience are entirely different, is the pinnacle of nonsense. Nor can one understand the application of penalties such as . . . suspension of political rights. . . . Transportation does not constitute a punishment, inasmuch as the black suffers no more in being exiled for a crime than in being taken from his country to enlist in a military contingent.

For a black who kills a white man there is only one useful penalty—death, which is today banished from our code of law.

And he had stigmatized as a dishonest farce the participation of the blacks in parliamentary and municipal elections.[14]

This aspect of "assimilation" (the name given to this policy) was not the sole, perhaps not the chief, objection to it from the administrators' point of view. What irked them more was the division of authority within each province and district that it infallibly brought about. Each of the departments within the Ministry of Marine—notably those of Finance and Public Works—had its own overseas staff, reporting direct to Lisbon and taking instructions only from Lisbon. The discretion allowed these officials was minimal; the district governor or governor-general had no control over them. "It is in Moçambique that Moçambique must be governed," Ennes had written in 1893. "In principle it is the Terreiro do Paço that governs the whole Portuguese world, but since the Terreiro do Paço cannot cope even with the routine of so much glory, it abdicates in favor . . . of the provincial authorities. This abdication is inevitable, and since legislation cannot abolish it, it must be regularized. . . . Already these functionaries [governors-general] have been told that *they can do what they like, so long as they do not ask for money*."[15] Mousinho had not found either Lisbon or the provincial departments so accommodating: in particular, the process by which the provincial budget was drawn up by the Financial Inspectorate in Lisbon, according to a rigorous series of rules and precedents and without regard to changing policies and circumstances, seemed to him absurd. Equally absurd were the attempts to prescribe every item of expenditure in advance and to prohibit any switches in expenditure, no matter how small or how urgent, without reference to Lisbon. Moreover, said Mousinho, the regulations required the provincial inspector of finance to have two attributes proper to the Almighty—omniscience and omnipresence; for he was charged with inspecting the tax-collecting and spending offices throughout the province, and yet was not permitted to be away from the capital (Moçambique) for more than three months in the year. He could not, Mousinho pointed out, get to outlying places like Zumbo and back in that time.[16]

The grant of exceptional powers to a Royal Commissioner was a way of cutting through red tape of this sort. But it had two disadvantages: first, it left the system, with all its vested interests, unchanged, instead of reforming it; second, it was calculated to provoke friction between the Royal Commissioner and any Minister of Marine who might feel that his constitutional powers were being infringed.[17] (Whereas Ennes had managed to work with the skeptical Ferreira d'Almeida, Mousinho had fallen foul of Dias Costa and the withdrawal of his special powers had followed.) Moreover, there was always the possibility that an active and determined minister might try to get the machine to work more effectively toward its own ends and so make matters worse. Thus, the impracticability of Barros Gomes' financial regulations of 1888 had been mitigated by his failure to set up the bureaucratic mechanism that would carry them out. Teixeira de Sousa, who became Minister of Marine in June 1900, describes the situation of the colonial finances as follows:

The colonies, as a rule, had no budgets and presented no accounts: none knew the legality or legitimacy of the expenditures, nor what was done with the receipts; and the outcome was an [annual] deficit of 2,000 contos ... not counting the extraordinary military expeditions, the costs of the Ambaca and Mormugão railroads, the compensation paid for the Lourenço Marques line, and the subsidies to telegraph cables.[18]

Accordingly, the new minister set up an Inspectorate-General of Overseas Finance and appointed the ablest man he could find to it. Shortly afterward, the new inspector-general asked to be relieved of his post because of harassment by a colleague of equal rank, who, he said, had blocked the entry to his department with numerous packing cases. Taxed with this, the colleague declared that he was only obeying the law of 1888 under which all colonial documents-of-account were to be sent to the chief of the colonial accounting section, then newly created. As neither Barros Gomes nor any subsequent minister had appointed any staff to that section, the documents had simply been left unopened until, after twelve years, there was someone whose job it was to deal with them. By that time their numbers ran, of course, into thousands.[19]

Teixeira de Sousa goes on to remark with pride that he reformed the whole system of colonial accounting and budgeting so that it became truly rigorous. Whereas a ministry circular of 1892 had sensibly (though unlawfully) put responsibility for provincial finances on the governor, Teixeira de Sousa's regulation removed him entirely from the financial picture.[20] It carried Barros Gomes' law of 1888, which Ornellas had described as "literally incapable of application," to its logical conclusion.* It was consistent with Teixeira de Sousa's general practice of keeping colonial policies in his own hands without undue reference to the man on the spot, of which the grant of the Williams concession is a conspicuous example.** But just as forceful governors-general ran into opposition, so did the forceful minister. The opposition to Teixeira de Sousa's methods was expressed in systematic form in a lengthy and detailed memorandum on civil administration in the African possessions that was presented by Eduardo da Costa to a Colonial Congress held in the later part of 1901, and that formed a logical corollary to the author's views on military policy.[21]

Though Costa appears not to have studied the practice of other metropolitan powers at first hand, his knowledge of the literature was considerable, and he ranged over every aspect of comparative colonial administration. His memorandum was thus much more than the distillation of his own experience, and provided a complete blueprint for would-be reformers. The principle underlying it, however, was simple: the concentration of authority and responsibility, within a given province, in the hands of the chief executive. According to Costa, there ought to be decentralization; but autonomy was sought "not for the colony, but for the governor," as a later critic put it.[22] The governor might be assisted by an advisory council composed of both official and nonofficial members, but the latter would be nominated, not elected. Representation of the provinces in the metropolitan parliament would cease. At lower levels of the administrative hierarchy the same concentration of authority would prevail: the

---

* Ramada Curto's project for administrative reform in Angola, put forward in 1905, would have made the governor legally responsible for provincial finances, and so (he said) would have enshrined the habitual practice "when not forbidden by regulations in the opposite sense." *Projecto de Reorganisação Administrativa da Província de Angola: elaborado na província em 1905* (Lisbon, Imprensa Nacional, 1905), p. 13.
** See above, p. 262.

district governor—who in Africa should be a military man—would be the delegate of the provincial governor in all matters save justice and religion; and the chief of the native circumscription (which, under Costa's plan, would have been the unit of local government in areas that, though pacified, did not contain sufficient Europeans to justify the establishment of municipalities) would likewise be solely answerable to the district governor. At this local level, specialist officers would be rare, and the administrator would therefore be empowered to communicate directly with officers at district or provincial level. The administration would need to be, like his analogue the Collector in British India, "judge, accountant, and administrator in one," as well as having "some knowledge of agriculture, engineering, and political economy."[23] Costa recognized that the selection of these key officials would need to be rigorous, and he devoted a whole section of his paper to the training, remuneration, and working conditions of a colonial civil service.[24] He did not, however, consider whether a sufficient number of recruits would be forthcoming even if his proposals were carried out.

One point on which Costa was particularly insistent was that the administrator should also be judge of first instance in all questions concerning natives that the tribal chiefs were unable to settle. Apart from administrative convenience, his main reason seems to have been that this practice corresponded to native custom and would therefore be more readily accepted and understood. There was no intention of taking away jurisdiction from the chiefs, for it was both politic and convenient that they should continue to deal with questions arising among their own subjects, leaving to the administrator only matters in which members of different tribes, or black men and white, were concerned; or offences against the chief's authority or that of the Portuguese. (Costa himself had attempted to establish such a system when district governor in Moçambique, and it had been endorsed by Mousinho—but Lisbon objected that it was "contrary to the custom of centuries.") Finally, Costa suggested that an attempt should be made to codify and purge of savagery the native law (the only law that should be applied to the African); and that in applying it, the administrator, and any superior court, should properly be assisted by native assessors.[25]

The Colonial Congress was sufficiently impressed by Costa's arguments to pass a motion in favor of granting financial and administrative autonomy to all the overseas provinces. In November 1904, a progressista Minister of Marine went so far as to invite proposals from the provincial governors for allowing the peoples of the territories to participate in their government, "consonant with their state of civilization, traditions and customs"—an idea that Costa and the other supporters of authoritarian decentralization frowned upon.* In May 1906, Ornellas, who had succeeded to his father's hereditary peerage, actually became Minister of Marine and Colonies: characteristically, in a dictatorial, "king's friend," antiparty administration headed by the dissident regenerador João Franco. A short while earlier, Costa himself had been appointed governor-general of Angola; later that year, Freire de Andrade was appointed governor-general of Moçambique. It looked as if Mousinho were to be posthumously avenged on the diehards of the Terreiro do Paço, for in May 1907 a decree was issued reorganizing the administration of Moçambique in accordance with the principles Costa had enunciated over five years earlier. The decree was preceded by a forthright preamble, in Ornellas' best style, appealing to the principles of decentralization laid down by Rebello da Silva in 1869, condemning the "dilution of local authority and its concentration in Lisbon" (particularly singling out the preparation of colonial budgets in the financial secretariat there), and defending at some length a decision that Mousinho would not have approved, but which by this time appeared inevitable: the transfer of the provincial capital from Moçambique Island to Lourenço Marques.** In one important respect the decree went beyond Costa's proposals: it established a separate provincial secretariat for native affairs. The need for this had become increasingly apparent since the turn of the century as the demands for Moçambique labor from the South African mines continued to grow.

It was Ornellas' intention to follow this decree with a similar reform for Angola, for which Costa had prepared a draft in November 1906, but he was denied the opportunity.[26] In February 1908, the João Franco regime was brought down abruptly by the assassination of the king and the heir apparent. (Costa himself had died in harness,

* José de Macedo, *Autonomia de Angola* (Lisbon, 1910), pp. 190–91. Ramada Curto's proposals of 1905, referred to above, were put forward in response to this circular.
** The decree and preamble are reprinted in Ornelas, *Colectânea*, Vol. III, pp. 267–338.

in May 1907.) In the period of short-lived ministries and political in-decision that followed, the policy of Ornellas was not merely halted but reversed. The decree of May 1907, issued at a time when the Côrtes was not sitting, required retrospective parliamentary sanction (and, even so, may have been unconstitutional).[27] Teixeira de Sousa, though out of office, carried great weight in the regenerador party; and he campaigned for a modification of the decree. Ornellas' suc-cessor as Minister of Marine was none other than Augusto de Cas-tilho, an ex-governor of the old school; in November 1908, he issued a decree which, in effect, restored most of the authority of the Inspec-torate of Finance over the Moçambique budget. The reaction was taken further in the early years of the Portuguese Republic, in decrees of December 1910 and August 1912 that emphasized the independence of the provincial inspector of finance, who was henceforth to report directly to the Minister of Colonies.[28]

By that time, however, it was clear that if the Costa-Ornellas doc-trine was too revolutionary for the bureaucrats in the Terreiro do Paço, it was too authoritarian for many other people—especially, per-haps, in Angola. Each of the five governors-general who served there in the first decade of the twentieth century produced his own paper constitution for the province, differing from the others in varying degrees. That presented by Ramada Curto in 1905, for instance, pro-posed to revive the provincial consultative committee (Junta Geral), which had been established in 1876 but had almost immediately fallen into desuetude, and to endow it with a budget, a staff, and certain administrative powers. It also proposed to incorporate S. Tomé and Príncipe in the province of Angola.[29] Ramada Curto's scheme would have permitted civilians to serve as district governors, except in two hinterland districts designated as military; Costa likewise had dis-tinguished between civilian and military districts in his Angolan scheme, whereas the plan actually adopted for Moçambique followed his earlier recommendation that all district governors be military.* But, as José de Macedo wrote in 1910, none of these plans corre-

---

* Compare Costa, "Relatório e Projecto de Reorganização," Titulo IV, *Colectânea*, Vol. I, pp. 260–62, with Ornellas' decree, Cap. XIII, pp. 317–20. Costa proposed dividing Angola into two provinces—the north to be governed by the governor-general, and the south by a lieutenant-governor at Benguela. He would really have preferred to set up a third province farther south. See *ibid.*, pp. 215–16.

sponded to the aspirations of the settlers: "The autonomy of Angola
... cannot be sketched within the narrow ambit of a governor's private office, preoccupied as he is with his personality and powers, and without the courage to break with the preconceptions by which he is contaminated.... [It] must be the work of the active and thinking elements of the province itself."[30]

Macedo added that it was not for Lisbon to send out constitutions as Jean-Jacques Rousseau had done for Poland. Nonetheless, and even under the Republic, Lisbon continued to do just that. At bottom the reason was financial—as was the reason for Teixeira de Sousa's persistent opposition to autonomy. As Minister of Marine he had been concerned to control the size of colonial budgetary deficits, if not to get rid of them altogether. He had also pursued the time-honored policy of using surpluses in one colony to compensate for deficits in another: "All the colonies had, so to speak, a common coffer." The chief beneficiary under this policy, other than the metropolitan exchequer, had always been Angola; the chief contributors, Macau, S. Tomé, and, latterly, Moçambique. Teixeira de Sousa justified S. Tomé's contribution as a recompense for the cocoa plantation labor there, which came, of course, from Angola; and he objected to the Ornellas decree of 1907 especially because it put an end to any contribution from Moçambique.[31]

III

Teixeira de Sousa was likewise opposed to the forward military policy of which the administrative reforms giving more power to governors-general were a corollary. He felt that in southern Angola particularly, where raids from the Ovampo tribes east of the river Cunene were a constant nuisance to the settled country to the west, and where fear of German intrigues furnished an additional incentive for asserting Portuguese authority, a policy of "peaceful attraction" was less risky, less costly, and more certain of success than were military expeditions.[32] As Minister of Finance in 1903, he opposed the plan of General Gorjão (who had followed him as Minister of Marine) to send an expedition into Ovampoland—only to be told, he says, that the German government had already been sounded and had raised no objection. As it turned out, a small expedition, amounting to no more than a reconnaissance force, was sent, and confirmed his fears: a large part of it fell into an ambush in the Cuamato country, just east of the Cunene, in September 1904, and suffered such crippling losses that it was forced to withdraw completely. Considerations of face, if no others, required that this defeat be avenged; and Eduardo da Costa was given the task of drawing up a plan of campaign—a task he performed with his habitual thoroughness and caution. But the government boggled at the scale and expense of the operation he proposed, and it was dropped, ostensibly on the ground (which those familiar with the country pooh-poohed) that sufficient native carriers and draft oxen could not be obtained in Angola.[33]

Instead of one campaign designed to complete the conquest of the troubled area in a single season, a series of small expeditions was conducted by successive governors of the Huíla district in each year from 1905 to 1910. In the earlier years, no more was accomplished than the consolidation of Portuguese authority west of the Cunene; and no decisive move was made against the Cuanhamas, the most feared of the Ovampo tribes. Some thought that this was due as much to over-caution (for which Costa, as governor-general, and Alves Roçadas, as governor of Huíla, were blamed) as to want of military strength: in September 1906, dissident officers in the column commanded by Roçadas, which was halted on the Cunene by Costa's orders, actually tried to telegraph the king for permission to advance.[34] Under their respective successors, Paiva Couceiro and João de Almeida, a bolder policy was pursued, though with meagre resources. Almeida conceived the plan of bypassing the Cuanhama country until it could be conquered; in 1909 he led a small force, largely composed of native irregulars, southeast and eastward along the Cubango River, which for a great part of its length forms the southern boundary of Angola, almost as far as the Barotseland boundary. Though unopposed, this march was important because it put a stop to infiltration across the Cubango by Germans posing as traders (*pseudofunantes*). Along with other mopping-up operations conducted by Almeida in 1910, it constituted a major contribution to the objectives laid down in Costa's 1901 memorandum.[35] But it did not dispense with the need to deal with the Cuanhamas. Moura Braz, Almeida's successor, wrote in 1912 that "the immediate occupation of the Cuanhama region is a question of prestige, administration and patriotism. . . . The other peoples, in their simple way, think we fear the Cuanhamas and are impotent against them. This does not conduce to maintaining among these people the necessary respect and submissiveness, and hence obliges us to maintain strong forces to defend what we already occupy: a state of rebellion is latent everywhere."[36]

The Cuanhamas, he added, were the "most intelligent and most civilized" blacks in southern Angola: they appreciated all that could be obtained from civilized parts by way of trade, and many dressed "most correctly" in the European fashion. Nevertheless they preferred to be independent, and so long as they could play off Portuguese against Germans, stood a good chance of remaining so. It was not, in fact, until World War I had started and the Germans of South-West Africa, isolated and outnumbered, had surrendered to the South African General Botha in 1915 that the Cuanhamas were finally overcome by a large-scale expedition under General Pereira de Eça.*

Teixeira de Sousa, writing in 1911, put the total cost of the Southern Angolan expeditions from 1904 onwards at 4,000 contos, or the best part of a million pounds sterling.[37] This was more than twice Costa's estimate for a single campaign on an adequate scale, and it bears out in the sphere of government the old maxim that the poor live far more expensively than the rich. Portugal's difficulties were put in a nutshell in a telegram that Ornellas, as Minister of Marine, sent to Costa in November 1906, saying that the Cabinet had resolved "that the evident necessity of occupying the Ovampo had to yield to the absolute necessity of balancing the budget."** There was no question of abandoning imperialist aims that were patently uneconomic; instead, they were deferred—almost, one might say, in order that they might be carried out more uneconomically still.

The Ovampoland campaigns had special importance in that their outcome might have borne on Portugal's chances of retaining southern Angola against external pressure, or even attack, such as was launched by the Germans toward the end of 1914 without the formality of a declaration of war. During the last decade of the monarchy, however, military activity both elsewhere in Angola and in Moçam-

---

* For a critical account of this campaign, see Júlio Botelho Moniz, *Conduta das Operações Coloniais* (Lisbon, 1944), pp. 81–90.

** Quoted by Costa in a private letter to Ornellas, December 24, 1906 (extract in Costa, *Colectânea*, Vol. I, p. 171). The whole extract (pp. 168–73) is eloquent testimony to the difficulties of the Portuguese at that time.

bique was all but incessant. Sometimes it was a question of repressing unrest in territory already occupied, as in the Bailundo campaign of 1902;* more often it was one of asserting authority in areas where the Portuguese writ had never run, or had ceased to run for a generation or more. In such instances, as also in Ovampoland, the Portuguese were entering what was, from an administrative or military point of view, terra incognita. Costa began work on his projected campaign by drawing up a detailed questionnaire about the country and its inhabitants, which was sent to all those persons, official and other, who were thought to know anything about it.[38] Before João de Almeida could contemplate pacifying the country of the Dembos, not a hundred miles from Luanda, which had been in defiance of Portuguese authority since 1872, he was forced to spend the best part of three months, accompanied by his white batman and six native soldiers, in an uncomfortable and hazardous journey of reconnaissance.**

The Dembos campaign itself, later the same year (1907), was marked by no major engagement—and for that very reason it was difficult, and, in terms of the numbers engaged, costly in casualties. It consisted of a lengthy march punctuated by numerous skirmishes, through mountainous country, on paths so narrow that the troops had to go in Indian file more than half a mile long. The scratch force was made up mainly of European military offenders (all the better troops having been sent south with Roçadas), and was short of water, food, and medical supplies. Of a total of 760 who began the march, 67 (of whom 23 were Europeans) were killed or died of wounds or disease; and 72 (of whom 39 were Europeans) were wounded. Such a proportion of casualties was without precedent for any successful Portuguese campaign, and it seems clear that the resolute leadership of Almeida alone turned the balance. Not only was the submission of the principal chiefs secured, but five fortified posts were established within the ter-

* Francisco Cabral de Moncada, *A Campanha do Bailundo em 1902* (2d revised ed., Lisbon, 1903). The author was governor-general of Angola at the time of the revolt, but this is not an official report, nor does one appear to have been published.
** The party was eventually captured. The two white men escaped by wading a crocodile-infested river, and arrived at Golungo Alto after they had been given up for lost. The account of their experience reads like something out of an adventure story for boys. See [Luna da Carvalho *et al.*], *O Coronel João de Almeida: Sua Acção Militar e Administrativa em Angola (1906–11); Publicação de Iniciativa dum Grupo de Companheiros e Amigos Coloniais* (Lisbon, 1927), pp. 35–40.

ritory. Even so, small punitive operations were necessary in 1908 and 1909.* Nor was the country of the Dembos the only comparatively accessible part of Angola where measures of occupation were needed. The approaches to the port of Ambriz were intercepted by tribesmen who levied tribute on passing caravans; the country behind Porto Amboim (Benguela-a-velha) and Novo Redondo was said to be in a state of unrest, and its peoples addicted to cannibalism. Further inland, the northeastern district of Lunda, bordering on the Congo Free State, was still in the course of occupation. When Couceiro was recalled in mid-1909, there was still an unsubdued people there, the Bengalas, who had been rebels since they had massacred a Portuguese force fifty years earlier.[39] But by that time it could no longer be said, as it might have been around the turn of the century, that four-fifths of the area of Angola was only nominally under Portuguese control. The change had been accomplished by a handful of military leaders with a minimum of help from the metropolitan government, and occasionally in defiance of it—as when Almeida, in September 1909, ignored an order not to proceed further down the Cubango, lest there be trouble with the Germans. Henrique Galvão might well remark that the diplomatic pressure put on Lisbon to discourage the military occupation of Southern Angola was an index of the value of Almeida's services.[40]

IV

In Moçambique there was at least some diplomatic pressure of a more benevolent kind. The British in Nyasaland were troubled by raids across the Portuguese border, from the territory of the Yao chief Mataka on the east side of Lake Nyasa. In September 1898, an agreement was reached in Lisbon between British and Portuguese representatives, providing, inter alia, for the establishment of a Portuguese military post to control Mataka's raiding; but months passed without any sign of action on their part, and meanwhile the raids continued.[41]

* [Luna da Carvalho *et al.*], *O Coronel João de Almeida*, p. 42. Paiva Couceiro, who was governor-general at the time, gives a different set of figures. See Henrique de Paiva Couceiro, *Angola: Dois Anos de Governo, Junho 1907–Junho 1909. História e Comentarios*, 2d ed. (Lisbon, 1948), p. 51. I can find no warrant for the statement by Duffy, *Portuguese Africa*, p. 229, that "the fatalities in battle were almost exclusively African" —though it is fair to add that this was an exceptional campaign.

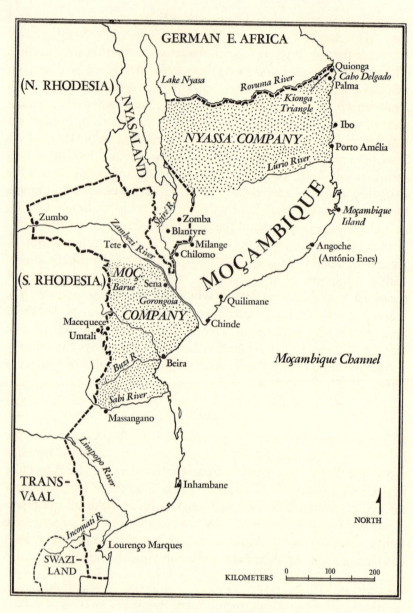

Moçambique Before 1914

The British, who possessed sufficient force to deal with Mataka, naturally chafed at being unable to do so, and eventually went so far as to propose to Lisbon that they be allowed to move against him, either with the Portuguese or separately. This initiative may account for the setting aside of a plan Eduardo da Costa had prepared for the Nyassa Company, under which Mataka would have been attacked overland from Ibo on the east.[42] Instead, a column of some 250 regular troops, together with ten times that number each of irregulars from the Zambezi prazos and native carriers, was sent out northwards from Chilomo under the direct auspices of the governor-general. The British assisted by providing food storage for the column on their side of the frontier, at Fort Johnston, Zomba, and Milange. Apart from occasional skirmishes, there was little or no resistance; and apart from burning villages in the absence of their occupants, the expedition accomplished little beyond the establishment of two fortified posts, named after the king and the heir apparent, on the edge of Mataka's country. These proved to be an insufficient deterrent: further expeditions had to be mounted within a few years, and it was not until 1912 that Mataka's headquarters was occupied and he himself fled into German East Africa.[43]

The British also gave useful support to their old adversary Coutinho in his Barué campaign of 1902.* Barué and the adjacent Gorongoza district, which lie along the Rhodesian frontier between the Zambezi and the Pungué rivers, had for a generation before 1890 been part of the dominion of Manuel António de Sousa. His modus operandi had been to establish a series of stockades (*aringas*) at strategic points, in each of which he posted one of his highborn native concubines, together with a subordinate captain. But in 1890, Manuel António had been taken prisoner at Umtasa's kraal by Captain Forbes and the Chartered Police,** and in his absence his empire fell apart: the Macombe chiefs at whose expense he had built it up returned from exile, and though he attempted to reestablish his power as soon as he was

---

* João de Azevedo Coutinho, *A Campanha do Barué em 1902* (Lisbon, 1904†). This, though bearing the imprint of a private publisher, is described as the "official report" of the campaign. A short account is in Teixeira Botelho, *História Militar (1833–   )*, pp. 577–96.
** See p. 141.

released, he was killed in an attack on a rebel kraal in December 1891. An expedition in his support, led by Coutinho, had met with disaster a month earlier, when a powder magazine exploded during an attack on another kraal, forcing the attackers to retire. For the next ten years the territory remained outside all control: for a time one Taylor, variously described as an Englishman and an American, appears to have ruled it on his own account, for though appointed capitão-mor by the Moçambique Company, he allegedly levied the head-tax for the Chartered Company.[44] Subsequent appointees appear not to have taken up residence there, and though Colonel Arnold[45] led an expedition to Barué in 1900 and secured the submission of one of the principal chiefs, nothing came of it. The neighboring territory of Gorongoza, under the muzungo Luiz Santiago, likewise defied efforts by the company to bring it under direct administration.

Coutinho, by reason of his position as district governor of Zambézia, his long experience, and his high personal prestige in the region, was well equipped to put an end to this situation. In particular, he was able to command the services of large numbers of native troops (*sipais*, or *cypaes*) from the Zambezi prazos: an indispensable requirement, for the *baruístas* were reputed well armed and numerous.* The number of cypaes and carriers contributed by the prazo holders—some of whom came along at the head of their troops—amounted to over 15,000: the regular force was 1,000 strong, of which not quite half were Europeans. A force of this size could have been raised nowhere else in Portuguese Africa, and could scarcely have been sustained in the field had it not been possible to base it firmly on the Zambezi. Having these advantages, Coutinho was bent on making the most of them: "When we prepare a campaign to punish rebels, we ought to do it with so much care and caution, and in such a way, as to be virtually certain of crushing them completely." A defeat at the hands of rebellious subjects, he adds, is far worse than one inflicted by an ex-

---

* They were also reputed to possess powerful fetishes, which could turn the bullets emerging from their enemies' guns into water. The leaders of the cypaes on the Portuguese side consulted many native sorcerers in an effort to offset these evil influences; the most effective advice, says João de Azevedo Coutinho, *A Campanha do Barue,* pp. 191–92, was given by a sorceress who claimed that a hippo accustomed to sunning itself on a particular sandbank in the Zambesi was actually a Barué chieftain who had fled his country in the form of a mouse. When the hippo was sought out and killed, the conviction spread through Zambézia that the baruístas would be defeated.

ternal enemy. Coutinho's plan of campaign consisted of isolating the Barué chieftains from possible ways of escape—and from possible allies—by sending three subsidiary columns along their borders. The Rhodesian authorities mobilized a force along their frontier so as to complete the *cordon sanitaire,* and at the same time Coutinho's main force advanced directly upon the aringas belonging to the two principal chiefs. The campaign, the active part of which occupied a little more than the two months of August and September 1902, was so successful as to be an anticlimax.[46] In his official report, Coutinho remarks that if he had known how things would turn out, he would have dispensed with so large a force. Except for one or two ineffectual attempts at ambush, which resulted in sharp skirmishes, there was very little resistance: the total casualties, almost all of them among the auxiliaries, numbered eight dead and less than fifty wounded. No European was killed in combat, though two died of disease and one was accidentally drowned. The chiefs were formally deposed and the whole country handed over to the Moçambique Company's administration.*

The remaining unsettled areas of the province were on the coast. The operations of Mousinho and Costa against the namarraes, opposite Moçambique Island, had not been conclusive; and in 1906, Coutinho, who was now governor-general, determined on the pacification of the district. The task, which occupied five years (1906–10), was entrusted to the new governor, Massano de Amorim, who had taken a leading part in ending the Bailundo troubles in Angola.[47] Whereas Mousinho had envisaged occupying a series of zones parallel to the coast (but had not taken the process beyond the first stage), Massano's plan consisted in striking inland by a number of routes, on which fortified posts would be established: the same kind of linear penetration that was advocated by Costa and carried out by Almeida in the south of Angola. For want of resources, the process could not be carried out simultaneously in all of the four captaincies into which the district was divided: it was this, rather than any large-scale resistance from the tribes, that accounted for the time taken to complete the

---

* In Zambézia, it came to be known as "the champagne war." My authority for this is an anonymous but evidently well-informed annotator of a copy of *Districto de Quelimane: Relatorio do Governador, 1907 a 1909* (Lourenço Marques, Imprensa Nacional, 1909) belonging to Stanford University. This note appears on p. 57.

pacification. Only in the Angoche region, which had a long tradition of recalcitrance (it had supposedly been brought under control as long ago as 1861, and had been re-pacified in 1877, 1887, and 1890) did a sizeable expedition have to be mounted, with two separate columns composed of over six hundred regular troops and two thousand each of cypaes and carriers. In the course of eight weeks' march (June–August 1910), which included a number of skirmishes, this force proved sufficient to secure the submission of the majority of the chiefs and the capture of the remainder.[48] However, further operations were necessary in the years 1911–13.[49]

v

By the time of the fall of the House of Bragança in October 1910, the greater part of the military program Costa had put forward nine years earlier had been carried out—small thanks, if one were to believe the men on the spot, to the politicians and bureaucrats of Lisbon, who had been unwilling even to provide money for the purpose. Freire de Andrade, who succeeded Coutinho as governor-general of Moçambique in 1906, flatly denied that the province was, or for the last ten years had been, a burden on the national exchequer. On the contrary, he said, the mother country was living at the expense of the colonies: "Since I have known East Africa, its administration has been a model one compared with that of the metropolis, in spite of the close relations between the two. . . . In the last ten years this Province has sent to Portugal, at the very least, twenty-five million milreis in gold."[50] This figure was made up of the budget surpluses arising in the province; the remittances to cover its imports from Portugal; and its obligatory subsidies, open or concealed, to the national shipping line, the *Empresa Nacional de Navegação*. Moçambique's balance of trade was, of course, already marked by the two large "invisible exports" that characterize it still. "The Province," wrote Freire de Andrade in 1909, "now lives almost exclusively on the Lourenço Marques railway and the profits of [native] emigration to Johannesburg."[51] In an earlier memorandum he had drawn attention to the decline in trade in other parts of the province, notably the districts of Inhambane and Quilimane: "All this comes, in my view, from having tied Lourenço Marques to the destinies of the Transvaal and neglected the development of the Province itself; this was . . . put on one side almost entirely, people thinking only of the port and railway."[52]

This was a cry that was to go up repeatedly in subsequent years against a policy that, though profitable, represented the line of least resistance: the creation of what would nowadays be termed enclaves of commercial development in an otherwise undeveloped country. It was indeed the misfortune of Lourenço Marques to incur obloquy from both British and Portuguese nationalists. Lord Selborne, in his famous memorandum of 1907 on British South Africa, almost invariably refers to it disdainfully as a "foreign harbor," while for men like Ornellas and Eduardo Saldanha it was a kind of outpost of British imperialism, dominated by British banks and commercial houses and, like Beira, largely English-speaking.* Whether any other kind of economic—as distinct from uneconomic—development was feasible at that time may well be doubted.

Without accepting the *suggestio falsi* that Moçambique was doing the mother country some kind of special favor by paying for imports thence in gold earned from invisible exports, rather than in goods, one may concur with Freire that the province was, broadly, paying its way. The situation in Angola was more complex. It is true that budgetary deficits there were endemic, and that their cumulative amount, over upwards of half a century, amounted to more than 10,000 contos (over two million pounds sterling). It is true also that the cumulative subsidy from the metropolitan exchequer to the Luanda-Ambaca railway, over the years 1889–1912, amounted to about 11,500 contos.[53] Unfortunately this represented, not a major contribution to the economic development of the district but an index of the extent to which economic development had fallen short of expectations— the government having guaranteed (illegally, it appears) not merely the interest on the construction bonds but also the gross receipts, at the rate of 1.2 contos per kilometer annually.[54] As Couceiro pointed out, this constituted an incentive to the railway company to keep its traffics, and

---

* The Selborne memorandum was first published as a British Command Paper (Cd. 2104) and was later reprinted commercially, with an introduction by Basil Williams which explained its origins and importance (*The Selborne Memorandum*, London, 1925). It is also included in A. P. Newton, ed., *Select Documents Relating to the Unification of South Africa*, 2 vols. (London, 1924). Page references herein are to the Williams edition. See Freire de Andrade, *Relatórios de Moçambique*, Vol. I, pp. 43ff.

hence its costs, as low as it could. It was an arrangement, moreover, for which the provincial authorities were in no way responsible.[55] On the other hand, military and naval expenses falling on the colonial budget over the half-century (mostly expenses of sovereignty that in France, for instance, would have been charged to the metropolitan country) amounted to some 20,000 contos. Critics in Angola naturally contrasted this amount with the 5,000 contos allocated for public works, the 2,800 allocated for public health, and the 370 spent for education over the same period, and they identified centralization with exploitation.[56]

Almeida Ribeiro, who as Minister of Colonies under the Republic propounded sweeping constitutional and financial reforms of a decentralizing sort, accompanied his legislation by a memorandum, dated June 1913, which constitutes the most searching analysis ever made of colonial financial policy under the monarchy—at once brilliantly written and free from the gratuitous polemics that often mar Portuguese state papers. He found no method whatever in the allocation of expenditures, whether as between metropolitan and colonial revenues or in categories within each: every successive Minister of Marine had apparently been a law unto himself. He did, however, detect a general bias in favor of loading expenses onto the colonies wherever possible, sometimes to an extent that bordered on absurdity. If, for instance, it made some sense that the cost of the Portuguese consulate in Hong Kong should be charged to the revenues of Macau, it made none at all that the same revenues should bear the entire interest charges on a loan raised in 1863 to pay for the construction of a new bridge in the naval arsenal in Lisbon.[57] Again, all kinds of miscellaneous charges in respect of various central activities of interest to the colonies were levied on their individual budgets, but on no sort of principle. The cost of the School of Tropical Medicine, established in 1902, was charged entirely to the colonies; that of the Cartographical Commission was paid out of the metropolitan budget; and there was a catchall category in the latter, labeled "sovereignty, civilization, and general administration," which did not, however, comprise all the items paid for out of metropolitan funds that might be so classified, and did not signify that items that were included were paid for wholly out of those funds. Any quotas that might be demanded from the colonies under this head were not specified. When one adds that the budget for the joint Ministry of Marine and Colonies did not make any apportionment of central administrative costs between the two services, Almeida Ribeiro's word for the situation, "incoherence," appears to be more than justified.[58] He failed to understand, for instance, why the staff of the Cartographical Commission should be paid out of "general administration" funds, while the materials they used were charged to "sovereignty and civilization"; or why the subsidy to the Lisbon Geographical Society came under the former, and that to the Scientific Society for Colonial Agronomy under the latter. That the incoherence of which he complained was not always innocent appears from a comment in Ennes' famous memorandum of 1893. The inclusion in provincial budgets of items relating to general colonial administration, authorized and paid for in Portugal, was, Ennes declared,

a political and administrative *expedient,* adopted so as to evade the laws relating to the public accounts, which operate up to a point in the Kingdom, but have never been observed overseas. For instance, it is sought to reform the organization of some service . . . but it is feared that the resulting increase in expenditure will not please Parliament and public. What does one do? It is decreed . . . that the Provinces, or some Province, shall pay for the increase, either in itself or with some bit of the former cost added, and Parliament and public opinion are satisfied and even believe that an economy has been effected. More, and worse. It is sought to authorize some expenditure, permanent or casual, within the Kingdom, and there is no allocation in the general budget from which it can be drawn: one orders that it be included in a provincial budget, or split up between all the provincial budgets, and this will suffice for the home government to pay it out of its own resources, but *on account of the overseas provinces.* On their account, and without their knowledge, astonishing things have been paid for in Portugal: subsidies to newspapers, pensions to widows, books, tips to employees, expenses of festivities, and I know not what![59]

These abuses, however, were symptoms of loose administration rather than important influences on the size of the colonial expenditures incurred by the metropolitan government. Of the 70,000 contos spent between 1870 and 1912, approximately half went to make up deficits in colonial budgets, and another third was spent on subsidies to railroads, steamship lines, and submarine cable companies. The remainder was accounted for by general administrative expenses (1,500 contos), and military and naval expeditions or construction financed directly from Portugal (8,000 contos). This last figure Almeida Ribeiro described as almost derisory, considering the number of operations it covered. He might better have described it as unreal, for to the extent that deficits on the colonial budgets were brought about by charging them with military expenses that might more properly have been borne by the metropolitan exchequer, no advantage, except perhaps a political one, redounded to the central government.[60] Thus, the budget for Angola in 1906–07 forecast receipts of 1,517 contos; and an expenditure of 2,777 contos, of which 1,410 contos was military. Because receipts fell short of the forecast by 133 contos, the whole of the revenue and more was, in effect, earmarked for warlike purposes.[61] It is clear that this kind of budgeting (for which, of course, not the province but the Terreiro do Paço was responsible) corresponded to no intelligent or intelligible administrative norms. It meant a series of reluctant remittances from Lisbon to Luanda to keep an embarrassed provincial government, not indeed in funds but at least from getting too hopelessly in debt to its employees and suppliers. No wonder Couceiro remarked acidly that the bureaucrats at home, instead of introducing reforms that every one else knew were necessary, constituted themselves a Holy Inquisition to persecute the lapses of their own appointees—all the while doling out sums "drop by drop, like alms at the porter's lodge of a monastery," to the creditors who shouted the loudest.[62]

Almeida Ribeiro made some instructive calculations of the effect, in a given year, of applying to Portuguese colonial budgets the French system of charging all military expenses to the metropolitan country, and, conversely, of applying the Portuguese system to French colonial budgets. In both cases the effect was spectacular: thus, in 1912/13 the Moçambique surplus would have risen from 25 contos to over 1,000 contos; and Angola, where military expenditures more than accounted for a deficit of 1,135 contos, would have had a surplus of 100 contos. Even provinces like Cape Verde and S. Tomé, where no military activity was going on, would have been affected: the first, instead of having a tiny paper deficit, would have had a surplus of 112 contos, equal to one quarter of its revenues; and the surplus in the second would have risen from 100 to 250 contos. Timor alone of the Portuguese colonies would still have been in deficit. On the other hand, if French Equatorial Africa and French West Africa had had to bear their total military costs, their deficits in 1912 would have equaled

2,428 contos and 3,136 contos—"high enough to overturn the whole system of financial autonomy and drive the moneylenders far away." Almeida Ribeiro concluded that, contrary to the opinion of those who would have sold Moçambique in the nineties, and of contemporaries who wrote about the "colonial cancer," the cost of the colonies was not an undue burden either absolutely, or in relation to the colonial area, or to the number of metropolitan taxpayers. "Strange though it may seem, these charges are, proportionately, far less than those falling on France and Germany, and possibly on other colonial powers."[63]

Such a comparison ignored altogether the difference in national wealth between Portugal and the other colonial powers—a difference that more than made up for any advantage she might derive from running her possessions cheaply. If, by 1910, the period of high military expenditures showed some prospect of coming to an end, that of expenditure on development—Lourenço Marques and the extravagant Luanda-Ambaca railway aside—had scarcely begun. "Virtually everything in Angola remains to be done," wrote José de Macedo in 1910.[64] He was referring to what nowadays would be termed the provision of an "infrastructure." "In point of economic exploitation," wrote Couceiro a little earlier, "the Colony is situated as if the glorious *padrão* of St. George, the first of the four set up by Diogo Cão along the coast of Angola to mark our occupation in the fifteenth century, had been put up yesterday."[65] "How can a colony like Moçambique," asked Freire de Andrade in 1909, "that is only now beginning to develop, be expected not merely to be administered without a deficit, but to deliver funds out of its income somewhere else at will? Are its sands somehow made of gold and its mountains of diamonds?"[66] "The central government," declared Almeida Ribeiro, "forgot that before one can regulate one must create."[67] For him, a surplus in a colonial budget signified that indispensable measures of development had been neglected: he felt that, in any event, larger enterprises such as railways and irrigation schemes ought not to be paid for from current income, since this would unduly burden the existing generation, but from loans. One of his objections to the absence of financial autonomy in the Portuguese colonies was that they were thereby prohibited from raising their own loans for development—though he recognized (as who could not?) that there had been good political reasons in the eighteen-nineties for introducing such a prohibition.[68]

VI

Running through all this discussion of financial policy and economic development was an assumption that has a very modern ring: namely, that government, rather than private enterprise, had to do whatever needed to be done. The assumption was in no sense doctrinaire: it came partly from the long-standing unwillingness of Portuguese investors to have anything to do with colonial enterprise, and partly from disenchantment with the various companies that had been granted concessions in the eighteen-nineties. "The *Montepio Geral* (savings bank) is replete with Portuguese funds," wrote Freire de Andrade in 1907, "yet of all the thousands of milreis deposited therein, not one is drawn out to be invested in Moçambique."[69]

As for the privileged companies, I do not believe that the Mother Country has benefited from them and I only hope that they will not someday give rise to disappointment and vexation. Set up in order that they might bring into the Province the many thousands of contos of which it was in need, they have not done so, except for the Moçambique Company: it indeed accomplished something, albeit little, in this direction, but it did much more for those who, at the expense of our Province, made millions by gambling in the shares on the stock exchanges of Europe, forcing the price up to nearly five pounds and then letting it fall below par.

The Nyassa Company is a stain on our Province; and the Zambézia Company has fought bravely but uselessly against a want of capital from which it has suffered from the beginning.

Fortunately . . . it was not possible to organize a *companhia majestática* for Inhambane which . . . would have taken away from the Province a great part of its current receipts. One might say that Providence watched over Moçambique at a time when some wanted to sell it and others to give it away in pieces to unscrupulous financiers of diverse origin.[70]

Couceiro, writing of Angola at the same period, was no less emphatic:

The way in which the economic life of Angola unrolls itself calls to mind an assault on a defenseless country by various groups of *francs-tireurs,* each acting independently. . . . We see the industrialists of Portugal snugly savoring a protectionism that has gone unchanged for eighteen years; . . . the Empresa Nacional de Navegação, taking advantage of the comfortable monopoly conferred by flag discrimination to maintain shipping charges devised rather for its own dividends . . . than the development of the Province; the Trans-African Railway Company freely practicing, thanks to the guaranteed dividend, its own special method of exploitation, putting into force by means of prohibitive freight charges the maxim, "the less traffic the more profits"; the Banco Nacional Ultramarino, carrying on undisturbed its right of note issue, limiting itself to being the state's banker, and to discount and foreign exchange dealings, without participating as an active promoter of trade and agriculture; the *emigrant agency,* pocketing improper gains as intermediary of the Junta in S. Tomé, and, moreover, depopulating [Angola].... There is the Moçâmedes Company wasting sixteen years of its concession without carrying out its due contractual obligations and without contributing anything, virtually, to the progress of the Country.[71]

Such an atmosphere of monopoly and restrictive practice was not, indeed, calculated to promote economic growth even in much more favorable circumstances than those of early twentieth-century Moçambique and Angola. Nevertheless, it by no means follows that spectacular growth would have taken place given freedom of trade and shipping, or a less demimondaine group of foreign capitalists than most of those attracted to invest in the Portuguese colonies. When Couceiro suggested that the State take over the Ambaca line—and indeed all the Angola railroads—in order to be able to reduce rate charges to the point at which they would stimulate traffic, he had in mind that this would be a more rational use of a subsidy than "putting a muleteer's load on wheels." The State, he argued, could afford to take a view of rates broader than one governed by the accounts of the railroad company—"It sees its profits in the expansion of wealth generally—the consequent revenue more than making up for any loss on railroad income. Moreover, "with the railway in hand, a whole region can be governed.... This instrument *par excellence* of dominion and public security cannot, without grave disadvantages, be left in the hands of foreigners." [72] This last remark presumably referred to the Benguela railway rather than to the foreign bondholders of the older Ambaca line—an object of fear and suspicion for Marianno some years earlier. Couceiro, though he might employ arguments in favor of economic development, would certainly have recommended uneconomic development if the alternative were the sacrifice of Portuguese sovereignty over Angola. Some measures of the kind were imperative, if only, as the Portuguese say, *para o inglês ver* (for the Englishman to see), for the absence of development was more than ever before a pretext for those who would have liked to end Portuguese colonial rule— notably Sir Edward Grey, the British Foreign Secretary. A year or so after Couceiro's report on Angola, Grey wrote to the ambassador in Berlin:*

* Grey-Goschen, private, December 29, 1911 (B.D., Vol. X, Part II, No. 266). The

The Germans would like the division of the Portuguese Colonies to take place as soon as possible. So should I. These Colonies are worse than derelict so long as Portugal has them: *they are sinks of iniquity.* The Union of South Africa will never rest till it has Delagoa Bay. On every ground—material, and moral, and even Portuguese—it would be better that Portugal should sell her Colonies. But how can we, of all people, put pressure on Portugal to sell—we who are bound by an Alliance ... renewed secretly for value received during the Boer War?

Doubtless Grey would have received with pain and surprise a suggestion that the Nyasaland Protectorate, which had not shown conspicuous economic progress by comparison with neighboring Portuguese Zambézia, should be handed over to the Germans.* Such a suggestion might have brought home to him that there was more to the problem than getting rid of the "hopelessly bad" administration of the Portuguese colonies and the "abominable" prazo system.[73] His permanent officials, notably Nicolson and Eyre Crowe, were anxious, like Lister a generation earlier, to be fair to the Portuguese: Crowe was inclined to discount the agitation against conditions in their colonies as being got up in the German interest.**

Behind the rhetoric of Couceiro's reference to Diogo Cão lay the hard fact that the economy of Angola had not undergone the transformation that idealists like Sá de Bandeira and Andrade Corvo foresaw as a result of the end of slavery, and that was still confidently expected in the eighties from the coming of the railroad, the steamship, and the telegraph. When work on the line to Ambaca was inaugurated in October 1886, Brito Capello, the governor-general, who was by no means starry-eyed, made a speech forecasting a great extension of plantation agriculture owing to a reduction in transport costs, and a great increase in exports to Europe.[74] But in Couceiro's time, twenty years later, the amount of traffic reaching Luanda by rail from the in-

---

words in italics were omitted by Gooch and Temperley "for reasons of international courtesy": to my mind, they reflect rather on their writer than on the Portuguese. They have been supplied from the original in F.O. 800/61. Compare Grey–Goschen, July 4 1912, No. 70 Africa (B.D., Vol. X, Part II, No. 312).
* For some comparative figures, see *Districto de Quelimane: Relatorio* ..., pp. 215–16.
** See, for example, the minute by Eyre Crowe, June 5, 1913, on a proposal by Germany to include an "anti-slavery" clause in the revised agreement on the Portuguese colonies: "The present introduction of the subject is due not to any humanitarian sympathy with the victims of slavery, but to the desire to find an additional pretext for intervention in the Portuguese colonies" (B.D., Vol. X, Part II, p. 532).

terior was a mere 8,500 metric tons annually: no more than that carried by the Cuanza river steamers it had superseded, if as much.[75] Exports continued to be what they had always been, consisting of products derived almost entirely from the barter trade with the African; but whereas in the eighties the predominant commodities had been coffee, wild rubber, and wax (generally in that order), by the turn of the century rubber had outdistanced all others in importance.[76] Coffee exports, which had reached a peak both in terms of quantity and of price in the early nineties, had fallen back ten years later to their previous level: the peak for rubber exports was reached in 1898 and 1899, when some 3,300 metric tons were exported, valued at 5,600 contos, or four-fifths of the total value of exports in those years. Angola had, in fact, been caught up in the great rubber boom that brought the Congo Free State both riches and notoriety. There was a slump from 1900 onward, but in only one year (from 1900 to 1908 inclusive) did rubber account for less than sixty per cent of exports. One might speak of monoculture were it not that all these exports grew wild and were merely gathered by the natives.

Supplies of rubber, as indeed of other products so gathered, were highly sensitive to price; and it so happened that the world price of rubber was reflected to the native producer by means of a highly distorted mirror operated by world humanitarians in his supposed interest; an operation complicated, moreover, by the literal way in which the Portuguese government interpreted one of its treaty obligations. Among Africans, the most sought-after item of barter, exceeding even cotton piece goods and firearms, was, of course, potable spirits—of which the cheapest was Hamburg gin. It was widely felt in Europe that spirits constituted a menace to the welfare of primitive peoples; and at the Brussels Conference of 1889–90—which the British had induced Belgium to call as a kind of lightning conductor for the energies of Cardinal Lavigerie's anti-slavery crusade, but which had, to a degree, confounded the skeptics—measures had been adopted whose purpose was to make the terms of trade less favorable to the (black) African drinker.[77] The signatory powers, including Portugal, agreed to establish a prescribed rate of customs duty on imported liquor (basis, fifteen gold francs per hectolitre for three years, and twenty-five thereafter), and an excise duty at least equal in amount.

In Angola, the principal activity of such European plantations as existed was the production of sugarcane for *aguardente,* and in the eighties some had even been exported.[78] The planters had apparently turned to this activity as being more profitable than cotton-growing, once the boom resulting from the American civil war had subsided; but they had found it difficult to compete with the European product, at a price, landed in Luanda, of 45 reis (under five cents) a litre. As part of the new policy of protective tariffs introduced by Dias Ferreira's administration, however, a customs duty well in excess of that prescribed by the Brussels Convention was introduced in April 1892; and this was increased by one-half in April 1895.* In neither case was the internal excise duty increased. Though not, apparently, a breach of the letter of the convention, this policy, as was later admitted, was wholly at variance with its spirit, and, for a small power unable to defy world humanitarian opinion, astonishingly maladroit. Ernesto de Vilhena, in his maiden speech in the Côrtes in June 1908, characterized it, and the policy of which it formed a part, in biting terms:

The legislator of 1892 did not seem to think. His spirit was untroubled by any doubt such as naturally would attack any statesman confronted with some great financial, economic, or political problem. The legislator of 1892 was positive, categorical, and absolute: he simply protected.

He looked about the kingdom and beheld the cotton industry. He did not ask himself whether it was, so to speak, a natural industry like winegrowing; he did not ask himself if Portuguese conditions would permit the industry to develop and perfect itself without recourse to excessive protective measures that in the last analysis would fall on the consumer; he did not ask himself whether the forcible introduction of its wares into the colonies would be prejudicial to their economy. No; he simply protected it. He looked far afield to Angola and saw the alcohol industry. He did not ask ... whether alcohol was bad for the native, whether the successive Brussels conferences would not make production increasingly difficult, whether it would not be more advantageous from the outset to convert the manufacture of alcohol into that of sugar. No: he simply protected it. And he protected it in such a way ... as to place us between the horns of the following dilemma: either to allow the financial and economic ruin of Angola to occur, or to put into the street, without work, ten or fifteen thousand workers in Portugal.[79]

---

* The whole problem is ably summarized in a report that João de Azevedo Coutinho, as Minister of Marine, made to the Côrtes in 1910: *A Questão do Alcool de Angola: Proposta de Lei* (Lisbon, Imprensa Nacional, 1910).

The combined effect of the rubber boom and the protective tariff was to promote a spectacular growth in the output of aguardente which more than matched the fall in imports. These, which as late as 1894 had amounted to over a million litres, fell by 1899 to less than one-tenth of that amount: but by that time production within Angola from sugarcane and sweet potatoes was estimated at fifteen million litres. The prosperity of the industry appeared so great that the government imposed an additional excise tax on it, the proceeds of which were designated for the building of the Benguela railroad, but were, in fact, used, after the contract with Robert Williams made their original purpose unnecessary, to build the extension of the Ambaca line to Malange.

It was all too good to last, and it did not last. The collapse of the rubber market coincided with a second Brussels conference which raised the minimum customs and excise duties to 70 gold francs per hectolitre.[80] The years 1900/1902 were years of crisis for the Europeans in Angola: a straw in the wind was the bankruptcy of Newton, Carnegie, and Company, a British firm that had played a leading part in the trade of Luanda for nearly forty years.[81] The majority of planters were in no position to incur the expenses of abandoning the monoculture of alcohol for such alternatives as sugar milling, or the raising of cotton or rubber: the one Angolan bank was not disposed to grant credits for such purposes. Moreover, the new excise tax regulations provided that the aguardente producer could compound his liability by an annual payment on the basis of an assessment that could neither be accurately determined in the first instance nor kept current; and though the area he planted might not be increased without license previously granted, the principle of compounding offered an incentive to evade a regulation that in any case would have been difficult to enforce. Growers, therefore, tended to hang on in hope of better times; production remained far higher—some six million liters annually—than could be justified in view of the manifest intention of the Brussels signatories; and the effective yield of the excise was about one-quarter of what it should have been. In short, as an official report of 1910 put it, "the life of a dying man was being prolonged by the use of oxygen cylinders."[82]

VII

In 1906, a third Brussels conference took a further step along the path marked out sixteen years previously, by raising the import and excise duties another fifty per cent. The Portuguese delegation obtained a special dispensation for Angola, under which thirty per cent of the proceeds might be given to producers to finance a changeover to sugar production. But an attempt to put this policy into force ran into insuperable difficulties. It was a question not merely of financing a technical change, but of creating an export industry out of one contrived—and, in part, located—to suit the domestic market. At once there appeared a conflict of interest between the few large coast distilleries, some of which were producing liquor as a by-product of sugar manufacture, and the two hundred or so small, quasi-domestic enterprises scattered over the hinterland as far inland as Malange, which, even if they turned over to sugar, would not have been able to get it to the seaboard at a competitive price. It was these inland farms, moreover, that Governor-General Paiva Couceiro cherished as possible "centers of culture, instruction, and wealth, roots of our influence, claws [sic] of our dominion, instruments of our civilizing mission."[83] Couceiro wished to assist these people by establishing a kind of cartel (*grémio*) under government auspices, which would serve as a means of collecting the increased tax from its members; by fixing a minimum price for alcohol; and by applying the subsidy authorized by the Brussels Convention to the promotion of forms of agriculture other than cane-growing. But away from the coast it proved impossible to enforce the minimum price or to collect the tax; and traders took advantage of the situation to buy for stock. Couceiro therefore announced that, inasmuch as the tax was officially one on consumption (though it was levied on the producer for the sake of convenience), stocks remaining at the end of the fiscal year would be deemed liable for tax in the ensuing year. This stopped hoarding and apparently brought the majority of growers to an acceptance of Couceiro's plan. Early in 1909, the cartel was actually formed in Luanda. Meanwhile, however, the sugar interests had raised an outcry in Lisbon against a monopoly: an outcry that Couceiro described as humbug and inspired by their desire to turn their lower costs of production into a de facto monopoly. Thereupon, the central government annulled his measures—only to revive them in somewhat different form a few months after his recall in mid-1909. In the following year, a new Minister of Marine, Azevedo Coutinho, was obliged to admit that all these efforts to kill the liquor industry by kindness had failed:

They all held out hopes that the established industry might continue and, despite measures that were adopted to promote [other forms of] agriculture, they failed to divert people's attention away from alcohol to other crops. This is shown by the fact that sugar mills that could have earned a bounty by exporting sugar to continental Portugal still persisted in concentrating on producing alcohol.[84]

Coutinho therefore proposed to abolish the industry outright, paying compensation in *Angolan* three per cent bonds—a virtual innovation, which the proponents of colonial autonomy were not slow to notice—on the basis of one conto per hectare of cane under cultivation at the end of 1909. The bonds would form a prior charge on the customs duties on wines and spirits entering Angola for the use of European residents: it was hoped thus to relieve the endemic glut of wine in Portugal and at the same time to compensate the Angolan producer. Legislation on these lines was, in fact, passed by the new Republican government in 1911; but though it clinched the fate of the industry, inevitable since 1890, the drinking of spirits by Africans continued to vex administrators for at least a decade thereafter.[85]

In Moçambique, the Brussels Conventions did not apply south of the 22nd parallel of latitude, but it was precisely there, in the districts of Lourenço Marques and Inhambane, that the problem of alcohol was most troublesome. Spirits do not appear to have been a major item of barter in any part of the province; and though the effect of the increased duties in Zambézia was to make it unprofitable to use the residues of the sugar factories for distilling, they could be disposed of otherwise—for instance, as fertilizer. Further south, the natives preferred a variety of fermented drinks such as *sópe, sura,* and *pombe* to spirits, though they would resort to distilling their own spirits if supplies of the other drinks—which they were accustomed to buy from Europeans or Asiatics—were scarce or expensive. In 1902 —less, it would seem, from consideration for native welfare than from a desire to help winegrowers in Portugal—a law was passed prohibiting the manufacture of "fermented Kaffir drinks" as well as the distillation of spirits in the areas south of the 22nd parallel. Like so much Portuguese colonial legislation, it was based on insufficient local knowledge, and it did not work well. In the first place, ordinary table wine was too weak in alcohol to appeal to native consumers, and in any case it had to be fortified with spirits as a preservative. This necessary practice lent itself to abuse: "I have already had occasion to analyse *a wine for blacks,*" wrote Freire de Andrade, "into the composition of which grape juice did not enter."[86] Secondly, being deprived of their habitual drinks, the consumers had recourse to illicit distilling of even less desirable products like spirits of cassava, overindulgence in which, according to a governor of Inhambane, "leaves the native for three or four days in a state of abject moral and physical depression which has to be seen to be believed."[87] Moreover, the restriction threatened to bring about permanent depopulation of the districts south of the Save, through migration either into the Moçambique Company's territories or into the Transvaal. "I draw your excellency's notice," wrote the same governor of Inhambane (the younger Almeida Garrett) "to the fact that in the Transvaal the blacks are supplied with . . . fermented Kaffir drinks [as part of] a plan to attract our population into that territory." Finally, not only were the Portuguese settlers who had been suppliers of these drinks deprived of a source of livelihood, but they found it difficult, as they had not before 1902, to obtain native labor: "As long as the native is able to buy his favorite drink, he will work willingly, and relatively assiduously; and if, in addition to his wages, he can obtain (as once he could), a daily ration of *sópe* or *sura*, the farmer will be able to secure as many hands as he wishes—which he cannot do at present."*

The problem continued to vex Freire de Andrade throughout his four years' tenure as governor-general (1906–10). He tried to suppress illicit distilling by recruiting a special force of native police, who were rewarded with a proportion of the fines; but this led to such abuses ("it is common knowledge that the native is cruel to his fellows") that the effort had to be abandoned.[88] He arranged for a provincial levy on wines imported from Portugal, to be used to enforce standards of quality; but this was disallowed by the home government at the instigation of interested parties. Far from rising, as the law of

---

* Alfredo Freire de Andrade, *Relatórios de Moçambique,* Vol. IV (Lourenço Marques, Imprensa Nacional, 1909); compare with Thomaz de Almeida Garrett, *Um Governo em Africa* (Lisbon, 1907), pp. 136–48, for the effect of the law of 1902 on his district (Inhambane).

1902 had intended, the imports of wine steadily fell. In the end, the *status quo ante*—at any rate, in practice—was restored, for Eduardo Saldanha wrote in 1919 that "the majority of [white] farmers live by growing sugarcane: from this they squeeze the juice and sell it fermented to the blacks (sópe); or occasionally, in Inhambane, [they live] by growing palms for sura, for the same purpose."[89] He added that, aside from supplying the needs of government departments and individual functionaries, the sale of liquor was virtually the only commercial activity in which Portuguese were engaged. In contrast to Angola, where the bush-trader had, at any rate, a Portuguese name, the petty trade of Moçambique was still, as it had been for centuries, in the hands of Asiatics. Their modus operandi was vividly described by Ernesto de Vilhena in 1905:

Only someone who has observed him plying his trade on the spot can appreciate to what extent the *monhé* (Asiatic trader) has made himself indispensable to the Negro. For instance, take any prazo in Zambézia. On the banks of a *mucurro* (creek), hard by a deadly mangrove swamp, rises a *palhota* (hut), small and low, whose only mark of luxury, perhaps, is that it is plastered outside. Inside dwell two or three beings, lean, yellow, dressed in filthy tunics, their heads covered with greasy skullcaps, squatting round the brass cooking pot containing their dinner: rice and curry, made with one or two scrawny fowls and a great quantity of *tempera*—that is, a yellow mixture of ginger, saffron, pepper, cloves, and other condiments. The remaining furniture consists of a kettle of water, for the ablutions prescribed by religion; the indispensable teapot; a few Kaffir chairs, consisting of coco-fibre net stretched on wooden frames; a few mats; and one or two Indian chests, with many drawers and pigeonholes. On the walls are shelves loaded with sundry pieces of cloth, bead necklaces, sun hats, and other miscellanea. On the floor, baskets of mexoeira, beans, and other grains [sic], which have been bought from the Negro and will later be sold to him for twice what they are worth. Everywhere starving skeletons of cats are mewing.

Now the customers appear on the scene. There are seven or eight Negroes from distant parts, carrying a tusk of ivory. Their main interest is not, perhaps, so much to sell the tusk as to carry out a piece of business: that is, to journey eight or ten days in caravan through the bush, showing others that they are going to sell ivory—a matter that will be revived at length over the evening campfire in every village where they spend the night—and having reached their destination, to spend three or four days in discussing, with an air of great importance, the sale itself. The monhé is, as it were, cousin to the recent arrivals, for every monhé is cousin and friend to the black. The argument begins. The owners of the tusk begin by asking three or four times its value, knowing that they will not get it, but simply wishing to put a price on the merchandise. The monhé refuses. Seated at their side, talking in their language, he tells them that the ivory is split, that it is too old, that the tusk is too small or too curved; that he rejected five or six similar ones a few days before. The Negro, happy to enter into a discussion that in itself will increase his self-esteem, makes grand gestures, waxes enthusiastic, stands up, describes at length how he obtained the tusk, utters exclamations, and appeals to the others. At times the discussion grows heated, and the monhé is given blows or is otherwise maltreated. Then the customers will be put out of the hut and the door closed until, after a little while, tempers have cooled and the negotiation is resumed. The monhé is tireless. He will take two, three, or ten days in discussion if necessary. He makes the customers little presents of mirrors, needles, or other trivial things, and in the end gains the tusk for half or a third its value, paid in kind. Is it possible to conceive a European, no matter how "Kaffirized" he may be—and there are some that differ but little from the blacks—doing business under these circumstances? Evidently not.[90]

This description was written in no spirit of hostility to the Asiatic trader. Whereas Ennes had grudgingly admitted his usefulness, and Mousinho counseled his gradual elimination through penal taxation, Vilhena considered him as the advance guard of commerce, the indispensable element of white penetration: "It is to be noted that the black flees from places that are occupied by the military; he has a horror of the soldier that is perhaps well justified."[91] Petty trade, therefore, at this incomplete stage of occupation, depended on agents who did not inculcate this fear nor were themselves fearful of operating in territory outside the immediate jurisdiction of the white man. Far from being harassed by discriminatory taxation which favored trading establishments within that jurisdiction, the Asiatics ought, in Vilhena's view, to be encouraged to the greatest extent possible. His attitude was characteristically enlightened, for all that it was to some extent prompted by observation of the commercial policy pursued by the Germans to the north of Portuguese Nyasaland. Their export taxes—on ivory and cloves, for instance—were higher than those of Portugal; but their charges for trading licenses were markedly less. Traders not unnaturally preferred a tax on turnover to one that imposed heavy overhead costs; and as in Angola, the Portuguese could not afford to be indifferent to the policies of their neighbors if they wished to preserve the trade and revenues of their territories.[92]

Chapter eleven

The Export of Labor

It was common form among colonial Portuguese, whether planters or officials, to point to the shortage of native labor rather than the absence of adequate export markets, for instance, as a reason for economic stagnation. The devising of effective means whereby the African could be induced to work—whether for himself or (preferably) for a European employer—had been a frequent preoccupation of the central government from the time the decision to abolish slavery was taken. António Ennes took a special interest in the question and, as chairman of an official committee of enquiry set up in October 1898 to enquire into it, was mainly responsible for the law of 1899 that imposed a general obligation to work on the *indígena*. It would be idle to argue about the merits or defects of this law, or the provincial regulations that ensued at the time it was passed. As Couceiro, who had been a member of the committee, later remarked, the law presupposed an administrative cadre able to exercise real authority throughout a province—and this had yet to be brought into existence. Like its predecessor, the more liberal regulation of 1878 that, by analogy with European practice, prescribed forced labor only for those deemed vagrants, the labor legislation of the early twentieth century remained an example of what Couceiro indignantly and almost untranslatably called *"o carácter hiperpapeloso, ultra-chinês e superchicaneiro do nosso praxismo official"* ("the paper-addicted, over-devious, and super-dishonest character of our official practices").

Looking as he did upon the labor regulations as a means of promoting economic progress, Couceiro classified their ineffectiveness as an example of the "DEAD LETTER which all legislation for colonial development promulgated in Lisbon has been in Angola" (emphasis in original).[1] What irked white settlers and planters in both Angola and Moçambique increasingly was not only their own inability to get labor (at the price they were able or willing to pay) and the provincial government's seeming inability to help them to do so in orderly fashion but also the fact that both provinces were actually exporting labor, just as the metropolitan country did. The implication that economic progress was in all three cases being promoted somewhere else was cold comfort, even in Moçambique where the returning laborers brought grist to the provincial balance of payments. Self-interest suggested that emigration, even more than employment within a province, needed to be brought under control, and reinforced any concern that might be felt on humanitarian grounds for the welfare of the emigrants. Coupled with a renewal of foreign, particularly British, interest in social conditions in the Portuguese colonies, it was responsible for the emergence of a *cause célèbre*—the case of the S. Tomé *serviçaes*—in the first decade of the twentieth century. If some Portuguese had had their way, this issue would have been submerged by, instead of partially submerging, another case that indeed involved far more migrants from a Portuguese colony: those who worked in the Transvaal mines.

I

Although the abuses to which these migratory movements gave rise came to a head (that is to say, attracted public notice) at approximately the same time, their similarity ended there. The most notable difference between them, and one that accounts for the furore over the S. Tomé case, was that while the emigrants from Moçambique went of their own accord, those from Angola manifestly did not, save in legal form. The movement thence to S. Tomé was really a survival from the days of slavery that had somehow contrived to escape notice and hence appeared the more shocking once it was exposed to world opinion. In a sense, the inhumanities that accompanied it and that occasioned a great mass of atrocity stories, denials, charges, and countercharges were beside the point: however humanely conducted, "A

Modern Slavery" was not to be tolerated in the twentieth century.*
The story of the humanitarian agitation and its eventual outcome
has been frequently told and will scarcely bear further repetition;
but there are one or two aspects of the case on which some fresh light
can be thrown.

The first of these is the origin of the system. The province of S.
Tomé consists of two small volcanic islands in the Gulf of Guinea
some eighty miles apart, S. Tomé and Príncipe. These were occupied by the Portuguese in the second half of the fifteenth century,
along with two other islands, Fernando Po and Annobon, which were
subsequently ceded to Spain. Except for a comparatively short time
in the sixteenth century, when they produced sugarcane on a considerable scale, the islands had remained a backwater for centuries and
their turbulent local history had had little connection with that of
the outside world. The provincial revenues had been derived wholly
from the dues paid by the slave ships en route to Brazil (for which
the province was a statutory port of call) and from a subsidy paid out
of the customs revenues of the port of Bahia. In the early nineteenth
century these sources were cut off, and the province passed from stagnation into decay. In a characteristic passage, Andrade Corvo wrote:

The whole industry of the islands was artificial; it was founded on the slave
traffic, which was its principal commerce; and the revenues proceeded from
absurd grants of privilege. When political circumstances and the progress of civilization put an end to this state of things, decadence was prompt and disastrous.
Misery invaded everything, in the midst of Nature's providence; the islands fell
almost into the state of savagery in which the Portuguese found them, save only
for the deep-seated vices that flourished among a scanty and demoralized population. This was the state of affairs when the great principles of modern civilization began to draw Portugal out of the long abasement in which she had lain for
many years, under the pressure of fanaticism and tyranny.

It took many years for the beneficent influence of modern institutions to reach
... S. Tomé and Príncipe. ... When the law put a definite end to the last vestiges
of slavery, it was still S. Tomé that showed itself most adverse to the civilizing
statute. From thence were raised clamors, complaints, and even extravagant
threats against the mother country.[2]

---

* The title of H. W. Nevinson's book (London, 1906), in which his *Harper's Magazine*
articles were reprinted. See James Duffy, *Portuguese Africa* (Cambridge, Mass., 1959),
pp. 157–65, for the most modern account of the controversy.

The reason, as Corvo went on to explain, was that such plantation agriculture as there was in the province was entirely dependent on slave labor. The reason lay in the incredible fertility of the islands, which enabled the free inhabitants to live at least tolerably without working for wages. In a population which, at the time of the first official census taken in 1878, numbered less than 21,000, a striking social diversity had grown up over the centuries. There were many proprietors of large estates (*roças*), not all of them white. There were about 2,500 peasant proprietors and tenant farmers. There were some 1,200 *Angolares,* descendants of a slave ship wrecked on the coast centuries before, who lived in their own village of Santa Cruz and held themselves aloof from the rest of the population.* Like those of the Cape Verde Islands, the free inhabitants of S. Tomé and Príncipe spoke a kind of Portuguese patois and practiced a Catholicism that had become strongly tinged with fetishism; they loved religious processions but seldom went to Mass and even more rarely to confession. The native priest, through educated and ordained in Portugal or Brazil, was esteemed, but the European priest was distrusted. For the men of this group, the idea of farm work for wages was unheard of: even the poorest among them, the socalled *forros* who often were former slaves or libertos, preferred, it was said, to live by thieving from the roças rather than demean themselves by manual labor. So strong was the belief that such work was only for slaves that it was shared by the slaves themselves; and the emancipation, which took place in S. Tomé in 1876, led to a great increase in vagrancy. A great number of the former slaves hired themselves out, not to their old masters, but to anyone else who would enable them to conform with the law: "The ex-libertos did not care whether they were paid: all they wanted was a life of leisure and the assurance of not being ill-treated."[3] In a land where the fruits of the earth were as plentiful as they were in S. Tomé, a very little casual labor would keep a man going.

There was, in fact, no way in which the "beneficent influence of modern institutions" could be brought to bear on the little province in such a way as to bring about an orderly and easy transfer from slavery to free labor. The transfer was made more difficult because, during the very years in which emancipation was decreed to take

* Only the occupations of a few, who were fishermen, are given in the census.

place by stages, the *roçeiros*—many of them wealthy newcomers from Portugal—were increasing their plantings of coffee and cocoa (which had been introduced earlier in the century) and thereby increasing their need for slave labor. Beyond complaining to Lisbon, they had done little to help themselves; moreover, it was notorious that they continued to treat their libertos as if they were slaves. A governor of the province wrote in 1865 that the constant rebellion of slaves against their masters was not to be wondered at, so badly were they treated. Manuel Ferreira Ribeiro, who served as director of public health in the same period, wrote in an official report of 1869 that the libertos were badly fed and clothed, and that this accounted for the high mortality and morbidity rates among them. Sá da Bandeira, commenting on this situation in 1873, observed that the importation of blacks from Angola into S. Tomé was impermissible so long as there were libertos there, since this would amount to authorizing the continuance of slavery both on the islands and on the African continent. He counseled the planters to accept the inevitable: to begin freeing their "better libertos" in advance of complete legal emancipation; and, at the same time, to recruit free Kroomen for work on the roças, "thus avoiding precipitancy, in which the danger consists."[4]

Far from heeding Sá da Bandeira's advice, the planters had, it seems, never really believed that the "extraordinary, indeterminate, and anarchical" status of the liberto would ever end. They found themselves faced overnight with the necessity of hiring paid labor and without the wherewithal to do so. The Banco Nacional Ultramarino (which had established a branch in S. Tomé a few years earlier) came to their help with loans; and a number of Kroomen and other free West Africans were hired on two-year contracts.[5] But difficulties arose about repatriation—perhaps because there was no regular shipping service between the islands and that source of labor. Allegations of bad faith on the part of planters spread, and they found it impossible to hire further labor on the coast.*

The regulations for bringing emancipation into effect, issued at the

---

* In the British colony of Sierra Leone, an official notice was issued in April 1877 warning prospective workers that they would only be able to return via Luanda at an expense of about £4 and advising them not to accept employment on S. Tomé or Príncipe unless they could speak Portuguese. See annexures to Derby–Morier, May 28, 1877, No. 49 Slave Trade (C.P. 3686, No. 299).

end of 1875, had provided for a period of two years' tutelage, under which libertos who could not read and write would be obliged to contract themselves to an employer under prescribed conditions administered by a provincial official (*Curador-geral*) appointed for the purpose. Specific provision had been made, doubtless with the needs of S. Tomé in mind, for the shipping of ex-libertos so contracted from one overseas province to another; and, in fact, some three thousand men, women and children reached S. Tomé and Príncipe from Angola during the years 1877 and 1878. They would, under the law, have been entitled to repatriation at the master's expense after two years, but there is no evidence that any were returned to Angola. In 1878, moreover, fresh regulations were issued formally abolishing the state of tutelage for all ex-libertos and thereafter extending it, in effect, to any who might voluntarily enter into contracts, whether as servants (*serviçaes*) or working settlers on the land (*colonos*). Except that the maximum term of contract was extended from two years to five, the stipulations of the new regulations were, in all important matters, identical with those of the old. On paper they appeared enlightened: Robert Morier even went so far as to report to his government that those of 1878 were "framed in a spirit of humanity towards the Negro, and of equity towards his employer—two qualities not always successfully combined."*

The Foreign Office was more skeptical. Already, in 1877, there had been at least one report of alleged slave trading at Novo Redondo under the guise of contract labor. In February 1878 the elder Wylde, head of the Slave Trade Department, had put the whole problem, as it was to remain for the next quarter-century, forcibly and succinctly:

If we are . . . to be debarred from inquiring into the status of the passengers on board Portge. vessels, our S[lave] T[rade] treaty with Portugal at once becomes a dead letter—for Portg. subjects have only to purchase or "ransom" any number of slaves they please and ship them as free men, and their Colonies will be amply supplied with laborers who, notwithstanding the Portge. law abolishing the status of slavery, will, in fact, be slaves in everything else but the name.

---

* Vicente Pinheiro Lobo Machado de Mello e Almada, *As Ilhas de S. Thomé e Príncipe: (Notas de uma Administração Colonial)* (Lisbon, 1884), p. 35. English translations of the two sets of regulations are annexed to Lytton–Derby, December 31, 1875, No. 15 Slave Trade (C.P. 3263, No. 106), and Morier–Derby, December 24, 1878, No. 55 Slave Trade (C.P. 4286, No. 91), respectively. The second dispatch contains Morier's comment.

As long as the Slave Dealers can get rid of their Captives, it matters little to them whether they are sold in the market as slaves or are "ransomed" to the Portuguese as criminals awaiting the punishment of death: the demand for the Article is the same and it will be supplied. Slave Hunts will be perpetuated.[6]

The Law Officers of the Crown, to whom the case was put, reported that the "ransoming" of slaves in this way was not a breach of the slave trade treaties. Nevertheless, in 1882, following a visit by the British Consul at Luanda to the island of S. Tomé, the British did address a mild remonstrance to the Portuguese government. Consul Cohen had described the system of recruitment in language that left no doubt as to its character:

Captured in the interior, they are brought to Novo Redondo and Benguela, there sold to agents of the planters at San Tomé at prices varying from £4 to £6 in goods, [and] registered and contracted by the Government authority for a period of five years—on the expiration of which term a return passage is to be provided to those who wish to repatriate. Inasmuch, however, as the offer is never made, or the opportunity afforded, they can never leave the island, are made to re-contract, and so become permanent indentured laborers.[7]

He added that they appeared well fed, and were properly cared for if they fell sick, but that there was much sickness and a high death rate among them. The Foreign Secretary (Granville), in forwarding Cohen's report to the chargé d'affaires in Lisbon, described the system as "simply a form of slave trade," and though the chargé did not see fit to use these words in his letter to Serpa Pimentel, there is no reason to suppose that the point was not made clear. The British had, in fact, been making representations at the same time about the shipment of contract laborers from Ibo to the French islands of Mayotte and Nossi-bé; but in this case, since shipment was not within the Portuguese dominions, they obviously had a better locus standi. Though Cohen's report and the action taken thereon were duly published in the annual Blue Book on the slave trade, they do not appear to have evoked any public interest, and the matter was allowed to drop. Far from intro-ducing a new era, it appeared that the regulations of 1878 had per-petuated the old one: a cynic might say that the Curador-geral, with his register of contracts, was the secular reincarnation of the bishops of Luanda who, according to tradition, used to baptize the slaves on their way to the New World. It was, consequently, academic—or, perhaps, cynical—for later critics such as Ennes to condemn the regulations for undue liberalism.[8]

II

Whether the Foreign Office could have brought sufficient pressure on Portugal at that time to end the abuses in the system is doubtful. Apart from the fact that shipments of laborers to S. Tomé were not covered by the slave trade treaties, it would have been difficult to resist the plea that the new regulations be given a trial before sentence was passed on them. But, as is always liable to happen in such instances, the long-standing tolerance of abuses tended to provide prescriptive sanction for them and make the task of reform, when at length it was undertaken, the more difficult. The planters of S. Tomé prospered during the last quarter of the nineteenth century, especially after 1890, when cocoa had replaced coffee as the principal crop. As leaders of the only Portuguese colony that consistently paid its way, they were highly influential in Lisbon: as early as 1881 they had been successful in ending the transportation of criminals to the islands.[9] But their very economic success recoiled upon them in the end, by turning a piece of moral obliquity into a public nuisance.

For many years after 1876, the number of serviçaes going to the islands had been on the order of two thousand annually: a figure that could be met by normal and traditional methods of recruitment in the far interior, beyond Portuguese jurisdiction, without upsetting either the chiefs who controlled the supply or the employers on the mainland of Angola who competed for it.[10] Around the turn of the century, this equilibrium began to be upset from both sides. With rising exports from the island plantations came an increasing demand for labor: over 3,300 men and women were officially reported as having been shipped in 1898/99; over 4,200 in 1899/1900; and 5,100 in 1900/01.* This increase, moreover, was taking place at a time when parts of Angola, notably the coffee-growing district of Cazengo, were being invaded by sleeping sickness. The British consul in Luanda re-

---

* Antonio Teixeira de Sousa, *Relatorio, Propostas de Lei e Documentos Relativos ás Possessões Ultramarinos Apresentados... pelo Ministro e Secretario dos Negócios da Marinha e Ultramar* (Lisbon, Imprensa Nacional, 1902†), p. 387. These official figures are for years other than calendar years and therefore do not agree with those from British sources, which are presumably based on them.

ported that by 1899, the price of a pair of serviçaes, a man and a woman, landed in S. Tomé, was quoted as fifty pounds—something like five times the traditional figure. The temptation that this represented in a country where military and civilian officers were chronically underpaid needs no stressing. In September 1901, the home government actually issued a decree providing for the issue in Angola of safe-conducts, free on request, to native caravans coming and going from market; for the shelter of such caravans at military posts; and for their armed escort between posts, if requested. Any attempt to seize the persons of natives coming to or from market, with a view to forcing them to become contracted laborers, was to be punishable with six months' to two years' imprisonment and a fine of two hundred to one thousand milreis. The decree, for which Teixeira de Sousa was responsible, was accompanied by an outspoken preamble:

It is urgent ... to give commercial caravans all possible facilities, else we run the risk that they will be diverted to seek markets outside the Portuguese dominion [i.e., in the Congo Free State].

Latterly, more than one shameful episode has occurred, the authors of which were not savage Negroes, resistant to civilization and the duties of humanity.... The fever to contract serviçaes, the sizeable profits obtained by middlemen, and the lust for gain that incites those devoid of all scruple, have brought about acts that are in themselves irregular and to be condemned, as well as pernicious for the economy of the province. Native caravans loaded with trade goods have been attacked, and on more than one occasion Negroes taken thus have been forced to become contracted laborers. These acts have taken place within a short distance of the seaboard, and the news of them has caused caravans to disperse even after arriving at the very gates of the market centers to which they had brought goods for barter!

It is one thing to allow the contracting of serviçaes when entered into freely— quite another to allow violence to be used against the black, who comes peaceably to the coast on business, and who is the most important means of commerce in the province.[11]

Less than a year later, the Bailundo revolt broke out in the back country of Benguela—the very area that was traditionally the source of slaves and serviçaes. Cabral Moncada, the governor-general, frankly acknowledged that it had been brought about by misconduct on the part of local officials, several of whom were afterwards brought to trial. (Teixeira de Sousa, on the other hand, blamed it on the machinations of American missionaries.)[12] In 1903, the government made a further effort to regulate the export of serviçaes by establishing a quota system; licensing recruiting agencies; and setting up a system of deferred pay for the laborers, under which a lump sum, previously deducted in installments from their wages, would be paid over to them, on repatriation, at the port of arrival.[13]

These measures, it should be noted, were undertaken before the English writer Henry W. Nevinson published the first of his famous articles in *Harper's Magazine*; and this may help to explain the sense of outrage felt by the Portuguese public—who, of course, knew little or nothing of either Angola or S. Tomé—at this and subsequent newspaper attacks. Though for many years exposed to the combination of hectoring and patronage to which British missionaries and journalists habitually treated them, the Portuguese never learned to bear it with silent contempt.* Nor does it seem to have occurred to many of their critics that discourtesy and accusations of bad faith might make the task of British diplomacy more difficult, or even that a good case benefits from temperate presentation. The wordy battle that went on from 1905 until the outbreak of World War I generated a great deal of heat without a commensurate accompaniment of light; and while some advantage for the serviçaes undoubtedly resulted, it is by no means certain that this could not have been accomplished by diplomatic means alone. Certainly if the Portuguese government had needed external persuasion to reform the system, it would have taken more than fulminations in the foreign press to do the trick. From the outset, therefore, the British government was, and moreover knew itself to be, a principal target of the anti-Portuguese agitation; and its attitude is therefore crucial to an understanding of what occurred.

When the *Harper's Magazine* articles began to appear, the Foreign Secretary (Lansdowne) deputed Consul Nightingale, who had previously served in Luanda and was now at Boma, to make an investigation in the islands. He spent the best part of three months—November 24, 1905, to February 9, 1906—visiting the principal roças on both islands. But his report, though it went into considerable detail, added very little to that of Consul Cohen, more than two decades before. (The most important change had been the appearance of the deadly sleeping sickness on Príncipe.) The laborers, in his view, were "well

---

* The *Punch* and *Moonshine* cartoons referred to above (p. 131n) are examples.

treated in every respect," and "great credit" was due to the planters for the care they took of them. They were better treated than the free laborers working in Spanish Fernando Po, and better fed and housed than those working in the trading factories on the coast. Moreover, there was a complete absence of armed force or even police on the roças, which would hardly have been possible had there been generally harsh treatment of the workers. The real evil lay elsewhere: in the manner they were obtained in Angola and in the failure to repatriate them. Commenting on the regulations of 1903, Nightingale observed that "the appointment of special emigration agents has in no way improved the situation—it has merely made them authorized slave dealers, and they not only buy from the merchants but send their own agents into the interior to purchase people."[14] In short, the same old loophole in the law still existed that Sá da Bandeira had wished to close, nearly half a century earlier, in the case of the barque *Charles et Georges*; and there was now, as there had not been in 1857, a powerful lobby in Lisbon that wished it to be kept open.[15]

By the time the Nightingale Report was received in London, in August 1906, the Conservative government under Balfour had fallen and had been replaced by a Liberal government headed by Campbell-Bannerman. One of the planks in the winning platform had been the exclusion of Chinese indentured laborers from the Transvaal mines, and hence the retention of the arrangement under which Moçambique laborers were permitted by the Portuguese to work there. As mortality among these laborers was very high, it would have been awkward for the British to argue simultaneously in favor of continuing their employment and against sending workers to S. Tomé, even though there was no comparison between the methods of recruitment in the two cases. Grey, the Foreign Secretary, therefore decided that no representations on the point should be made to Portugal for the present, and that an edited copy of the Nightingale Report should "be communicated, *not for publication*, to the Aborigines [Protection] Society," in order to keep them from pressing for publication: "the portions which relate to past history may give rise to unnecessary controversy and annoyance."[16] It was not, however, merely these portions that were suppressed, but the essential point of the report—its reference to the virtual slave trading on the mainland. Once this garbled version had been given in confidence to the Aborigines Protection Society, its later publication in authentic form was precluded—as the Foreign Office subsequently realized. (It was, however, transmitted to the Portuguese government.)[17] Though it would be naïve to complain of the Foreign Secretary's want of candor, one may question his judgment—at least in the light of later events—for the publication of the Nightingale Report might have forestalled the long series of allegations of cruelty made against the S. Tomé planters by the missionary J. H. Harris and others on what seems to have been the flimsiest of evidence, and concentrated criticism at the point where the Portuguese government, by reason of its admittedly inadequate control of the Angolan interior, would have found rebuttal the most difficult. Any ill-feeling that might have been generated by publication could scarcely have been greater than that which arose as a result of the long agitation and the eventual boycott of S. Tomé cocoa by the firms of Cadbury, Rowntree, Fry, and Stollwerck.

In 1903, when the boycott had first been mooted, Foreign Office officials had been delighted; but by 1907, both they and the cocoa firms had come around to the view that the most promising course of action was to damp down public agitation and to rely on diplomatic pressure, which might get the Portuguese government to remedy abuses whose existence it could not but deny on open challenge.[18] The continued prevalence of slave hunting in the country around the headwaters of the Zambezi was beyond question. "The Ovimbundu," wrote the missionary Walter Fisher to Consul Nightingale in 1902, "still continue their wretched slave traffic."[19] By 1908 things were no better: Nightingale's successor Mackie, who had toured the back country extensively, reported that the system of recruiting labor was "closely akin to slavery," and that villages in the Caconda district were systematically raided by parties who forcibly carried away men, women, and children; and that "the purchase and sale of serviçaes were openly spoken of."[20] Similar reports came from the Rhodesian side of the border with Angola, from district officers who put the blame on the absence of effective Portuguese administration. This was something that the more candid of Portuguese officials would admit. Couceiro, for instance, declared that the allegations against the recruiting system amounted to a detailed indictment "whose insistent and acrimonious assaults we seek to deter with successive parades of paper regulations which, in their haste to appear, destroy one another." Given the want of a police force in the interior, he said, one could assert a priori that there would be abuses beyond remedy; though he pointed out that in March and April 1909 four alleged slave dealers had been expelled from the province. Couceiro admitted that the absence of repatriation was the root evil, and he was prepared to make repatriation, if not obligatory, at least the rule: the existing provision for it was, he thought, unduly hedged about with qualifications that might entail the survival of "the present beautiful system, to which we owe ... the charge of being slavers. ... '*Via recta, via certa*' should be the watchword of Portuguese policy."[21]

In July 1909, the Portuguese government took the decisive step toward reform by prohibiting recruitment of serviçaes in Angola altogether, pending the introduction of new and more effective regulations. Though put into force in the first instance for only three months, the prohibition was eventually sustained for nearly four years. The cocoa manufacturers' boycott had preceded it by about four months —having been imposed at a time when they knew that an official inquiry was being made, and knew also the reforms it would propose. This, the Portuguese not unnaturally felt, was unfair: it might almost have been designed to suggest that they would make no change except under compulsion. More probably it was prompted by the notorious *Standard* leading article of September 28, 1908, accusing the Cadbury firm of dragging its feet and, indeed, conniving at the "slavery" of S. Tomé—the article that occasioned the libel action of December 1909 in which the jury awarded a farthing damages and in which, in effect, the rulers of S. Tomé were put on trial without benefit of counsel. Nevinson later wrote that the trial had established the facts of the slave traffic and the system of forced labor in Angola and the Islands as he had reported them; and it was true that neither side in the action attempted to dispute what he had written nearly five years earlier.[22] What Portuguese officials would have argued was that this was not only exaggerated, but no longer relevant; that they were doing their best in adverse circumstances and earning not credit but abuse. They conveniently forgot that not all this abuse came from foreigners. If Harris referred to "Pecksniffian decrees and regulations,"[23] it was a pamphlet published in Luanda in 1903 that referred to the new labor law of that year as "merely an ornate lie."*

The controversy continued through the early years of the Republic, and echoes of it were heard even after World War I, by which time a system of regular repatriation had been firmly established. How far this may be attributed to the continuance of agitation and the watchfulness of British consular officers appointed ad hoc (with the consent of the Republican government) is a matter of opinion. It has to be remembered that the controversy did not turn solely on whether or not there had been abuses, or whether the system of recruitment was, as a Foreign Office official put it in 1903, "in practice not to be distinguished from slavery; but ... so different in theory that it is difficult to attack it successfully."[24] Aside from any question of administrative malpractice, there remained the question of whether it was proper to impose forced labor on the African at all. Ennes and Couceiro thought it not merely proper but essential to do so as part of the civilizing process; they merely wanted it done in decent and orderly fashion. One result of strengthening the administrative machine in the colonies might thus be to increase the amount of forced labor that was demanded: the system would be fairer, perhaps, but harder to dodge and hence more oppressive. (The very inefficiency of Portuguese rule might well account for its tolerance by the African over the centuries.) For this reason, if for no other, it was unlikely that the Portuguese would be free for long from humanitarian criticism. As Freire de Andrade had remarked in 1907 with Moçambique in mind:

Inasmuch as any form of imposition of work, or, for that matter, any measures tending to induce the native to work, can always be dubbed slavery, I would like to know what is meant nowadays by the term. ... Slavery or forced labor are words that sound terrible to the ears of our century and perhaps this is why they are used to menace those who wish to take away the black man from the idle state so dear to him. ... I do not desire slavery in any form or aspect, but I do want the duty of labor, imposed by that great law of nature that is embodied in

---

* See pamphlet, *Ao Paiz: O Povo de Luanda contra O Renovamento dos Contractos de Serviçaes* (Luanda, 1903), copy in F.O. 63/1447. A sustained and detailed polemic against the regulations of 1903 is in *Os Contractos de Serviçaes em Angola: ao Paiz e á Sociedade de Geographia: Manifesto da Grande Commissão de Luanda* (Lisbon, 1904). José de Macedo, whose work has been frequently cited, was a member of the "Grand Commission."

our statutes, and I do not think the black should escape it through the leniency of the law and through the practice of that veritable slavery he imposes upon the woman.[25]

III

Freire de Andrade had himself been responsible for abolishing—at any rate temporarily—one particular form of forced labor known as *chibalo*, which he found in operation in the district of Lourenço Marques. Under this system, anyone desiring native labor would apply to the government, which would requisition it through one of the *chefes de circumscrição* at a standard rate per day for a number of months. The credentials of the employer were apparently not inquired into, and he was free to hire out the labor so acquired at a profit. "Naturally," says Freire de Andrade, "there arose abuses": one such, involving two hundred men from the Gaza district, was found to involve falsification of contracts, whereby men who thought they had hired themselves for 120 days found themselves bound for 180. Other abuses consisted in the refusal of employers to pay sums due on account of alleged absenteeism; or to pay even a part of the wages of laborers who left before the appointed time. Eighty workers did, in fact, complain to the authorities, who referred the case to the courts; but judgment was so long in coming that the men got tired of waiting and left without being paid. Another practice was to use chibalo to provide servants, paid for out of the local treasury, to public officials who might then use them for unsuitable purposes: as carriers for prostitutes under an official's protection, or as "rickshaw" men hired out for their employers' profit.[26] It was presumably chibalo (which was prohibited by an order dated December 7, 1906) to which the Anglican Bishop of Lebombo referred when he wrote, a few months earlier: "The new railways [in Moçambique] are all being built with forced labor. It was for the latter purpose that the police fetched one of our subdeacons out of church while he was conducting service not long ago."[27] About the same time, the British vice-consul in Inhambane was reporting that compulsory recruiting for the Transvaal mines was going on in the district: "These boys are being caught like wild animals by the police boys in the employ of the Commandants. . . . I have seen them myself arriving here in town under strong guard." A colleague sent from Lourenço Marques to investigate confirmed the story, adding that it was an innovation for natives to be forced to work outside Portuguese territory.[28] If the bishop is to be believed, it was an unnecessary innovation: "There is absolutely no force used or required to get laborers for the Transvaal.... as things are in this country, W[itwatersrand] N[ative] L[abor] A[ssociation] stands for justice and freedom."[29]

For a generation it had been the habit of the natives of the Portuguese districts adjoining the Transvaal and Natal to seek work there. Consul O'Neill noted in April 1888 that this practice was "getting every day commoner," adding that the willingness of men to contract themselves without seeing something of the work was, however, lessening. The migratory movement does not seem to have attained sizeable proportions, however, until the opening of the railway line through to Johannesburg, in January 1895. Ennes, in his memorandum of 1893, does not mention it beyond saying that the returned laborers from Natal "spent their pounds, exchanged at a vile price by the monhés, on drunken bouts."[30] For his successor Mousinho it was already an administrative problem: he found in existence a prohibition on native emigration which was enforceable only on those traveling by train. Mousinho persuaded Dr. Leyds, and through him the Transvaal government, to do what it had hitherto declined to do: license the agents recruiting for the mines and allow the Portuguese to appoint a resident curator in Johannesburg to look after the interests of their emigrants. "The regulations did not aim at encouraging emigration, but merely at regularizing it," Mousinho wrote. Nevertheless, he seems to have regarded the movement as advantageous: besides stimulating the economy of the province through the spending of returned emigrants, it would benefit the emigrants themselves by bringing them into contact with civilization.[31]

However, just two years after Mousinho made his *entente* with the Transvaal the Boer War broke out. Mining on the Rand was suspended, and traffic on the Lourenço Marques line heavily reduced. Toward the end of 1901, when the outcome of the war was already beyond doubt, Governor-General Gorjão and Captain Crowe, the British consul-general in Lourenço Marques, negotiated a modus vivendi providing for the restoration of the previous arrangements "pending the conclusion of a definite convention." This was done in order that gold mining, which was dependent on immigrant labor from Moçambique, might be resumed as quickly as possible; and as a quid pro quo the British agreed, among other things, to restore the prewar through freight rate differentials between Johannesburg and Lourenço Marques on the one hand, and Johannesburg and the British South African ports on the other. The British were in a position to do this because one of the incidental results of the war had been the nationalization—if that be the right term in the circumstances—of the Transvaal railroads.*

In view of the tendentious account of this and related transactions that was later compiled by a member of Milner's "kindergarten," Lionel Curtis, and thereafter published over the signature of Milner's successor Selborne, it must be emphasized that these differentials did not constitute a favor to the port of Lourenço Marques. It was, as it had always been, the nearest and best outlet for the Transvaal, and the lower freight rates to it reflected the economic advantage of a shorter haul. To that advantage before the war had been added the political one of not being under British control; but even in the new political situation Transvaal shippers showed persistent and even increasing preference for Lourenço Marques. "In November 1902," Curtis indignantly remarked, "79 per cent of the trade is going to British ports, 21 per cent to the foreign port. Four years have passed under the British flag and 44 per cent is going to British ports and 56 per cent to the foreign port." In these circumstances, cries began to be heard for a modification of the modus vivendi that would reduce the economic advantage of the Lourenço Marques route; and one of the advantages urged for the creation of a union of South Africa was that it would end the rivalries between the railway systems of the separate colonies and enable them to present a united front on freight rates to the foreigner.

From the national point of view the result [of railroad disunity] has been calamitous, for it has developed a port outside British South Africa at the expense of her own ports, and introduced the foreign complications of continental Europe into the domestic affairs of this country—as shown by the fact that matters which involve the relation of one South African Colony to another have now to be dealt with by the Foreign Office of the Imperial Government.

The political naïveté revealed by this passage is evident; the economic fallacy that lay behind it scarcely less so. Its writer viewed the

---

* *Selborne Memorandum,* pp. 69–71. The Transvaal-Portugal treaty of 1875 (above, p. 83) was, of course, binding on the British as the suzerain power.

competition between the various routes to the seaboard solely in terms of railway receipts: "Under federation, the gross receipts, on whatever line they were earned, would go into a common pocket" and the Transvaal and Orange River Colony would no longer have "so great an interest in exploiting Delagoa Bay."[32] It never occurred to him that they would be exploiting the railway users instead if they equalized rates between the lines, much less that, to the extent that other lines were used to the exclusion of Delagoa Bay, there would be an economic loss resulting from a wasteful use of resources. Federation or no federation, what he proposed to do was to keep the Cape and Natal happy at the expense of the Transvaal shipper. Freire de Andrade, commenting on the Selborne memorandum at the time it was published, made the point clearly:

Once federation is completed, any disadvantage suffered by the Transvaal's line from Ressano Garcia to Johannesburg, or any measure that prejudices its natural economic development, will be injurious to the commonwealth as a whole.... Moreover, there are the lines to Swaziland and Zoutpansberg: would the federation seek to divert the traffic of these districts from their natural harbor ... or leave them unproductive just in order not to *enrich the "foreign port"*? Does the *Review* [memorandum] want to divert the traffic of Rhodesia to the Cape?

Freire de Andrade went on to show, by reference to the accounts of the various lines, how absurd was the claim that the competition of Lourenço Marques was ruining the remaining railroads. The increase in gross receipts on the Portuguese section of the line, corresponding to the large percentage gain in tonnage between 1902 and 1906, was the paltry sum of £1,214: so much for the argument that the diversion of traffic from British ports was building up a foreign community. There had, of course, been a sharp fall in receipts on the British lines, but this was due to the failure of the expected postwar boom to materialize. South African railway building had, in fact, been excessively sanguine: there were five lines converging on the Transvaal from the seaboard, each capable of handling all the traffic on offer. Some apportionment of it between them could be defended as a way of preserving capital assets that would be needed later on, and had indeed been discussed as early as 1895; but to dwell on the "foreignness" of Lourenço Marques was to excite prejudice on what was at best a side issue—the more so since most of the capital invested in the town was British.

What irked the Portuguese was the persistent effort by the British, led by Milner, to whittle down the terms of the modus vivendi by pressure or unilateral action. An example of the latter was a proposal to reduce freight charges generally on the South African railroads, thus cutting down the absolute advantage of the Lourenço Marques line while leaving relative rates untouched. According to the Selborne memorandum, the "highest legal authority" (presumably the British Law Officers) had ruled that this would not be a breach of Article IV of the modus vivendi. But, as Freire de Andrade pointed out, it was wholly improper to seek this way of circumventing an agreement that could be denounced, should its interpretation become a matter of dispute:

Why were the negotiators of the modus vivendi not consulted about the meaning of Article Four? As they are both alive, this would seem the natural course; moreover, the modus vivendi was not denounced—for all that some maintain that that document represented an extortion practiced by the Portuguese Government on the Transvaal, by threatening to prevent it from recruiting blacks in Moçambique. Instead of that, they had recourse to an anonymous "high legal authority," which reached conclusions that were promptly accepted, in order to be able to "deprive Lourenço Marques immediately of the advantages that it enjoyed from the modus vivendi" and that this Province would continue to enjoy for a year, were the agreement to be denounced. Thus the aim was accomplished of making the modus vivendi, only five years after its signature, a worthless document, almost completely disregarded in any respect that was of advantage to us.

Perhaps because I am not *au fait* with the nature of diplomacy, I judge that a signed document capable of rescission ought either to be complied with by the signatory or rescinded.

The barefaced explanation in the memorandum of why the British had taken that course made matters worse: "What advantage is there in publishing these facts gratuitously, unless the end be to provoke disunion among those whose interests it professes to reconcile?"[33]

IV

In imputing underhand motives to the Selborne memorandum, Freire de Andrade was evidently mistaken; its imperialist aims were as transparent as its history and its economics. But in general, his comments were shrewd and to the point, and would have made salutary reading for the Milner "kindergarten." Thus, a lengthy passage culminating in a piece of rhetoric about the conflict of railway interests vanishing "like a foul mist before the sun of South African Federation" was cited derisively as something that "nobody but a visionary or a poet could have written"; and a reference to the white races peacefully leading the Africans "on the upward path of Christianity and of civilization" was dubbed "poetic," for nothing of the sort had happened up to the present. Freire de Andrade noted that this remark was followed by another rejecting slavery but avoiding any positive proposals on native labor: "It is sufficient to say only when full responsibility is assumed by the people of this country [South Africa] as a whole will the wisdom to foresee, the courage to begin, and the endurance to persevere to the end, without which no native policy is worth calling a policy at all, be summoned into action."[34] "Social questions," commented the Portuguese administrator, "are not resolved with pious sentiments (*sentimentalismos*) but by actions which need to be discussed and then put into effect. Slavery must be set aside, but the labor question in Africa cannot be resolved merely with . . . words."[35]

Freire de Andrade was convinced that the Transvaal would not readily sacrifice the advantages of the Lourenço Marques line in the face of pleas for unity, and that the supply of labor was a strong card in the hands of the Portuguese, who had, he thought, given up too easily some of the advantages the original modus vivendi conferred on them—most notably, that of free entry of goods produced in Moçambique into the Transvaal, and vice versa. Had this right been fully maintained, it would have encouraged the establishment in Lourenço Marques of certain port industries such as flour milling, oilseed crushing, and sugar refining. But in June 1904 the Portuguese had allowed it to be restricted to goods originating in the province: a limitation from which members of the South African Customs Union, set up in 1903, were exempt. This and similar policies aimed at eroding the position of the "foreign port" seemed poor recompense for the harbor improvements that had been undertaken at Lourenço Marques since 1901 on the strength of the modus vivendi, to say nothing of the railroad to the Swaziland border that the Portuguese had built in the belief that it would be continued on the farther side. Freire de Andrade was, therefore, in favor of taking a tough line with the Transvaal: inasmuch as the port and railroad had been built for its benefit, there was no reason why Portugal should agree to run them at a loss. "If the Transvaal cares to face the facts, so much the better for her and for us; if not, she will suffer the consequences of her want of foresight, and will recognize this sooner or later."[36]

This estimate of the position proved to be nearer the mark than that of the Selborne memorandum; though the Portuguese government lacked the nerve to test it fully in negotiation. The Transvaal, though obliged, in February 1909, to make an agreement with Natal and Cape Colony under which fifty per cent of rail-freight traffic between the Witwatersrand and the seaboard would be divided between their ports had already initiated negotiations for guaranteeing Lourenço Marques the remainder. By an agreement signed at Pretoria in April 1909 by Selborne, as governor of the Transvaal, and the special Portuguese representative Garcia Rosado, rates were to be so adjusted as to ensure the port not less than fifty per cent and not more than fifty-five per cent of the total goods traffic by weight. For this purpose, and to advise on port improvements, a joint committee of two Transvaal and two Portuguese representatives (one of whom would be chairman) was set up in Lourenço Marques. The quid pro quo, the recruitment of labor for the mines, was to take place more or less under the same conditions as before. The same rule applied to the tariff concessions: that is, the limitation accepted by Portugal in 1904 was maintained. The treaty was to last for ten years in the first instance, after which it would be automatically renewed annually unless denounced.[37] It is noteworthy that it took precedence in South Africa over the inter-colonial agreement: Article 148(1) of the Act establishing the Union of South Africa made it, along with other treaties made by the separate colonies, binding on the Union government, whereas Article 148(2) declared merely that the railway agreement should be enforced "as far as practicable."* In fact, the Lourenço Marques line took two-thirds of the Transvaal traffic both in 1909 and in 1910, the first year in which the agreement began to operate.[38]

* "An Act to Constitute the Union of South Africa, 1909" (9. Edw. 7, c. 9); reprinted in, *inter alia*, R. H. Brand, *The Union of South Africa* (London, 1909), pp. 142–92. On the other hand, the agreement was unconstitutional in Portugal. See Ernesto de Vilhena, *Questões Coloniais*, Vol. I, p. 98.

V

The Transvaal-Moçambique Convention naturally caused indignation in South Africa, especially Natal: "At one moment it looked as if
the Union itself was jeopardized."[39] There was sharp criticism—not
all of it factious—in Portugal, where the government was blamed for
not submitting the agreement to Parliament before signature. The
establishment of the joint committee was attacked as a step toward
the "denationalization" of Moçambique—an indication of the way in
which the southernmost tip of the province had become identified
with the whole in the minds of many. In an impressive series of articles
published in the Lisbon *Diário Popular* during May–August 1909,
Ernesto de Vilhena went further and attacked the whole policy of
making Moçambique into a compound for supplying labor to the
Transvaal.[40] He did not suggest that laborers be prohibited from going to work there: as Mousinho had recognized more than a decade
earlier, this would have been impracticable. He did, however, argue
that the area of recruitment and the numbers to be recruited should
have been limited; that a guarantee of repatriation should have been
exacted; that recruitment should have been in the hands of Portuguese officials, instead of the W.N.L.A., which was virtually a state
within a state; that the export tax levied in respect of each migrant
should have been sharply raised, and the proceeds devoted to foment-
ing agriculture within the Province; and that the agreement should
have contained provisos about working conditions and welfare in the
mines. True, the British government had taken measures in this last
respect, but they were evidently not sufficient.

Even if they were, even if we only wanted to show the civilized world that we
were not unmindful of a subject which deserves the greatest attention from all
colonial administrators, while in reality we attached no importance to it, it seems
to me that some articles [in the agreement] ought to have been devoted to the
matter. As it is, the convention—its only interest in the profits—treats the black
like a veritable animal, exporting him without care of any kind. This is an un-
pardonable deficiency in it from the moral point of view.[41]

Vilhena did not suggest that the monopoly of recruitment given
to the W.N.L.A. had led or would lead to individual abuses. His objection to it went deeper: that its very efficiency was likely to have dis-
integrating effects on the economy of the province and the morale of
its inhabitants. Odious comparisons were likely to be drawn between

the British recruiter, with his uniformed black "runners," and the Portuguese administrator, worse housed, worse paid, and with fewer, less smart-looking subordinates.

Already in the comparison of burdens and profits the advantage is with the Englishman. He gives him [the black] abundant drams, blankets, and presents of all kinds to encourage him to set out, pays him on the Rand far more liberally than we do, and advances him the amount of the hut tax—while the administrator of the circumscrição is merely the man who exacts the tax at fixed and inexorable intervals, who calls upon him for labor service without pay on public works, or for low rates for private individuals.

One gives, the other takes, and as the Negro is still too backward to understand that the state cannot maintain itself without taxes whose payment, moreover, brings him no material or moral advantage in return . . . neither better food, nor instruction, nor a cure for smallpox, nor riddance of locusts, it is not difficult to see why the activity of the recruiter encourages the Negro to become English.[42]

To this objection it was added that the absence of adult males abroad was likely to be dysgenic—the more so as they were liable to return suffering from silicosis, "miner's phthisis," tuberculosis, or syphilis—and socially disruptive as well:

The recruitment of natives as hitherto practiced . . . denationalizes the native, upsets the institution of property, decimates his numbers, weakens his constitution, brings about race degeneration and perverts his morals. . . . This is a repugnant industry which reduces the black once more to the level of a slave, and the recruiter to the position of a civilized slave dealer, protected by treaties and diplomatic notes—cleaner, but no more scrupulous.[43]

One might almost be reading Nevinson or Harris on the serviçaes of S. Tomé. Yet there is no reason for doubting Vilhena's sincerity, or that of men like Eduardo Saldanha who were later to campaign endlessly against the recruitment of labor for the mines. It does appear that Garcia Rosado may have lost an opportunity to get better terms for the province, though this can hardly have been altogether his fault, since there were three Ministers of Marine during the period of the period of the negotiations. Whether Vilhena and other critics were right in condemning his acceptance of a quota of rail traffic markedly lower than that enjoyed by Lourenço Marques during the later years of the modus vivendi is less certain. The formation of the Union of South Africa did not constitute a specifically Portuguese interest, but a railway agreement had been made a sine qua non of union, which in its turn was a key aim of British imperial policy at the time. To have become the economic rock on which union split might have been politically awkward for Portugal. Moreover, if the agreement of 1909 were to bring about the expected "Kaffir boom," the increase in total traffic would be more than compensatory for any reduction in Lourenço Marques' quota. On this railroad question it is difficult to exculpate the critics from the charge of wanting to have it both ways. Freire de Andrade had frequently argued that any South African economic arrangements ought to include Lourenço Marques instead of being directed against it. General Smuts' comment on the April 1909 treaty, that "the Portuguese would no longer have a free hand with their own railways, and that "Delagoa Bay would really be treated as a part of the Transvaal and of South Africa," was perhaps tactlessly worded; but the joint committee, being almost purely advisory, was not very convincing in the part of a Trojan Horse whereby the Union could infringe Portuguese sovereignty.[44]

It is clear that Vilhena was under no illusions about the short-run possibility of changing the situation. He categorically rejected any idea of taking the matter to the British government:

This would be to change certainty, with all its deficiencies and inconveniences, for something absolutely uncertain and unforeseeable. If we were a great power it would be worth our while, on the immediate and restricted issue of the treaty, to oppose the realization of the South African Union; but we are not, and it might happen that we should be obliged to modify the agreement, not in our interest but in the interest of the other party.... Our efforts with the Pretoria government having failed, we can only resign ourselves to our lot.

The only chance of getting the economy of the province of Moçambique on to the right lines has been lost.... We shall continue, as hitherto, to be towed along by others, very pleased when they throw us the rope.[45]

Conclusion

"We are not a great power." That regretful admission runs through
Vilhena's articles, as it does through so much more Portuguese writing on colonial affairs. It is the converse of the claim of the German
colonial party that because the Bismarckian Reich was a great power,
she—unlike Portugal—was entitled to African possessions. The historian is not called upon to adduce a single overriding motive for the
"scramble for Africa"; but if one were wanted, the Veblenian notion
of conspicuous consumption seems nearer the mark than the urgings
of Hobsonian capitalists bent on enlarging export markets in improbable places. As Yves Guyot wrote in 1885: "Our [the French] colonies
are an outlet, not for our industry and commerce, but for the taxpayers' money"—a sentiment with which Goschen would have doubtless agreed.[1] A generation later, when the growth of colonial empire
could be seen to have been accompanied, if not matched, by an
assumption of increasing responsibility for the welfare of primitive
peoples, this skeptical view still appeared justified. True, there were
examples of successful economic development that the critics might
term exploitation; but for each of these there was at least one counter-
vailing instance where the attempt to exploit had proved sanguine. By
1910, if not earlier, it was clear that the expenditure of large sums of
money in Africa, whether by investors or taxpayers, was a necessary,
but by no means a sufficient, condition of economic growth and financial profit. Part of the trouble with Hobson's theory was that it
took the exceptional case—that of the Rand goldfields—as typical, and

did not look at a more representative case such as the African railways. The history of most of these might have been designed as a punning illustration of Veblen's too-little-known reductio ad absurdum of marginal utility economics: "The production of utilities is . . . a function of the pigheaded optimism of mankind."[2]

For supporters of the imperial idea in Portugal, the failure of the colonies to come up to economic expectations was evidently more serious than it would have been in a wealthier country; the ability of the Rand mine-owners to attract some eighty thousand natives from Moçambique for arduous and dangerous work was as ominous a sign as the inability of the roceiros of S. Tomé to recruit their labor in a genuinely free market, or the failure of the Moçambique and Nyassa Companies to pay dividends. If the price of continued dominion were development, and uneconomic development at that, who in Portugal could be found to pay it? If the Germans and the Union of South Africa were intent upon putting Portugal out of business as a colonial power—not by war, necessarily, but by economic competition and encroachment—how could they be stopped unless by each other? How could Portugal cope with the forces of world humanitarianism, seemingly allied with her colonial rivals, which had ruined the only prosperous industry in Angola and delivered the S. Tomé cocoa market into the hands of the Gold Coast? Such questions were the more daunting if one contemplated the state of Portuguese politics after the assassination of King Carlos and his heir apparent in February 1908. Far from rallying Royalist politicians in support of Manuel II— if only for a last-ditch battle against a Republican open conspiracy— that event had completed the disintegration of the old rotativist parties that, with all their faults, had provided the country with a certain continuity of administration, and with leaders who had at least experience to recommend them. Men like Teixeira de Sousa and Ayres d'Ornellas had even been able to stay at the Ministry of Marine long enough to formulate and put into effect something that could be called a colonial policy. But in the thirty-two months of Manuel II's reign there were no less than six ministries, and five different Ministers of Marine and Colonies: "wills-o'-the-wisp," Vilhena called them. Moreover—and this may have been nothing new—colonial affairs had the lowest priority in ministerial discussions: "The Ministry of Marine is the 'ragpicker among ministries.' Matters concerning it are the last to be presented and discussed, when indeed they are presented at all; the sessions begin work at ten, and by midnight everyone is exhausted; a general lassitude, invading tired bodies and spirits that were never fresh, sets ministers a-nodding over the mass of paper."

This was the picture conveyed by Augusto de Castilho, Minister of Marine at the time of the Transvaal-Moçambique Convention of 1909, in a parliamentary speech. "Anyone who saw," adds Vilhena, "the pleasure with which the Republican members of the House received Senhor Castilho's declarations, will have understood what splendid weapons he was handing them, not only against the government but against the regime that employed such governments."[3]

The House of Bragança was to disappear from the scene in October 1910, after an uprising in the Lisbon streets, provoked by the slaying of a prominent Republican and alienist, Dr. Miguel Bombarda, by a deranged patient. A display of resolution and tolerable efficiency on the side of the Royalists could scarcely have failed to save the régime on this occasion, though one may doubt whether it could have been saved in the long run—not that in the long run the change to a republican form of government was to make much difference to the conduct of affairs in Portugal. As the democratic leader Cunha Leal was ruefully to observe from political exile a generation later, the intelligent but inexperienced politicians who came to power in 1910 took the line of least resistance—"changing the label, but keeping the same merchandise." He went on:

The Republicans left intact ... the same state organization with its defects and its monarchical conformation, the same inefficient armed forces, the same incompetent diplomatists, the same idle bureaucrats, the same reactionary professors, the same servile judges, the same impotent ruling class [forças vivas].... Instead of a severe earthquake, the proclamation of the republic was a mere storm in a teacup.[4]

The implications of these Republican omissions were long-lived and weighty, but slow to emerge: in the colonies especially a new era seemed to be dawning in which prospects of radical reform were but slightly obscured by current administrative confusion. The making of colonial administration into a virtual preserve for military and naval officers had occasioned criticism under the monarchy;[5] now it was to have an unforeseen disadvantage in that some of them took their allegiance to the person of the Crown at its face value. Couceiro, Coutinho, Ornellas, João de Almeida—all went so far as to lead insurrections, or incursions from Spain, designed to restore the monarchy. Freire de Andrade, arguably the ablest of his generation, accepted the new regime, though (it was commonly believed) with reservations; as Director-General of the Ministry of Colonies, now for the first time separated from that of Marine, he was a powerful influence on colonial policy during the first years of the Republic, as was his junior Ernesto de Vilhena. But in the colonies themselves the inferior quality of Republican appointees—sometimes chosen for their political services to the cause—was frequently remarked upon.* There has never been enough administrative talent in Portugal for any government to be able to dispense with large portions of it on political grounds.

Of the dominant figure of these years, Afonso Costa, Cunha Leal remarks that he was perhaps a conservative without knowing it: only his language was radical.[6] In nothing was the conservatism of the Republic evinced more clearly than in the absence of anti-imperialist feeling, such as was to be found among contemporary British radicals, or of any recrudescence of proposals to reduce the size of the empire. Twenty years earlier, in June 1891, Costa Lobo, speaking in the House of Peers on the Anglo-Portuguese Treaty, could insist that the African colonies and Portugal herself were not to be regarded as all of a piece: "There is much talk of the integrity of the Motherland, but it is needful that neither explicitly nor implicitly, in word or in thought, should the sacrosanct soil of Portugal be confounded with that of Moçambique, which is governed by Mutasas and such. They are two completely different things."[7]

Casal Ribeiro, speaking in the same House a few weeks later, could commend Ferreira d'Almeida for proposing the sale of some of the colonial possessions, and question the claim that Portugal's raison d'être as a nation depended on her possession of a colonial empire. Oliveira Martins, writing to A. F. Nogueira in January 1893, could say: "We cannot aspire in Moçambique to more than suzerain rights."[8] None of these people was anti-imperialist in principle: on the con-

---

* Hardinge–Grey, March 3, 1913, No. 23 Africa, recounting an interview with Freire de Andrade in Lisbon (C.P. 10466, No. 24): "Unfortunate as has been for Portugal the establishment of the Republic, its results have perhaps proved, if anything, more harmful in her colonies, and, above all, in the province of Mozambique, whose administration is the most difficult of all."

trary, they were truly economic imperialists in that they wanted the Portuguese to cease imitating Aesop's frog. "What would be best," wrote Nogueira, "would be to limit our dominion on the east coast of Africa to Lourenço Marques . . . get rid of Guiné and Timor, and use the proceeds to extend the so-called Trans-African railroad from Ambaca to Malange...and build the Benguela and Moçâmedes lines."[9]

It is, of course, possible that even in the nineties, the radical nature of these proposals was—as George Orwell once wrote of some people's revolutionary views—in part derived from a secret conviction that nothing could be changed. They always constituted a minority view. But at any rate they were not unthinkable, as they seem to have become by 1910, for all that the economic weakness of the country would seem to have been as palpable as ever. The facts of uneconomic empire had not changed in essence; yet no politician or publicist with any standing was now to be found arguing that Portugal should try to get away from them by a deliberate act of policy. The pessimism of Oliveira Martins might almost be said to have been buried with him, no doubt partly because his more apocalyptic prophecies had failed to materialize. Like many another reformer, he underrated both the resilience of human societies in face of misgovernment and the ability of governments to survive their own mistakes: odd errors for a historian of Portugal to fall into.

One might argue that the imperial effort of Portugal in the two decades that separated the ultimatum of 1890 from its logical but delayed consequence, the fall of the House of Bragança, was no more than running hard to keep in the same place: on the edge of the abyss. There must often have been times when it seemed like that to Portuguese contemporaries. Such a judgment, however, would underrate what was actually accomplished during those years. It was not so much that the African territories left to Portugal by treaty had almost all been effectively occupied, some for the first time in history; successive challenges from black potentates and white imperialist rivals warded off; and the eager hands of foreign moneylenders evaded. All this had been possible, it might be said, because the dangers themselves had been overrated: Gungunhana was a bluffer, the British and Germans mistrustful of each other, the financial crisis less serious than orthodox opinion supposed. Moreover, though few Portuguese have

been ready to admit it, the British, far from being consistently predatory, had helped them time and again both in their colonial campaigns and their financial dealings. The fact remains that sufficient
courage and tenacity had been forthcoming to confound both foreign
critics and domestic prophets of disaster; and that the results were an
encouragement—indeed, a commitment—to persevere in the task. It
was no longer necessary to invoke the spirits of Vasco da Gama and
Alfonso de Albuquerque so as to confute the rationalism of Ferreira
d'Almeida and Oliveira Martins, now that one could point to the gov-
ernance of Ennes and Freire de Andrade and the exploits of Mousinho,
Paiva Couceiro, and João de Almeida. These men indeed brought a
fresh infusion of strength to the Portuguese mystique of empire at a
time when empire and mystique seemed sick beyond recovery.

Notes

Notes

The following abbreviations are used in both notes and text. For a fuller explanation of their meaning, see the Note on Documentary Sources, pp. xiii–xv.

B.D.   British Documents on the Origins of the First World War (eds., G. P. Gooch and H. W. V. Temperley).

B.P.P.   British Parliamentary Papers.

C.O.   Colonial Office (Great Britain).

C.P.   Foreign Office Confidential Print (Great Britain).

D.D.F.   Documents Diplomatiques Françaises.

F.O.   Foreign Office (Great Britain).

Since it is often difficult to determine whether a Portuguese publication is government authorized or inspired, it has been thought best to designate doubtful cases by a dagger (†). The asterisks after the numbers of certain Confidential Prints appear on the official Prints themselves.

CHAPTER I

1. Vicente Ferreira, *Regimen Monetário e Bancário nas Colónias Portuguesas* (Lisbon, 1924), pp. 128–29; reprinted in his *Estudos Ultramarinos,* Vol. I (Lisbon, 1953†), p. 181.

2. Patrick Balfour, *Lords of the Equator* (London, 1938), p. 81. Gilberto Freyre, *Aventura e Rotina* (Lisbon, 1952), *passim*. Vicente Ferreira describes an earlier work of Freyre's as "having little scientific value," *Estudos Ultramarinos,* Vol. III (Lisbon, 1955†), p. 207, n. 1.

3. Dan Stanislawski, *The Individuality of Portugal* (Austin, Texas, 1959), *passim*.

4. Sir Charles W. C. Oman, *History of the Peninsular War,* Vol. III (London, 1908), pp. 153–66.

5. A full description of Olivença is given in Raul Proença, ed., *Guia de Portugal,* Vol. II (Lisbon, Biblioteca Nacional, 1928), pp. 450–53.

6. Alphonse de Figueiredo, *Le Portugal: Considérations sur l'état de l'administration, des finances, de l'industrie et du commerce de ce royaume* (Lisbon, 1866), pp. 177–78.

7. Aquilino Ribeiro, "Introdução Etnográfica," in *Guia de Portugal,* Vol. I (Lisbon, Biblioteca Nacional, 1924), p. 76. The quotation, attributed to Guerra Junqueiro, is on pp. 64–65.

8. Frank Huggett, *South of Lisbon* (London, 1960).

9. Aquilino Ribeiro, "Introdução Etnográfica," p. 68.

10. Ezequiel de Campos, *A Conservação da Riqueza Nacional* (Oporto, 1913), p. 108; Vogel, *Le Portugal et ses colonies, tableau politique et commercial de la monarchie portugaise dans son état actuel* (Paris, 1860), p. 204.

11. De Campos, *Conservação,* p. 139.

12. *Ibid.,* p. 147.

13. J. C. Russell, *British Medieval Population* (Albuquerque, New Mexico, 1948), pp. 22–23.

14. Manuel Severim de Faria, "Dos Remédios para a Falta de Gente," in *Noticias de Portugal, 1655,* reprinted in António Sérgio, ed., *Antologia dos Economistas Portugueses: Seculo XVII. Obras em Português* (Lisbon, Biblioteca Nacional, 1924), p. 188.

15. Sérgio, ed., *Antologia,* pp. vi–vii.

16. De Campos, *A Conservação,* pp. 142–43. See Basílio Telles, *O Problema Agricola (Credito e Imposto)* (Oporto, 1899), pp. 142–46.

17. J. P. Oliveira Martins, *História de Portugal,* Vol. II, pp. 23, 47–48. Subsequent quotations are from the seventh edition, published in Lisbon in 1908.

18. *Ibid.,* pp. 149, 151.

19. *Ibid.,* p. 154; K. G. Jayne, "Portugal," *Encyclopaedia Britannica,* 11th ed.; Paulo Freire, "Mafra," *Guia de Portugal,* Vol. I, pp. 559–60.

20. Quoted in Oliveira Martins, *História de Portugal,* Vol. II, p. 153.

21. *Ibid.,* p. 158.

22. *Ibid.,* p. 208.

23. Ameal, *História de Portugal,* p. 500.

24. Vogel, *Le Portugal,* p. 173.

25. Oliveira Martins, *História de Portugal,* Vol. II, p. 229.

26. Oman, *Peninsular War,* Vol. I, pp. 26–29.

27. Oliveira Martins, *O Brazil e as Colónias Portuguezas,* 5th augmented edition (Lisbon, 1920), pp. 102–4.

28. Oliveira Martins, *Portugal Contemporaneo,* 5th edition (Lisbon, 1919), p. ix. The passage quoted is in a reprint from an article entitled "Portugal," which originally appeared in a Rio de Janeiro newspaper, but the author does not give the date, beyond saying it was written after the events of the "past three years" (he was writing in 1894).

29. Oliveira Martins, *História de Portugal,* Vol. II, p. 250.

30. A. Balbi, *Variétés Politico-Statistiques* (Paris, 1822), quoted by Bento Carqueja, *O Povo Portuguez* (Oporto, 1916), p. 35.

31. Oliveria Martins, *História de Portugal*, Vol. II, p. 250.

32. Vogel, *Le Portugal*, p. 220.

33. Oliveira Martins, *Portugal Contemporaneo*, Vol. I, pp. 66–67.

34. *Ibid.*, p. 216.

35. Quoted in Oliveira Martins, *Portugal Contemporaneo*, Vol. I, p. 426.

36. Oliveira Martins, *Portugal Contemporaneo*, Vol. I, p. 408.

37. Almeida Garrett, "Memória Histórica de J. Xavier Mousinho da Silveira" (Lisbon, 1849), reprinted in his *Obras Completas,* ed. Theophilo Braga, Vol. XXII (Lisbon, 1904), pp. 77–103.

38. Oliveira Martins, *Portugal Contemporaneo*, Vol. II, Chapter I, *passim.*

39. Alexandre Herculano, "Mousinho da Silveira ou La Revolucion Portugaise" (in French, 1859), reprinted in *Opusculos, Tomo II: Questões Publicas* (Lisbon, 1904), p. 205.

40. Almeida Garrett, *Memória*, p. 94.

41. Herculano, "Mousinho da Silveira," pp. 177–78.

42. Oliveira Martins, *Portugal Contemporaneo*, Vol. II, p. 231.

43. Alexandre Herculano, article in *O Paiz,* October 29, 1851 (?), quoted in Oliveira Martins, *Portugal Contemporaneo*, Vol. II, p. 298.

44. *Ibid.*, pp. 73–84.

45. *Ibid.*, p. 170.

46. Quoted in H. C. F. Bell, *Lord Palmerston* (London, 1936), Vol. I, pp. 394–95.

47. Quoted in José de Macedo, *Autonomia de Angola* (Lisbon, 1910), p. 22.

48. Almeida Garrett, *Viagens de Minha Terra*, in *Obras Completas,* Vol. XVIII (1910), p. 22; quoted in Oliveira Martins, *Portugal Contemporaneo*, Vol. II, pp. 299–300.

49. *Guia de Portugal*, Vol. I, pp. 60–61.

50. Oliveira Martins, in *Política e Economia Nacional* (Lisbon, 1885). See his reference in the newspaper article already cited (reprinted as Preface to the third and subsequent editions of *Portugal Contemporaneo*—see note 34).

51. Herculano, article in *O Paiz,* July 24, 1851 (?), quoted in Oliveira Martins, *Portugal Contemporaneo*, Vol. II, p. 299.

52. Huggett, *South of Lisbon,* especially pp. 72–78.

53. Carqueja, *O Povo Portuguez,* pp. 187–204, *passim.*

54. Vogel, *Le Portugal,* p. 164.

55. Letter, Crawfurd to Morgan, January 23, 1890; enclosure No. 4 in Petre–Salisbury, No. 39 Africa, January 31, 1890 (British Foreign Office, Confidential Print 6061, No. 158). Confidential Prints are hereafter cited as C.P.

56. Adam Smith, *Wealth of Nations,* ed. Cannan (London, 1904), pp. 47–51.

57. For example, Angel Marvaud, *Le Portugal et Ses Colonies* (Paris, 1912), p. 54.

58. Teixeira Bastos, *A Crise* (Oporto, 1894), pp. 316–19.

59. Vogel, *Le Portugal,* pp. 75, 105, 112–18.

60. Oswald Crawfurd, *Portugal Old and New* (London, 1879), pp. 118–19; a view confirmed by Marvaud, *Le Portugal,* p. 118.

61. Marvaud, *Le Portugal,* pp. 168–71; Léon Poinsard, *Le Portugal Inconnu,* I: *Paysans, Marins et Mineurs* (Paris, 1910), pp. 58–61, 70, 107, 120, 148, 157.

62. Basílio Telles, *O Problema Agricola,* pp. 96–97.

63. Gerardo A. Pery, *Geographia e Estatistica Geral de Portugal e Colonias* (Lisbon, Imprensa Nacional, 1875), p. 110; E. A. Lima Basto, *Inquérito Económico-Agricola: Vol. IV, Alguns Aspectos Económicos da Agricultura em Portugal* (Lisbon, 1936), pp. 41–62.

64. Crawfurd, *Portugal,* pp. 157, 176; 160–61.

65. Lima Basto, *Inquérito,* pp. 25–33 and Gráfico IV.

66. Carqueja, *O Povo Portuguez,* pp. 399, 401, 403; de Campos, *A Conservacão,* pp. 41ff.; Affonso Costa, *O Problema da Emigração,* No. 1 in *Estudos de Economia Nacional* (Lisbon, 1911), especially pp. 71–93.

67. The description of Portugal as "the sick man of Western Europe" is Oliveira Martins'.

68. *Portugal Contemporaneo,* Vol. II, pp. 429–30. The passage quoted was first published in 1881.

CHAPTER 2

1. Marquez de Sá da Bandeira, *O Trabalho Rural Africano e a Administração Colonial* (Lisbon, Imprensa Nacional, 1873), pp. 13–14. He was writing, of course, after the formal abolition of slavery in the Portuguese dominions.

2. Vicente Ferreira, "Regiões de Povoamento Europeu nos Planaltos de Angola" (1938, reprinted in his *Estudos Ultramarinos,* Vol. III, Lisbon, 1954†), pp. 103ff., 99, 111.

3. Alexandre Lobato, "Colonização Senhorial da Zambézia," in *Colonização Senhorial da Zambézia e Outros Estudos* (Lisbon, 1962†), pp. 96–116, *passim.*

4. *Ibid.,* p. 113; see J. J. Teixeira Botelho, *História Militar e Política dos Portugueses em Moçambique da Descoberta a 1833* (Lisbon, 1934†), pp. 336–37.

5. Lobato, "Colonização Senhorial," p. 113.

6. Teixeira Botelho, *História Militar,* p. 606. For life on the seventeenth-century *prazos,* see, for example, James Duffy, *Portuguese Africa* (Cambridge, Mass., 1959), p. 84. An account of conditions in Moçambique c. 1800, marred by misprints in Portuguese, will be found in M. V. Jackson, *European Powers and South-East Africa* (London, 1942), pp. 19–41.

7. Manuel Joaquim Mendes de Vasconcellos e Cirne, *Memória sobre a Provincia de Moçambique* (reprinted, Lisbon, Imprensa Nacional, 1890†), p. 17; Duffy, *Portuguese Africa,* p. 85; Teixeira Botelho, *História Militar,* pp. 525–26.

8. For a recent discussion of the economics of the slave trade, see S. Daniel Neumark, *Foreign Trade and Economic Development in Africa* (Food Research Institute, Stanford University, 1964), pp. 50–57.

9. Oliveira Martins, *O Brazil e as Colónias Portuguezas,* pp. 53, 57–58.

10. Oliveira Martins, *Portugal Contemporaneo,* Vol. II, p. 130.

11. For example, José d'Arriaga, *A Inglaterra, Portugal e Suas Colonias* (Lisbon, 1882), pp. 182–219; Manuel Pinheiro Chagas, *As Colonias Portuguezas no Seculo XIX* (Lisbon, 1890), p. 73. The former work is a frank polemic against the British that strikes some shrewd blows.

12. Pinheiro Chagas, *As Colonias Portuguezas,* pp. 74–81.

13. *Ibid.,* pp. 178–82; Arriaga, p. 203; António José de Seixas, *A Questão Colonial Portugueza em Presença das Condições de Existencia da Metropole* (Lisbon, 1881), pp. 38–47.

14. Bell, *Lord Palmerston,* Vol. I, p. 234, and Webster, *Palmerston,* Vol. I, pp. 490–92, both convey this impression.

15. D'Arriaga, *A Inglaterra,* pp. 220–24; Jaime Walter, *Honório Pereira Barreto* (Bissau, 1947†), pp. 25, 52–65.

16. José Joaquim Lopes de Lima, *Ensaios sobre a Statistica das Possessões Portuguezas na Africa Occidental e Oriental; na Asia Occidental; na China, e na Oceania* (Lisbon, Imprensa Nacional, 1844†), Livro I, Parte 2, p. 111; A. Teixeira da Mota, *Guiné Portuguesa* (Lisbon, 1954†), Vol. II, p. 27.

17. Christopher Lloyd, *The Navy and the Slave Trade* (London, 1949), p. 97; Roger Anstey, *Britain and the Congo in the Nineteenth Century* (Oxford, 1962), p. 14.

18. The work of Jaime Walter, already cited, includes not only a biography of this remarkable man, but a selection of contemporary documents and a facsimile reprint of his pamphlet on the state of Portuguese Senegambia. See also Marquês de Lavradio, *Portugal em Africa depois de 1851* (Lisbon, 1936†), pp. 124–33.

19. Walter, *Barreto,* pp. 28–29, 79, 166. The color feeling displayed by the Minister is by no means uncharacteristic of the Portuguese governing class. See C. R. Boxer, *Race Relations in the Portuguese Colonial Empire, 1415–1825* (Oxford, 1963), *passim.*

20. Honório Pereira Barretto, *Memória Sobre o Estado Actual de Senegâmbia Portugueza, Causas de Sua Decadencia, e Meios de a Fazer Prosperar* (Lisbon, 1843, reprinted Bissau, 1947), especially pp. 3, 9, 44. See Joze Maria de Souza Monteiro, *Diccionario Geographico das Provincias e Possessões Portuguezas do Ultramar* (Lisbon, 1850), p. 285; Pinheiro Chagas, *As Colonias Portuguezas,* p. 86 ("Our dominion in Guiné at this time was a national disgrace.").

21. See A. J. de Seixas, *A Questão,* pp. 52–57. (The quotation is on p. 54.)

22. Walter, *Barreto,* pp. 173–83 (contemporary correspondence); Lavradio, *Portugal em Africa,* pp. 35–53.

23. Letter to Sá da Bandeira, dated from Lisbon, December 22, 1857; *Annaes do Conselho Ultramarino* (Parte Não Official, Serie II, Lisbon, Imprensa Nacional, 1867), pp. 17–20.

24. Pinheiro Chagas, *As Colonias Portuguezas,* p. 89.

25. Tams' account was published in German, translated into English, and thence into Portuguese. Of necessity I have used the Portuguese edition. George Tams, *Visita ás Possessões Portuguezas na Costa Occidental d'Africa* (Oporto, 1850), Vol. I, pp. 38–39, 186–87, 213–14, 225–26; Vol. II, pp. 108–110, 127.

26. See the Brazilian custom noted by Boxer, *Race Relations,* p. 114, n. 23.

27. Sá da Bandeira, *O Trabalho Rural Africana,* pp. 156–58; Anstey, *Britain and the Congo,* pp. 41–49.

28. The Portuguese texts of these treaties are to be found in José de Almada, ed., *Tratados Aplicáveis ao Ultramar,* Vol. I (Lisbon, 1942†), pp. 5–39.

29. Anstey, *Britain and the Congo,* p. 54, n. 3. In saying (p. 40) that the extension of Portuguese authority northward would have prevented British cruisers from hunting slavers in Portuguese waters, Anstey has overlooked altogether the treaty of 1842.

30. Sá da Bandeira, *O Trabalho,* p. 158.

31. *Ibid.,* pp. 159, 162; Anstey, *Britain and the Congo,* pp. 46–50; Pinheiro Chagas, *As Colonias Portuguezas,* p. 126.

The English trader and mining engineer Joachim John Monteiro, who was active in Angola for a number of years (and who was, presumably, of Portuguese extraction), claimed that the low duty was introduced by the governor-general on his advice. J. J. Monteiro, *Angola and the River Congo* (London, 1875), Vol. I, pp. 153–54.

32. Teixeira Botelho, *História Militar e Política dos Portugueses em Moçambique de 1833 aos Nossos Dias* (2d ed., revised, Lisbon, 1936†), pp. 149–56, 174, 233–36; Lavradio, *Portugal em Africa,* p. 10; Duffy, *Portuguese Africa,* pp. 88–89.

33. Lloyd, *The Navy and the Slave Trade,* pp. 217–28; Teixeira Botelho, *História Militar* (1833– ?), pp. 161–70.

34. Sá da Bandeira, *O Trabalho Rural Africano,* pp. 21–30.

35. Minutes by Lister, August 29, 1888; by Salisbury, September 1, 1888; letter, Kirk to Clement Hill, August 27, 1888. (Italics in original.) All in F.O. 84/1927.

36. Morier–Salisbury, May 14, 1878; No. 12 Slave Trade, C.P. 3928/152; Morier–E. D. Young, December 31, 1877 (Enclosure No. 2 in Morier-Salisbury, May 15, 1878; No. 13 Slave Trade, C.P.. 3928/153).

37. O'Neill–Granville, November 3, 1880; No. 50 Slave Trade, C.P. 4498/220.

38. Sá da Bandeira, *O Trabalho,* pp. 48–58.

39. Pinheiro Chagas, *As Colonias Portuguezas,* p. 86.

40. Reproduced in A. J. de Seixas, *A Questão Colonial,* pp. 22–26.

41. Oliveira Martins, *O Brazil e as Colonias Portuguezas,* pp. 284–86.

42. *Ibid.,* p. 241n (reprint of letter, Oliveira Martins–José Leopoldo Mira, November 18, 1884); p. 288.

43. Oliveira Martins, *Portugal em Africa,* 2d ed. (Lisbon, 1953), p. 77.

44. Pinheiro Chagas, *As Colonias Portuguezas,* p. 107. For the work of Coelho do Amaral, see Douglas L. Wheeler, *The Portuguese in Angola 1836–1891* (unpublished Ph.D. dissertation, Boston University, 1963), pp. 133–35.

45. Pinheiro Chagas, *As Colonias Portuguezas,* pp. 100–102; Duffy, *Portuguese Africa,* pp. 98–99.

46. Sá da Bandeira, *O Trabalho,* p. 149.

47. Pinheiro Chagas, *As Colonias Portuguezas,* pp. 129–30, 171. It is fair to

add that African utopias were by no means a monopoly of the Portuguese. Liberia and Sierra Leone were in some degree innately utopian.

48. Correia da Silva, "Viagem da Escuna 'Napier' a S. João Baptista de Ajudá," *Annaes do Conselho Ultramarino* (Parte Não Official, Serie VII, Lisbon, 1869), pp. 53–83. (Quotation on p. 73.)

49. *Ibid.*, p. 80.

50. *Ibid.*, p. 81; Pinheiro Chagas, *As Colonias Portuguezas*, p. 147.

51. Derby–Morier, March 28, 1877, No. 24 Slave Trade, C.P. 3686/252; Morier–Salisbury, November 14, 1878, No. 49 Slave Trade, C.P. 3928/204.

52. The text of the abortive Congo Treaty is in British Parliamentary Papers (BPP), 1884, LVI, 45 (C. 3886); reprinted in Anstey, *Britain and the Congo*, pp. 241–46.

53. Pinheiro Chagas, *As Colonias Portuguezas*, p. 153.

54. Teixeira Botelho, *História Militar* (1833–   ), pp. 193–225, *passim*.

55. Vincente Ferreira, "Regimen Monetario," pp. 22, 36, in *Estudos Ultramarinos*, Vol. I, pp. 41, 58.

56. Reports by Consul Hopkins (Loanda): 1874 (BPP, 1875, LXXV), pp. 233–36; 1875 (BPP, 1876, LXXVI), p. 1540; 1876 (BPP, 1877, LXXXIII), pp. 1485–86.

57. Pinheiro Chagas, *As Colonias Portuguezas*, p. 164. Hopkins, Reports: 1874, p. 237; 1875, pp. 1542–43; 1876, pp. 1482–83. Report by Consul Cohen (Loanda) for the year 1882 (BPP, 1884, LXXX), p. 702. Anstey, *Britain and the Congo*, pp. 28–33.

58. Report by Consul Elton (Moçambique) for the year 1875 (BPP, 1876, LXXIV), pp. 111, 104–5.

59. Report, Consul O'Neill (Moçambique) for the year 1880 (BPP, 1881, XC), p. 1025.

60. Charles Bright, *Submarine Telegraphs* (London, 1898), pp. 131, 135.

61. R. I. Lovell, *The Struggle for South Africa, 1875–1899* (New York, 1934), pp. 9–10.

CHAPTER 3

1. Lister, minute (undated) on Lisbon Dispatch No. 21 Slave Trade, March 6, 1886 (F.O. 84/1766).

2. José Maria da Ponte Horta, *Tratado de Lourenço Marques: Sua Historia Parlamentar, Seu Valor Technico e Social, Sua Conclusão* (Lisbon, Imprensa Nacional, 1882), p. 4.

3. João de Andrade Corvo, *Estudos sobre as Provincias Ultramarinas*, 4 vols. (Lisbon, 1883–87).

4. Corvo, *Perigos* (Lisbon, 1870), p. 160.

5. Lavradio, *Portugal em Africa depois de 1851*, p. 63.

6. Corvo, *Provincias Ultramarinas*, Vol. I, *passim*; Pinheiro Chagas, *As Colonias Portuguezas*, pp. 176–77.

7. Lavradio, *Portugal em Africa,* pp. 59–62; Arriaga, *A Inglaterra,* pp. 270–75 (differs in some details from the foregoing).

8. Lavradio, *Portugal em Africa,* p. 64; Ponte Horta, *Tratado de Lourenço Marques,* p. 42. The report of the Portuguese envoy who negotiated the treaty is reproduced in José de Almada, *Tratado de 1891* (Edicões do Estado Maior de Exército, Lisbon, 1947†), pp. 156–72, an extensive compilation which includes material from much earlier dates, but with a minimum of editorial comment and explanation.

9. Meade (C.O.)–Pauncefote (F.O.), August 17, 1878 (C.P. 4302, No. 1); Morier–Salisbury, October 3, 1878, No. 41 Slave Trade; *ibid.,* December 4, 1878, No. 49 Slave Trade (*ibid.,* Nos. 7, 20). Only the more important documents from these Confidential Prints will be cited severally.

10. Salisbury–Morier, telegram, February 6, 1879 (*ibid.,* No. 35); Morier–Salisbury, February 5 and 7, 1879, Nos. 11 and 13 Slave Trade (*ibid.,* Nos. 41 and 43).

11. Meade–Pauncefote, March 11, 1879 (*ibid.,* No. 52). L

12. Salisbury–Morier, telegram, March 12, 1879 (*ibid.,* No. 55); Morier–Salisbury, March 14, 1879, No. 32 Slave Trade (*ibid.,* No. 67).

13. Salisbury–Morier, May 23, 1879, No. 37 (*ibid.,* No. 86); Morier–Salisbury, May 28, 1879 (No. 45 Slave Trade), May 29, 1879 (No. 49 Slave Trade), covering text of the treaty; telegram, May 30, 1879 (*ibid.,* Nos. 99, 101, and 93).

14. Pauncefote, Memorandum, Foreign Office, June 25, 1880 (*ibid.,* No. 221).

15. Ponte Horta, *Tratado de Lourenço Marques,* p. 13; Anstey, *Britain and the Congo,* pp. 84–91.

16. Morier–Granville, June 6, 1880, No. 66 (C.P. 4302, No. 213).

17. Ponte Horta, *Tratado de Lourenço Marques,* pp. 12–13.

18. Ameal, *História de Portugal,* p. 686.

19. *Ibid.,* p. 687.

20. F. Reis dos Santos, "O Movimento Republicano e a Consciencia Nacional," in Luiz de Montalvor, comp., *História do Regímen Republicano em Portugal* (Lisbon, 1930), Vol. I, p. 285; cartoon by Raphael Bordallo Pinheiro, *O António Maria,* January 1, 1880, reproduced in Montalvor, facing p. 256, which (comments Reis dos Santos) depicts the *progressistas* using the royal cloak to obtain power.

21. Morier–Salisbury, June 1, 1879, No. 53 Slave Trade (C.P. 4302, No. 105).

22. Morier–Granville, May 20, 1880, No. 46 (*ibid.,* No. 193). Cartoon by Raphael Bordallo Pinheiro, "Preparativos para o Centenario," in *O António Maria,* May 20, 1880, pp. 168–69.

23. Memorandum (in French) communicated by D'Antas, July 5, 1880; Granville–Morier, same date, No. 65; memorandum by Morier, July 18, 1880 (C.P. 4302, Nos. 224–26).

24. C.P. 4395, *passim,* especially Morier–Granville, October 22, 1880, No. 128 (No. 34 of C.P.).

25. Morier–Granville, December 31, 1880, No. 170 (C.P. 4506, No. 10).

26. C.P. 4506, *passim,* and see, for example, Lovell, *Struggle for South Africa,* pp. 29–32.

27. Morier–Granville, March 15, 1881, No. 58 (C.P. 4506, No. 89).

28. Morier–Granville, May 7, 1881, No. 116 (*ibid.,* No. 179).

29. Morier–Granville, May 6, 1881, No. 115; May 9, No. 119; D'Antas–Granville, May 14; Herbert (C.O.)–Pauncefote (F.O.), May 18; Granville–Morier, May 18, telegram No. 18 (C.P. 4506, Nos. 178, 181, 187, 190, 191).

30. Morier–Granville, May 21, 1881, No. 129 (*ibid.,* No. 195); Anstey, *Britain and the Congo,* p. 100.

31. W. J. Leyds, *The First Annexation of the Transvaal* (London, 1906), p. 258.

32. Eça de Queiroz, "Os Inglezes no Egypto" (1882, reprinted in *Cartas da Inglaterra,* Oporto, 1905). The most striking passages are at pp. 163–83 of the reprint.

33. Anstey, *Britain and the Congo,* pp. 100–167; S. E. Crowe, *The Berlin West African Conference, 1884–1885* (London, 1942); A. Berriedale Keith, *The Belgian Congo and the Berlin Act* (London, 1919).

34. Quoted in Lavradio, *Portugal em Africa,* p. 92.

35. Anstey, *Britain and the Congo,* p. 105.

36. Crowe, *The Berlin West African Conference,* p. 171.

37. Quoted in Petre–Granville, March 18, 1884, No. 22 Africa (C.P. 4906, No. 117).

38. Corvo, *As Provincias Ultramarinas,* Vol. I, pp. 160–68.

39. Morier, memorandum dated August 17, 1877 (C.P. 3686, No. 325; quoted in part by Anstey, *Britain and the Congo,* p. 85); Morier–Granville, April 20, 1881, No. 101 (C.P. 4786, No. 36).

40. Morier–Granville, December 7, 1882, No. 172 (C.P. 4785, No. 39).

41. The quotation is from Anstey, *Britain and the Congo,* p. 105; an English translation of Bismarck's dispatch to Munster, June 7, 1884, is in C.P. 5000, No. 169.

42. Serpa–D'Antas, March 24, 1883 (translation in C.P. 4785, No. 137); Hertslet, memorandum, April 20, 1883 (C.P. 4807, No. 57); Granville–D'Antas, June 1, 1883 (C.P. 4865, No. 51); Serpa–D'Antas, June 26, 1883 (translation in C.P. 4865, No. 65); Crowe, *The Berlin West African Conference,* p. 21. The Portuguese White Book covering the negotiations during 1883, *Negocios Externos: Documentos Apresentados ás Cortes na Sessão Legislativa de 1884 pelo Ministro e Secretario D'Estado dos Negocios Estrangeiros: Questão do Zaire* (Lisbon, Imprensa Nacional, 1884), adds nothing to the British records.

43. Minute, Granville, December 6, 1883 (C.P. 4944, No. 88). The original is in Granville's private papers: see A. Ramm, ed., *The Political Correspondence of Mr. Gladstone and Lord Granville, 1876–1886* (Oxford, 1962), Vol. II, p. 122.

44. Minute, Lister–Granville, December 4, 1883 (C.P. 4944, No. 82).

45. Gladstone–Granville, December 8, 1883, in Ramm, *Gladstone and Granville,* No. 1163, Vol. II, p.121.

46. Anstey, *Britain and the Congo,* pp. 163–65 (a useful summary of the views of other writers); Bismarck–Munster, June 7, 1884 (C.P. 5000, No. 69).

47. Lavradio, *Portugal em Africa,* p. 87.

48. Bocage–Petre, October 28, 1884 (translation enclosed in Petre–Granville, October 29, No. 103; Africa, C.P. 5033, No. 4); quoted in part in Lavradio, *Portugal em Africa,* p. 82.

49. Lavradio, *Portugal em Africa,* p. 88.

50. Crowe, *Berlin West African Conference,* especially pp. 176–91.

CHAPTER 4

1. The salient parts of Barros Gomes' speech are reproduced in Almada, *Tratado de 1891,* pp. 94–95.

2. Júlio de Sousa e Costa, *O Rei Dom Carlos I: Factos Inéditos do Seu Tempo (1863–1908)* (Lisbon, 1943), p. 97.

3. Manuel Ferreira Ribeiro, *As Conferencias e o Itinerario do Viajante Serpa Pinto atravez das Terras da Africa Austral nos Limites das Provincias de Angola e Moçambique* (dated Lisbon, 1879, on title page, but dated January 1880 in text), p. 439; Ribeiro, *A Provincia de S. Thomé e Principe e Suas Dependencias* (Lisbon, Imprensa Nacional, 1877), p. 181.

4. J. P. Oliveira Martins, *O Brazil e as Colonias Portuguezas,* pp. 215–16; Pinheiro Chagas, *As Colonias Portuguezas,* p. 185.

5. J. P. Oliveira Martins, *O Brazil e as Colonias Portuguezas,* pp. 223–24.

6. *Diario do Governo,* 1886, No. 2; copy appended to Petre–Salisbury, No. 3 Africa, January 5, 1886 (F.O. 84/1766).

7. Bocage's memorandum is printed in F. M. Da Costa Lobo, *O Conselheiro José Luciano de Castro e o Segundo Período Constitucional Monarquico* (Coimbra, 1941), pp. 141–45; also see Luis Vieira de Castro, *D. Carlos I* (Lisbon, 1936), pp. 56–57.

8. Lavradio, *Portugal em Africa,* pp. 145–47. The text of the Convention, in French and Portuguese, and the rose-colored map itself are in a Portuguese White Book, *Documentos Apresentados as Cortes* (1887); *Negociações Relativas á Delimitação das Possessões Portuguezas e Francezas na Africa Occidental,* Segunda Parte, Protocollos, pp. 53–58 and facing p. 16. The Portuguese text is reproduced in Almada, *Tratados Aplicaveis á Ultramar,* Vol. IV, pp. 117–21. The French and German texts of the respective treaties were transmitted in Petre–Salisbury, Nos. 88 and 89 Africa (C.P. 5727, Nos. 1 and 2).

9. Vieira de Castro, *D. Carlos I,* p. 60.

10. Text in Almada, *Tratados Aplicaveis,* Vol. V, pp. 137–41. I have not been able to see the White Book relating to these negotiations, of which there is a useful account in the *Estudo Biográfico,* prefixed by F. A. Oliveira Martins to his selection of António Ennes' newspaper articles (*O "Ultimatum" Visto por António Enes,* Lisbon, 1946, pp. xxxiii–xxxix) and also printed separately for private circulation.

11. Almada, *Tratados Aplicaveis,* p. 93. A similar view is expressed by Costa

Lobo, *O Conselheiro,* p. 145; but the essential continuity is brought out by F. A. Oliveira Martins, *O "Ultimatum,"* p. xxxi.

12. This circular, dated November 22, 1889, was printed in a White Book, *Negócios da Africa Oriental e Central: Correspondencia com a Inglaterra e Documentos Correlativos até 13 e Janeiro de 1890* (Lisbon, Imprensa Nacional, 1890, No. 135), and extracted thence to be appended to a speech by Barros Gomes, dated June 10, 1891, *As Negociações com a Inglaterra no Periodo de 1886 á 1889; Discurso Proferido na Camara dos Dignos Pares do Reino* (Lisbon, Imprensa Nacional, 1891), pp. 39–59. Reference to relations with Great Britain on pp. 46–51.

13. Salisbury–Petre, August 2, 1887, No. 89 Africa; Bunsen–Barros Gomes, August 13, in Bunsen–Salisbury, No. 103 Africa; Barros Gomes–Bunsen, August 19, translation in *ibid.,* No. 108, August 22 (C.P. 5727, Nos. 5, 6, and 8).

14. Crowe, *The Berlin West African Conference,* pp. 181–82; Lister, F.O.–C.O., December 13, 1887 (C.P. 5727, No. 11).

15. Sir Travers Twiss, *The Law of Nations Considered as Independent Political Communities,* new ed. (Oxford, 1884), pp. 232–34; also see Hertslet, memorandum, undated, March 1888, on C.P. 5727, No. 21*.

16. Twiss, *The Law of Nations,* pp. 205, 210.

17. Pauncefote–Meade, September 10, 1879 (C.P. 4302, No. 119).

18. For example, Morier–Corvo, January 14, 1877 (enclosure, Morier–Derby, January 16, 1877, No. 6 Slave Trade; F.O. 84, No. 1476); quoted in A. J. Hanna, *The Beginnings of Nyasaland and North-Eastern Rhodesia* (Oxford, 1956), pp. 111–12.

19. Lister, quoted in Hanna, *Nyasaland,* p. 109.

20. Hanna, *Nyasaland,* p. 109.

21. O'Neill–Salisbury, November 24, 1879, enclosed correspondence, No. 53 Slave Trade; Pauncefote–O'Neill, January 24, 1880, No. 4 Slave Trade (C.P. 4498, Nos. 171, 176).

22. Hanna, *Nyasaland,* p. 123.

23. For example, Lister, note (undated) on O'Neill–Granville, November 12, 1884, No. 47 Slave Trade (F.O. 84/1671); Lister, minute, February 5, 1885, on O'Neill–Granville, No. 62 Slave Trade (*ibid.*); minute, February 20, 1885, on Petre–Granville, No. 22 Africa (F.O. 84/1708), cited in Hanna, *Nyasaland,* p. 126.

24. Petre–Rosebery, April 2, 1886, No. 23 Africa (F.O. 84/1766); Hanna, *Nyasaland,* p. 127, has slipped in referring to the Portuguese proposal about Matabeleland as being "made in the following April (1886)." It was, of course, made that same April.

25. Minutes by Anderson and Lister on letter from Lord Provost of Edinburgh to the Foreign Office, February 14, 1887 (F.O. 84/1858).

26. Minutes by Anderson, July 6, and Lister and Salisbury, July 7, on Petre–Salisbury, June 22, 1887, No. 88 Africa (F.O. 84/1844).

27. Minute on letter from Colonial Office, December 22, 1887 (F.O. 84/1876).

28. Pauncefote, minute, March 13, 1888 (F.O. 84/1901).

29. The correspondence relating to the passage of arms is in C.P. 5896.

30. Lister, Anderson, minutes, July 2, 1888 (F.O. 84/1899).

31. Hanna, *Nyasaland,* pp. 131–32.

32. Malet–Count Bismarck, December 23, 1888, enclosed in Malet–Salisbury, December 28, No. 150 Africa (C.P. 5727, No. 214).

33. Lister, minute, September 27, 1888 (F.O. 84/1929).

34. For the Moffat Treaty, see, for example, Lovell, *Struggle for South Africa,* pp. 137–38. Its text will be found in, inter alia, C.P. 5727, No. 61.

35. Anderson, minute, June 8, 1888, annexed to C.O.–F.O., May 23, 1888 (C.P. 5727, No. 52).

36. Lovell, *Struggle for South Africa,* p. 149; Bonham–Salisbury, August 1, 1888, No. 75 Africa; Petre–Salisbury, October 30 and 31, 1888, Nos. 145 and 147 Africa (C.P. 5727, Nos. 92, 169, 170).

37. Lister, note, September 25, 1888; Salisbury, minute on Petre, No. 145 Africa (both on F.O. 84/1900).

38. Barros Gomes, *As Negociações com a Inglaterra,* pp. 15–16.

39. Ennes, "A Questão Africana," *O Dia,* May 30, 1888; reprinted in F. A. Oliveira Martins, *O "Ultimatum,"* pp. 16–17.

40. Roland Oliver, *Sir Harry Johnston and the Scramble for Africa* (London, 1957), pp. 140–43.

41. Ennes, "Em Africa," *O Dia,* August 27, 1888, reprinted in *O Ultimatum,* pp. 30–31.

42. Oliver, *Sir Harry Johnston,* pp. 146–51.

43. Lovell, *Struggle for South Africa,* p. 207. The dispatch in which Johnston's terms were embodied is Petre–Salisbury, April 9, 1889, No. 39 Africa (C.P. 5970, No. 92*). Barros Gomes, *As Negociações com a Inglaterra,* pp. 16–18.

44. Johnston–Barros Gomes, April 8 and 18, 1889; extracts in Portuguese translation published in Barros Gomes, *As Negociações com a Inglaterra,* pp. 36–37. No trace of the originals, which were presumably in French, has been found in the British archives.

45. Salisbury–Petre, April 10, 1889, No. 57 Africa (C.P. 5970, No. 88; draft in Salisbury's hand in F.O. 84/1964, same date); Salisbury, minute, May 7, 1889 (F.O. 84/1994); Lister, memorandum, May 29, 1889; quoting Johnston's report of a letter received from a leading Scotch missionary *favoring* his proposals (C.P. 5970, No. 165).

46. Ennes, "A Questão Africana," *O Dia,* December 20–21, 1889, reprinted in *O Ultimatum,* p. 167.

47. Lovell, *Struggle for South Africa,* p. 207; Oliver, *Sir Harry Johnston,* pp. 152–54.

48. Ennes, "Portugal e a Inglaterra," *O Dia,* November 28–December 1, 1889, reprinted in *O Ultimatum,* pp. 129–30.

49. Fairfield, minute, January 18, 1889 (C.O. 417/36, file 1145).

50. *Ibid.,* January 18, 1890 (C.O. 417/50, file 1028).

51. Salisbury, Lister, minutes, April 26, 28, 29, 1889 (C.P. 5970, No. 107).

52. Fairfield, Herbert, minutes, August 10, 1889 (C.O. 417/36).

53. Oliver, *Sir Harry Johnston,* pp. 156–72 (with map).

54. Petre–Barros Gomes, May 14, 1889 (in Petre–Salisbury, *ibid.,* No. 68 Africa); *ibid.,* May 25, in No. 70 Africa; Barros Gomes–Petre, May 25, in No. 74 Africa (C.P. 5970, Nos. 149, 157, 170).

55. Petre–Salisbury, April 28, 1889, No. 49 Africa; *ibid.,* No. 105.

56. Smith (Moçambique)–Salisbury, June 23, 1889, No. 32; Anderson, minute on same, July 24 (F.O. 84/1969, Pt. II). The phrase "bifid garment" is Johnston's: Johnston–Salisbury, July 20, 1889, No. 4 Africa (C.P. 5970, No. 232).

57. Lister, Salisbury, minutes, c. September 4, 1888 (F.O. 84/1927).

58. Salisbury–Vivian, November 14, 1889, No. 89 Africa (F.O. 84/2010); *ibid.,* Wylde–Anderson, private, November 21.

59. Vivian and Kirk to Salisbury, November 23, 1889, Nos. 8 and 10, Slave Trade Conference (C.P. 5983, Nos. 188, 190: the second enclosing the Portuguese proposals); *ibid.,* November 30, No. 20 S.T.C., including the Portuguese memorandum (C.P. 5983, No. 223).

60. Vivian–Currie, private, December 8, 1889 (F.O. 84/2010); Vivian and Kirk–Salisbury, December 19, 1889, No. 46 S.T.C.; *ibid.,* also C.P. 5983, No. 295); Anderson, minute on No. 8 S.T.C. (F.O. 84/2010).

61. Teixeira Botelho, *História Militar (1883–),* pp. 249–64, 339–50, admits this in a chapter heading: "Precautions of the Portuguese government against the English expansion."

62. Petre–Salisbury, March 21, 1889, No. 26 Africa; *ibid.,* January 25, No. 9 Africa (C.P. 5970, Nos. 78, 33).

63. Hanna, *Nyasaland,* pp. 129–31; Lovell, *Struggle for South Africa,* pp. 203–18.

64. Vieira de Castro, *D. Carlos I,* pp. 64–65, 81. The salient documents relating to Couceiro's expedition are printed in J. M. R. Norton de Matos, *Angola: Ensaio sobre a Vida e Acção de Paiva Couceiro* (Lisbon, 1948), pp. 17–25.

65. Johnston–Salisbury, August 26, 1889, No. 9, received November 16 (C.P. 5970, No. 320); quoted in part in Oliver, *Sir Harry Johnston,* pp. 158–59.

66. Buchanan–Salisbury, September 25, 1889, No. 33 Central Africa, received November 26 (C.P. 5970, No. 344).

67. *Ibid.,* August 19, 1889, No. 28 Central Africa; *ibid.,* No. 291; Anderson, Salisbury, minutes on same, October 30 (F.O. 84/1942); Anderson, memorandum, c. November 26, 1889 (C.P. 5970, No. 348). Pinheiro Chagas, *As Negociações com a Inglaterra, 1887–1890* (Lisbon, 1890), p. 55, remarks sarcastically on the "informality with which the English establish Protectorates."

68. Barros Gomes–Petre, December 20, 1889, in Petre–Salisbury, December 22, No. 190 Africa; *ibid.,* No. 417; Pinheiro Chagas, *As Negociações,* pp. 56–57.

69. Teixeira Botelho, *História Militar (1833–),* pp. 347–50.

70. Lady Gwendolen Cecil, *Life of Robert, Marquis of Salisbury,* Vol. IV (London, 1932), pp. 261–64.

71. Ennes, "A Ordem do Dia," *O Dia,* December 15, 1889, reprinted in *O Ultimatum,* p. 148.

72. Petre–Salisbury, March 21, 1889, No. 27 Africa (C.P. 5970, No. 79).

73. Barros Gomes–Petre, December 20, 1889, in Petre–Salisbury, December 22, No. 190 Africa; Petre–Salisbury, telegram, December 28, No. 40 Africa (C.P. 5970, Nos. 417, 429); Salisbury–Petre, January 2, 1890, No. 1 Africa; *ibid.*, telegram, private, January 6 (C.P. 6061, Nos. 6, 25, 26).

74. Barros Gomes–Petre, January 8, 1890, in Petre–Salisbury, January 9, No. 6 Africa (also telegram, No. 4 Africa); Barros Gomes–Petre, private, January 9, in Petre–Salisbury, January 10, No. 10 Africa; Churchill–Salisbury, telegram, January 4; Salisbury–Petre, January 9, No. 8 Africa (also telegram, No. 2 Africa); *ibid.*, January 10, telegram, No. 3 Africa (C.P. 6061, Nos. 34, 34*, 42, 19, 35, 36, 45).

75. Petre–Salisbury, January 12, 1890, No. 12 Africa; also telegram, No. 8 Africa; Churchill–Salisbury, telegram, January 11 (C.P. 6061, Nos. 56, 57, 50).

76. Lister, minute, April 28, 1889 (C.P. 5970, No. 107).

77. Salisbury, minute, April 29, 1889 (*ibid.*).

78. Lavradio, *Portugal em Africa*, p. 170; José Gonçalo Santa-Rita, *A Africa nas Relações Internacionais depois de 1870* (Lisbon, 1959†), p. 118.

79. Memorandum by Sir Percy Anderson on the Portuguese campaign in Africa, 8 pp. (C.P. 5950: sole contents. Printed January 8, 1890).

80. Petre–Salisbury, January 2, 1890, No. 12 Africa.

81. Lavradio, *Portugal em Africa*, p. 173; Pinheiro Chagas, *As Negociações com a Inglaterra* (a powerful piece of polemic that makes effective use of all the published diplomatic documents).

82. Santa-Rita, *A Africa*, pp. 86–95; Vieira de Castro, *D. Carlos I*, pp. 111–13.

83. *Hansard*, 3d series, Vol. 341, cols. 227–35; February 13, 1890.

84. Lister, minute, March 23, 1889, on letter from Church of Scotland Foreign Missions Committee to Salisbury, same date (C.P. 5970, No. 77).

85. J. Mousinho de Albuquerque, *Moçambique, 1896–98* (Lisbon, 1899), p. 89. Vieira de Castro, *D. Carlos I*, p. 80, mistakenly attributes this remark to Aires de Ornelas.

CHAPTER 5

1. *Hansard*, 3d Series, Vol. 341, col. 34 (February 11, 1890).

2. Crawfurd–Petre, January 26, 1890, in Petre–Salisbury, January 27, No. 33 Africa (C.P. 6061, No. 142); Chaves de Aguiar, *A Administração Colonial* (Lisbon, 1891), p. 83.

3. Thomas Christy–Salisbury, July 23, 1890 (F.O. 84/2087).

4. Pinheiro Chagas, *As Negociações com a Inglaterra*, p. 61; Almada, *Tratado de 1891*, pp. 310–11n.

5. Lovell, *Struggle for South Africa*, p. 218; White Book, "Negociações do Tratado com a Inglaterra" (Lisbon, Imprensa Nacional, 1890), No. 32.

6. Petre–Salisbury, June 24, 1890, No. 163 Africa; (C.P. 6061, No. 511); *ibid.*, July 4, No. 169 Africa (C.P. 6069, No. 14); Johnston, memorandum, July 7, 1890, *ibid.*, No. 16.

7. Salisbury, minute, May 7, 1891 (F.O. 84/2164).

8. Lovell, *Struggle for South Africa,* pp. 218–19.

9. The text of the convention is printed in the White Book "Negociações do Tratado com a Inglaterra," No. 303.

10. Ennes, "O Consentimento da Inglaterra," *O Dia,* September 1, 1890; "O Tratado," *ibid.,* August 30; reprinted in F. A. Oliveira Martins, *O "Ultimatum,"* pp. 371, 368.

11. Petre–Salisbury, September 6, 1890, No. 212 Africa (C.P. 6069, No. 150).

12. Ennes, "As Vantagens do Tratado," *O Dia,* August 23, 1890, reprinted in *O Ultimatum,* pp. 352–61.

13. Ennes, "O Que se Há-de Fazer," and "A Rejeição do Tratado," *O Dia,* September 4–5, 1890, reprinted in *O Ultimatum* (see especially pp. 377, 381).

14. J. P. Oliveira Martins, *Portugal em Africa,* pp. 76–156, *passim.*

15. Reprinted in António Cabral, *Eça de Queiroz,* 2d ed. (Lisbon, 1920), pp. 431–32.

16. Eça de Queiroz, *Cartas da Inglaterra,* p. 210. The quotation from *The Times* is a retranslation from the Portuguese as given by Eça.

17. Oliver, *Sir Harry Johnston,* pp. 178–81.

18. F.O. 84/2086, 2087, *passim.*

19. Abercorn–Currie, September 9, 1890; Currie–Abercorn, September 11 (C.P. 6069, Nos. 151, 154); Cawston–Currie, September 7, 1890; Currie–Cawston, September 13 (F.O. 84/2090).

20. Hawksley–Lister, September 13, 1890; Lister, minute, *ibid.* (F.O. 84/2090).

21. J. P. Oliveira Martins, *Portugal em Africa,* pp. 141–55.

22. Petre–Salisbury, September 17, 1890, No. 223 Africa; *ibid.,* September 18, No. 226 Africa (C.P. 6069, Nos. 194, 197).

23. F. A. Oliveira Martins, *António Enes,* pp. clviii–clxi.

24. Barrington–Soveral, November 10, 1890 (C.P. 6069, No. 308).

25. F. Reis dos Santos, "O Movimento Republicano," in Montalvor, *Historia do Regimen Republicano,* pp. 333–34.

26. Harris–Bower, December 31, 1890 (enclosed in C.O.–F.O., January 31, 1891; C.P. 6086, No. 93).

27. Anderson, Salisbury, minutes on Fife–Salisbury, November 7, 1890 (F.O. 84/2094).

28. Anderson, minute, February 25, 1891 (F.O. 84/2156).

29. Lovell, *Struggle for South Africa,* p. 234; F.O. to B.S.A.C., May 14, 1891 (C.P. 6227, No. 267).

30. F.O.–C.O., December 6, 1890; C.O.–F.O., December 10 (C.P. 6069, Nos. 349, 359).

31. Salisbury, minute, April 17, 1891 (F.O. 84/2162).

32. *Ibid.,* April 3, 1891 (F.O. 84/2190).

33. Lovell, *Struggle for South Africa,* pp. 235–40; J. E. S. Green, *Rhodes Goes North* (London, 1936), pp. 261–64; P. R. Warhurst, *Anglo-Portuguese Relations in South-Central Africa, 1890–1900* (London, 1962), pp. 61–67.

34. Bocage–Petre, April 2, 1891, in Petre–Salisbury, April 3, No. 74 Africa (C.P. 6227, No. 37).

35. Currie, minute, April 6, 1891; Anderson, minute, April 10 (F.O. 84/2161).

36. Lovell, *Struggle for South Africa,* pp. 238–39.

37. Cecil, *Robert, Marquis of Salisbury,* Vol. IV, p. 272; Soveral-Bocage, telegram, April 22, 1891, White Book, 1891, No. 243.

38. Manuel Maria Coelho, "A revolta de 31 de Janeiro de 1891," in Montalvor, *História do Regimen Republicano,* Vol. I, pp. 339–73.

39. Cecil, *Robert, Marquis of Salisbury,* Vol. IV, p. 273.

40. Rhodes to B.S.A.C. (London), telegram, April 3, 1891 (C.P. 6227, No. 64).

41. José de Almada, *Tratado de 1891,* p. 375, n.2.

42. Text in, inter alia, Almada, *Tratado de 1891,* pp. 389–17, and in B.P.P., 1890–91, Vol. LVII (C. 6370).

43. F. A. Oliveira Martins, *António Enes,* pp. clvi–clvii.

44. Petre–Salisbury, June 3, 1891, No. 137 Africa (C.P. 6227, No. 370).

45. A summary of Hintze Ribeiro's speech is annexed to Petre–Salisbury, June 12, 1891, No. 148 Africa (C.P. 6227, No. 396); on the principal speeches, see Almada, *Tratado de 1891,* pp. 400–422. On Barros Gomes' speech, see text, p. 114.

46. Warhurst, *Anglo-Portuguese Relations,* pp. 22–24; E. F. P[into] B[asto], *Breve Exposição sobre as Diversas Tentativas para o Desinvolvimento das Riquezas da Província de Moçambique* (Lisbon, privately printed, 1889; copy with ms. translation in F.O. 84/2159).

47. Morier–Salisbury, July 28, 1879, No. 60 Slave Trade (C.P. 4286, No. 121).

48. Petre–Salisbury, August 1, 1889, No. 119 Africa (C.P. 5970, No. 210); November 11, 1889, No. 150 Africa (*ibid.,* No. 327); December 30, 1889 (C.P. 6061, No. 14).

49. For these various letters, C.P. 6069, Nos. 338, 340, 341; C.P. 6086, No. 5*, Petre–Salisbury, December 6, 1890, No. 272 Africa; December 17, telegrams, No. 83 Africa and No. 284 Africa; December 24, telegram, No. 88 Africa (C.P. 6069, Nos. 371, 400, 416, 425); paper "communicated by Mr. Barrington," December 24 (*ibid.,* No. 424); Petre–Salisbury, December 27, No. 296 Africa (C.P. 6086, No. 1). Letter in *The Times,* February 5, 1891, signed "J. H. Jeffreys."

50. Cawston–Philip Currie, March 13, 1891 (with documents); D. Currie to P. Currie, enclosing memorandum, March 18; enclosing memorandum, March 19; memorandum, D. Currie, March 24 (C.P. 6086, Nos. 242, 252, 260, 271). See statement by Moçambique Company in Petre–Salisbury, No. 112 Africa, May 6, 1891 (C.P. 6227, No. 240).

51. Clement Hill, memoranda, September 1, 4, 1891 (C.P. 6253, Nos. 85, 94).

52. B.S.A.C., London–F.O., September 17, 1891 (*ibid.,* Nos. 112, 117).

53. Van Laun–F.O., November 2, 1891 (C.P. 6265, No. 36).

54. Baron E. B. D'Erlanger, *The History of the Construction and Finance of the Rhodesian Transport System* (London, privately printed, 1938), p. 14.

55. Enes, *Moçambique: Relatório Apresentado ao Govêrno* (1893), 3d ed. (Lisbon, 1946†), pp. 27–30.

56. *Ibid.*, pp. 34–35.

57. *Ibid.*, pp. 333–43.

58. T. Christy–Salisbury, November 3, 1890 (F.O. 84/2094).

59. Enes, *Relatório*, pp. 61–62.

60. *Ibid.*, pp. 43, 45, 47–48, 49, 50.

61. *Ibid.*, pp. 73–74.

62. T. Christy–Salisbury, November 3, 1890 (F.O. 84/2094).

63. Keane–Henderson, March 21, 1890 (in Admiralty–F.O., April 27); Johnston–Salisbury, June 9, No. 25 (C.P. 6178, Nos. 36, 103).

64. *Relatório da Commissão Encarregada de Estudar as Reformas a Introduzir no Systema dos Prazos de Moçambique* (Lisbon, Imprensa Nacional, 1889), pp. 22–23. This report is reprinted in a compendium of official material relating to the prazo system, published in 1897, *Regimen dos Prazos da Corôa* (Lisbon, Imprensa Nacional), and in another, published in 1907, same title (Lourenço Marques, Imprensa Nacional).

65. Carr, Report, April 28, 1894 (F.O. 63/1286).

66. See note 64 above, and also see Duffy, *Portuguese Africa*, p. 353, n. 14.

67. Lobato, "Colonização Senhorial," pp. 96–116, *passim*.

68. Sebastião Xavier Botelho, *Memoria Estatistica sobre Os Dominios Portuguezas na Africa Oriental* (Lisbon, 1835), pp. 264–71.

69. Alfredo Augusto Caldas Xavier, *A Zambezia* (Nova Goa, Imprensa Nacional, 1888), especially pp. 24–36.

70. O'Neill–Granville, from Quilimane, September 1, 1884, No. 25 Africa (C.P. 5165, No. 73).

71. *Relatório da Commissão* ("Conclusões"), pp. 46–51, 53–55.

72. *Decreto de 18 de Novembro 1890 (Regimen dos Prazos da Corôa)*, 1897, pp. 85–94; *Regulamento de 7 de Julho*, 1892 (*ibid.*, pp. 95–133). See Enes, *Relatório*, pp. 495–513.

73. Caldas Xavier, *A Zambezia*, pp. 24–25.

74. *Ibid.*, p. 13.

75. *Ibid.*, p. 230.

76. Ernesto Jardim de Vilhena, "Algumas Palavras sôbre o Regimen dos Prazos da Corôa," 1908; reprinted in *Questões Coloniais*, Vol. II (Lisbon, 1910), pp. 520–26.

77. A. Freire de Andrade, *Relatórios sobre Moçambique*, Vol. I (Lourenço Marques, Imprensa Nacional, 1907), p. 165.

78. Pedro A. Alvares, *O Regime dos Prazos da Zambezia* (Lisbon, 1916), p. 37.

79. R. N. Lyne, *Mozambique: Its Agricultural Development* (London, 1913), p. 218.

80. Alvares, *O Regime dos Prazos*, pp. 29–32.

81. Mousinho de Albuquerque, *Moçambique, 1896–98*, pp. 125–27, 139–41, quotation on p. 127.

82. R. C. F. Maugham, *Zambezia* (London, 1910), p. 97.

83. Freire de Andrade, *Relatórios*, Vol. IV (1909), p. 234.

84. Lyne, *Mozambique*, p. 205.

85. Alvares, *O Regime dos Prazos,* pp. 33–36, 41.

86. Freire de Andrade, *Relatórios,* Vol. IV, pp. 232–33; see also Vol. I, pp. 150–61.

87. Alvares, *O Regime dos Prazos,* pp. 45–46.

CHAPTER 6

1. Abercorn–Rosebery, June 22, 1893 (C.P. 6484, No. 89).

2. Hertslet, memorandum, May 9, 1893; Anderson, memorandum, June 1; Ennes, memorandum (in French), enclosed in Soveral–Rosebery, June 7; Leverson, reply to foregoing, July 21; Hill, memorandum, August 1; Ennes, memorandum, enclosed in Soveral–Rosebery, October 30; Leverson, rejoinder, enclosed in Leverson–Rosebery, December 19 (C.P. 6484, Nos. 68, 80, 85, 97, 101*, 127, 167).

3. Minutes, Anderson, November 6, 1893; Currie, November 7; Rosebery, November 8 (C.P. 6484, No. 131). Ennes became embroiled with the Lisbon Geographical Society on the question: see enclosures, MacDonell–Rosebery, January 29, 1894, No. 3 Africa (C.P. 6606, No. 11).

4. Johnston–Rosebery, June 8, 1893, No. 20 Central Africa; MacDonell–Rosebery, September 4, No. 40 Africa; September 16, No. 44 Africa; September 23, No. 45 Africa (C.P. 6482, Nos. 141, 182, 205*, 206); Cameron–Foreign Office, March 9, 1894 (C.P. 6537, No. 64).

5. Anderson, memorandum, February 7, 1894; *ibid.,* March 2 (C.P. 6606, Nos. 10, 17).

6. Johnston–Rosebery, December 11, 1893, No. 66 Central Africa; Rosebery–Johnston, telegram, February 17, 1894, No. 4 (C.P. 6537, Nos. 32, 38).

7. Rosebery–Johnston, telegram, March 6, 1894, No. 6; Johnston–Kimberley, telegram, April 26, No. 2 (*ibid.,* Nos. 56, 133).

8. Johnston–Rosebery, February 20 and February 25, 1894, Nos. 20 and 21 Central Africa (*ibid.,* Nos. 110, 127).

9. Johnston, February 20, 1894; Anderson, memoranda, March 8, March 20 (Nos. 60, 80); Oliver, *Sir Harry Johnston,* pp. 231–43.

10. Loch–Ripon, February 27, 1894, enclosed in C.O.–F.O., March 21 (C.P. 6537, No. 82); Rosebery, Anderson, minutes, March 22 (F.O. 63/1286).

11. Anderson, memorandum (A), March 9, 1894 (C.P. 6606, No. 21); Rosebery, minute, March 2, on Anderson, memorandum (*ibid.,* No. 17); Kimberley–MacDonell, March 15, telegram, No. 6 Africa (*ibid.,* No. 24).

12. MacDonell–Salisbury, April 15, 1896, No. 45 Africa (C.P. 6910, No. 192).

13. Leverson–Hill, private, June 19, 1896 (C.P. 6910, No. 265); *ibid.,* also Leverson–Ford, July 21 (C.P. 6975, Nos. 36, 37); Leverson–Hill, private, August 16 (F.O. 63/1324).

14. Ford–Salisbury, February 1, 1897, Africa No. 2; B.S.A.C.–F.O., April 10; Leverson, observations on foregoing, April 15 (C.P. 7031, Nos. 13, 46, 52); Leverson–Hill, private, January 25, 1897 (F.O. 63/1340).

15. Junod–Ennes, February 23, 1895, in Marcello Caetano, ed., *As Campanhas*

de Moçambique em 1895 Segundo os Contemporáneos (Lisbon, 1947†), pp. 41–46; Teixeira Botelho, *História Militar* (1833–   ), pp. 437ff.

16. MacDonell–Kimberley, telegram, September 27, 1894, No. 16 Africa; Bernal–Kimberley, September 1, No. 11; Kimberley–Bernal, telegram, September 29; Bernal–Kimberley, *ibid.,* No. 12 (C.P. 6606, Nos. 98, 99, 101, 143).

17. Bernal–Kimberley, telegram, October 10; MacDonell–Kimberley, telegram, October 10, No. 17 Africa (*ibid.,* Nos. 108, 109).

18. Teixeira Botelho, *História Militar,* p. 443; see the reports of the officer commanding H.M.S. *Thrush,* in Admiralty–F.O., November 15 and 29, 1894 (C.P. 6606, Nos. 82, 203).

19. In Admiralty–F.O., December 10, 1894; see *ibid.,* December 5 (C.P. 6606, Nos. 225, 216); Kimberley, minute on No. 225 (F.O. 63/1287).

20. C.O.–F.O., November 7, 1894, with enclosures (C.P. 6606, No. 160; also *ibid.,* Nos. 118, 119); Lobo d'Avila–MacDonell, October 18, enclosed in MacDonell–Kimberley, October 19, No. 79 Africa (*ibid.,* No. 136).

21. The original French ran: "Remarquez ce fait: du jour où les journaux allemands ont commencé a laisser clairement entendre que leur Gouvernement devait s'opposer aux intrigues anglaises à Delagoa Bay, de ce jour les nouvelles qui avaient donné l'alarme ont cessé, comme par miracle, d'arriver; les nègres se sont subitement tenus tranquilles. C'est à croire qu'ils lisent la *Gazette de Cologne!*" (D.D.F., Série I, No. 317, October 29, 1894.)

22. Kimberley–MacDonell, November 21, 1894, No. 120A Africa; MacDonell–Kimberley, December 11, No. 95 Africa; Rhodes–Soveral, December [sic] 1894, in B.S.A.C.–Kimberley, December 21 (C.P. 6606, Nos. 187, 235, 245); Soveral–Rhodes, December 23, in B.S.A.C.–Kimberley, January 8, 1895 (C.P. 6773, No. 4).

23. The Portuguese were made aware of these proceedings. Salisbury–Petre, telegram, June 6, 1892, No. 37 Africa; Salisbury–De La Cour, telegram, June 6; De La Cour–Salisbury, telegram, June 11; Petre–Salisbury, June 15, No. 68 Africa; De La Cour–Salisbury, telegrams, June 25, 28; *ibid.,* dispatch, June 4, No. 20; Lister–De La Cour, July 14, No. 7; De La Cour–Salisbury, June 11, No. 22, and June 25, No. 26; telegram, July 25 (C.P. 6336, Nos. 86, 87, 88A, 88B, 92A, 92B, 101, 102*, 104, 106, 130).

24. António Enes, *Moçambique,* pp. 177–78. (Henceforward cited as Ennes I.)

25. Leverson–Hill, private, August 16, 1896 (F.O. 63/1324), where Ennes is referred to as "quarrelsome and difficult."

26. Trinidade Coelho, *Dezoito Annos em Africa* (Lisbon, 1898), p. 423.

27. *Ibid.,* pp. 422–34, especially p. 431, Almeida–Freire de Andrade, February 18, 1895.

28. For the "minutes" of the *banja,* see *ibid.,* pp. 439–41; compare with António Enes, *A Guerra de Africa em 1895* (Lisbon, 1898), pp. 198–200. This work will henceforward be cited as Ennes II.

29. Ennes II, p. 201.

30. *Ibid.,* p. 187. The quotation is on p. 35.

31. *Ibid.,* p. 85.

32. *Ibid.,* p. 107.

33. *Ibid.,* pp. 168–75.

34. *Ibid.,* pp. 188–93.

35. Eduardo da Costa, "Relatório acêrca da Missão Desempenhada em Moçambique de Janeiro a Dezembro de 1895" (Lisbon, September 3, 1896), reprinted in Costa, *Colectânea das Suas Principais Obras Militares e Coloniais* (Lisbon, 1939†), Vol. II, pp. 27–102; discussion at pp. 35–36.

36. Ennes, letter, March 29, 1895, *As Campanhas de Moçambique,* p. 59.

37. Ennes, letter, June 27, 1895, *ibid.,* pp. 104–5.

38. F. A. Oliveira Martins, *António Ennes,* p. cxcii.

39. MacDonell–Kimberley, January 28, 1895, No. 7 Africa (C.P. 6773, No. 18).

40. Ornelas, letter, November 17, 1895, *Colectânea,* Vol. I, p. 148.

41. Ennes II, pp. 285–87.

42. *Ibid.,* pp. 281–83.

43. Coelho, *Dezoito Annos,* especially pp. 502–8.

44. Ennes II, pp. 293–96.

45. Coelho, *Dezoito Annos,* especially pp. 340–52.

46. See Mousinho–Ennes, August 23, 1895 (Ennes II, 2d ed., pp. lviii–lvix, with the later tribute to Almeida (*Moçambique, 1896–98,* p. 156).

47. Ennes II, pp. 358–59; Couceiro, in Ennes II, 2d ed., p. xvii; Ornelas, "Missão a Gaza," *Colectânea,* Vol. I, pp. 175–91.

48. Almeida–Ennes, Telegramma J, August 12, 1895, *Dezoito Annos,* p. 521; also Ornelas, "Missão a Gaza," *Colectânea,* Vol. I, pp. 183–84; Ornelas, letter, September 17, *ibid.,* p. 139; Ornelas–Ennes, July 30, Ennes II, 2d ed., pp. xlii–xliv.

49. Ennes–Almeida, telegram, August 7, No. 36, *Dezoito Annos,* p. 519.

50. Correspondence about the *indunas* is enclosed in C.O.–F.O., August 27, 31, September 4, 12, 25, and October 5, 1895 (C.P. 6773, Nos. 130, 136, 137, 146, 157, 161); for the ignorance in which the mission to Gaza was kept, see Ornelas–Ennes, July 30, already cited.

51. Ennes II, pp. 396–98; Mousinho's letter, dated August 23, 1895, is printed in the 2d ed., p. lviii.

52. *Ibid.,* pp. 412–15.

53. *Ibid.,* pp. 493–98; Ornelas, letter, October 26, 1895, *Colectânea,* Vol. I, pp. 145–46.

54. Ennes, letter, October 5; Freire de Andrade–Couceiro, October 6, *As Campanhas de Moçambique,* pp. 305–11; Ennes II, p. 501.

55. Teixeira Botelho, *História Militar,* pp. 491–96; Ennes II, pp. 504ff; Ornelas, letters, October 22 and November 17, *Colectânea,* Vol. I, pp. 142, 147–53.

56. J. Mousinho de Albuquerque, "Chaimite; Relatório apresentado ao... Governador-Geral interino da provincia de Moçambique," January 16, 1896; reprinted in Mousinho de Albuquerque, *Livro das Campanhas* (Lisbon, 1935†), pp. 11–37; Diogo de Sà–Ennes, January 8, 1896, *As Campanhas de Moçambique,* pp. 376–79.

It should be noted that the titling of Mousinho's works in the 1934–35 reprint was muddled. There are but two volumes in all, of which the second, *Moçambique, 1896–98,* was issued first, in 1934, as No. IV in the *Biblioteca Colonial Portuguesa.* The first was issued in 1935, as No. V of the series; but the words "Volume I" were placed on the title page after *Livro das Campanhas,* making it appear that a second volume with the same title was to come. Hence, the two volumes are sometimes lumped together in book catalogs under this title. The reader is reminded that all citations from *Moçambique, 1896–98* are from the first (1899) edition.

57. MacDonell–Salisbury, February 25, 1896, No. 21 Africa (C.P. 6910/113).

58. See, for example, Lovell, *Struggle for South Africa,* pp. 361–78; Warhurst, *Anglo-Portuguese Relations,* pp. 133–35.

59. Mousinho de Albuquerque, *Moçambique, 1896–98,* p. 156, n. 1.

60. Ennes II, pp. 564–65, 569.

61. Coelho, *Dezoito Annos,* pp. 502–3.

62. *Pontos nos ii,* November 6, 1890, p. 343.

63. Ennes II, p. 567.

64. Ornelas, *Colectânea,* Vol. I, pp. 11–23.

65. Julião Quintinha and Francisco Toscano, *A Derrocado do Imperio Vátua e Mousinho d'Albuquerque,* 3d ed. (Lisbon, 1935), Vol. II, pp. 163–69.

66. F. A. Oliveira Martins, *António Enes,* pp. xi–xiii. The reference in the text is, of course, to J. P. Oliveira Martins.

67. Ennes, letter, June 27, 1895, *As Campanhas de Moçambique,* p. 104.

68. Eça de Queiroz, *Cartas da Inglaterra,* p. 210.

CHAPTER 7

1. Bower, memorandum, November 11, 1894 (enclosure No. 4, C.O.–F.O., December 7; C.P. 6606, No. 218). This was shown to Soveral, then Portuguese Foreign Minister, in April 1896; MacDonell–Salisbury, April 14, 1896, No. 45 Africa (C.P. 6910, No. 191).

2. For example, the *Morning Post,* October 20, 1894 (cited in Montalvor, *História do Regímen Republicano,* Vol. II, p. 180).

3. Gosselin–Kimberley, November 17, 1894 (C.P. 6606/183); Gosselin, memorandum, December 1; Kimberley, minute, December 4 (F.O. 64/1334); Kimberley–Gosselin, October 31, 1894, No. 174A Africa (C.P. 6606, No. 149).

4. Teixeira Bastos, *A Crise,* p. 290; *Relatorio, Propostas de Lei e Documentos Apresentados na Camara dos Senhores Deputados da Nação Portugueza na Sessão de 12 de Julho de 1897 pelo Ministro ... dos Negocios da Fazenda, Frederico Ressano Garcia* (Lisbon, Imprensa Nacional, 1897), pp. 28–29, *Quadros* X–XXI.

5. Quoted in Augusto Fuschini, *Fragmentos de Memorias. Vol. II: O Presente e o Futuro de Portugal* (Lisbon, 1899), p. 170. The whole of Fuschini's Chapter V, "Origens da actual crise," pp. 125–80, merits study.

6. Fuschini, *Fragmentos,* p. 151.

7. *Ibid.,* p. 21.

8. Fuschini, *Fragmentos de Memorias. Vol. I: Liquidações Politicas; Vermelhos e Azues* (Lisbon, 1896), pp. 170–72.

9. [Marianno de Carvalho] *Os Planos Financeiros do Sr. Marianno de Carvalho* (Lisbon, 1893), p. 181. This is a reprint of articles appearing in *O Popular* between February and April of 1893. While constituting an apologia for the author's policies, and critical of his opponents, they are temperate in tone and lucid in statement.

10. Albino Vieira da Rocha, *Situação Económica de Portugal: A Alta dos Preços* (Coimbra, 1913), pp. 174–78.

11. Fuschini, *Fragmentos,* Vol. II, pp. 230–31; but see also *ibid.,* Vol. I, pp. 253–54.

12. Carlos de Barros Soares Branco, *Aspectos da Questão Monetária Portuguesa* (Lisbon, 1950), p. 15. The author writes with the authority of a governor of the Bank of Portugal, but does not give the sources for his figures.

13. [Marianno de Carvalho] *Os Planos Financeiros,* pp. 178–81.

14. Lopes de Oliveira, "A obra da propaganda republica," in Montalvor, *História do Regimén Republicano,* Vol. II, pp. 99–100; Oliveira Martins–Carlos I, 1891 [sic], in F. A. Oliveira Martins, ed., *Correspondencia de J. P. Oliveira Martins* (Lisbon, 1926), pp. 168–72.

15. Lopes de Oliveira, "A obra da propaganda republica," p. 108; Teixeira Bastos, *A Crise,* pp. 130–31; Fuschini, *Fragmentos,* Vol. I, pp. 151–52.

16. [Marianno de Carvalho] *Os Planos Financeiros,* pp. 287–96; Oliveira Martins, *Correspondencia,* p. 203.

17. Fuschini, *Fragmentos,* Vol. I, pp. 154–55. The French is given by Fuschini: "Eh! Monsieur, est-ce que votre gouvernement se moque de nous?"

18. *Ibid.,* pp. 155–207. The French creditors, however, afterwards denied having agreed to anything.

19. Dudley Saurin, *Report on the Finances of Portugal* (B.P.P. [1880], Vol. LXXII, pp. 63–64); Teixeira Bastos, *A Crise,* pp. 168, 329–45; Fuschini, *Fragmentos,* Vol. I, pp. 239–41.

20. The quotation is from Saurin's *Report,* p. 68. Fuschini, *Fragmentos,* Vol. I, pp. 308–9; Lopes de Oliveira, "A obra da propaganda republica," pp. 117–18.

21. Fuschini, *Fragmentos,* Vol. I, pp. 316–17.

22. *Ibid.,* Vol. II, p. 169 (table), p. 242.

23. Soares Branco, *Aspectos,* p. 15; p. 54 (table).

24. Constantino Roque da Costa, "A crise financeira," *Jornal do Comercio e das Colonias,* December 25, 1912; reprinted in *Questões Economicas, Financeiras, Sociaes e Coloniaes* (Lisbon, 1916), p. 345.

25. Soares Branco, *Aspectos,* p. 53.

26. *Ibid.,* pp. 17–18, 33–34, 43.

27. Ressano Garcia, *Relatorio,* July 1897, pp. 9–10.

28. Soares Branco, *Aspectos,* pp. 17–18; Anselmo de Andrade, *Portugal Económico: Theorias e Factos,* new edition (Coimbra, 1918), Vol. I, p. 304, n. 1.

29. MacDonell–Kimberley, May 23, 1895, No. 43 Africa (C.P. 6688, No. 194), enclosing "Memorandum regarding the Nyassa Company," dated May 21.

30. A translation of the decree is annexed to Goschen–Salisbury, September 29, 1891, No. 176 Africa (C.P. 6178, No. 157). MacDonell's memorandum wrongly gives its date as 1890.

31. MacDonell, "Memorandum . . . ," May 21,1895; for the amendments to the concession, Petre–Salisbury, November 16, 1891, No. 191 Africa, enclosing translation of decree (C.P. 6178, No. 195*).

32. Salisbury–Kimberley, May 23, 1895, No. 43 Africa.

33. MacDonell–Salisbury, September 30, 1896, No. 109 Africa (C.P. 6911, No. 71).

34. Ayres d'Ornellas, letter to his father, June 21, 1896, in Ornelas, *Colectânea,* Vol. I, p. 221; Mousinho de Albuquerque, *Moçambique,* pp. 162–63.

35. *Ibid.,* pp. 151–54.

36. *Ibid.,* pp. 160–61, 159.

37. See, for example, Maugham–F.O., November 7, 1905 (F.O. 63/1446).

38. Meade, minute, August 15, 1894 (file 16S in C.O. 537/128).

39. J. E. S. Green, *Rhodes Goes North,* p. 1.

40. J. S. Marais, *The Fall of Kruger's Republic* (Oxford, 1961), pp. 46ff.

41. Warhurst, *Anglo-Portuguese Relations,* p. 146. Two volumes of documents in the Foreign Office Archives (F.O. 63/1440, 1441) are devoted to these concessions in southern Moçambique between 1893 and 1905.

42. C.O.–F.O. April 14, 1897 (C.P. 7031, No. 49). There are numerous papers about the Inhambane concession on C.P. 6910 (Nos. 107, 122, 134, 152A, 160, 161, 174, 183, 211, 220, 236, 238, 241, 246, and 254*).

43. Greene–Rosmead, telegram, April 14, 1897, in C.O.–F.O., April 20 (C.P. 7031, No. 53).

44. C.O.–F.O., December 5, 1898; MacDonell–Salisbury, December 14, No. 104 Africa (C.P. 7213, Nos. 117, 122).

CHAPTER 8

1. Mario Simões dos Reis, *Arbitragens de Lourenço Marques* (Lisbon, 1936), Segunda Parte, p. 135; report by Machado, April 4, 1884, Green Book, "Documentos Relativos ao Caminho de Ferro de Lourenço Marques (Contrato de 14 Dezembro de 1883)" (Lisbon, Imprensa Nacional, 1889), No. 25.

2. McMurdo–Pinheiro Chagas, June 27, 1884, and departmental comment, June (July) 12 (*ibid.,* Nos. 56 and 57).

3. Simões dos Reis, *Arbitragens,* pp. 142–44.

4. *Ibid.,* p. 152; for the assurance, see Green Book, "Caminho de Ferro de Lourenço Marques," No. 79.

5. For the two versions, see enclosures in Petre–Salisbury, May 2, 1889, No. 53 Africa (C.P. 5988, No. 26); see also Bocage–Beelaerts van Blokland, May 17, 1884; Bocage–Pinheiro Chagas, May 19 (Green Book, "Caminho de Ferro de Lourenço Marques," Nos. 46, 50).

6. Tito de Carvalho, memorandum, March 22, 1884 (Green Book, "Caminho de Ferro de Lourenço Marques," No. 21); *ibid.,* May 8 (*ibid.,* No. 36); Machado, memorandum, April 4 (*ibid.,* No. 23); decree, May 14 (*ibid.,* No. 43).

7. Tito de Carvalho, memorandum, November 13, 1886 (*ibid.,* No. 259).

8. Sir James Fergusson, memorandum, July 3, 1889 (C.P. 5988, No. 108).

9. Tito de Carvalho, notes, December 18, 1885 (Green Book, "Caminho de Ferro de Lourenço Marques," Nos. 100, 101); Pinheiro Chagas, minutes, December 21 (*ibid.,* Nos. 103, 104); decree, December 28 (*ibid.,* No. 107).

10. Tito de Carvalho, memorandum, March 31, 1886 (*ibid.,* No. 134).

11. P. H. Leemans–Pinheiro Chagas, Brussels, June 4, 1886; McMurdo–Pinheiro Chagas, June 6 (*ibid.,* Nos. 172, 174).

12. McMurdo–Pinheiro Chagas, June 18, 1886; to *The Times,* June 23 (*ibid.,* Nos. 185, 192).

13. W. G. S. Mockford–Henrique de Macedo, December 28, 1886 (*ibid.,* No. 252).

14. Minutes of meeting, February 1, 1887; decree, March 3; Serpa–Macedo, March 3; Ministry of Marine–Serpa, March 5 (*ibid.,* Nos. 262, 290, 291, 292).

15. Company prospectuses, February 14, March 7, 1887 (*ibid.,* Nos. 287, 293); *The Times,* March 19 (*ibid.,* No. 316).

16. Cecil Hartridge, stockbroker, to F.O., April 9, 1890 (F.O. 63/1261; not included in C.P.).

17. *The Statist,* September 1, 1888 (Green Book, "Caminho de Ferro de Lourenço Marques," No. 555).

18. *Ibid.,* August 18, 1888 (*ibid.,* No. 550).

19. See below, p. 237.

20. *Portaria,* October 30, 1884 (*ibid.,* No. 69).

21. Machado, memoranda, August 20, 1884; August 2, 1887 (*ibid.,* Nos. 84, 386).

22. Macedo–Pinheiro Chagas, November 7, 1887; Pinheiro Chagas–Macedo, November 14 (*ibid.,* Nos. 437, 440).

23. Macedo–Pinheiro Chagas, January 31, 1888; Macedo–Barros Gomes, June 26 (*ibid.,* Nos. 488, 556).

24. A. J. de Araujo, director of public works, Lourenço Marques, to Ministry of Marine, Lisbon, April 12 and May 10, 1888 (*ibid.,* Nos. 508, 511).

25. McMurdo–A. D. Oyens (Amsterdam), June 6, 1888; Araujo, enclosing same, to Ministry of Marine, August 2 (*ibid.,* Nos. 524, 543).

26. Beelaerts van Blokland, answering questions from the Portuguese government, January 6, 1891. Quoted in *Tribunal du Delagoa: Sentence Finale . . . concernant le Chemin de Fer de Lourenço Marques* (Berne, 1900), pp. 66–67.

27. Opinion of Crown Procurator-General, August 31, 1888 (Green Book, "Caminho de Ferro de Lourenço Marques," No. 554).

28. Barros Gomes–Pinheiro Chagas, September 5, 1888 (*ibid.,* No. 556; translation annexed to Delagoa Bay Railway Company–Salisbury, October 10 [C.P. 5988, No. 2]); reply from Lisbon Company, October 12 (Green Book, "Caminho de Ferro de Lourenço Marques," No. 567).

29. *Portarias,* October 24, 29, 1888 (*ibid.,* Nos. 574, 576).

30. *Sentence Finale,* p. 82.

31. McMurdo–Barros Gomes, October 4, 1888 (Green Book, "Caminho de Ferro de Lourenço Marques," No. 565).

32. As reported in *The European Mail,* January 4, 1889 (quoted in Araujo–Ministry of Marine, March 9, 1890 (*ibid.,* No. 630, at p. 509).

33. Petre–Salisbury, April 27, 1889, No. 46 Africa (C.P. 5988, No. 24).

34. [Draft] memorandum of contract, April 11, 1889 (Green Book, "Caminho de Ferro de Lourenço Marques," No. 655).

35. Larcom, memorandum, May 31, 1889; Sanderson, memorandum, June 11 (C.P. 5988, Nos. 34, 50).

36. Correspondence enclosed in Admiralty–F.O., August 16, 1889 (*ibid.,* No. 172).

37. Enclosure in Petre–Salisbury, July 2, 1889, No. 104 Africa (*ibid.,* No. 115).

38. Fairfield, minute, September 23, 1892 (file 691S[ecret] in C.O. 537/127).

39. *Ibid.,* February 14, 1891 (file 3234 in C.O. 417/70).

40. Anderson, Lister, minutes on Rumbold (The Hague)–Salisbury, July 7, 1889, No. 123 (F.O. 84/1963). (Dispatch alone printed, C.P. 5988, No. 119.)

41. Salisbury–Petre, September 10, 1889, No. 153 Africa; Blaine–Loring, November 8, 1889; compare Petre–Salisbury, August 15, 1889, No. 124 Africa (C.P. 5988, Nos. 153, 220, 171).

42. Treasury–F.O., August 26, 1889 (*ibid.,* No. 178); Welby–Lister, October 6, 1889; Salisbury, minutes, September 29, October 16 (F.O. 63/1265).

43. Blaine–Lincoln, October 13, 1890, enclosure, Lincoln–Salisbury, October 23 (C.P. 6058, No. 233).

44. For example, Petre–Salisbury, June 28, 1889, No. 91 Africa (C.P. 5988, No. 84); Magniac–Hintze Ribeiro, March 1, 1890, enclosure (5) in Petre–Salisbury, March 8, No. 80 Africa (C.P. 6058, No. 29).

45. Report, enclosure (1) in Petre–Salisbury, May 2, 1889, No. 53 Africa; *ibid.,* March 8, 1890, No. 80 Africa (C.P. 6058, No. 29).

46. For example, Sanderson, minute, July 20, 1896 (F.O. 63/1326).

47. F.O. 63/1371 *passim.*

48. *Sentence Finale.* See note 26.

49. *Sentence Finale,* pp. 132, 102–7, 156–67, 179.

50. For the detailed calculations, see *ibid.,* pp. 182–90.

51. Quoted and endorsed by Simões dos Reis, *Arbitragens,* pp. 274–76.

52. This is the point argued by Simões dos Reis, *Arbitragens,* pp. 254–63.

53. Bertie, minute, June 13, 1900 (F.O. 63/1371).

CHAPTER 9

1. Fairfield, minute, September 23, 1892 (file 6865S, C.O. 537/127).

2. These exchanges are in C.O. 537/124B, files 693S, 694S, 695S.

3. Many of these activities are recounted in Warhurst, *Anglo-Portuguese Relations,* pp. 115–26.

4. For the Davis scheme, see C.P. 6606, Nos. 132, 137, 138; for Henderson, see Bertie, minute, May 18, 1897 (F.O. 63/1341).

5. Chamberlain, minute, July 27, 1897 (F.O. 63/1342).

6. Fiddes, memorandum, "Delagoa Bay Railway," October 11, 1895 (C.O. Confidenial Print, African [South], No. 508), pp. 36–38.

7. Fairfield, minute, August 31, 1895 (file 89S, in C.O. 537/129). It was after this minute that Chamberlain instructed that the memorandum of October 11 be drawn up.

8. MacDonell–Bertie, February 24, 1897; Bertie, Salisbury, minutes, March 1, and subsequent papers, on F.O. 63/1359.

Grenville, *Lord Salisbury,* pp. 182–83, seems not to distinguish between the two schemes.

9. Chamberlain–Bertie, private, April 10, 1897 (F.O. 63/1359; omitted from B.D.).

10. MacDonell–Salisbury, April 23, 1897, No. 43 Africa (C.P. 7031, No. 60); the position is recapitulated in a memorandum by Bertie, dated May 1, 1898—the first document printed by Gooch and Temperley in their section on the Anglo-German treaties (B.D., Vol. I, No. 65).

11. Bertie, minute, January 10, 1898 (F.O. 63/1359).

12. Sanderson, minute, March 21 (F.O. 64/1466; F.O. 63/1359, *passim*; Mac-Donell–Salisbury, telegram, May 27, 1898, No. 15 Africa (C.P. 7213, No. 80).

13. Bertie, note, June 6, 1898 (F.O. 63/1359).

14. Warhurst, *Anglo-Portuguese Relations,* pp. 141–42. I have not seen the dispatch cited therein (F.O. 179/338, No. 62), but the reference to the "customs of Angola" should certainly read "customs of Mozambique" (see Salisbury–MacDonell, June 29, 1898, in C.P. 7303, No. 10). See also Bertie, memorandum, May 1, 1898 (B.D., Vol. I, No. 65).

15. Salisbury–Gough, June 17, 1898, No. 94 Africa (C.P. 7303, No. 2; not in B.D.); *ibid.,* June 14, 21 (*ibid.,* Nos. 1, 3; B.D., Vol. I, Nos. 66, 67).

16. Salisbury–MacDonell, June 22, 1898, No. 72 Africa (C.P. 7303, No. 4; B.D., Vol. I, No. 68).

17. Vieira de Castro, *D. Carlos I,* pp. 143–44, quoting the official German publication *Die Grosse Politik,* Vol. 14, Part I, Document 3813.

18. MacDonell–Bertie, private, June 30, 1898 (F.O. 63/1359).

19. Chamberlain, minute, July 6, 1898 (F.O. 63/1359); Chamberlain–Salisbury, June 27, quoted in Grenville, *Lord Salisbury,* p. 190.

20. Salisbury–Gough, July 9, 1898, No. 122 Africa (C.P. 7303, No. 10; B.D., Vol. I, No. 74).

21. Grey, note (secret), January 25, 1911, in B.D., Vol. X, Part II (London, 1938), p. 427 (from the *Grey Papers*); J. L. Garvin, *The Life of Joseph Chamberlain,* Vol. III (London, 1934), p. 314.

22. Marais, *Kruger's Republic,* pp. 100, 150.

23. Noailles–Nisard, *Documents Diplomatiques Françaises,* Série I, Tom. 14, Document No. 232, June 19, 1898.

24. Eyre Crowe, minute, June 4, 1912 (B.D., Vol. X, Part II, p. 472).

25. Bertie–Salisbury, private, September 14, 1898 (F.O. 64/1467).

26. Thornton–Bertie, private, September 12, 1898 (*ibid.*).

27. Salisbury–Thornton, September 28, 1898, No. 106 Africa (C.P. 7303, No. 51; not in B.D.); Thornton–Salisbury, September 11, 1898, No. 83 Africa (*ibid.*, No. 45); Thornton–Bertie, private, September 22, 1898 (F.O. 64/1467).

28. Garvin, *Joseph Chamberlain*, Vol. III, pp. 315–19; W. L. Langer, *The Diplomacy of Imperialism* (New York, 1935), p. 529.

29. See Salisbury–Lansdowne, August 30, 1899 (quoted in, *inter alia*, Marais, p. 318); Rouvier–Delcassé, April 12, 1899 (D.D.F., Série II, Tom. 2, No. 423).

30. Marais, *Kruger's Republic*, pp. 205–12; Lovell, *Struggle for South Africa*, pp. 379–421 *passim*.

31. MacDonell–Bertie, private, September 18, 1899 (F.O. 2/228; B.D., Vol. I, No. 115).

32. Grenville, *Lord Salisbury*, pp. 260–61; Salisbury–MacDonell, September 13, 1899, No. 92 Africa (F.O. 2/227; B.D., Vol. I, No. 113); correspondence between Soveral and Salisbury, annexed to Salisbury–MacDonell, October 7, 1899, No. 102 Africa (*ibid.*, B.D., Vol. I, No. 117).

33. António Cabral, ed., *Cartas d'El Rei*, p. 251; Vieira de Castro, p. 170.

34. Text in, *inter alia*, B.D., Vol. I, No. 118 (see editorial note immediately following text).

35. Bernhard von Bülow, *Memoirs*, translated by F. A. Voigt (Boston, 1931), Vol. I, p. 385, also pp. 320–21.

36. See especially Grey–Goschen, December 15, 1913, No. 71 Africa (B.D., Vol. X, Part II, No. 352).

37. See Goschen–Grey, private and secret, March 28, 1914 (*ibid.*, No. 370).

38. Grey, minute, undated, appended to Grey–Goschen, January 11, 1913, No. 5 Africa (B.D., Vol. X, Part II, No. 323, p. 502).

39. J. A. Hobson, *Imperialism: A Study* (London, 1902; new and revised edition, 1938).

40. For example, Grey–Goschen, July 4, 1912, No. 70 Africa (B.D., Vol. X, Part II, No. 312); see also Article 7 (1) of the 1913 agreement (*ibid.*, enclosure No. 341, p. 539).

41. Bertie, memorandum, November 17, 1898 (C.P. 7303, No. 69; not in B.D.).

42. MacDonell–Bertie, private, January 24, 1899 (F.O. 63/1440).

43. F.O. 63/1441 *passim*.

44. These exchanges and anonymous notes are on F.O. 63/1357. For the German interest, Rouvier–Delcassé, January 3, 1902 (D.D.F., Série II, Tom. 2, No. 3).

45. B.D., Vol. X, Part II, p. 427; António Teixeira da Sousa, *Para a Historia da Revolução* (Coimbra, 1912), Vol. I, pp. 206–13; José de Almada, *Para a História do Caminho do Ferro de Benguela* (privately printed, 1951), pp. 35–42.

46. A number of newspaper articles were reprinted as a pamphlet: *Perda da Angola: A Concessão Williams* (Lisbon, 1903).

47. José de Almada, *passim*; report by Consul Mackie (Luanda) for the year 1905 (F.O. Commercial Reports, No. 3704).

48. Farnall, minute, November 10, 1903 (F.O. 63/1445).

49. Warhurst, *Anglo-Portuguese Relations,* p. 139; see text, p. 246; F.O. 63/1440 *passim.*

50. Arnold (Beira)–Sanderson, October 12, 1903 (F.O. 63/1446).

51. Lansdowne, minute, August 12, 1903 (*ibid.*).

52. Note, Bertie–Salisbury, January 12, 1899 (F.O. 63/1440).

53. For this correspondence, F.O. 367/88 (files 23081, 28073, 29660, 34097, 36139).

54. *Ibid.,* file 29098.

55. Spilsbury–Lansdowne, January 31, 1900; minute, March 1; Admiralty–F.O., April 9, 1900, with minute (F.O. 2/667).

56. The negotiations with the bondholders are covered, from the British point of view, by F.O. 63/1381 and 63/1410; see also C.P. 7537, 8535.

57. Cabral, *Cartas d'El Rei,* p. 259. King Carlos' view is found in a letter to José Luciano, March 31, 1900.

58. MacDonell–Lansdowne, January 4, 1901, No. 2 (C.P. 7537/36); Paul Cambon–Delcassé, March 8, 1901 (D.D.F., Série II, Tom. I, No. 128).

59. Rouvier–Delcassé, October 10, 13, 1898 (D.D.F., Série I, Tom. 14, Nos. 427, 434).

60. Bertie–Lansdowne, December 25, 1901 (F.O. 63/1410).

61. MacDonell–Lansdowne, April 15, May 10, May 12, 1902 (Nos. 19, 25, 27) (C.P. 8535, Nos. 39, 40, 41).

62. Soares Branco, *Aspectos,* pp. 41–54 *passim.*

63. Roque da Costa, "A questão financeira," *Jornal do Comercio,* December 24, 1912; reprinted in *Questões Económicas,* p. 348.

64. Roque da Costa, "Ainda a Economia e Finanças," October 9, 1913; reprinted in *Questões Económicas,* p. 322.

65. F.O. 63/1381.

66. For example, MacDonell–Lansdowne, December 31, 1900, No. 43 (C.P. 7537, No. 35).

67. Villiers–Grey, November 5, 1907, No. 31, and minute (F.O. 371/315).

CHAPTER 10

1. Eduardo da Costa, "Ocupação Militar e Domínio Efectivo nas Nossas Colónias," first published 1903; reprinted in Costa, *Colectânea,* Vol. IV, pp. 19–40.

2. For example, Amadeo Cunha, *Mousinho: a Sua Obra e a Sua Época* (Lisbon, 1944†); Ameal, *História de Portugal.*

3. MacDonell–Salisbury, December 22, 1896, No. 149 Africa (C.P. 6975, No. 119); Ross (Lourenço Marques)–Salisbury, April 28, 1899, No. 28 (F.O. 2/230).

4. Ornelas, *Colectânea,* letter, July 16, 1896, pp. 226–27; letter, September 6, 1896, p. 233.

5. Ameal, *História de Portugal,* p. 713.

6. See the Bertie memorandum of May 1, 1898 (B.D., Vol. I, No. 65).

7. This case was the subject of an anonymous pamphlet, *Escândalos Inauditos: Arbitrariedades Inqualificáveis e Processo Tumultário contra Cinco Cidadãos Inocentes Presos em Moçambique* (Lisbon, 1898); but see also Ornelas, letter, September 6, 1896, *Colectânea*, pp. 231–32.

8. Mousinho de Albuquerque, *Livro das Campanhas*, pp. 339–441 (the official report); Teixeira Botelho, *História Militar* (1833–), pp. 533–47.

9. Costa, "Ocupação Militar," p. 38.

10. Quintinha and Toscano, *A Derrocada*, Vol. II, pp. 217–36.

11. Costa, "Ocupação Militar," p. 31.

12. Mousinho de Albuquerque, *Moçambique*, pp. 32–33; see also Eduardo da Costa, *O Território de Manica e Sofala e a Administração da Companhia de Moçambique*, first published 1902; reprinted in *Colectânea*, Vol. III, p. 282.

13. Costa, "Ocupação Militar," pp. 35–36.

14. Mousinho de Albuquerque, *Moçambique*, pp. 182–83, 56.

15. Enes, *Moçambique*, pp. 230–31.

16. Mousinho de Albuquerque, *Moçambique*, pp. 263–78.

17. Almeida Ribeiro, *Administração Financeira das Provincias Ultramarinas: Proposta de Lei Organica e Relatório Apresentados ao Congresso pelo Ministro das Colonias Artur R. de Almeida Ribeiro* (Coimbra, 1917†), p. 137. (This work is hereinafter cited as Almeida Ribeiro, *Administração Financeira*.)

18. Texeira de Sousa, *Para a Historia da Revolução*, pp. 257–58.

19. *Ibid.*, pp. 259–61.

20. Almeida Ribeiro, *Administração Financeira*, pp. 112–14.

21. Costa, *Estudo sobre a Administração Civil das Nossas Possessões Africanas* (1901), reprinted, *Colectânea*, Vol. IV, pp. 43–350.

22. José de Macedo, *Autonomia de Angola* (Lisbon, 1910), p. 143, referring to Ornelas' reforms in Moçambique.

23. Costa, *Estudo*, p. 130.

24. *Ibid.*, pp. 316–35.

25. *Ibid.*, p. 128, n. 1; pp. 257–65; Mousinho, *Moçambique*, p. 184.

26. Costa, *Relatório e Projecto de Reorganização Administrativa de Angola* (November 1906), printed in *Colectânea*, Vol. I, pp. 211–78.

27. Almeida Ribeiro, *Administração Financeira*, pp. 133–34.

28. *Ibid.*, pp. 115–16.

29. Ramada Curto, *Projecto de Reorganização*, Cap. VI, sec. (i), Articles 86–115.

30. Macedo, *Autonomia de Angola*, pp. 234–36.

31. Teixeira de Sousa, *Para a Historia da Revolução*, Vol. I, pp. 268, 275–76.

32. *Ibid.*, pp. 230–32.

33. Costa, *A Questão de Cuanhama: Sul de Angola* (Lisbon, 1906; reprinted, *Colectânea*, Vol. IV, pp. 399–548.)

34. [Luna da Carvalho, *et al.*], *O Coronel João de Almeida; sua Accão Militar e Administrativa em Angola, 1906–11; Publicação de Iniciativa dum Grupo de Companheiros e Amigos Coloniais* (Lisbon, 1927), pp. 14–15.

35. *Ibid.*, pp. 66–87; João de Almeida, *Sul de Angola: Relatorio de um Go-*

verno de Distrito, 1908–10 (Lisbon, 1911; 2d ed., 1936†), pp. 127–254; Henrique Galvão, *Accão e Obra de João de Almeida* (Lisbon, 2d ed., 1934), pp. 261–331.

36. *Distrito da Huíla: Relatório do Governador* [Cesar Augusto de Oliveira Moura Braz], Ano de 1912 (Coimbra, 1918†), p. 75.

37. Teixeira de Sousa, *Para a Historia da Revolução*, Vol. I, p. 232.

38. Costa, *A Questão de Cuanhama*, pp. 529–33.

39. Henrique de Paiva Couceiro, *Angola: Dois Anos de Governo, Junho 1907–Junho 1909: História e Comentarios*, 2d ed. (Lisbon, 1948), pp. 53–60.

40. Galvão, *João de Almeida*, p. 307.

41. Enclosures (2), Thornton–Salisbury, September 14, 1898, No. 84 Africa (C.P. 7143, No. 64).

42. Teixeira Botelho, *História Militar (1833–   )*, pp. 564–73.

43. Duffy, *Portuguese Africa*, p. 234.

44. Coutinho, *A Campanha do Barué*, pp. 23–25.

45. See text, p. 263.

46. Coutinho, *A Campanha do Barué*, pp. 61–62.

47. Teixeira Botelho, *História Militar (1833–   )*, pp. 596–609.

48. *Ibid.*, pp. 233–38; and Alfredo Brandão Cró de Castro Ferreri, *Angoche: Breves Considerações sobre o Estado d'este Districto em 1881* (Lisbon, 1881), pp. 13–26.

49. [Duarte Ferreira], *Relatório dos Trabalhos Militares no Districto de Moçambique, 1911–13* (Lourenço Marques, 1915†).

50. Alfredo Freire de Andrade, *Relatórios de Moçambique*, Vol. IV (Lourenço Marques, Imprensa Nacional, 1909), p. 327.

51. *Ibid.*, p. 103.

52. *Ibid.*, Vol. I, p. 109.

53. Almeida Ribeiro, *Administração Financeira*, p. 175.

54. [Marianno de Carvalho] *Planos Financeiros*, pp. 106–12.

55. Couceiro, *Angola*, p. 109.

56. José de Macedo, *Autonomia de Angola*, p. 61.

57. Almeida Ribeiro, *Administração Financeira*, p. 80.

58. *Ibid.*, p. 72.

59. Enes, *Moçambique*, pp. 104–5; quoted in part by Almeida Ribeiro, *Administração Financeira*, p. 71.

60. *Administração Financeira*, p. 177.

61. Macedo, *Autonomia de Angola*, p. 56; Couceiro, *Angola: 1907–09*, p. 412.

62. Couceiro, *Angola*, pp. 413–14; see the reports from the British Consulate in Luanda on F.O. 367/89.

63. Almeida Ribeiro, *Administração Financeira*, pp. 182–84.

64. Macedo, *Autonomia de Angola*, p. 66.

65. Couceiro, *Angola*, p. xviii.

66. Freire de Andrade, *Relatórios de Moçambique*, Vol. IV, p. 5.

67. Almeida Ribeiro, *Administração Financeira*, p. 119.

68. *Ibid.*, pp. 10, 91.

69. Freire de Andrade, *Relatórios de Moçambique*, Vol. III, p. 5.

70. *Ibid.,* p. 50.

71. Couceiro, *Angola,* pp. 391–92.

72. *Ibid.,* pp. 107, 109, 111–12.

73. Grey, minute to the Cabinet, July 17, 1912 (B.D., Vol. X, Part II, p. 485, n. 1).

74. [Guilherme Augusto de Brito Capello], *Relatório do Governador da Provincia de Angola* (Lisbon, Imprensa Nacional, 1889), pp. 160–61.

75. Couceiro, *Angola,* pp. 108–9.

76. Compare Brito Capello, *Relatório,* Table ("Mappa") 7, p. 33, with Couceiro, *Angola,* pp. 305, 311, 443.

77. See text, pp. 121–22, and compare Ennes' gibe, p. 155.

78. Capello, *Relatório,* Table 7, p. 33, and Table 9, pp. 40–41.

79. Reprinted in Ernesto de Vilhena, *Questões Coloniais,* Vol. I, pp. 4–6.

80. João de Azevedo Coutinho, *A Questão do Alcool de Angola: Proposta de Lei* (Lisbon, Imprensa Nacional, 1910), p. 9.

81. Nightingale (Luanda)–Lansdowne, May 25, 1902, No. 15 (F.O. 2/640).

82. Coutinho, *A Questão do Alcool,* pp. 15–17.

83. Couceiro, *Angola,* p. 275.

84. *Ibid.,* pp. 273–74; quotation from *A Questão do Alcool,* pp. 29–30.

85. J. M. R. Norton de Matos, *A Provincia de Angola* (Oporto, 1926), pp. 142–45.

86. Freire de Andrade, *Relatórios de Moçambique,* Vol. I, p. 10.

87. *Ibid.,* p. 20.

88. Freire de Andrade, *Relatórios de Moçambique,* Vol. V, pp. 127–49 (quotation from p. 135).

89. *Ibid.,* pp. 128–29; Eduardo d'Almeida Saldanha, article, "Perigos sobre Moçambique" (1919), reprinted in his *O Sul de Save* (Lisbon, 1928), p. 21.

90. Companhia do Nyassa: *Relatorios e Memorias sobre os Territorios, pelo Governador Ernesto Jardim de Vilhena* (Lisbon, 1905), pp. 134–35.

91. *Ibid.,* p. 133. For the views of Ennes, see his *Moçambique,* pp. 51–58; compare Mousinho de Albuquerque, *Moçambique,* pp. 139–41.

92. Companhia do Nyassa: *Relatorios e Memorias,* pp. 132, 136.

CHAPTER II

1. Couceiro, *Angola,* pp. 226–28.

2. João de Andrade Corvo, *Estudos sobre as Provincias Ultramarinas,* Vol. I, pp. 113–14.

3. Vicente Pinheiro Lobo Machado de Mello e Almada, *As Ilhas de S. Thomé e Príncipe: Notas de uma Administração Colonial* (Lisbon, 1884), pp. 12–13, 29.

4. Sá da Bandeira, *O Trabalho Rural Africano,* pp. 95–99.

5. Vicente Pinheiro, *As Ilhas de S. Thomé e Príncipe,* pp. 84–87.

6. Wylde, minute, February 11, 1878, on Hopkins (Luanda)–Derby, No. 4 Slave Trade (F.O. 84/1478—bound in Consular Section of volume).

7. Cohen–Granville, July 16, 1882; Granville–Baring, November 27, 1882;

Baring–Serpa, December 7, 1882 (in Baring–Granville, December 7, 1882), B.P.P. Slave Trade, No. 1, 1883, Nos. 52, 53, 57, Vol. LXVI. See also, for example, Baring–Granville, October 27, 1882 (*ibid.*, No. 48).

8. Duffy, *Portuguese Africa*, pp. 153–54.

9. Pinheiro, *As Ilhas de S. Thomé e Príncipe*, pp. 47–64.

10. Report by Consul Roger Casement (Luanda) for the years 1897/98 (F.O. Annual Series, Diplomatic and Consular Reports on Trade and Finance, No. 2363; B.P.P. [1899] Vol. CI).

11. Antonio Teixeira de Sousa, *Relatorio, Propostas de Lei e Documentos Relativos ás Possessões Ultramarinos Apresentados ... pelo Ministro e Secretario dos Negócios da Marinha e Ultramar* (Lisbon, Imprensa Nacional, 1902†), p. 228; see also Teixeira de Sousa, *Para a Historia da Revolução*, Vol. I, p. 194.

12. Cabral Moncada, *A Campanha do Bailundo*, pp. 211–28; Teixeira de Sousa, *Para a Historia da Revolução*, p. 189.

13. *Report* [by Consul Nightingale (Boma)] *on the Treatment of the "Serviçaes," or Contract Labourers, in the Portuguese Islands known as the Province of São Thome and Principe*, July 28, 1906 (C.P. 8806), pp. 3–9. (Hereinafter cited as Nightingale, *Report*.)

14. Nightingale, *Report*, pp. 8, 9.

15. See text, p. 58.

16. Grey, minute, undated, on file 28370/06 (F.O. 367/18).

17. File 69/07 (F.O. 367/46) *passim*.

18. F.O. 63/1447 *passim*.

19. Enclosure, Nightingale (Luanda)–Lansdowne, June 20, 1902, No. 2 Africa (F.O. 2/640).

20. Mackie (Luanda)–Grey, March 15, 1908, No. 5 Africa (file 19896/08, F.O. 367/87).

21. Couceiro, *Angola*, pp. 254–57.

22. H. W. Nevinson, *More Changes, More Chances* (New York, 1925), pp. 87–93.

23. Quoted in Duffy, *Portuguese Africa*, p. 163.

24. Farnall, minute, May 14, 1903, on Gosselin–Lansdowne, May 3, No. 89 Africa (F.O. 63/1447).

25. Freire de Andrade, *Relatorios sobre Moçambique*, Vol. II, p. 65.

26. *Ibid.*, pp. 10–11.

27. Bishop of Lebombo–Godfrey Lagden, May 7, 1906 (copy on file 26127/06, F.O. 367/19).

28. Baldwin (Lourenço Marques)–F.O., June 4, July 11, 1906 (file 28852/06, *ibid.*).

29. File 26127/06 (F.O. 367/19).

30. Ennes I, p. 49.

31. Mousinho de Albuquerque, *Moçambique*, pp. 103–9.

32. *Selborne Memorandum*, pp. 57, 79, 86. The Selborne memorandum was first published as a British Command Paper (Cd. 2104), and was later reprinted commercially, with an introduction by Basil Williams which explained

its origins and importance: *The Selborne Memorandum* (London, 1925). Page references herein are to the Williams edition. It is also included in A. P. Newton, ed., *Select Documents Relating to the Unification of South Africa,* 2 vols. (London, 1924).

33. Freire de Andrade, *Relatorios sobre Moçambique,* Vol. II, pp. 47, 48, 52–53, 62.

34. *Selborne Memorandum,* p. 114.

35. Freire de Andrade, *Relatorios sobre Moçambique,* Vol. II, p. 65.

36. *Ibid.,* Vol. III, pp. 363–89, especially pp. 372–74; quotation on p. 387.

37. Angel Marvaud, *Le Portugal et ses Colonies,* pp. 251–56; Teixeira de Sousa, *Para a Historia da Revolução,* Vol. I, p. 171. Text of the Transvaal-Portuguese Convention in Command Paper, Cd. 4587 (B.P.P. 1909, Vol. LXI).

38. Marvaud, *Portugal et ses Colonies,* p. 256.

39. R. H. Brand, *The Union of South Africa* (London, 1909), p. 94.

40. Ernesto de Vilhena, *Questões Coloniais,* Vol. I, pp. 63–345.

41. *Ibid.,* p. 322.

42. *Ibid.,* pp. 233–34.

43. *Ibid.,* p. 118.

44. *Ibid.,* pp. 316–17 (quoting *Transvaal Leader,* June 26, 1909).

45. *Ibid.,* pp. 127–28.

CONCLUSION

1. Yves Guyot, *Lettres sur la Politique Coloniale* (Paris, 1885), p. 99.

2. Thorstein Veblen, "Professor Clark's Economics," *Quarterly Journal of Economics,* February 1908, reprinted in Veblen, *The Place of Science in Modern Civilization, and Other Essays* (New York, 1919), p. 229.

3. Vilhena, *Questões Coloniais,* Vol. I, p. 75.

4. Cunha Leal, *Os Partidos Politicos na Republica Portuguesa* (Corunna, 1932), pp. 82–83.

5. José de Macedo, *Autonomia de Angola,* pp. 164–65.

6. Cunha Leal, *Os Partidos Politicos,* p. 87.

7. Quoted in A. F. Nogueira, *A Ilha de S. Thomé, a Questão Bancaria no Ultramar e o Nosso Problema Colonial* (Lisbon, 1893), p. 157.

8. Nogueira, *A Ilha de S. Thomé,* p. v.

9. *Ibid.,* pp. xiii–xiv.

Index